MONDAY NIGHT MAYHEM

MONDAY NIGHT MAYHEM

||||||||| ★ |||||||||

The Inside Story of
ABC's Monday Night Football

Marc Gunther & Bill Carter

BTB
BEECH TREE BOOKS
WILLIAM MORROW
New York

Library of Congress Cataloging-in-Publication Data

Gunther, Marc. 1951—
    Monday night mayhem: the inside story of ABC's Monday night football / Marc Gunther and Bill Carter.
      p.   cm
    Bibliography: p.
    ISBN 0-688-07553-3
    1. Monday night football (Television program)—History.
I. Carter, Bill, 1949–   . II. Title.
GV742.3.G86   1988
791.45'72—dc19

Printed in the United States of America.

First Edition

1 2 3 4 5 6 7 8 9 10

BOOK DESIGN BY LINEY LI

To my brothers, Noel and Andrew Gunther—M. G.

To my father and mother, Richard and Teresa Carter—B. C.

Contents

MONDAY NIGHT MAYHEM

1.

ROONE
ON THE RISE

"There was opposition almost everywhere. It was only through fear that I finally got it on the air."—ROONE ARLEDGE

Art Modell, dripping with perspiration in the steamy September night, sat in a box in the end zone of Cleveland's Municipal Stadium.

His Browns were preparing to take the field against the New York Jets, and Modell was worried.

He was not worried about losing the game; he was worried about losing his shirt.

The phone rang. He picked it up, listened for a moment, then smiled. The news was good: Outside the stadium, the parking lots were jammed a half hour before game time. In every direction, the ticket sellers could see people—people in packs, people in waves, people filling West Third Street, the main thoroughfare leading to the stadium. They poured out of cars and buses in a building stream.

The closer it got to nine P.M., the longer the lines stretched. The ticket manager called back and told Modell that all the seats were sold, but that people were still lined up—to buy standing room.

Then and there, long before the final ticket count was completed and the Cleveland Browns set an all-time,

11

never-to-be-broken attendance record of 85,703, Art Modell smelled the sweet aroma of something big.

It was an especially gratifying moment for the Browns' owner, who had put his franchise—and even his owner's box on the 50-yard line, which he had sacrificed for a camera position—behind the conviction that football could work as a prime-time television attraction. Modell, one of the men who negotiated the NFL's first prime-time deal, had volunteered to host the first regular-season game of *Monday Night Football* after several of his fellow owners expressed a distinct absence of interest in that privilege. Many of them predicted that *Monday Night Football*, coming on the heels of a big weekend of college and pro games, would be a disaster at the gate.

Before the ball was kicked off that night, September 21, 1970, Art Modell was ready to accept congratulations from the skeptics.

Halfway across the stadium, from his spot in the executive boxes, Pete Rozelle took in the scene—the crowd, the noise, the electricity in the stands, the starlit sky, the bright lights glinting off the players' helmets. He concluded immediately that his league had just crossed the threshold of a new and almost limitless prosperity. The commissioner of the National Football League was struck by how the very presence of darkness as a backdrop made the whole atmosphere in the stadium more dramatic. *No matter how this thing plays on TV*, Rozelle thought, *Monday night football is going to have a huge impact on the league as word spreads about how exciting it can be to attend an NFL game at night.*

Rozelle, the man who had conceived the idea of *Monday Night Football*, was already feeling great pride at what he had wrought.

Inside a trailer-truck parked outside the stadium, another man faced a bank of television monitors and a console cluttered with buttons, dials, and half-empty Styrofoam cups. He sat calmly, even coolly, in defiance of the stifling heat and the opening-night tension surrounding him.

In the past decade, this man had sat in production trucks all over the world and created new ways to present television. He had emerged from the ranks of network bureaucrats to popu-larize such technical advances as slow-motion replays and isolated cameras. He had elevated the Olympics to a television spectacle. He had produced the most famous sports anthology program in the history of television. He had imposed his personal vision on the industry of sports television.

Until now he had mostly performed his magic outside the bright lights of prime time. So, like Art Modell and Pete Rozelle, he had high stakes riding on *Monday Night Football*. He had sold the idea for the show to his company, planned its production, and cast its stars.

As the countdown to airtime began, it was too soon for this man to celebrate. He had work to do: He was preparing to transform the game that was about to begin into a show of arresting creativity and unprecedented popularity. Football on television would never be the same.

Within a few moments, he would demonstrate once more that the wide world of sports television belonged to ABC Sports, and that the attention of the nation could belong to Roone Arledge.

Like so much else about him, his distinctive first name set him apart. As his legend grew, everyone in television would know him simply as Roone.

Roone Pinckney Arledge, Jr., was born on July 8, 1931, in Forest Hills, New York, into a family of Scottish heritage and substantial means. His father, an attorney, had moved the family from North Carolina to New York, where they settled in suburban Merrick, Long Island.

Roone grew up in comfortable surroundings, so his drive to succeed could not be explained by any conventional rags-to-riches formula. His father did encourage him to be intellectually curious; the family discussed politics and world events around the dinner table, and avidly followed the accounts of World War II that were broadcast over the radio.

In high school, Roone wrestled, played baseball, and edited the sports page of the student newspaper.

In 1949, Arledge entered Columbia University. There he majored in business and studied the great works of literature under Columbia's renowned English faculty, including Lionel Trilling, whose instruction in the art of the narrative struck a responsive chord in Arledge that would continue to ring throughout his career. Arledge became part of a remarkable circle of friends, including Lawrence K. Grossman, who would become president of first the Public Broadcasting Service and then NBC News; Richard Wald, who would edit the *New York Herald Tribune*, run NBC News, and later work for Arledge at ABC News; and Max Frankel, who would go on to serve as executive editor of *The New York Times*. They were all interested in journalism, passionate about ideas, and determined to make something of themselves. The world, they thought, presented limitless opportunities to young men with ambition and intelligence.

Arledge had ambition, intelligence, and enormous energy. Under his picture in the Columbia yearbook were twelve lines listing his activities—no one else in his graduating class had more than seven. In addition to being on the wrestling team, he was a campus politician, active in both his fraternity and the student government. He was not, however, the class president, though his ABC biography for years stated he had been. He majored in business and pursued his interest in journalism by editing the yearbook; the first two words in the book, which appeared even before the title page, were *Roone Arledge*.

After he graduated in 1952, Arledge first spent a few months in Columbia's graduate school of international relations, then decided to look for a job as a sportswriter. He wound up being hired as a gofer by the fading Dumont Television Network. He never needed further career counseling. Television, an industry still struggling to define itself in the 1950s, provided the perfect arena for Arledge's talents.

Still, his climb to the top was by no means direct. He was drafted, and by the time he got out of the army in 1955, Dumont had folded. He moved on to NBC as a stage manager, and finally got his first credit as a producer for a puppet show called *Hi Mom* with Shari Lewis. For this, he won his first Emmy award in 1959.

But Arledge wanted to make a contribution to society that went beyond puppets. With his friend Larry Grossman, who lived in the same Brooklyn neighborhood, Arledge developed a grand plan for a television series that would do nothing less than dramatize the stories behind the greatest works of art, music, and literature in history: Michelangelo's Sistine Chapel,

Beethoven's *Eroica* Symphony, Walt Whitman's *Drum Taps*. It was a romantic notion, and Arledge and Grossman spent nearly two years giving it form, spreading out their rough drafts over an ironing board in Grossman's apartment. They called it *Masterpiece*.

As a low-level puppet-show producer, Arledge knew all along that he needed a daring plan to get his idea considered in high places. Big ideas, bold execution: Arledge's entire career would be built on that approach.

His wife, Joan, just happened to be the personal secretary to David Sarnoff, chairman of RCA, parent company to NBC. Arledge persuaded her first to type the proposal for *Masterpiece* on Sarnoff's stationery, then to get him to initial it, and finally to steer it onto the desk of Pat Weaver, president of NBC.

Weaver and his aides seriously considered *Masterpiece*. But they eventually turned the proposal down.

Arledge soon had another idea—this one not quite so lofty. He developed a magazine show called *For Men Only*, modeled on *Playboy*—as much as a television program could be in the 1950s. The show was tilted heavily toward sports, but it also included a jazz segment and a starlet clad in a bathing suit parading back and forth on the set. This time, Arledge was authorized to produce a pilot.

Again, he was rejected. The pilot never aired.

But a friend of Arledge's brought *For Men Only* to the attention of a man named Edgar Scherick, then the head of a company called Sports Programs Inc., which functioned as the sports arm of ABC. Something about *For Men Only* caught his eye.

Scherick wanted to meet the producer, and when he did, he was impressed. The two men talked awhile before Scherick asked an important question: "Do you know anything about sports?" Arledge said he was a sports fanatic, then proved it by correctly identifying every athlete in every picture on the walls of Scherick's office.

It was April 1960. Scherick needed an assistant to help him with the broadcasts of a package of college-football games he had just acquired for ABC.

Arledge was intrigued, though leaving the prestige of NBC for Scherick's rinky-dink organization would be an unconventional career move. Still, he liked sports, he was fed up with the network bureaucracy, and he was excited by the opportunity to go someplace where he could make an immediate impact.

So, when Scherick offered him a job, he accepted on the spot. It was a turning point for Arledge—and for the television industry.

The running joke had labeled ABC the Almost Broadcasting Company. Formed in 1943 when Washington regulators had forced NBC to spin off one of its radio networks, ABC had struggled ever since to overcome its competitive disadvantages. It had fewer and weaker stations than CBS and NBC, little money to invest in programming and equipment, and no tradition to build on.

The very absence of tradition ultimately turned out to be a blessing. Unlike its bigger rivals on Broadcast Row, ABC welcomed mavericks, even gamblers, to come in and take a shot at making television. ABC's chairman, Leonard Goldenson, later concluded that *Monday Night Football* was one of those gambles, but he said, "We were gambling in our growth all along the line." ABC affected a shirt-sleeved informality as its corporate style, and encouraged innovation, usually because the company had nothing to lose. ABC was perfectly suited for Roone Arledge.

Sports was perfect too. ABC had sports on the air, but nothing worth bragging about—bowling, boxing, and a golf show that was not even live. At CBS and NBC, top management had a lackadaisical attitude toward sports. Sports had neither the prestige of news nor the glamour of entertainment and, besides, sports programs were messy; they could run long and play havoc with the important parts of the broadcast schedule. To the top men at the networks, most sports also had a decidedly proletarian scent. CBS's first ventures into sports were horse racing, the sport of kings, and golf, the sport of broadcasting executives. Television sports meant the Derby, the Masters, and the World Series.

Nor did the sports establishment welcome the networks in those years. The colleges and professional leagues liked the networks' money, of course, but the conventional wisdom was that television exposure could ruin a sport.

Baseball owners, worried about shrinking crowds, blacked

out Saturday telecasts in major-league cities. And when they did allow cameras into the ball park, they limited what they could do. The prevailing attitude was summed up by baseball commissioner Ford Frick. "The view a fan gets at home," Frick once said, "should not be any better than that of the fan in the worst seat of the ball park."

The production values the networks brought to sports coverage barely exceeded Frick's expectations. They took a passive approach, pointing a few stationary cameras at the field and hoping the plays didn't happen too fast for them to focus. But the viewers of the 1950s were satisfied. They were still marveling at the technology that could bring a faraway contest right into their living rooms.

Into this Neanderthal world came Arledge, a man with creative ideas, an innovator, a visionary. He arrived with a simple question: What if I tried this?

"That's the difference between those who are very good and those who are mediocre," Arledge would say. "First to be curious, and second to say, what if I tried this?"

From the day he was hired by Scherick, and for the rest of his career, Arledge would ask that question about television. The past was irrelevant. Television was young, ever changing, the ultimate tabula rasa; the creative mind could write whatever it wanted on it.

Arledge began by questioning the very purpose of sports television.

His first heretical idea was that sports television did not exist to promote sports. Television was not in the business of selling tickets, or of telling viewers to turn off their sets and come to the ball park because there were still great seats available.

Sports television, Arledge decided, was like the rest of television. Its job was to entertain the audience at home. That led him to the belief that television had to do more than just document the game.

It became the Arledge credo: The show, not the contest, is what counts. It was a simple idea, but one with revolutionary implications.

As he put the idea into practice, Arledge plumbed every corner of his own life for inspiration. As a sports fan, he wanted to see and appreciate better all the intricacies of a game. His wife, Joan, who was uninterested in sports, got him thinking about color and spectacle as well as the score when, at a Notre Dame–Army football game, she borrowed his binoculars to get a close-up look at the plumes on the Notre Dame band. And from his undergraduate days at Columbia, Arledge remembered his lessons about dramatic narratives and their power to move audiences.

"What we set out to do was get the audience involved emotionally," he said. "If they didn't give a damn about the game, they still might enjoy the program."

Arledge thought it all out in detail, then wrote it down in a memo to Scherick. The memo presented an eerily accurate preview of the future of television sports in America:

> Heretofore, television has done a remarkable job of bringing the game to the viewer—now we are going to take the viewer to the game!!
>
> We will utilize every production technique ... to heighten the viewer's feeling of actually sitting in the stands and participating personally in the excitement and color ...
>
> We must gain and hold the interest of women and others who are not fanatic followers of the sport we happen to be televising. Women come to football games, not so much to marvel at the deftness of the quarterback in calling an end sweep or a lineman pulling out to lead a play, but to sit in a crowd, see what everyone else is wearing, watch the cheerleaders and experience the countless things that make up the feeling of the game. Incidentally, very few men have ever switched channels when a nicely proportioned girl was leaping into the air or leading a band downfield ...
>
> We will have cameras mounted in jeeps, on mike booms, in risers or helicopters, or anything necessary to get the complete story of the game. We will use a "creepy-peepy" camera to get the impact shots that we cannot get from a fixed camera—a coach's face as a man drops a pass in the clear—a pretty cheerleader just after her hero has scored a touchdown—a co-ed who brings her infant baby to the game in her arms—the referee as he calls a particularly difficult play—a student hawking programs in the stands—two romantic students sharing a blanket late in the game on a cold day—the beaming face of a substitute halfback as he comes off the field after running seventy yards for a touchdown, on his first play for the varsity—

all the excitement, wonder, jubilation and despair that make this America's Number One sports spectacle, and human drama to match bullfights and heavyweight championships in intensity. In short—*We are going to add show business to sports!*

The memo ended with a prediction that demonstrated both the size of Arledge's ego and the clarity of his vision: "We will be setting the standards that everyone will be talking about and that others in the industry will spend years trying to equal."

Edgar Scherick needed only one look at that memo to know who should be producing college football for ABC.

On the warm afternoon of Saturday, September 17, 1960, in Birmingham, Alabama, Roone Arledge climbed into a mobile-unit truck to produce a live sports telecast for the first time in his life.

It was not just any telecast. It was the first game in the college-football package ABC had just bought for more than $6 million, more money than the network had ever spent for any kind of programming.

The top executives of the network were all in attendance that afternoon at Legion Field in Birmingham, watching over Arledge's shoulder like anxious parents. He was under intense pressure to fashion a success for ABC.

And yet, Arledge climbed into that truck like a man stepping gracefully into his element. He even told Scherick, his boss, to get lost so that he could do his job.

The University of Alabama, under Bear Bryant, faced a Georgia team led by a spectacular quarterback named Fran Tarkenton. This game would attract the hardcore fan, but Arledge was about to deliver more than a football game. He was going to give the fans—and anyone else who was watching—a captivating experience.

From the moment the telecast hit the air, it was different from anything television had ever done with sports. Standing in front of his bank of monitors, calmly plotting each camera move like a film director blocking his big battle scene, Arledge shifted the focus from the field to the stands to the sidelines to the entire stadium as seen from on high.

He spoke with authority and precision to the announcers in the booth, Curt Gowdy and Paul Christman, who were working their first game together, telling them to emphasize the developing story of the game, the contrast between the Bryant-drilled unit of Alabama and the soaring individual ability of Tarkenton for Georgia.

He drew the faces of the athletes into tight focus, then swept back to capture entire sections of delirious fans after a big play. He turned up the sound on his phalanx of remote microphones to convey both the thudding impact of the line play and the festive din of the stadium.

With an intimacy that was unprecedented, Arledge displayed the calm concentration of Bryant on the sideline before an important call, the youthful elation of Tarkenton after a scrambling first down, the sweet exuberance of the Alabama cheerleaders, and the anguish of a rooter with a Georgia pennant.

For the first time, the television screen was filled with more than helmets and numbers colliding almost soundlessly in the distance; it was filled with emotion, the same emotion a spectator would have felt inside Legion Field. Arledge's plan had worked; he had used more microphones and more cameras in different locations to bring the *feeling* of the event to the spectators in their living rooms.

Sports events had been on television for years. But as presented by CBS and NBC, they were one-dimensional displays of action, seen from afar and devoid of passion. Compared to the way Arledge would produce, array, and animate them, the games on the other networks would begin to look like stick-figure drawings on the wall of a cave.

Sports television was reborn that afternoon. And Roone Arledge discovered a wide-open field for his own breakaway talent.

Roone Arledge only thought like a maverick; he did not look like one. His appearance was thoroughly average. He was of medium height, with the hint of a bulge around his waist. He had a ruddy, freckled complexion, twinkling blue eyes, and unruly, wiry, sandy-red hair. He wore a pair of unhip, thick-framed, black glasses; without them, he bore a faint resemblance to Jack Nicklaus.

As Arledge became a figure on the sports scene, he affected for a time a bold look of striped shirts, safari jackets, aviator glasses, and gold bracelets, topped off with a cigar. He got into hunting and fishing, and went on safaris for big game. Even on the job, his clothes were aggressively casual, setting him apart from the businessmen who ran the company.

But what really set Arledge apart was his work. Within months of his triumph with college football, he had thrown himself into a new show that would become the foundation of ABC Sports.

Starting with a list of events compiled from back issues of *The New York Times*, Arledge began working the phones and traveling the world, trying to secure the rights to sports events ranging from college track meets to demolition derbies. He would call someone who was involved in a minor sport and tell him that there was this new show that might or might not go on the air, that he might or might not use the event, and that he might or might not pay him, but would be hold the event open for ABC? Surprisingly, some of those he called said yes.

Wide World of Sports premiered on April 29, 1961, with a pair of track meets. Patched together and tape-delayed, mixing obscure competitions with the occasional big fight or international track meet, the show was a perfect expression of the Arledge credo. *Wide World* thrived because of the way he presented the events. It was not about who won or lost, or even about the games themselves; it was about "the human drama of athletic competition," as the famous signature line said, about "the thrill of victory and the agony of defeat."

Arledge was usually given credit for the line. In a widely told tale, he was said to have written the phrase on the back of an airline-ticket envelope as he flew back from Japan before *Wide World*'s second season.

He didn't. Arledge was working on a new opening for *Wide World* in a New York studio in January 1962. With him was the man he hired to host the series, Jim McKay. Arledge and McKay both frantically scribbled many phrases that day in an effort to capture the essence of the show. "I do think it was eventually scribbled down on an envelope," McKay said, "but my recollection is that it was, well, a *joint* effort. I can tell you for sure that I was involved in writing it."

What Arledge indisputably did author was the idea behind the phrases, that the heart and soul of sports television is human emotion. With the always curious McKay serving as tour guide, Arledge also introduced *Wide World* viewers to unknown people and distant places.

In the show's first year, without even attempting to get official permission, Arledge mounted a camera on a car and drove down the streets of Prague, Czechoslovakia, to set the scene for the World Figure Skating Championships. His show was about the wide world as much as it was about sports.

The Olympics, which had been only a minor television attraction, were a natural outgrowth of *Wide World,* which popularized so many Olympic sports. ABC bought the rights to Arledge's first Olympics—in Innsbruck, Austria, 1964—for just $200,000. Tape of each day's competition was shipped by plane to New York and broadcast a day later.

Arledge wasn't satisfied with that. He was always asking his technical people, What if? Using *Wide World* as a laboratory, Arledge pushed them to develop a myriad of video break-throughs. And soon ABC Sports telecasts were enlivened with slow motion, stop action, split screens, isolated replays, hand-held cameras, and sophisticated graphics.

In the early years of *Wide World,* Arledge produced nearly all the events himself. Even though he took control of ABC Sports when Scherick sold Sports Programs to the network in 1961, he loved the action too much to chain himself to a desk. "The image that ultimately appears on the tube is what TV is all about," Arledge said. "So, for me, the most rewarding and exciting part of my job is making pictures and words that move people. . . . During a major sporting event, the action isn't in the commissioner's box, where every other TV executive sits, but in the mobile unit. That's the place to be."

His employees admired his willingness to climb into the trenches. While other executives negotiated contracts or planned budgets, Arledge would show up in jeans and a windbreaker to get a program on the air. "There was a real camaraderie there," said Joe Aceti, who was an ABC director for many years. "He wasn't some guy in a suit and tie."

Arledge also knew how to make money for ABC. For several years, ABC Sports was the only division of the network to show a profit. This naturally helped win Arledge promotions—he became a vice-president in 1964, and president of ABC Sports in 1968. He was given a free hand to run Sports and a special place in the corporate hierarchy. Citing the need to get this program or that one on the air, he would skip top management meetings, sending a deputy in his stead. No one objected and, when he did appear, "Leonard Goldenson would greet him like the lost son," said one executive. "Roone intimidated ABC management. He does something that no other executive at his level at ABC can do. He knows how to push the buttons."

As a manager, he ran a loose ship. He worked long but irregular hours, preferred bull sessions to formal meetings, and sometimes would disappear for hours or days. Even top aides such as Chuck Howard and Jim Spence, who were left to clean up many an administrative mess, had trouble tracking him down. "Roone could have something going on in *The American Sportsman* and disappear, oh, a day planning it, or three days doing it, while there were some major, major things that had to be done. You just couldn't get Roone," Howard said.

"Roone's day was just starting when everybody else was going home. And he did it deliberately," another aide said. "He had more time to think. He did not clutter up his day with administrative bullshit." By arriving and staying late, Arledge also avoided the phone. His reluctance to return phone messages later would reach epic proportions.

It didn't matter. ABC Sports was flourishing. People were watching the programs. And, if he could not always be found in the office, Arledge did manage to spend enough time on the twenty-eighth floor to make it an exciting place to work. Most people were in awe of Arledge. He was a remote, hard-to-know figure who set high standards and rarely handed out compliments. But that only made everyone work even harder to please him and advance the glory of ABC Sports. "When you got off that elevator," said one longtime aide, "you knew you were special."

"The people in the ABC building hated and yet respected ABC Sports," said Dick Ebersol, who came to work for Arledge in the late 1960s. "Respected it because it was about the only part of the network that was successful and original. Hated it because the one thing that Roone insisted on was that all of us would live well." Salaries were not exceptional then, but the people at ABC Sports traveled the world with Arledge, and they stayed in the best hotels and ate in the finest restaurants.

If Arledge was hard to find around the office, and harder still to reach on the phone, he never let anyone doubt who was in charge at ABC Sports. Not his employees, not his superiors, not his rivals at the other networks, not even the viewers at home. They would soon become familiar with a simple nine-word declarative sentence that was intoned, with a touch of reverence, at the close of each and every sports telecast on ABC: "The executive producer of ABC Sports is Roone Arledge." His signature was stamped on every program that left ABC Sports—whether he saw it or not. The signature meant something to him, and so did the fee he got every time the credit was read.

He was everywhere and nowhere. It all contributed to the mystique, to the sense that this man was unlike any other who walked the halls of network television. Dorrance Smith, a producer under Arledge in Sports and later in News, spent some time in between his stints at ABC at the White House as an aide to President Gerald Ford. Smith felt that there was always an aura about Arledge. "I've worked for the president of the United States, and for the president of ABC Sports," he said. "Roone is a much more commanding figure."

As the 1960s drew to an end, Arledge was the acknowledged master of sports television. He hungered for more. It was time to take his act onto a bigger stage.

The NFL championship game of 1958, an overtime thriller in Yankee Stadium in which the Baltimore Colts defeated the New York Giants, launched football as America's sport.

And yet, until the unlikely ascendancy of Alvin "Pete" Rozelle to the commissioner's office a little more than a year later, the pro-football owners were not sure how to capitalize on their newfound popularity. Soon enough, Rozelle would show them.

In January 1960, the owners of the twelve National Football League teams met in Miami to elect a commissioner to replace the late Bert Bell. Rozelle, the general manager of the Los Angeles Rams, was not initially a contender for the job.

Rozelle, then thirty-three, had been a successful public-relations man before taking the Rams job three years earlier.

While serving as general manager, he had eased tensions between the team's feuding owners, and had made the club a good deal of money by creating such souvenirs as Rams seat cushions and cocktail glasses.

Dan Reeves, the Rams' principal owner, was grateful. When the NFL owners were deadlocked after a week of bitter fighting over whom to elect as commissioner, he proposed Rozelle as a compromise choice. "I was the only candidate who hadn't already alienated most of the people in that meeting," Rozelle said later. He posed no apparent threat to the old-line owners, who were accustomed to having things their way. Washington Redskins owner George Marshall praised him as a "good boy," and the press, with just a hint of scorn, dubbed him the "boy czar."

Rozelle's new empire was no prize. Four decades of NFL football had been marred by teams going broke, franchises jumping from city to city, and constant internal strife. Even after the league achieved stability in the 1950s, no one expected to make much money from pro football. Games rarely sold out and, as a television attraction, NFL football had a lingering image problem. Network executives saw the pro game as a blue-collar property, appealing mostly to men with no college loyalties. Worse, each franchise negotiated its own television contracts in a scatter-shot manner.

Rozelle's first step was to move the league offices from the back of a Pennsylvania bank building to Manhattan, instantly giving the league new visibility. Soon afterward, he tackled the television problem.

The commissioner saw television as a cash drawer he wanted to get his hand in. Football, he thought, was well-suited for the medium, once you overcame the difficulty of getting viewers to identify with men hidden beneath layers of shoulder pads and helmets. The action was fairly predictable, so cameras could follow the flow of play as teams marched up and down the field. And the sport was exciting. Rozelle saw, as Arledge did at about the same time, that the contest could stir emotions and deliver high drama with winners and losers, heroes and goats. He liked to contrast the appeal of football to the rest of television, saying, "You don't find people telling their parking attendant, 'God, wasn't Lassie magnificent putting out that forest fire last night.' But after a pro-football game, that does happen."

Rozelle recommended that the league sell its collective television rights as single package, then share the proceeds equally among all franchises. Getting the owners to buy that idea, with its socialistic overtones, was a struggle, but in early 1961, he got them to agree. Then Rozelle went to Washington and obtained a special act of Congress to exempt the NFL from the antitrust laws.

In less than two years, Rozelle had created a classic monopoly. He had a product to sell—professional football—that was valuable and hard to duplicate. He had three potential buyers— ABC, CBS, and NBC. So he set to work, with consummate skill. Rozelle was ready to marry pro football to television. It would not always be a smooth union.

Smooth, though, was the word most often used to describe Pete Rozelle. Detractors preferred *slick*. Tall, tanned year-round, impeccably tailored, and well spoken, Rozelle ran the league like a modern corporate executive. If his tact had won him the commissioner's job almost by accident, his toughness soon sent a message to everyone that he planned to keep it. He wasn't afraid to square off with the owners, some of whom were twice his age; he slapped a heavy fine on George Halas, patriarch of the Chicago Bears, for criticizing an official. Nor did he hesitate when Paul Hornung and Alex Karras, two of the NFL's most prominent stars, admitted to betting on games. Rozelle threw both men out of football for a year. There was, the owners discovered, more czar than boy in Pete Rozelle.

Now the networks would learn that same lesson.

By the middle of the 1960s, Pete Rozelle was on a roll. He had sold the NFL television rights in 1964 to CBS for $14.1 million a year. NBC then agreed to pay $8.4 million to the upstart American Football League for the rights to its games. Before the new commissioner had gone to work in 1960, pro football had generated less than $2 million a year in television money.

Now ABC wanted a piece of the action. All the bidding had been on Sunday afternoon games, but Tom Moore, the network president, was getting ready to ditch Gillette's Friday night fights. Would Rozelle consider scheduling some NFL games in prime time?

Rozelle was interested in exploring it. So were the NFL owners, who were drooling at the prospect of even more rights money. And so, most important, was the J. Walter Thompson advertising agency and its biggest client, Ford, whose marketing manager was a dynamic young comer out of sales named Lee Iacocca. Iacocca was ready to commit Ford to sponsor an entire night of prime-time football.

But before the games had been scheduled, Ford received batches of letters protesting the company's plan to sponsor football on Fridays. The letters, part of an organized campaign, complained that the telecasts would harm attendance at high school games. The men who hatched the plan, afflicted with New York myopia, had forgotten that in other parts of the country high schools played football on Fridays.

Friday Night Football was dead. Neither Ford nor the NFL wanted any public-relations problems. "The last thing we wanted to do was to tackle the high schools," Rozelle said. He sat down again with Tom Moore, but their options were limited.

Midweek games were out; they would disrupt practice schedules. Saturday night was too valuable to the network to dislodge entertainment shows. "What about Mondays?" Rozelle asked. No way, said Moore. _Ben Casey_, the most popular show on ABC, was going to run on Mondays in the fall of 1964.

That September, though, Rozelle did get a taste of Monday night football. A Monday night game was scheduled between Green Bay and Detroit, though it was not televised. Despite the Lions' worries that fans might not accept the departure from tradition, the game drew 69,203, then the largest home crowd in the club's history.

Two years later, Rozelle prevailed upon CBS to telecast a Monday night game between the Chicago Bears and the St. Louis Cardinals as a onetime experiment. "They weren't anxious to do it," Rozelle said. CBS had its own lineup of Monday hits, anchored by _The Lucy Show_. "But," the commissioner said, "we insisted." He could be a very insistent man.

*   *   *

In October 1968, Pete Rozelle spoke at a luncheon of the International Radio and Television Society, and Monday night football was again on his mind. The room was packed. By then, network executives knew that it was good business to listen to Rozelle.

He began his pitch for prime-time football in predictable fashion. Everyone, he said, stood to gain—the networks, the fans, and, of course, the league itself. Then he dropped a bombshell. If none of the Big Three networks is interested in Monday games, he said, "we'll go to Las Vegas and see what Dick and his friend can do."

The network people in the audience knew that "Dick" was Dick Bailey, who had left ABC in the 1950s to set up his own company to distribute sports programming. "His friend" was Howard Hughes. The reclusive millionaire had recently bought the company from Bailey and announced that he intended to make a mark in the world of sports. Surely, Hughes had the money to do it.

Not long after the lunch, Art Modell, the owner of the Cleveland Browns, arrived in Las Vegas on behalf of the NFL. Modell, the chairman of the league's television committee and a Rozelle ally, had scheduled a meeting, not with Hughes, of course, but with two of his top aides, General Nigro and Robert Maheu.

A man driving an old Chevrolet met Modell and his fiancée, Patricia, at the airport, dropped Patricia off at a casino, and then escorted Modell through a series of back entrances, automatic doors, and hallways monitored by television cameras. Modell couldn't believe what was happening.

The proposal from the Hughes people was just as unbelievable. They made a pitch to Modell for all NFL football—not just Monday nights but the complete package of Sunday games as well. Modell listened quietly and managed to ascertain that, if nothing else was available, Hughes would certainly bid on a Monday night package. Word to that effect was soon discreetly passed to the Big Three.

The ploy was classic Rozelle. Just two years earlier, Rozelle had threatened a reluctant CBS by telling them that he would sell games directly to television stations if they did not agree to a sizable rights increase. The commissioner got his price increase, to $18.8 million. Rozelle's merger of the NFL and AFL in 1966 had created the most valuable television property of all time—the Super Bowl. All that was left was to extend his reach into prime time.

Shortly after Joe Namath led the AFL's New York Jets to a 16–7 upset over the Baltimore Colts in Super Bowl III in January 1969, Rozelle began making the rounds of the networks with his Monday night package.

His first stop was CBS. Bill MacPhail, who ran Sports, was intrigued, but knew he had no chance at all with CBS chieftain William S. Paley. CBS's Monday lineup was too strong.

NBC was mildly interested. Its Monday schedule was built around movies, which could easily be preempted for fourteen weeks of the year. But NBC had a compelling reason to reject prime-time football; his name was Johnny Carson. Carson, the network's most important star, had refused to do the *Tonight* show when it had been delayed by another one of Rozelle's experimental Monday night games. Fearing a blowup from Johnny, NBC politely declined.

That left ABC and Roone Arledge, who would have snapped up the package in a moment. He had been talking for months with Rozelle and the NFL's television executive, Bob Cochran.

But Tom Moore, who was a strong supporter of sports, had been replaced as president of the network by Elton Rule, the former manager of ABC's station in Los Angeles. Rule's lieutenants all warned him against Monday night football. Not enough women would watch, they said. Even men might tune out since few would have any rooting interest in most games. The affiliates wouldn't like the idea, since late games would disrupt their newscasts. And ABC's salesmen were nervous. They would not have any postseason games; traditionally, advertisers were enticed to buy regular-season sports with the promise of time in more desirable postseason events. Arledge reported back to Rozelle: "Everybody is really down on it."

Rozelle was unfazed. He reopened his talks with Hughes. Dick Bailey, figuring he could sell the games to one station at a time, put his offer on the table. He would pay $9 million a year for the Monday night games.

The commissioner had the bargaining chip he needed. And so, finally, did Arledge.

"I'm going to try to brainwash you," Arledge said as he sat down for a final meeting with Elton Rule and the top managers of the network.

Arledge was surrounded by skeptics: I. Martin Pompadur, who was Rule's right-hand man; and Martin Starger, who ran the entertainment division and wanted to keep Monday nights under his control. But, armed with the news from Rozelle, Arledge made a prediction. If we don't take Monday night football, he said, Hughes will sell the games to many of ABC's own affiliates, who will happily dump the network's low-rated offerings. Arledge had made some inquiries and found out that affiliates in major markets, such as Philadelphia and Cleveland, would be among the defectors. "We're going to lose one hundred stations," Arledge said bluntly.

Rule remained uncommitted. He suspected that the Hughes threat might be a typical bargaining ploy. The decision was left to Leonard Goldenson. He too thought Rozelle might be using Hughes to pressure ABC; but he couldn't risk losing the stations. Goldenson, who had great confidence in his Sports chief, gave his go-ahead to Monday night football.

A few last-minute details remained, one of which was price. Hughes's $9-million offer was outstanding, but Rozelle never really wanted to do business with Hughes, a company without a set station lineup. However, ABC insisted that it could not afford to pay that much. They compromised on $8.5 million.

Before going public, Rozelle also felt obligated to pass word of the deal to NBC and CBS. Arledge was galled, but he could do nothing except sit and wait. To everyone's surprise, NBC said it wanted to take one last look at the package. The decision went right up to General Sarnoff, who, at the very last minute, said no.

In the ballroom of the Fairmont Hotel in San Francisco, where ABC was holding its affiliates meeting in May 1969, several hundred well-dressed men sipping cocktails were interrupted by a piercing siren and bursts of red light from a flashing beacon on the ceiling.

Most of them were station managers, accustomed to pyrotechnics from ABC when the network had nothing else to offer—which was often. They didn't expect this sideshow to signal anything of momentous significance.

But when Elton Rule stepped to the microphone and said he had a major announcement, every head turned his way.

Rule had been called by Arledge as soon as Rozelle got off the phone with Sarnoff. The Monday night football deal was done.

Just moments ago, Rule told the affiliates, ABC Sports purchased a package of Monday night football games from the National Football League. The games would begin in the fall of 1970, when a new deal between the NFL and, for the first time, three network partners would go into effect.

Most of the men in the room applauded, but their feelings were mixed. Many knew that Rozelle had been shopping the package around and that CBS and NBC had passed. Didn't that mean it was a questionable deal? Then there were questions about when the games would start, how late they would run in the East, how early in the West.

The crowd was abruptly quieted by another announcement. Roone Arledge was about to speak.

"Now, you must realize why I could not be with you," Arledge said over a speaker phone from New York. He told the station men that he was sitting right next to Pete Rozelle, and that the two of them were about to hold a joint press conference in New York. But first he wanted to assure the affiliates that ABC's football games on Monday night would be "the best football package on the air." He had great confidence that the games would attract a big audience and, he added, "they would help maintain ABC's position as number one in sports."

Arledge signed off and stood up with Rozelle. They shook hands. In a sense, the two men had spent the past decade preparing for this adventure.

Arledge knew better than anybody what sports could do for television. Rozelle knew better than anybody what television could do for sports.

Now the two of them would find out what they could do for each other.

At the news conference in the NFL offices, Arledge and Rozelle fielded questions from the New York press. How much did the package cost? They wouldn't say. Will football play in prime time? They said it was a sure thing. Does this mean the NFL is overexposed? Not at all.

In the crowd was a tall, slightly stooped figure covering the story for a local television station. He was happy about the news, because it was good for ABC and ABC was his company.

The prospect that he would play a role on *Monday Night Football* never entered the mind of Howard Cosell.

2.

THREE FOR
THE SHOW

"You don't sell prime-time football with two dullards in the booth."—CHET FORTE

The first casting call for *Monday Night Football* went out in the middle of a fairway.

After months of brainstorming, Roone Arledge knew what he wanted to do with his new prize attraction, prime-time football. But before he took the most crucial step, putting the stars' names on the marquee, he wanted to confer with a key consultant—his golf partner.

Roone Arledge and Frank Gifford had been friends for almost a decade. Arledge was a fan—some would say idolater—of Gifford, a celebrated, glamorous, All-Pro halfback who had played for the New York Giants, Arledge's favorite team. Their friendship was an early example of an Arledge trait inelegantly described by some as "star-fucking." Arledge loved the company of famous people, even after he became well known himself.

Their paths crossed in the surprisingly small world of New York broadcasting. Gifford, during a one-year retirement inflicted on him by a brain-rattling tackle delivered by Philadelphia's Chuck Bednarik in 1960, took a job as a sports reporter for WCBS Radio. He soon branched into television.

When he met Arledge, he took a liking to his swashbuckling style. Soon they were playing golf together or watching sports at Gifford's house in Mamaroneck. The friendship would become one of the most important in each man's life.

As Arledge set out for his golf date with Gifford, it was the spring of 1970, a year after he closed the deal with the NFL. They met at the Winged Foot Golf Club, very much the right club among New York's chic sports set.

In the course of their round that day, Arledge laid out his grand plan:

Monday Night Football would be as much entertainment as football, he said. It would be a spectacle that people would watch whether or not they cared about the game. It would appeal to women viewers as well as men.

The key player, though he had not been told yet, would be Howard Cosell. Flamboyant and controversial, Cosell would play a role that Arledge described as akin to the one played by Dorothy Kilgallen, the New York newspaper columnist, on *What's My Line*, the game show of the 1950s and 1960s.

What's My Line was the longest-running game show in the history of prime-time television, not because of the game but because of the interplay among the panelists. As Arledge saw it, people tuned in hoping to see Kilgallen fall on her face because she was so abrasive. But she was also smart; Arledge thought her sharp-edged personality gave the show its bite. She was the provocateur.

Nobody had thought that pro-football coverage needed to be provocative. That was one reason why Arledge liked the idea. He wanted *Monday Night Football*, his most high-profile show, to be daringly new.

Yet the show could not be so jarring that it turned away traditional football fans. That was where Gifford came in. He was then doing color commentary on the NFL for CBS. In Arledge's scheme, ABC would need a color man to go along with Cosell and analyze the game while a play-by-play man followed the action.

The math was out of the ordinary, even revolutionary—all the better as far as Arledge was concerned. He was going to up the ante in the broadcast booth by creating the first three-man announcing team in television history. It was just one of many precedents set by Arledge on Monday nights, but it would be the one that dominated attention. To his critics, the three-men-in-the-booth gambit would forever stand as the epitome of the Arledge approach: More is better. ABC, they said, simply put on more events for more hours with more cameras, more replays, more graphics, more sound, and, worst of all, more announcers.

Arledge never conceived of his breakthroughs in such simple terms. He was going to use more announcers, but he had a well-defined job description for each of the three men in the booth.

Cosell would provide the bite, Arledge told Gifford, so the color man had to supply the more basic football information: how Number 81 managed to get free on the deep route.

That was the job Gifford was suited for—and wanted. When ABC landed *Monday Night Football*, Gifford was eager to go to work for Arledge. He could stay tied to football and to the NFL, which he loved unabashedly, while gaining entry to Arledge's wide world of sportscasting opportunities, from the Olympics to skiing to Evel Knievel bus jumps, all of which Gifford would eventually cover for ABC.

As they walked the verdant hills of Winged Foot, Gifford said he wanted to be the color man on *Monday Night Football* "more than anything in the world." That was what Arledge wanted to hear, so he went on to outline some of the other, not-so-traditional job requirements.

The color guy also would have to be irreverent, Arledge said. He wanted to smash the attitude of adorational toadyism that prevailed at the other networks. "I'm tired of football being treated like a religion," he would say. "The games aren't played in Westminster Abbey." Arledge and his superconfident minions at ABC Sports saw themselves as Young Turks, ready to overthrow the network sports establishment. They ridiculed the reigning style of television football, personified by men like Ray Scott, CBS's voice of the NFL, who was long associated with the mighty Green Bay Packers.

"When Scott called a game, it was almost sepulchral," Arledge said, imitating a voice booming down from on high: " 'Boyd Dowler—good for fifteen yards.' "

Gifford had once been paired with Scott on a CBS Super Bowl telecast, an irony that somehow escaped Arledge's notice.

Gifford was also a good friend of Pete Rozelle, and a man so closely identified with the NFL establishment and so faithful a practitioner of the TV-football-as-Holy-Writ style that some of Arledge's associates were amazed that he would think Gifford could make the transition to ABC. But Arledge had an enduring blindspot where Gifford was concerned.

Beyond the irreverence, Arledge continued in his pitch to Gifford, he wanted his color man to play off Cosell, to puncture his pomposities and react to his outrages—and Arledge definitely expected, and wanted, Cosell to be outrageous.

Gifford listened carefully as Arledge elaborated on the job description. He knew he could provide the football mechanics. Otherwise he didn't hear anything that sounded like Frank Gifford—except maybe the part about expanding the appeal of football to women. Gifford had once been under contract to a Hollywood studio, a result of his well-acknowledged sex appeal; so he had reason to believe he had something to offer in that department.

There was also the matter of Gifford's obligations to CBS. That was no obstacle to Arledge. But Gifford had a year remaining on his contract and a well-deserved image as a man of principle. Loyalty was high on his list.

Gifford's enthusiasm for the job faded. The timing was wrong; so was the job description. He told Arledge that he didn't see himself fitting into the plans for *Monday Night Football*. A man with an unerring sense of self, Gifford knew the color-commentator role that Arledge had in mind was all wrong for him.

But it sounded awfully right for someone else.

"There's only one guy you should talk to about this job, Roone," Gifford said, shrugging off his own disappointment and thinking instantly, as he often did, of how he could be of service to a valued friend, a friend who happened to need a break like this very badly.

"Who's that?" Arledge asked.

"Don Meredith."

Gifford agreed to set up a lunch with Meredith for Arledge. In the meantime, Arledge decided that the time had come to make his first formal *Monday Night Football* appointment. He would let Howard Cosell in on his plans.

Arledge had settled on Cosell much earlier, but he had put off talking to him because he was not sure precisely where he would fit into the telecast. He knew that Cosell's main asset, beyond his thundering personality, was his unmatched skill as a sports reporter on television. At one point, Arledge thought about using Cosell on a pregame show. But the starting time the network had set for the games, nine P.M. in the East, was so late that there would be little time before the kickoff. Any delay in the action might be fatal, especially with NBC's movie rolling and *Mayberry R.F.D.* into the second burst of canned laughter on CBS.

Arledge also considered splitting away from the game in mid-stream to go to Cosell for editorial commentary, but decided that would disrupt the flow of the telecast. Besides, it would deprive the telecast of another of Cosell's talents: the ability to find a story line in a sports event and build tension around it. In that pursuit, he was the perfect disciple of the Arledge School of Drama.

But even after defining Cosell's role as commentator and lightning rod, Arledge was slow to give him the good news. The same man who easily made dozens of split-second judgments in the control room preferred to keep his options open until the last minute back at the office.

In the year since Cosell had covered the announcement of the deal for *Monday Night Football*, he had heard nothing from the ABC hierarchy about the show. Nor had he lobbied for a job. It didn't seem a likely prospect to Cosell, given the traditional practice of pairing a play-by-play man with an ex-jock in the booth.

The only time Cosell heard his name connected to *Monday Night Football*, he was taken aback by the source—Pete Rozelle. Several weeks before Arledge's golf date with Gifford, Cosell had interviewed Rozelle on his local television show in New York. When they met later for drinks at Tavern on the Green in Central Park, Rozelle told Cosell he thought it would be great if ABC put him on the telecast. Rozelle had never shown any dissatisfaction with the old ways of presenting football, but he understood that a prime-time show had to be different.

Cosell later became convinced that Rozelle had instigated his being hired for the package. But Arledge had ensured, in his negotiations with Rozelle a year earlier, that the choice of announcers would be his alone. He had compelled Rozelle, after some haggling, to delete from the standard NFL television contract a clause giving the league final approval on announcers. Arledge wore as a badge of honor his unbending refusal to allow any rights-holder, no matter how powerful, veto power over his announcer selections. It was part of his drive to make journalistic integrity a trademark of ABC's sports coverage.

That too put Arledge ahead of the competition. Just a few months earlier, CBS had demonstrated its devotion to the image of the National Football League by getting through its entire broadcast of the Super Bowl without once confronting the big story leading up to the game—allegations that Kansas City Chiefs quarterback Len Dawson had ties to a bookmaker who had been arrested a few days earlier for taking bets on NFL games. The charge put enormous pressure on Dawson, but the issue was too hot for CBS to handle. ABC and Cosell, of course, would have built the entire broadcast around the controversy.

Arledge believed that naming Cosell to *Monday Night Football* would amount to tossing a gauntlet at the NFL's feet. Instead, Rozelle told him that Cosell would prove helpful in developing a wider audience for football.

So it was that on a hot June afternoon, Arledge finally decided to approach Cosell. He learned that Cosell was having lunch at Jimmy Weston's, a Manhattan restaurant, and paged him there. After months of delay, talking to Cosell was suddenly a priority. Arledge told Cosell he had to see him immediately.

Cosell went directly to Arledge's office in the ABC building at 1330 Avenue of the Americas. He had no inkling of why he had been summoned so urgently.

Arledge got right to the point. He told Cosell in his usual matter-of-fact way that he wanted him on the new pro-football package. Cosell accepted the offer coolly—but in reality he was astounded.

He had every reason to be.

In 1955, Howard Cosell, then an obscure radio reporter touring baseball's spring-training camps with a sportswriter friend, Ray Robinson, made a stunning prediction. "I'm going to be the top guy in sports television," he said.

Robinson didn't know whether to laugh out loud or feel sorry for Cosell, an odd-looking man in his mid-thirties with thinning hair and an oversized nose. Instead, Robinson asked his friend how he intended to reach that lofty goal.

"Easy," Cosell replied. "The rest of them are all asses."

The remark was pure Cosell: brash, blunt, egotistical, profane, and, if not exactly truthful, close enough. Television sportscasters of the mid-1950s were not all asses, but most followed along after each other like sheep. Howard Cosell followed along after nobody.

While most sports at that time were described over the air in the gentle twangs of the South, the sturdy accents of the Midwest, or the new ideal—words that were rooted nowhere and spoken in bland, made-for-television tones—Cosell stood out as the voice of New York. He was an unmistakable product of Brooklyn, an ethnic borough populated by big talkers and big dreamers, and of the Great Depression of the 1930s, which produced an entire generation of men and women who were determined to give their children material wealth that they never had.

Howard Cohen was born on March 25, 1918. He changed his name back to its original form of Cosell at the request of his father, who had been given the name Cohen by immigration officials when he came to the United States. He also changed his birthdate—for less benign reasons. For years, Cosell gave the year of his birth as 1920, evidently trying to improve his prospects in a young man's business. He even gave the wrong date in his first book, *Cosell*, a mistake, he said many years later, that "must have been a typo."

Cosell's father was a clothing-company accountant who was sometimes out of work, so the family was occasionally without money; they would manage without light after their power was shut off by the electric company. His mother was overprotective and a hypochondriac, a trait that her son refined to an art. Cosell's early experiences shaped his belief that success, no matter how great, was always precarious. Especially after he met and married his beloved wife, Emmy, Cosell was driven by a desire to achieve lasting financial security.

He began traditionally—with college, a stint as a major in World War II, marriage, law school at New York University, and a successful legal practice, where he got a taste of the broadcasting business by representing a newswriters' union and entered the sports world through such clients as Monte Irvin and Willie Mays. He had always been an avid fan of sports, especially baseball, football, and boxing. However, Cosell was successful but unhappy at the law, frustrated by the slow workings of justice and eager to perform in a more public arena.

In 1954, he left law—and a $30,000 salary—for a radio job that paid $250 a week: In hindsight, his first assignment seems ludicrous—he was invited to moderate a show on the ABC radio network in which famous athletes were questioned by a panel of Little Leaguers. He got the job because he had drafted a legal charter for the New York Little League. But even then Cosell could make something out of nothing. He fed the youngsters tough questions to ask the stars, and the show gained enough notice to earn Cosell a weekend job as a sports reporter.

He arrived with so many negatives—the wrong voice, the wrong face, the wrong religion—that a lesser man would have quit before getting started. Yet sports reporting on radio and television in those days was so primitive that Cosell saw an opening. If the other guys were rip-and-read artists, content to recite the scores provided by wire services, Cosell would cover the sports scene from the field, lugging a refrigerator-sized tape recorder on his back and logging dozens of interviews each week. The clumsy, slouching figure who asked those abrasive questions was scorned by some veterans of the sports scene. The Yankees' Ralph Houk once told him, "You're like shit— you're everywhere." Cosell took it as a compliment.

Cosell's talents forced his bosses to take notice. He had a remarkable memory for detail, recalling the events of a contest held years earlier or the lineups of famous sports teams. He could use his memory as a party curiosity, or as a weapon; he had the names and numbers right, so who was going to say that he wasn't right about everything else?

His ability to ad-lib also became legendary. Cosell would deliver coherent, literate reports and commentaries without ever committing a word to paper. The words would be perfectly paced and the sentences would parse. Cosell was also a master of timing in the literal sense, though his comic timing was superb as well. He could speak for thirty seconds; he could speak for ten minutes. Either way, he would speak for exactly as long as he was told to speak. All he needed was a clock. He would turn on his microphone and deliver his simple request with supreme confidence: "Just tell me when to go."

He even managed to turn his voice to his advantage. While some men might have tried to disguise the nasal echoes of Brooklyn, Cosell made them his signature, using his voice with consummate skill: pausing here, accenting the wrong syllable there, changing inflection, cranking the volume up and down, virtually grabbing listeners and demanding that they pay attention. Later, of course, he became an inviting target for mimics. Among the most memorable was Bill Cosby with his line: "Five thousand people [pause] died in floods [pause] yesterday. They all [pause] deserved it."

Yet Cosell, even after refining his act, did not enjoy a smooth ride to the top. He had a daily radio show and, for a brief time in the late 1950s, appeared regularly on network television. But in 1959, just as his career was taking off—and just before Arledge's arrival would invigorate ABC Sports—Cosell was removed from ABC television. The president of the network, Tom Moore, didn't like him, and sent out word that he didn't want Cosell on television.

Others suggested that anti-Semitism was at work, but Cosell stopped short of making that charge. He chose to explain his exile as the result of "prejudice against truth in the sports world," a version that cast him as an even more noble victim. Yet Cosell mentioned Moore's Mississippi upbringing and described Ted Shaker, another ABC executive who fought to keep him off the air, as a Darien WASP. Certainly the experience reinforced Cosell's sense that he was an outsider and his view that the television business was a "colossal jungle."

Cosell then worked off-camera, producing a series of acclaimed sports documentaries for local television that impressed even Tom Moore. Moore suggested that Cosell get together with Arledge to talk about making documentaries for ABC.

Arledge had other ideas. He had once run into Cosell and told him he liked his work and wanted to find a way to get him onto the network. In 1965, Arledge began using Cosell on the pregame show before ABC's Saturday baseball telecasts. After that, he weaved him into *Wide World of Sports*, mostly on boxing.

On *Wide World*, Cosell came upon the brash and talented Muhammad Ali, who inspired the most memorable moments as well as the finest hour of his broadcasting career. His early years with Ali—when they staged their unpredictable, highly entertaining vaudeville act in boxing arenas all over the world—first brought Cosell and all his gifts, quirks, and bombast to the attention of a wide audience. Then, after Ali was illegally stripped of his title and barred from boxing for refusing induction into the armed services, it was Cosell's lonely and courageous defense of the fighter that forever branded him as a sportscaster with convictions, principles, and raw guts like no other who ever lived.

His support for Ali was unflagging, even though its most tangible result was the hate mail that piled up on his desk, letters that often began by calling him a "nigger-loving Jew."

In the long run, Cosell's crusade served him well. He emerged as a sportscaster with a cause, a man who was not afraid to challenge the sports establishment at the very moment that a generation was embracing antiestablishment causes. Cosell appealed to that generation; polls showed that Cosell was most popular with young people and blacks.

Cosell was drawn to the athletes who challenged the dusty traditions of American sports: Olympians Tommie Smith and John Carlos, who raised their fists in black-power salutes in Mexico City; Curt Flood, who challenged baseball's reserve clause; Pete Gent and Dave Meggysey, who wrote books attacking the pro-football establishment; and his first and most important sports hero, the man Cosell liked to call "Jackie Roosevelt Robinson." Robinson's fight to integrate the big leagues was such an emotional issue for Cosell that whenever he discussed it, he seemed to feel Robinson's victories and defeats as his own.

But, then, most issues were emotional for Cosell. Some became obsessions. He led personal crusades that permitted no room for doubt: Ali was entitled to fight and Robinson had been entitled to play in the big leagues, just as Cosell's enemy, Walter O'Malley, had no right to rip Howard's beloved boyhood team, the Dodgers, out of Brooklyn. Cosell took it all personally.

Off the air, Cosell was no different. He did *The New York Times* crossword puzzle every morning—in ink. He pierced the air after a pronouncement with a massive cigar as a kind of visual exclamation point. And he was just as definitive in his judgments of people; they were either heroes or villains. The world according to Cosell was black and white, open to no shading. And rarely did he fail to have an opinion about something.

Now his opinions would provoke millions. Not everyone would like him, but no one who saw and heard him on *Monday Night Football* would ever forget him. Cosell, at fifty-two, was well paid and well known, but his success had come at great cost. In candid moments, he admitted that the flip side of the Olympic-sized ego he displayed in public was a deep and nagging insecurity.

The condition would remain chronic, and its side effects would have lasting repercussions for *Monday Night Football.*

Arledge had great respect for Cosell's opinion. So, after he invited him to be part of *Monday Night Football,* he gave him the rundown on his plans, solicited his reactions to Meredith, and talked briefly about the possibilities for play-by-play announcer. Nothing was resolved that afternoon. It was to be a drawn-out process of elimination.

Arledge was inclined to go for a well-known personality. He wanted maximum star power on the series because he was convinced that he needed to stage a sideshow in the broadcast booth when the game on the field was either a blowout or a contest between teams with no national following. The success of Rozelle's Monday night experiments on CBS and NBC was explained largely by the presence of the league's top names, notably the Green Bay Packers and the Dallas Cowboys. Arledge had to make his show work when Cleveland played Houston and Pittsburgh played Cincinnati.

The man he wanted—and tried to get even before his talk with Gifford—was the leading play-by-play announcer in television and another friend, Curt Gowdy. Gowdy, who was also close to Cosell, was the voice of the NFL and major-league baseball for NBC. He had done play-by-play on the first sports event ever produced by Arledge, the Georgia-Alabama game, and became the voice first of the NCAA, then of the AFL, for ABC. Now Gowdy considered Arledge his best friend.

What linked the two men in their souls was *The American Sportsman*, an outdoors show that Gowdy had hosted for ABC since 1964. Arledge, an avid hunter, was introduced to fishing by Gowdy, a Wyoming native and master fly-fisherman. Arledge grew to love *The American Sportsman*, not just because it won dozens of awards but for the opportunities it gave him and Gowdy to get together in midstream. Gowdy felt so strongly about the show that he insisted on staying with it, even after he was hired by NBC.

In the spring of 1970, Arledge insisted that Gowdy join him for dinner in Manhattan. They ate at a small Italian place, and Arledge tried to persuade Gowdy to leave NBC to become the play-by-play man on *Monday Night Football*.

"It's going to be the biggest thing in television sports," Arledge said.

Gowdy was sure he was right. He believed Arledge was a genius who could pull off anything. Gowdy told him that he very much wanted the job—even though it would mean giving up the Super Bowl, the World Series, and the Rose Bowl, all events he called for NBC. The problem, Gowdy said, was his contract. It had two years to run. He didn't see how he could break it.

Arledge had an idea. He suggested that Gowdy spend the next three months gradually, but persistently, telling NBC that he was unhappy and wanted to leave. Gowdy was uncomfortable with that plan. Instead, he told Arledge, he would confront NBC head on, then report back, yes or no, in a couple of days.

Gowdy made the request to Carl Lindemann, the vice-president of NBC Sports. Lindemann blew up; he was already jealous of Arledge and all he had accomplished at ABC. He threatened to sue Gowdy if he jumped to ABC.

That was as far as Gowdy was willing to go. He called Arledge and told him he was sorry, but he would have to skip the ride to the funhouse.

Arledge then considered Chris Schenkel, who had become well known as the play-by-play man on ABC's college-football telecasts. Schenkel, as square a man as Cosell was multiedged, hardly seemed to fit the Monday night blueprint. But he was then the number-one announcer at ABC, and he was steadfastly loyal.

However, naming Schenkel could create problems with the NCAA, whose officials already felt threatened by the arrival of the NFL on ABC. Arledge had no obligation to the colleges, but he decided there was no reason to upset NCAA officials further by taking away their favorite play-by-play man.

Schenkel was crossed off the list.

Another ABC staff announcer was available, but Arledge was reluctant to use him. His name was Keith Jackson. It was not a name Arledge expected the nation to know. Jackson had worked regional NCAA games and a multitude of the lesser events that crowded their way onto *Wide World of Sports*. He was a pro, but that was not enough for Arledge, who continued to look elsewhere.

One possibility remained that Arledge knew would qualify as a play-by-play coup, exactly the kind of headline-making hire that would put the publicity mill at full grind. Arledge tried to lure Vin Scully to *Monday Night Football*.

Although he worked for a team and not a network, Scully was the most famous voice in baseball. The team was the Los Angeles Dodgers, whom Scully had followed west from Brooklyn. With his stylish, melodic delivery, Scully had brought a touch of poetry to play-to-play and attained the status of legend in Los Angeles.

Arledge felt him out through intermediaries. The response was not encouraging.

Scully had done a smattering of football on radio for CBS, but he was not comfortable calling the sport. In addition, he had a large family and was reluctant to add four more months of cross-country travel to his schedule. Besides, the early football season would conflict with his Dodger commitments.

The negatives piled high enough for Arledge, who often went to great lengths to entice major talents, to give up on this one.

The short list of play-by-play names with star power was exhausted. Arledge certainly wasn't going to try to pry Ray Scott away from CBS.

A few of Arledge's sports lieutenants spoke up again for Keith Jackson. That had some impact. But Arledge listened more attentively when Elton Rule, now president of ABC broadcasting, came forward as a strong Jackson advocate. Rule had hired Jackson as a sports reporter when he ran KABC-TV, the company-owned station in Los Angeles. He liked Jackson's no-nonsense demeanor and thorough professionalism.

It was getting harder for Arledge to say no to Jackson. Most of the alternatives were exhausted. Still, he hesitated. Then Arledge had an idea. If he could not find the right man for the job, he would find the right job for the man.

Without a star in the role, Arledge decided to take the play-by-play character off the top of the bill altogether and bury it down in the credits with the supporting players. Instead of a "Mr. Golden Throat" who would host the game, set the scene, and report on the action, Arledge envisioned a play-by-play role that he likened to the stadium announcer—a near-anonymous disembodied voice who would record nothing but basic information such as down, distance to go, and who made the last tackle.

Arledge presumed that Keith Jackson not only would be well suited for the stripped-down assignment but also that he would accept it happily because it would be a big leap in his career.

He was right. Jackson, then forty-one, did see it as a major career jump, and he was willing to take the job as outlined by Arledge—that is, as Arledge's outline was relayed to him by one of his vice-presidents, Jim Spence. In a move characteristic of the entire course of their professional relationship, Arledge did not hire Keith Jackson in person for *Monday Night Football.* Jackson was the only member of the broadcast team given secondhand treatment.

Keith Jackson was perfectly happy to become what he called "the highest-priced public announcer in the country." He could take that. He'd been through worse, he said, notably "four years and thirty-seven days" as a marine in China after World War II.

There was still some marine in Jackson. He was tall and broad-shouldered, tough-minded and stubborn, and, while he was willing to play a supporting role in the *Monday Night* booth, he did not intend to allow himself to be demeaned. He had faith in his professional abilities, even if Arledge did not.

As long as the jobs kept coming and the paychecks didn't bounce, Jackson didn't care much about Arledge's opinions.

The two men were as different as Carrollton, Georgia, is from New York, New York.

Born in 1928, Jackson was proud to label himself a Georgia farm boy. He talked about how he rode a horse to school and milked six cows a day, even though he had left the South long before and had raised his own family in the upscale hills of Sherman Oaks, California. He and his wife, Turi, had three children and a strong marriage.

Jackson had taken an indirect route to ABC Sports. He spent ten years as a television newsman and sportscaster in Seattle, then moved to Los Angeles to work for ABC Radio, cover sports for the ABC-owned television station, and freelance for the network. He had never worked in New York, and never wanted to, an attitude not likely to endear him to the ultimate New Yorker, Roone Arledge.

New York, Jackson said, was "a town that worked overtime trying to defeat you." From his vantage point out West, Jackson thought the people running ABC Sports suffered from the "New York syndrome. . . . You become insulated, get tunnel vision and forget it's a big country."

Jackson's lack of glamour probably landed him some of his early *Wide World* assignments. He would turn up at such arcane events as Scottish caber tossing, and for years he was the voice of the legendary World Wrist Wrestling Championships in Petaluma, California.

It was a long way from Petaluma to the seat beside Howard Cosell in the *Monday Night Football* booth.

Don Meredith had been calling and leaving messages at Roone Arledge's office for a week. It was no surprise that his calls were not returned. By then, Arledge was already notorious for ignoring phone messages. He once explained by saying, "I've never trusted anybody who's available to return calls. If they've got time for that, they're probably not doing their job."

Don Meredith didn't know that.

All he knew was that, thanks to his friend Frank Gifford, he had been invited to New York to discuss an offer from CBS to do regional telecasts of Dallas Cowboy games for $20,000 a year. Now Gifford was urging him to call Arledge too.

Meredith needed the money. Only a year after walking away from a $100,000 contract to play quarterback for the Cowboys, he was just about broke. He had spent the year as a stockbroker in Dallas. It had been a terrible year for the market. Meredith, by his own admission, had been a "miserable failure."

He had no reason to believe he would be any better at color commentary, but he had decided to try it for a year. He wasn't really sure what he wanted to do, though acting, country-and-western singing, and writing a novel had all crossed his mind. He saw himself not as a Texas cowboy, but as a creative guy.

When Arledge ignored his calls, Meredith was exasperated. He decided to go to New York and make a deal with Bill MacPhail at CBS.

The day he was leaving, Arledge called back. He invited Meredith to have lunch with him and Gifford the next afternoon. By then, Meredith didn't much care. He laid into Arledge for not calling back. Arledge was apologetic and soothing. Meredith, the CBS job effectively in hand, was rude.

"Hey, okay," he told Arledge. "I just want to see you and tell you what a horse's ass I think you are." Arledge wasn't sure if he was kidding.

In New York, Meredith first saw MacPhail. The CBS offer sounded fine. He told MacPhail that everything was set—but he just had to go have this lunch with Roone Arledge, which he was sure would amount to nothing.

That set a pattern for Meredith's dealing with the networks—even after he gave his word, the negotiations were not necessarily over.

Gifford set up lunch at a favorite haunt, Toots Shor's, the ultimate New York jock hangout. Things began badly. Meredith, raising his voice, said he was still angry about Arledge's phone etiquette. Arledge let it ride, and both men relaxed.

Arledge, always impulsive about hiring, was taken with Meredith: He was certainly irreverent; he was a former quarterback, so he knew the game; he was funny and country; and he might be sexy to women—all of which would set up an ideal contrast to Cosell. Arledge decided he was perfect.

Gifford left after lunch to do a radio show. Arledge and Meredith lingered for an hour or more, and Meredith told him that CBS was willing to pay him $20,000. Arledge had intended to pay the same amount, but he wanted Meredith. He saw no reason to wait, so he offered Meredith the job.

They talked money, scribbling figures down on cocktail napkins and passing them back and forth.

A few napkins later, they settled on a three-year deal at $30,000 a year, with an option for a fourth year.

As they were getting ready to leave, Meredith hesitated. By now, he knew Arledge wanted him badly for his prize show. It didn't seem right to him that he should make the same salary each year for three years. "I want a ten percent raise each year," he said.

Now Arledge was exasperated, but he said nothing. The lunch had begun badly and it was ending badly. But he wanted a strong personality on *Monday Night Football*. He could put his ego aside. The needs of the show came first.

Arledge went back to the napkins for a minute before agreeing to Meredith's raise. They shook hands.

"There's something I want you to know, Don," Arledge said. "This lunch cost me ten thousand dollars more than I expected to pay."

Meredith flashed his dandiest grin. "It's the best ten thousand dollars you'll ever spend," he said.

He was right.

Don Meredith's decision to quit football in 1969 was unexpected, but then Meredith, who conformed to no one else's standards of behavior, was constantly surprising people. Some people—among them Tom Landry and Howard Cosell—tried to figure out Don Meredith; they came away frustrated and mystified. Others, such as his bosom pal Frank Gifford, accepted him and his eccentricities, and came away charmed for life.

Meredith, at only thirty-two, was still able to play in the NFL, but he quit the game because it was no longer fun. "If it ain't fun," he would say, "it ain't worth doing." Football had been fun for him until he became a Dallas Cowboy.

He was one of those blessed children of Texas, an athlete as natural as the morning dew on the south forty. Born in 1938 and raised on a ranch in tiny Mount Vernon, the man who later called himself "Jeff and Hazel's baby boy" grew up tall and rangy and rifle-armed. He excelled at all sports, even making All-State in basketball. But in Texas, those who can, play football.

Meredith chose a college near home, Southern Methodist University in Dallas, where he had a spectacular career and, just as important, found playing football an uncomplicated delight. He was known there as "Dandy Don," a nickname his brother had given him to celebrate his talents. The nickname later would take on a life of its own, much to his chagrin, but his college days were indeed dandy. His coach, Bill Meek, encouraged his freewheeling style. As one of his later pals put it, "Don wanted to run around and dance around and throw the ball between his legs and just give him a bunch of good ol' boys out there and let's do it."

Meredith's personal style was freewheeling too. Handsome and charming, he married the campus beauty queen, then divorced her, then married and divorced her again before settling down with his second wife, Cheryl. He and Cheryl had a son and a daughter.

Meredith was such a local hero that he was signed to a contract by Dallas millionaire Clint Murchison before he had secured an NFL franchise. If Murchison did not get a team, Meredith was supposed to go to law school and work for one of his companies. It was a half-baked idea; not the first, and surely not the last, for Meredith.

When Murchison did get the franchise, Meredith was its first player, a rookie quarterback on a rookie team in the NFL. It nearly killed him. The Cowboys were a joke in the early years, though Dallas wasn't laughing. Meredith was booed ferociously by the fans and battered by the pass rushers. He did not get a lot of sympathy from the Cowboy coach, Tom Landry.

No coach has ever been dedicated to a system more than Landry. No player has ever viewed football as a form of personal expression more than Meredith. "Their personalities were just about as opposite as daylight and darkness," said Ralph Neely, Meredith's closest friend on the Cowboys. The pain felt by Meredith as he chafed under Landry's rigidly structured system was worse—or at least deeper—than that caused by the multiple fractures and sprains of nose, ankle, thumbs, ribs, shoulders, and knees that became part of his NFL résumé.

Their biggest battles were over play-calling. In the NFL of the 1960s, top quarterbacks called their own plays. Meredith thought that "one of the most exciting aspects of the position was sticking your head in the huddle with ten guys looking at you and working out what you're going to do next." Landry put a stop to that, virtually single-handedly, sending in a substitute with the play on every down.

Meredith eventually rebelled. "Tom, I don't want to talk to you," he would tell Landry on the night before a game. "Just slip your game plan under the door."

Landry, surprisingly, agreed, and the compromise worked. With the support of an improving young team, Meredith led the Cowboys to the NFL championship game against the veteran Packers in 1966. The Cowboys, who weren't expected to win, fell behind 14–0 before Meredith and his offensive unit got their hands on the ball.

The Cowboy huddle was somber as the team prepared to run its first play—until a voice began singing, "I didn't know God made honky-tonk angels." It was Meredith. "Folks," he said, grinning, "it looks like we're in a heap of shit." Everyone relaxed, and Meredith rallied the team to keep them in the game until the closing moments. Dallas had served notice on the NFL that they were an up-and-coming team, and that their quarterback had the chance to be the next John Unitas or Bart Starr.

Dallas and Green Bay met for the championship a year later, but now the Cowboys had grown up. They expected to win and go on to the second Super Bowl.

The game was played in Green Bay on December 31. It was 13 degrees below zero. The teams struggled to survive as much as win, and the Cowboys led with sixteen seconds to play. Then Bart Starr sneaked over the goal line from the 1 to give the Packers a 21–17 win.

Meredith played another season, but in a way that second championship game against the Packers ended his first career as a football star and began his second career—as a television star. CBS carried that game, which, because of the cold, had been played with unprecedented haste. When it was over, CBS had nearly forty minutes of airtime to fill.

No one had planned interviews in the losers' locker room— that element of drama had never occurred to the best minds at CBS Sports. But Gifford, who was part of the CBS broadcast team, had been sent to the Cowboys' locker room to await a Dallas win.

As the Packers celebrated on the air, Gifford sat and talked to an emotionally spent Meredith. The two men were already pals; they had become close while traveling the world together for Jantzen, promoting sportswear, partying, and playing golf. During a commercial, Gifford told a CBS producer that he thought it might be worth putting some Dallas players on the air, especially since almost every Packer except the official ball warmer had been accounted for.

With the postgame interview, Gifford was bringing his friend into television, a medium that would embrace Meredith's infectious, appealing personality.

By the time CBS finally got to the Dallas locker room, most of the Cowboys had showered. Meredith still sat on his stool with his T-shirt on and his uniform pants bloodied and caked with hunks of frozen tundra.

Gifford put the mike under his mouth, and Meredith was off and running, pouring out his feelings with such passion that it seemed he might break down: how hard his team had played; how they were the best bunch of guys you ever could know; how bad it felt; how bad he felt for them; how it almost felt like being killed, or worse.

Unintentionally, CBS had stumbled onto a moment straight out of Roone Arledge's playbook. Meredith was the personification of "the agony of defeat." He emerged a celebrity, if not a winner.

The next day, he was on talk shows. Mail poured into CBS, expressions of sympathy for the true-hearted gladiator who blamed himself for his team's loss.

Meredith had not meant to blame himself, but he did feel awful. On the plane ride home, he talked about quitting. He talked about the defeat for months—and was haunted by it for years. Some who met him later, including Arledge, thought Meredith was tormented by his Green Bay "demons." Arledge had seen Meredith, after a couple of drinks, replay the losses to Green Bay play by play, explaining how Pettis Norman dropped this pass, Bob Hayes missed that one, someone else missed a block. "Obviously," said Arledge, "he was not as free a soul as he appeared to be." Arledge was not the only one to suspect that the happy-go-lucky Meredith had a darker side.

Meredith played on in 1968, a season that ended in yet

another bitter disappointment as the Cowboys lost a playoff game to the Cleveland Browns. Meredith started the game poorly, and Landry replaced him with Craig Morton. It capped a year during which Meredith all but severed relations with Landry.

Gifford, who was again there for CBS, got on a plane for New York that night and was surprised to see Meredith and his pal Pete Gent aboard. Both players were supposed to be on the team plane back to Dallas.

They began talking and had a few drinks. Somewhere along the way, Meredith told Gifford that he could not go back to Dallas. Gifford said immediately, "So why don't you just come home with me?" He didn't want Meredith running around New York on his own. Up at Gifford's place in Mamaroneck, Meredith flopped out in the sun room and stayed three days. They took long walks together, and Meredith cleared his head. Then he flew back to Dallas to play once more for Landry, in a meaning-less game called the Playoff Bowl, which matched the losers from the division playoffs.

So much for the Dallas Cowboys. So much for Tom Landry. So much for Texas football, and training camp, and total dedication to the team. Don Meredith was going to set out on his own to see what was over the next hill.

Later, when he broadcast Cowboy games on Monday nights, everyone assumed Meredith was rooting for his old team. It was not as simple as that. Nothing was ever simple with Don.

Once Arledge assembled the stars of the show, he turned to his area of expertise: the production. Here too he was driven by the forces that shaped his announcing scheme. He was com-peting with entertainment, so he had to present football in a way that engaged the casual fan.

Fortunately, ABC had a built-in advantage. CBS and NBC had to spread their efforts over five or six games on Sundays, while ABC could throw all its resources—including every bell and whistle that Arledge and his team could conjure up—into one telecast.

As always, ABC's production story was tied up in numbers, numbers that would attract notice—and publicity: three men in the booth, nine cameras on the field, and, in a real departure, two fully independent production units in separate trailer-trucks parked outside the stadium, each staffed by a producer and a director. The other networks called it overkill.

The nine cameras seemed a particular extravagance, since everyone else made do with four or five. But Arledge had a unique deployment plan. While others located their main coverage camera at the 50-yard line—the so-called best seat in the house—Arledge put one at the 50- and two more at the 30-yard lines. He reasoned that the 50-yard line was not the best vantage point when the action moved to one end of the field or the other. Each camera was used for wide shots of the entire play or close-ups of the action. So were cameras in each end zone, which were well placed for following pass receivers on their routes.

A man with a hand-held camera worked each sideline, looking for the intimate reaction shots of players and coaches that were unseen on the other networks. Two more cameras were mounted on a wooden platform built over a golf cart, called a marketeer, which began each play at the line of scrimmage. They provided eye-level views of the offense and defense, as well as an ABC innovation—the tight shot of the ball as the players approached the line of scrimmage.

Every camera had a microphone, and two men walked the field with "shotgun" mikes, getting as close to the action as the NFL would allow. Arledge also pointed microphones at the crowds; he was always asking his technicians to crank up the volume on the mikes in the stands to deliver more crowd noise. The crunch of pads, grunts of players, sounds of bedlam from the stands—all this, he thought, brought the game to life.

If Arledge had an inspiration, it was the cinematic look of the highlight reels produced by NFL Films, a production company formed by the league in 1962. Using low angles and tight close-ups as well as stirring music and a powerful narration, NFL Films thrived by providing what weekend football did not: lyrical pictures, heightened sound, and a human dimension added to the action. Arledge and his staff wanted all that and more.

His second production unit was the most grandiose part of the scheme. The B-unit was devoted solely to isolated cameras and instant replays; the producer and director there would not have to worry about live action or, for that matter, breaking for commercials or promos. Instead, they would seek out matchups—a pass receiver against a defensive back, or an offensive tackle against a blitzing linebacker—to personalize the action.

The man chosen by Arledge to run the production, the man whose hands controlled the throttle of the television rocket that *Monday Night Football* would become, was an intense, loud, vulgar, dynamic ex–college-basketball star named Chet Forte.

Other than Roone Arledge and Howard Cosell, no one had more impact on *Monday Night Football* than Chester "Chet" Forte. Forte, who was then thirty-four, olive-skinned, short, compact, and forceful—a blunt instrument of a man—was named producer and director of the series in 1970.

Forte had won the biggest production assignment on ABC's biggest sports series because he was talented, and also because he had a good relationship with Cosell. Cosell, from the start, was the linchpin of the series, and the producer needed his support. Forte was Cosell's favorite producer; the two men had grown close as they tracked the Ali saga around the world. In Forte's typical argot, they were "asshole buddies."

Their friendship had an unlikely beginning. As a star basketball player at Columbia in the late 1950s, Forte was a nervous guest on Cosell's radio show. "Don't worry, kid," Cosell assured him. "It'll be a fine show." Cosell delivered a warm introduction, calling Forte a dazzling little man with a great shooting touch. Then he asked his first question: "Chet, is it true that some of your teammates hate to pass to you because you shoot so much?" Forte was speechless, a rare state for him.

Both men were brash New Yorkers with outsized egos and consuming ambitions. Forte was a man of bacchanalian appetites—for food, cigarettes, gambling, and women. Cosell shared some of his vices and tolerated others. Forte loved to play cards, and the two men would play gin rummy for hours on the road or in Cosell's office, trading high-decibel ethnic slurs.

"You fucking guinea," Cosell would say. Forte would respond

by bellowing, "You Jew bastard." Both men were as volatile as gelignite, so they produced countless explosions, some in jest and some real. Still, Forte said, "I was probably the only guy that got along with Howard."

Forte's crudeness belied his middle-class upbringing. He grew up in Hackensack, New Jersey, the son of a doctor. Basketball was his ticket to the Ivy League, but he struggled in class and was declared academically ineligible for his junior year.

He came back for a glorious All-American senior season, scoring 28.9 points per game. A five-foot-nine-inch guard, Forte had a dead-eye jump shot that he demonstrated years later when, as producer of the NBA for ABC, he would challenge the pros to shooting contests and, as he put it, "clean their clocks"—and their wallets.

The Cincinnati Royals drafted Forte, but cut him before the season began. He played instead for the Williamsport Billies of the Eastern League, then was offered an entry-level job at CBS Sports by a personnel officer who had followed his basketball career. Forte was enough of a star to become part of a social circle that included Bill MacPhail, the head of CBS Sports, and Pete Rozelle.

Forte moved quickly up the ladder to producer, but he felt great pressure hanging around with all those big shots. "I had to get out of that fast lane, or I wasn't going to live another five years in the business," he said. He moved to ABC in 1963, ready to gamble on Arledge. He also vowed never again to become chummy with his boss and, in all his years at ABC, he never shared a drink or a meal with Arledge.

They did, however, develop a good working relationship. Arledge, a Columbia graduate himself, remembered Forte from the director's basketball days. "I think that's why I got the job," Forte said. At ABC, Forte instantly took to Arledge's approach to sports television, and Arledge recognized Forte's talents by making him a director.

Forte had quicksilver reflexes and a brilliant feel for sports; with his great athletic instincts and concentration, he could anticipate the action. "I never saw anybody direct with such a passion," said one associate. "If he had been on the field, he would have grabbed the ball and run with it."

He was also an exacting and short-tempered—some said cruel—boss, who ruled his shows like a malevolent dictator. "I'll come down there and cut your fucking fingers off," he would threaten if a production assistant blew a statistic or punched up the wrong slide.

The sensitive tried to avoid him. But he was beloved by his hand-picked crew of skilled camera operators. Forte took care of his favorites when it came time to hand out assignments, pay overtime, or pick up the tab at a hotel. "You liked the guy, but he was a two-edged sword," said Joe Aceti, an associate director who worked the Ali fights with Forte and Cosell. "He was awful during the show, but afterwards he was a very nice guy." Others were less charitable. One longtime *Monday Night* staffer said, "Chet was a great director, but he was the biggest prick who ever walked the face of the earth."

Another friend of Howard Cosell assumed a key role on *Monday Night Football*. His name was Herb Granath, and his job was to sell the games to advertisers.

Granath was the temperamental opposite of Chet Forte—charming and cultured, patient, soft-spoken, well liked, and devoted to his family. He was known as a class act. "Herb Granath is the only guy who lived in New York City all his life and never stepped in dogshit," said another ABC executive. Granath's name was never spoken on the air, and that was fine with him. Money, more than ego, motivated Granath.

But if Granath had not been as creative, in his way, as Arledge, Forte, and Cosell, *Monday Night Football* would have failed the test that really counted—the test of the bottom line.

In the spring of 1970, Granath had a lot more to worry about than Monday nights. Arledge was in the midst of a spending spree, the likes of which had never before been seen in television. ABC had bought *Monday Night Football* for four years at $8.5 million a year, NCAA football for two years at $12 million a year, NBA basketball for three years at $5.5 million a year, and the 1972 Munich Olympics for $13.5 million. The bill came to $88 million.

It fell to Granath to turn that investment into profit, by somehow persuading advertisers to buy time on ABC at rates that exceeded anything they had previously been asked to pay for a sports show. The task was so daunting that ABC created a Sports sales department, the first at any network, in January 1970, and put Granath in charge.

Granath, forty-one at the time, had joined ABC in 1960, rising to become head of sales for network radio. He and Cosell became friends during their radio days; Cosell was in trouble with the top brass at ABC Radio for a time until Granath sold Mennen a fifty-two-week sponsorship of his radio show. Both men had grown up in Brooklyn. They also shared a strong sense of family. Granath was married to Ann Flood, an actress who starred for many years on the soap opera *Edge of Night;* though he worked long hours, he would get to work at 6:30 A.M. so that he could be home for dinner with his wife and four children.

Soon after forming the Sports sales department, Granath hired an aggressive young man named John Lazarus as his assistant. While they could call on the rest of ABC's sales staff for help, the financial future of ABC Sports rested heavily on the shoulders of these two men.

Granath and Lazarus had one clear advantage over the competition: Unlike just about every other salesman in television, Granath didn't have to worry about the daytime soaps or the evening news or whether *The Mod Squad* could knock off *The Beverly Hillbillies* on Tuesdays at seven-thirty. He spent all his time selling sports. ABC soon was selling sports better than anybody else.

Better meant at a higher price. Granath knew that the pricing of television advertising is more art than science. No one, after all, can say in advance what a minute of television time will be worth, since that depends on how many people will be watching. And, even after the commercial has run, its impact is hard to measure. So the time, in effect, is "worth" whatever a buyer is willing to pay for it—or whatever a good salesman can get for it.

Granath set out to get $65,000 a minute for *Monday Night Football.* It was a steep price, only a few thousand dollars less than what CBS was asking for *Here's Lucy,* a proven Monday night commodity that was certain to outdraw the NFL by a comfortable margin. But the NFL, unlike Lucy, could deliver men; and some advertisers were willing to pay a premium to reach a heavily male audience.

Granath looked first to Detroit. The automakers had been carrying on a long romance with televised football, not only because they sold to men but also because their selling season matched the football season. The people who ran General Motors, Ford, and Chrysler all believed that if the public was not sold on the new cars between October and December, the model year was shot. So they looked to football as the perfect sales vehicle.

Several car manufacturers looked at *Monday Night Football*, but Granath decided to sell it to just one company. That posed some risk—he was, after all, eliminating buyers in a market where they might be scarce—but it enabled him to charge a premium price. With exclusivity, an advertiser would pay more to keep out the competition. Once the price was set, Granath could try to apply it to all other advertisers.

Chevrolet, Buick, and Oldsmobile all considered the show. But, while mammoth GM was trying to get untracked, Granath struck a deal with Ford and its agency, J. Walter Thompson. Ford took five minutes of time per week and paid full price.

Of all the automakers, Ford was closest to the NFL. It had been the exclusive NFL advertiser on CBS since 1960, and Henry Ford's brother, William Clay Ford, who was a director of the company, also owned the Detroit Lions.

The support from Ford and J. Walter Thompson was crucial. JWT also bought time for Firestone and several smaller clients. Soon they were joined by other male-oriented marketers, including Schick and Hertz.

Granath had persuaded them that *Monday Night Football* would reach a new group of viewers—those casual fans who did not watch sports on the weekends. It was a pitch that would be used again and again over the years.

"There's this hardcore sports nut who is oversaturated with all the same advertisers," Granath would tell prospective buyers. "With a prime-time offering, we'll attract other male viewers who are kind of virgin territory." Many bought the argument. That was one way to justify paying ABC's inflated prices.

Granath had another brainstorm. Sponsors who came in early and paid top dollar would be given special treatment. Their care and feeding would be attended to by another new ABC department, set up to entertain important clients. They would get tickets to the games and invitations to splashy pregame parties. Other networks entertained clients, but not on the same scale as ABC.

Monday Night Football sold out in May. Granath had plugged holes on Mondays by stealing clients away from the Saturday NCAA package, where sales were lagging behind the previous year's level. Within ABC, the message was clear: NCAA football had launched ABC Sports ten years earlier, but that was history. *Monday Night* was taking over.

The *Monday Night* team assembled for the first time in Detroit to document, for internal use only, a preseason game between the Lions and the Kansas City Chiefs. It was an expensive rehearsal, with ABC transporting its entire operation to Tiger Stadium. But Arledge wanted to get a sense of how his complicated new approach to televising football would play without having to face criticism if he fell flat on his face.

Keith Jackson, Howard Cosell, and Don Meredith sat behind the microphones. Dennis Lewin, a young producer, called the replays in the B-unit with veteran director Lou Volpicelli. Chet Forte directed in the A-unit. He was not producing that night, not with the executive producer on the scene.

Arledge sat on his stool behind Forte and Jim Feeney, who had the title of co-producer, watching the action, monitoring the replays, and listening to the commentary.

Cosell began by saying that Len Dawson, the Kansas City quarterback, had an impressive completion percentage only because he threw mostly safe passes for short yards. Arledge liked that. It was a taste of what he wanted from Cosell— tough-minded judgments, not just blind praise for the men on the field.

Forte was having no trouble using all nine cameras. The two cameras on the moving marketeer were delivering stirring pictures of the battles along the scrimmage line that had never before been seen on television.

Jackson moved the game along in his brisk professional way.

Otherwise, Arledge was not enjoying the show.

Cosell talked too much. When Arledge said so, Cosell's insecurities surfaced. He pouted and said nothing for a while.

Meredith was having a terrible time. He began goofily, by saying, "Hello, football fans everywhere." He talked at the wrong time, spilling over into the live action.

The replay system was a disaster. Meredith was supposed to watch a bank of monitors and tell the B-unit whom to isolate on, but he was overwhelmed by the task. Lewin, trying to jazz up the show, was calling replays from obscure, oddball angles. He seemed to view the game as an occasion to experiment in abstract television art.

As the game unfolded, everyone realized that *Monday Night Football* had a serious traffic problem. No one knew how and when to use the replays. The announcers were undisciplined. Pictures and words rarely meshed.

Arledge broke off the coverage early. He wanted to analyze the tape with Forte before addressing the problems.

Meredith didn't have to wait for the report card. He realized he had been uptight, falling back on the most banal clichés, straining to be funny. *What am I doing in Detroit?* he wondered. *What is all this? Why am I doing this?* He was already under strain at home. That week, Meredith was struggling to decide whether to commit his daughter, Heather, born with severe birth defects, to an institution. He never used that as an excuse for his performance, but others were aware of his troubles.

The critique session took place a few days later in the ABC Sports conference room. It was a tough meeting. Arledge was not mean-spirited, but he had serious points to make, problems he wanted solved by the time they went on the air live for the first time to telecast a preseason game from Pittsburgh.

Arledge, in a rare display of frustration, chewed out Lewin and Volpicelli. He demanded to know where all the crazy replays had come from. He wanted to know why he wasn't getting the tight shots he had ordered. "If the guy wears a moustache, I want to see the fucking thing," he said. He concluded by saying pointedly, "When I make an assignment, it's because I think I've put the best person that I can on the job, and I don't want to have to change that assignment."

He was gentler with the announcers, but said that they hadn't clicked. He began to suggest some specific guidelines.

Meredith took it glumly for a while. Then he got up and

made an announcement. He wanted out. "I'm not qualified for this," he said.

Arledge and Forte tried to smooth his feathers. This was only constructive criticism, they said. They had confidence in him.

Meredith stayed and listened.

Cosell was not feeling much better about his own position after the dismal dry run, but he thought the show might collapse without Meredith.

After the meeting, Cosell invited Meredith to the bar in the Warwick Hotel, across the street from ABC. In a magnanimous mood, he tried to prop up Meredith over a few drinks. He gave him a speech about how much America—the press and the audience—was going to love him, the droll, appealing country boy, as they directed their venom at the abrasive New York Jew.

"You'll wear the white hat, and I'll wear the black hat," Cosell said, summing up the soap-opera appeal of *Monday Night Football* with startling foresight.

Meredith flew back to Dallas mildly reassured, and at least willing to hang in awhile. But in the turbulent months to come, he would require a near-steady stream of reassurance and support.

He would not be alone.

One evening shortly before the premiere of *Monday Night Football*, Cosell, who never drove a car, ordered up his regular limousine service to take him to his home in Pound Ridge, New York. Arledge, who was living in nearby Bedford Hills, ran into him on the way out. Cosell invited Arledge to share the limousine.

First, they stepped into the Warwick for a couple of drinks to take with them in the car. As the drinks soaked slowly into his system, Cosell settled back in his seat and looked over at Arledge, mischief in his eye.

"I suppose," he said with grandly affected disinterest, "that in a strange way it matters to you whether this succeeds or not."

Arledge rose to the bait and replied, pungently, "Yes, Howard, it does. And it better damn well matter to you!"

3.

LIGHTS, CAMERA, FOOTBALL!

"What do people talk about on Tuesday morning? They talk about me and Dandy and even Keith. We have become, if I may continue to tell it like it is—which is my nature—bigger than the game."—HOWARD COSELL

The camera panned the two antiquated decks of Municipal Stadium in Cleveland, the milling crowd blurred by the smoky aura from the stadium light towers.

Over the picture on the screen came the voice, the cadence distinctive yet the power oddly muted, as though reined in either by design or simply by the tension of the moment:

"It is a hot . . . sultry . . . almost windless night here at Municipal Stadium in Cleveland, Ohio, where the Browns *will* play host to the New York Jets.

"Good evening, everyone, I'm Howard Cosell and *welcome* to ABC's Monday night prime-time National Football League television series.

"As you already know, each team has a superstar. The extraordinary running back, Number Forty-four, Leroy Kelly, of the Browns; the premier quarterback, Number Twelve, Joe Willie Namath, of the Jets. . . ."

As the crowd shot faded, the head and shoulders of the man himself appeared on the screen.

He was standing on the field wearing a maroon blazer that stood out against the green of the grass, with a slicked-back toupee on his head, his hand shaking noticeably as he held the microphone under his mouth. His face was blank except for the eyes, which revealed, above the heavy, sagging bags at the top of his cheekbones, neither delight nor relaxation in their steady, almost frozen gaze.

Monday Night Football was on the air, and Howard Cosell was having no fun at all.

He had waited nearly an hour for Namath to do the pregame interview that had been set up to open the show. After some desperate cajoling, Cosell had convinced Jet coach Weeb Ewbank to let him have Namath, but the interview had to be rushed, with Ewbank standing off to one side insisting he needed his quarterback.

Cosell lumbered off the field toward the runway that would take him upstairs to the booth. He had no more time to fret over the rushed quality of the opening; he was consumed with uncertainty about his upcoming performance.

None of that uncertainty found its way into his official pronouncement, delivered to the press before the game. "With the intelligent viewers," he had said, "I'll destroy the parrots in the cages who have been providing us with their fatigued litany for years."

But Cosell confided to a friend, "I question seriously if I will have time to be myself." And he wondered out loud whether Forte would go berserk, showing off his new technical toys. His nerves showed.

Not even Arledge, watching his monitors in the truck, was completely convinced that the broadcast was ready. With Cosell so obviously on edge, he was feeling some anxiety too.

The telecast, he thought, had shaped up since the fiasco in Detroit. Everyone had performed better at an exhibition game in Pittsburgh, where the product went out over the air. Forte had mastered his nine cameras, and Lewin had delivered the replays he wanted.

By now, Arledge was sure that ABC's brand of pro football would look, sound, and feel strikingly different. He had come up with a distinctive halftime attraction—a package of highlights from Sunday's NFL games, delivered by the classy NFL Films unit and narrated with impassioned drama by Cosell. Arledge had no use for marching bands or the Kilgore Rangerettes in prime time. They could drive viewers to check out what Carol Burnett was up to on CBS, and she might be up to something funny.

Arledge had even devised a plan to help the announcers clear up their vocal traffic jam. Jackson, who sat on the far left of the booth, would speak first on every play, followed by Cosell, who sat in the middle, and finally Meredith, who sat on the right. One, two, three—left to right.

But where Cosell was concerned, nothing was as simple as one, two, three. He felt constrained by the rules. At the game in Pittsburgh, he had pouted, just as he had in Detroit. The next day, he had threatened to quit. And tonight he was clearly uneasy.

As Arledge tried to concentrate on the opening of the show, one major question gnawed at him—are these three guys going to work? It was a question that had gnawed at him for weeks.

On the screen, he saw the beginnings of an answer. Cosell had just introduced Keith Jackson and now he was talking about Don Meredith, saying that the fans might remember Dandy Don from his playing days with Dallas.

That cued a film package that had been put together to set up Meredith's comic persona—a personal-lowlight reel consisting of sacks, interceptions, fumbles, and botched handoffs.

The gag worked; it sparked sympathy immediately for the just-folks new announcer, even if it presented a grossly distorted picture of Meredith's mostly stellar career on the field.

Meredith didn't know he was going to be roasted in the film clip, but his aw-shucks reaction completed the impression: Cosell came on sour; Meredith came on sweet. Black hat/white hat. An act was born.

As a showcase for Arledge's brave new wide world of football, Game One supplied the most serendipitous sort of magic. The Jets and Browns played a near classic pro-football game, full of action, big plays, points, and, most important of all to ABC, drama.

In the booth, Cosell felt he was having an extraordinary

game. He was supremely prepared, confident he knew the Jets and Namath as well as the coaches did. Along with Meredith, Cosell had visited Namath at his apartment during the week to discuss the Jets' game plan. Now, on the air, Cosell could point out with assurance that the Jets were exploiting the Browns' rookie defensive lineman, Jerry Sherk, because that was exactly what Namath had told him they were going to do. When the Browns' offense began working on a gimpy Jets safety, Jim Hudson, Cosell said that Cleveland quarterback Bill Nelsen knew a weakness when he spotted one. At a practice on Sunday, Nelsen had told him that he was going to throw at Hudson.

This was Cosell the reporter doing his job. Cosell the commentator made an appearance as well.

First, Cosell praised Nelsen, saying that the unheralded Browns quarterback did not get as much publicity as Namath because he did not play in New York. Later, in the third period, Cosell said that Cleveland's star runner, Leroy Kelly, who had been held to forty-four yards, had not been "a compelling factor in the game." He then added, "But make no mistake about it, he will have his days of glory, such are his talents."

The second half of the comment about Kelly might as well have been spoken in Urdu, for all it was noticed.

Meredith, though his stomach had churned before the telecast, exactly as it used to before big games on the field, sounded relaxed and natural all night, as though he were chatting about the game with some friends on the front porch of the ranch. Cosell called him Dandy Don so many times that it sounded like he wanted to give him the status of a mascot—or maybe a sagebrush sidekick from a two-reeler.

At one point, Cosell went on at length about how the Jets' defense faced a critical test. "As long as Cleveland keeps possession," Cosell declared, "Namath can't score."

Meredith said, with a near-audible grin, "You've got a point there, Howard."

Later, when Cosell asked Don to explain an interference call, Meredith gave it a few halting tries before announcing, "I don't know for sure what it is, but it's a no-no."

But Meredith's moment of reckless abandon came after Cleveland wide receiver Fair Hooker pulled in a pass from Nelsen.

"Isn't Fair Hooker a great name?" Meredith asked, with the implications hanging.

"I pass," Jackson said.

Cosell, perhaps reluctant to hear what might come next, said nothing.

Meredith went on anyway. "Fair Hooker," he mused. "I haven't met one yet."

Nothing Meredith said that night qualified him for enshrinement in Bartlett's *Familiar Quotations*, but in homes all over America, where viewers were used to hearing football described as a clash of titans, he sounded breathtakingly fresh.

In the truck, it all sounded good to Arledge. He sat on his stool of authority—which his staff sometimes referred to as God's chair—calmly giving instructions, occasionally suggesting themes and story lines to the announcers. Forte directed intensely, as always, but his temper remained under wraps, as it did whenever Arledge sat behind him in the truck.

Visually, the game was eye-opening. The replays came back in slow motion and stop action, many displayed from several angles. Arledge and Forte called up split-screen shots to show receivers and defenders. For the football viewer of 1970, it was outrageously fancy stuff.

But the most striking aspect of the *Monday Night Football* look was its intimacy. Forte's marketeers, roving the sidelines, caught Namath's eyes as he looked down the line of scrimmage. The hand-held cameras delivered close-ups of the coaches as they reacted to big plays and penalties. At one point, Cleveland receiver Gary Collins was slammed to the turf and lay motionless. The convention on the other two networks was to pan to the crowd, the scoreboard, the sky, anywhere but the field and the injured player, lest the public get the impression that people really got hurt playing in the NFL. On ABC, the marketeer with its powerful lens bore in on Collins and caught him sitting up, shaking his head, looking groggy. On ABC, Collins had become more than Number 86 in the program. He had become a man with a headache.

Game One established a new visual standard for football on television, a standard symbolized in one shot, a shot so memorable that it came to be regarded as the "signature shot" of *Monday Night Football*.

The moment came late in the fourth quarter. On their last drive, Namath had moved the Jets to a touchdown with pulsating flair. Now, trailing 24–21 with less than a minute to play, New York had the ball again deep in its own territory with one last chance for victory. This was unscripted drama far more compelling than the stale detective shows and westerns that dominated prime time.

Namath, under pressure, had to hurry his first pass. The ball was picked off by Billy Andrews, a Browns linebacker, who raced 25 yards into the end zone for the clinching score.

The crowd erupted. In the truck, Forte—scanning the row of monitors, one for each camera—followed Andrews into the end zone, then called for a shot of the crowd, then returned to Andrews and his jubilant teammates. Suddenly, Arledge shouted out, "Look at Namath!" And Forte saw the image on the monitor.

"Take six!" he commanded.

The marketeer camera framed the dejected Namath, head bowed, shoulders hunched, hands planted on his hips, standing absolutely still and looking frail and beaten. The camera stayed right there, framing Namath, milking the image, as other players trotted on and off the field. Forte knew instantly that he had one of the greatest shots of his career—and Roone Arledge had called it for him.

Arledge, with all his emphasis on close-ups and reaction shots, had been seeking exactly that kind of moment. Throughout the game he had been thinking about Namath, about how drama so naturally attached to him as it did to other singular athletes in the midst of battle: Ted Williams at the plate; Valery Brumel pacing before a high-jump attempt; Jack Nicklaus lining up a putt to win a tournament. The Namath shot distilled into one arresting image Arledge's contributions to sports television: the human dimension, the climax of the drama, the agony of defeat.

With the Namath shot, Arledge attained a goal that had seemed quixotic: to bring the art of still photography to the kinetic medium of television. He had always wanted to capture a great sports moment in a way that would match anything seen on the cover of *Life* or *Sports Illustrated*. And in the very first edition of the most important program of his sports career, he had done it.

*   *   *

Leaving the stadium that night, Arledge and his men were convinced that they had done what they had set out to do. Measured against the efforts of CBS and NBC, they knew they had produced exceptional television. They had every expectation that their accomplishments would be acclaimed by the public, the press, the advertisers, and especially their own company.

They were wrong on every count.

By the next day the calls and letters were pouring in. Nobody wanted to talk about the Namath shot. Everybody wanted to talk about the loud-mouthed New Yorker who didn't know anything about football. Jet fans attacked him for denigrating Namath in favor of Nelsen; Cleveland followers ripped him for exalting Joe Willie and dismissing the great Kelly with his heinous remark about the Cleveland star not being a compelling factor in the game. If nothing else, the reactions to Cosell's innocuous comments proved that football fans expected nothing stronger than pabulum from network sportscasters.

The critics, with some important exceptions, were stridently negative. In *The New York Times*, Jack Gould said Cosell's "parochial partisanship for the Jets was grating enough but his miscalls of what happened on the field suggested that boxing is his bag." The Washington *Star* said Cosell delivered a "retching prattle" and "took the fun out of watching a really good football game." In the Newark *Evening News*, Cosell was called "the master of the verbal cheap shot." The Dallas *Times Herald* said he displayed a "towering ignorance of football."

Writers began calling Arledge to ask if Cosell was going to be dumped from the telecasts. Arledge could brush off those questions as nonsense. But other callers had to be taken more seriously: Some of the advertising agencies were on the phone, saying their clients were getting skittish about the negative reaction to Cosell.

ABC had a firestorm on its hands, and the blast of its heat was aimed directly at Howard Cosell.

The calls reached the highest levels of ABC. The day after the game, in the office of Leonard Goldenson, the chairman of the board of ABC, a figure of overwhelming influence was on the line. Henry Ford, owner of the motor company that was the principal sponsor of *Monday Night Football*, wanted to talk about the game.

Goldenson took the call.

"I listened to that gab between Don Meredith and Howard Cosell last night," Ford said. "I couldn't concentrate on the football. Take that guy Cosell off."

Goldenson listened with concern. He knew the loss of Ford's support would be a catastrophe for the series—and the company. "Well, we just got started, Henry," he said.

Ford repeated his demand: "As far as I'm concerned, you should take Cosell off."

Goldenson told Ford he'd get back to him. Then he summoned Arledge and Elton Rule to his office.

Goldenson did not mince words. He told them about the Ford call and its obvious implications. "Shouldn't we reconsider this Cosell thing?" he said.

Arledge thought fast. His commitment to Cosell went deep. He had put him on the network when others wouldn't; his instincts as a producer told him that Cosell, with all his outrageousness, was all-important to prime-time football; he had taken a public stand about backing his announcers against outside interference. But Henry Ford was Henry Ford, and there was no way he could overrule a command decision by Goldenson to fire Cosell.

"Give me four weeks, Leonard," Arledge said, "and if Howard is hogging the mike, I'll pull the plug on him."

It was a play for time that Arledge knew was so reasonable, Goldenson would have no choice but to grant it. Arledge was well aware that he shone brightly in Goldenson's eye, thanks to the profits and prestige his Sports division had brought to ABC.

Arledge got his four weeks.

Almost immediately, the picture brightened, if only slightly. Reviews that appeared the following week in publications most likely to respond to ABC's style—*Sports Illustrated* and *Newsweek*—were full of praise, if not always for Cosell, at least for the network's new approach.

In *Sports Illustrated*, Frank Deford called the announcers "a team to keep an eye on" and singled out the "magnificent shot of a defeated Namath."

In _Newsweek_, Pete Axthelm said _Monday Night Football_ had "more imagination and fewer clichés than any football telecast in memory." He enjoyed Meredith's "refreshing wit." He wrote, "Cosell is, well, Cosell: Authoritative, energetic, Olympian in his proclamation. He grates on some but his perception far outstrips that of anyone else in the business."

More important, the ratings were strong. Projected by the ad agencies to reach a 26 to 32 percent share of the audience, the first edition of _Monday Night Football_ drew a mighty 34 share. Each share point equaled 1 percent of the nation's television sets in use during those hours. ABC had broken even against the CBS comedy lineup and had beaten the NBC movie, _Boom_, an Elizabeth Taylor–Richard Burton vehicle expressly chosen for its presumed appeal to women. ABC had every reason to be elated with those results. The previous year, its Monday lineup of shows, including _The Survivors_ and _Love, American Style_, had averaged a pitiful 20 share for the season.

Arledge was optimistic, if a little apprehensive, as he looked to the weeks ahead. He had no intention of telling Cosell about his tenuous status, so he kept his conversation with Goldenson to himself. Cosell, he knew, could become terribly clingy, and he was already reeling to the point where his work might be affected. His best hope was that Cosell would be able to ride out the storm, maybe make a few converts. He sensed that a lot of the opposition was coming from people opposed to Cosell for the same old reasons—his defense of Ali, his New York accent, his ethnic background—and not because of what he was saying on _Monday Night Football_.

Just to make sure he was right, Arledge called in Forte. They replayed the tape of the first game, listening to every word Cosell had uttered. When it was over, Arledge turned to Forte and said, "What do you think?"

Forte didn't hold back: "I don't think he's done a fucking thing wrong."

"I don't either," Arledge said. "This is why I put him there. To bring out things the other color announcers don't."

He didn't tell Forte that they had only four weeks to bring Leonard Goldenson and Henry Ford and the rest of the world around to their point of view.

*   *   *

Cosell displayed none of the anxiety that was churning inside him when he arrived in Baltimore for the second *Monday Night* game, between the Colts and the Kansas City Chiefs. On Sunday night, he had dinner at the Chesapeake restaurant downtown and gave a few interviews to Baltimore sportswriters. One of the legendary Colts, Lenny Moore, dropped in to say hello. He threw his arm around Cosell and announced to the room, "This man is the greatest broadcaster in the world."

"Lenny, you're exactly right," Cosell responded.

Cosell acknowledged that many of the early reviews had been nasty, but he ascribed that to the "$180-a-week mediocrities" who had written them. Besides, the audience share had been outstanding, he pointed out. "And you know why they're tuning in?" he asked grandiloquently. "To see me."

The bravado was entirely false. Cosell had been so unnerved by the torrent of criticism that he had asked a football friend, former Lions quarterback Bobby Layne, to come to Baltimore just to say a few kind words about him to the press as a show of support. Layne showed up, though he didn't do much to turn the anti-Cosell tide.

Before the game, Arledge gave Cosell a pep talk. There was nothing desperate in Arledge's tone—there never was. He didn't want to spook Cosell further. But he did suggest that it might make sense for Cosell to hold back just a little, not to stick his neck out unnecessarily in this telecast. Cosell agreed.

But the opening of the show that night brought Cosell right back into the critics' bull's-eye. He stood on the field interviewing the two great quarterbacks matched in the game, Johnny Unitas of the Colts and Len Dawson of the Chiefs. Cosell noted that Unitas surely ranked as one of the greats of the game, but then said: "Some of the would-be experts have said you throw the short one with all of the old brilliance but the ability to throw the long one is no longer there: true or not true?"

Cosell had not said he didn't think Unitas could throw the long pass anymore, but his inquisitional style made it sound as though he wanted to prosecute Unitas for his deficiencies in arm strength. It didn't quite rank as toning down to Arledge's ears—or those of the Cosell haters in the press.

In the course of the game, Cosell repeated the comment that Arledge had liked during the practice game in Detroit. He said Dawson's predilection for throwing short passes inflated his statistics without necessarily advancing the cause of the team. The insight was valid, but mistimed. Dawson and the Chiefs were on their way to a 31–0 halftime lead.

Otherwise, Cosell was restrained—as restrained as he could be. He did, naturally, utter a few Cosellisms, including one following a fumble by Unitas: "That's exactly right, Keith. The official adjudged that the arm was not moving forward, in which case it would have been adjudged to be a forward pass, incomplete. Since it was not moving forward it was a fumble and ruled accordingly."

In the second period, Kansas City's star runner, Mike Garrett, pulled up lame after being tackled and headed for the sideline. The hand-held camera caught him, helmet off, talking to a teammate. He wondered, loud enough for the nation to hear, "what Cosell is saying tonight."

The next thing Cosell was saying was, "That Garrett is a tough, slippery kid. He'll be back. Very quickly."

In an instant, Arledge was on the interrupted feedback line, known as the IFB, which enabled him to speak to each announcer. "Howard, that's exactly the kind of thing that's going to get you into trouble," he snapped. "What if he doesn't come back?"

Cosell was stunned. *Even the boss is coming down on me now,* he thought. Cosell could only conclude that Arledge was worried about his own reputation. Arledge, he thought, was "probably the single most reactive person to print criticism I have ever known in the entire industry—other than myself."

It was more than Cosell could bear. He reacted predictably: He pouted. Cosell had next to nothing to say for the rest of the game.

He felt no better when the next round of press clips arrived, slamming him for the Unitas interview—and his wrongheaded prediction that the injured Garrett would return to the game. He hadn't.

Cosell hit bottom after the game in Baltimore. Rumors that company board members were agitating against him spread through the ABC building. Cosell suspected he was about to be fired; naturally, that made him think about quitting first.

The following Sunday night in Detroit, Cosell told Jackson and Meredith over drinks that he couldn't take it anymore.

Jackson piped up and agreed. The pressure was weighing on him too, especially since he was getting the strong impression that he was barely tolerated by Arledge and Forte. They seemed to be reminding him constantly that his job was to say only the minimum, to be the traffic cop, to set up the platform for Cosell and Meredith to play on.

Meredith now was getting rave reviews, even from columnists critical of the series. In the *Los Angeles Times*, Jim Murray said, "Meredith comes on like a riverboat gambler with a heart of gold." Joe Falls of *The Detroit Free Press* called him "the brightest thing to hit TV since somebody got the idea of inventing color." Meredith now found the talk of quitting absurd. He was making money and winning love. Life was good—so was television.

Unaware that he was under the close scrutiny of Henry Ford, Cosell had an outstanding game in Detroit as the Lions beat the Chicago Bears. Arledge, aware that his deadline with Goldenson was approaching, tried to boost Cosell's morale, praising his effort lavishly.

The anti-Cosell columns were still being ground out, but the ratings were holding—the Detroit game amazed the television industry when it was able to equal the rating for a pair of NBC specials starring Bob Hope and Jack Paar. And the show was being talked about everywhere. *Variety* reported that movie attendance took a "real nose dive" on Monday nights. That caught the interest of the ABC publicity factory, and soon every item about the impact of *Monday Night Football* was sent out to wire services and newspapers all over the country—and much of it was getting printed. A man in Long Beach, California, built a three-thousand-dollar den in his garage solely to get away from his family to watch the Monday night games in peace. A Seattle hospital tried to decree that no babies could be born between the hours of seven and ten on Monday nights. Bars and restaurants were said to be investing in large-screen television sets to bring back patrons who were staying home on Monday nights. The Lions game was followed by a report about how the television blackout of Detroit-area viewers had turned the nearby Canadian communities of Leamington and Kingsville into overnight boomtowns because they could pick up the signals from Cleveland's ABC station across Lake Erie.

All of it made an impression on Henry Ford. The week after the game in Detroit, he called Goldenson back.

"Leonard, I want to apologize," Ford said. "Despite my complaints on opening night, I like that patter that's going on between Cosell and Meredith. I'm enjoying that along with the game, and I want to withdraw my objections."

Goldenson passed the word on to Arledge—Howard had passed his probation.

Now Arledge turned his attention to Meredith, who, on the surface, was sailing. But Arledge felt Meredith might be getting a reputation for being a little too breezy, adding more quips than substantial insights. He wanted him to inject some perspective based on his experience as a player.

Meredith would have a perfect opportunity in Game Five between the Oakland Raiders and the Washington Redskins, teams run by big-name quarterbacks Daryle Lamonica and Sonny Jurgensen, respectively. At the Monday production meeting, Arledge suggested that Meredith work in some colorful anecdotes about the quarterbacks, something beyond the one-liners that made up most of his act to that point.

Meredith didn't wait long. That night, Lamonica fired a touchdown pass only two minutes into the game. Cosell, setting him up as always, fed Meredith a line about Lamonica's ability to capitalize on opportunities.

"He sure does," Don said, launching into a meandering anecdote that somehow moved from Lamonica's quarterbacking talents to the trip Don had taken with Daryle for an edition of _The American Sportsman_ about hunting Cape buffalo in Africa, and then finally to a description of how Meredith had contracted amoebic dysentery while on safari.

The silence from his stunned and mildly disgusted broadcast partners seemed endless. Finally Jackson went on with his call of the next play while the irritated voice of Arledge came through their earpieces: "Fuck the anecdotes."

A while later, Meredith reverted to form. As the marketeer zoomed in on Jurgensen in the Washington huddle, his paunch hanging over the top of his football pants like a section of firehose, Meredith said: "Now, there is an example of what clean living can do for you."

The graph charting Cosell's psyche took a sharp dive the following week in Minnesota, the night before a game between the Vikings and the Los Angeles Rams. As would happen often, the local newspaper columns, radio talk shows, and television sports reports were filled with denunciations of him. The attacks were driving him crazy.

In the lobby of the Marriott Hotel in Bloomington, Cosell ran into Don Weiss, an aide to Rozelle. In Cosell's mind, Weiss, as a representative of the football establishment, was somehow to blame for his bad press. Cosell tore into the unsuspecting Weiss, a mild-mannered man who could do little but take the abuse and report back to Rozelle that Cosell was deeply unsettled by all the sticks and stones being tossed his way.

Cosell's funk was Stygian this time. All weekend he ranted at the rest of the crew, to the point where Arledge felt he had to step in. He told Cosell to quit if he felt like it, but not to ruin the upcoming telecast with his childishness. It was a tactic that worked well with Cosell early in his *Monday Night* career. In those days, Arledge had an uncanny capacity for stroking or poking Cosell with seemingly perfect timing. Cosell apologized and turned in another solid performance.

Meredith hit for one of his more memorable lines in the Minnesota game. As the camera settled on Minnesota coach Bud Grant, Meredith, who had conducted a desultory interview with Grant before the game, said, "If Bud Grant and my old coach Tom Landry were in a personality contest, there'd be no winner."

The next evening, having heard Weiss's report on Cosell, Rozelle decided to drop by Cosell's apartment in Manhattan. He was greeted warmly by Howard and Emmy. They all shared a real friendship in those days.

Over drinks, Rozelle tried to allay Cosell's concerns about the bad press he was getting. "You have confidence in your ability," Rozelle told him. "Shake off this criticism. . . . Just have some fun with the games."

Cosell responded to the encouragement. He was deeply grateful to Rozelle.

Meredith, in that first season, was his own harshest critic. As warmly as he had been received by the press and the public, he was still leaving the booth after every game feeling drained. As the series moved into November, Meredith could not point to a single game in which he felt he had done especially well. There was always something else he wished he had said, or something he wished he had not said. In that way, television was even less satisfying to him than football. After many games, as a Cowboy, Meredith had been convinced he had played as well as he possibly could. He never had that feeling in television.

Jackson found himself pumping Meredith up before every game, and all but dragging him from the hotel to the stadium. Despite his burgeoning stardom, in private moments Meredith was talking about moving on, and about his desire to hit Hollywood after the season.

On a rainy night in Pittsburgh, seven games into the season, Meredith's morale sank further.

The Steelers, then 2-and-4, were playing the Cincinnati Bengals, who were even worse, 1-and-5. It was a terrible game. The crowd was soaked and spiritless. Early in the second quarter, Pittsburgh middle linebacker Chuck Allen made a passably good play to stop a run. Forte, desperate for action of any sort, decided to play it back. He cued Cosell, who led Meredith by saying, "Well, Dandy, our old friend Fifty-eight made the play on that one."

Meredith, unprepared as usual, did not know who wore number 58 on the Steelers. So he quickly scanned the player charts in front of him. "Yeah, look at our buddy Al Beauchamp fill that hole and make the play."

Beauchamp was number 58 for Cincinnati, not Pittsburgh.

In the truck, Forte exploded. "That fucker has the wrong player on the wrong team," he yelled into Cosell's earpiece.

Then he opened up on Meredith: "Listen, you stupid son of a bitch, you had the wrong guy on the wrong team. Not another word unless Howard asks you a direct question."

Meredith was floored by the outburst. Cosell tried to settle him by saying that Forte always became more volatile in the absence of Arledge. This was the first *Monday Night* game Arledge missed; he had gone to Europe on business.

That night, Meredith walked back to the Hilton in the rain with Jackson, who finished off a perfect evening by slipping off the side of the road into a mudhole. Jackson was less concerned about his mud-covered pants than he was about Meredith's state of mind. Don, he thought, was just terribly depressed. "It was one of those nights where you want to take all the sharp items out of the room," he said.

Meredith survived that night. But the next week brought more unhappiness. During a game in Milwaukee, he was interrupted in mid-sentence by Forte whispering in his ear over the IFB. Forte had gotten a call from Arledge, who was back in New York. He thought Meredith was going too far with the silly anecdotes.

Meredith fumed to Cosell after the game, again talking of quitting. But instead he resolved to go into the following week's game prepared as he had never been before. The time was right for Meredith to try to win back some respect, because the game featured the team he knew best—the Dallas Cowboys.

Arledge went to Meredith early in the week and reinforced the point. "You played with these guys only two years ago," he said. "You should really be able to give us great insights—and anecdotes." Arledge apparently thought it was again safe to ask for anecdotes. He asked Meredith to get inside stuff from some of the assistant coaches and even Landry, if he could stand to talk to him.

Meredith talked to everybody. He had the Cowboy game plan down, as cold as if he had been preparing to call the plays that night himself. He was also confident that his Cowboys were ready to chase the St. Louis Cardinals clean out of the Cotton Bowl.

What happened that night worked because it was utterly unexpected. It was the night that convinced the nation that *Monday Night Football* was much more about interplay than it was about interference.

The performance began in the first period, when Cowboy star Bob Hayes muffed a punt. Meredith blurted out, "Dadgum it. Things like that get the Cowboys in a hole." Realizing he was getting emotionally involved, he confessed: "Think I'm not biased tonight? Well I am. But I'll do the very best I can."

With his shrewd performing sense, Cosell recognized at once the potential for a running gag. So he exploited every pang of pain Meredith felt as his old team committed one blunder after another.

After a Cowboy punt was run back for a touchdown, Meredith said with chagrin, "There's not much tackling going on down there, boys." After the Cowboys failed to move the ball again, he said, "If we're going to have any fun on this broadcast, the Cowboys are going to have to start playing better ball." Then St. Louis scored again. "I'm going to get upset in a minute," Meredith said, sounding depressed. "In fact, I already am."

Cosell jumped in: "I wish the viewers could see Don Meredith right now. He's upset, gritting his teeth. It may make a better picture than the game."

Meredith added sadly, "I had so many funny stories to tell. I can't tell funny stories when something like this is going on."

By the time the score mounted to 17–0 near the half, the Dallas crowd started up a chant: "We want Meredith. We want Meredith." Forte ordered up shots of the crowd waving up to the broadcast booth, beckoning their lost hero.

"I'm not going down there," Meredith said. "Not on a night like this."

When the rout ended with a score of 38–0, Meredith, forlorn and contrite, apologized with disarming sincerity for the "bad job" he'd done. "I'll try to do better next week."

In the truck, Arledge's mood had shifted from concern, when the game turned one-sided so quickly, to delight. There had been no need for insight or anecdotes on this night. On this night the real fun—the only fun—was the act.

It was as if Arledge's credo had been written across the *Monday Night* screen: The show, not the contest, is what counts.

Later that week, when the ratings came out, a terrible game on *Monday Night Football* had won its time period over a Johnny Carson special on NBC. The announcers, Chet Forte boasted, had "overpowered the game."

*   *   *

A week later in Philadelphia, Howard Cosell was in no condition to overpower anything. It was November 23, 1970, and the New York Giants were in town to take on the Eagles. The fall had turned bitter cold in the East. But Philadelphia was in a festive mood because *Monday Night Football* had come to town. In one of the first examples of civic excitement over the Monday night phenomenon, Leonard Tose, the owner of the Eagles and an acquaintance of Cosell, hosted a party for the *Monday Night* stars on the evening of the game at the lounge in the University of Pennsylvania, adjacent to Franklin Field, home of the Eagles.

Cosell showed up about six-thirty, just back from the stadium where he had laid down the voice track over the halftime highlights. He did not tell anyone he felt sick.

Keith Jackson turned up late, mainly because he had been compelled to make a side trip on his way to the stadium. As he checked out of the Marriott Hotel at about four P.M., Jackson had put his suitcase on the floor behind him with his topcoat folded over it. After settling the bill, Jackson turned to pick up his bag. His topcoat had vanished. After a brief search, he decided that it had been lifted quietly by someone on the way out of the hotel.

Jackson had heard the weather reports. He knew the Franklin Field announcing booth was exposed to the open air. And he was a Georgia native, now living in Southern California. He looked across the street and saw a near-completed shopping mall. The only big store that was open was a branch of Saks Fifth Avenue. Jackson picked out the warmest-looking coat he could find. Real beaver, the sales clerk said. And tweed. Jackson eyed the price: $650. Fortunately for Jackson, the clerk had seen *Monday Night Football.* He sold Jackson the coat for $450.

By the time Jackson arrived at Franklin Field, Cosell had left Tose's party to do his pregame interview with Ron Johnson of the Giants. After about half an hour, Cosell rejoined the festivities. Arledge thought that during the two trips to the party Cosell had had a couple of martinis. Jackson thought Cosell had been drinking his usual, vodka straight up. Neither said anything to Cosell. They'd both seen Howard drinking casually at parties before the games. They were all aware, as Jackson put it, that "Howard could tote a lot."

Arledge had his own worries that night. He had consented to allow reporters from *The New York Times* and the Philadelphia *Bulletin* to sit in the A-unit for the telecast. This went against a rule Arledge himself had instituted—no reporters in the mobile unit during a live telecast. He felt it would inhibit his crew in the heat of a game. But Arledge had a weekly prime-time series to promote, so, just for this one night, he relented. The reporters were given seats in the back of the truck.

ABC's announcing position was on an overhang of the top deck, in a booth the ABC crew had been forced to construct. It was unheated. The cold, painful all day, had become piercing by game time. Jackson, Meredith, and Cosell huddled behind their table, all bundled in overcoats and gloves. On this night, for no particular reason, Meredith sat between Jackson and Cosell.

Soon after the game started, an officer of the Philadelphia fire department appeared at the back of the booth, carrying two large fire buckets. During a commercial he walked down and placed one beside Meredith and the other beside Cosell. In the first bucket was a generous bottle of Courvoisier cognac. In the other, an equally generous jug of vodka martinis. Compliments of the generous Mr. Tose.

Cosell was soon bracing himself against the cold with the help of the second fire bucket.

The game began smoothly, more or less. Cosell took note of Jackson's resplendent new overcoat and regaled the public on Keith's exquisite taste in outerwear. A little while later, an Eagle runner named Billy Walik broke a punt return for 45 yards. "Folks," Howard interjected into the replay, "I'd like to tell you about my partner, Dandy. On the way up to the booth tonight, he told me to watch this boy Walik. He was gonna break one tonight."

Meredith had said no such thing. "I don't remember saying that, Howard, but if you say I did, well I'll stick to it." He paused and added, "Howard, why do you do that to me?"

But the merriment faded a short time later, when Cosell started to have increasing difficulty getting his sentences out whole.

In the truck, Arledge was getting edgy. After another fluff by Cosell, he was exasperated. He leaned forward toward Forte and said, "What the hell is the matter with Howard? Goddammit, he's really screwed up."

Forte snapped his head around and blurted out: "That son of a bitch is drunk!"

Arledge practically tackled him. He gestured to the reporters sitting in the back of the truck and whispered to Forte through clenched teeth: "Jesus Christ! Shut up, will you!" He spun Forte back toward the monitors and told him to stay quiet about Cosell. Forte softly told Arledge he thought they should get Cosell off the air immediately. "Leave him on," Arledge said. "Maybe he'll straighten himself out."

But the situation in the booth was deteriorating. Cosell's mouth seemed to be slowing down. Jackson, taking in Cosell's erratic performance, concluded to himself that he'd been "kicked in the butt" by the combination of the cold and the martini jug.

Suddenly, with a few minutes to go in the second quarter, Cosell went white. He pitched forward and threw up all over Meredith's cowboy boots.

Dandy pressed on gracefully, ignoring what had transpired down at his feet. But Cosell was clearly in trouble. He remained quiet for the rest of the half.

At the break, Arledge got on the line to Cosell and told him to get some coffee and see if he felt any better. The highlights package, prerecorded that afternoon, was rolling. But Cosell had to come on live at the finish of the highlights to do a transition into the next commercial. When he tried to get out the score, he discovered what a pronunciation challenge *Philadelphia* can be. It came out "Full-a-dull-fa."

Arledge had heard enough. He gave Cosell the rest of the night off.

Everyone assumed that Cosell would go back to the hotel and sleep it off. But Cosell depended on his Emmy—especially in times of crisis. Without telling anyone where he was going, Cosell left the stadium with the assistance of a security guard and climbed directly into a taxi for the airport. He intended to fly home to New York. By the time he arrived at the airport, however, there were no more flights to New York. So Cosell went back into the cold night air, hailed another cab, and asked to be driven all the way to Manhattan—no matter what the cost.

Cosell arrived at his Manhattan apartment at close to four A.M.

The ride cost ninety-two dollars. Emmy took him in and put him straight to bed.

Back in Philadelphia, Meredith told the public that Howard had taken ill, but that he and Keith hoped he'd be back. Nobody with ABC knew where Cosell was. Jackson and Meredith finished up what turned out to be an exciting game—the Eagles upset the Giants, 23–20, and derailed New York's playoff hopes—as a twosome.

As soon as the game ended, ABC's production people started a frantic search for Cosell. They quickly determined that he had not checked back into the hotel. Everyone, including Arledge, got on the phones. They called every hospital in Philadelphia, even checked with the police. They kept right on calling until four A.M., when someone suggested they try Emmy. She answered and said yes, Howard was home and in bed.

Somehow, Cosell roused himself to do his five-minute radio broadcast the next morning. But when the calls started coming in soon afterward, he had gone back to bed and was reported to be under a doctor's care. Arledge, meanwhile, had been called by his ABC superiors, who shared the widespread suspicion that Cosell had gone on the air drunk. They were appalled. Arledge told them that Cosell deserved a chance to defend himself. The reporters who called ABC got an official denial that Cosell had been drunk, though there was a candid admission that he probably had had a drink at the cocktail party before the game.

Astoundingly, the only reporters in a position to provide a firsthand account missed the story. The *Times* made no mention of Cosell's disappearing act and the Philadelphia *Bulletin* said only that Cosell had become unexpectedly ill.

When Arledge finally reached Cosell, he expected him to have his defense ready. He did. It was a preposterous insult to accuse him of being drunk, he said. He'd never been drunk a day in his life. The erratic performance, the slurred words, the unfortunate incident with Dandy's boots, all that had occurred because he had pushed himself to do the telecast under inhuman conditions while suffering from a "virulent virus" that had attacked his inner ear.

Only Howard Cosell could have a virulent virus, Arledge thought. But he didn't question the veracity of the story. He realized that Cosell had to be handled with utmost care at this moment if he was to be saved. Ten games into a stunningly successful first season of *Monday Night Football,* Arledge was not about to see the star of his package run off the job because he may or may not have been drunk one night in Philadelphia. The heat was already on Cosell; Arledge had no desire to apply more.

So he did the opposite. He backed Cosell's story in public and he bucked him up in private. Arledge had planned to skip the next week's game in Atlanta, but he changed his plans, to show his support for Cosell. Arledge stayed by Cosell's side most of the evening, walking him to the booth and even sitting up there for half the game.

That night Cosell had another strong telecast—the crisis had faded quickly. *Monday Night Football* had grown too big, too special, too phenomenal, to be felled—even by a virulent virus.

The *Monday Night* act ended the season in a swirl of celebrity. The season-ending reviews were far more complimentary than critical. *Time* magazine said, "The Don and Howard show has become so entertaining that at times it comes close to upstaging the action on the field below."

Even Cosell was winning friends. He was invited to do guest shots on other television shows, including *The Partridge Family* and *Nanny and the Professor.* Since he was always drawn even more to show business than to sports, he was thrilled.

Meredith trumped Cosell that first year by walking off with the Emmy award as the year's top sports personality on television. Cosell was outwardly gracious, inwardly jealous. Years later he was still citing the Pittsburgh-Cincinnati game as the one he was *certain* had cemented the Emmy for Meredith. That, of course, was the game in which Meredith had been dressed down so harshly by Forte for his middle-linebacker foul-up. Cosell was implicitly trying to devalue Meredith's Emmy.

Taking full advantage of his raging popularity, Meredith hit the lecture circuit with a frenzy. He was going to make only $33,000 the next season, so he wanted to cash in on every side deal *Monday Night Football* could bring him. His Hollywood aspirations were put aside—temporarily.

Most important, thirteen weeks of *Monday Night Football*

had proved that Roone Arledge was right. Sports, if produced with style and flair, could thrive in the bright lights of prime time. The Monday night games had finished with an outstanding average rating of 18.5, with a 31 percent share of the audience. The numbers meant that during a typical Monday night minute, 18.5 percent of all the households in America with television were watching the game, and that 31 percent of the households that had their sets on were tuned to *Monday Night Football.* Of the twenty-two new television shows to premiere in 1970, *Monday Night Football* was ranked third, behind *The Flip Wilson Show* and *The Mary Tyler Moore Show*—two famed series of the 1970s that it would long outlive.

Television sports had established a beachhead in prime time. The World Series had always meant long lunches and transistor radios on weekday afternoons, but the next fall, one of the games between the Baltimore Orioles and the Pittsburgh Pirates was scheduled at night. Sixty-one million viewers—the biggest audience of the fall television season—watched it on NBC, and commissioner Bowie Kuhn decreed that from then on, all weekday games would be played under the lights.

The Super Bowl too was slowly eased into prime time during the 1970s, and the NCAA basketball finals were also moved, not just to prime time but to Monday nights. Organizers of the Olympic Games learned that if they wanted to maximize their income from television, they would have to schedule their premiere events to play to nighttime audiences. Rights fees for all sports escalated dramatically as the networks and the sports establishment recognized the profit potential of prime-time advertising spots.

Pro basketball felt the impact of the Monday night experiment immediately. ABC decided to air twenty-eight NBA games during the 1970–71 season, up from eighteen the year before. Ad prices were raised from $19,000 to $21,000 a minute. And Arledge scheduled the first of those games for Monday, December 21, the week after the end of the football season. He was hoping to capitalize on the sports-viewing habit he had established, and to keep the time period alive for ABC Sports.

Arledge had a grand design for Mondays. He envisioned a year-round sports night: pro football in the fall, basketball in the winter, occasional big events, and an assortment of family-oriented sports such as gymnastics and figure skating, which, with a little help from ABC, could be packaged and sold to mass audiences. Some ABC people described it as a prime-time version of *Wide World of Sports*.

However, NBA games were not the answer. The Monday night ratings collapsed immediately. ABC plugged the gap with movies, and the opportunity passed.

But Arledge had other ideas. He always had other ideas.

Keith Jackson didn't get even one week off. He remained the Monday night voice of ABC Sports the week following the last *Monday Night* game at an NBA game in Atlanta. By then, Jackson had reason to believe that his *Monday Night Football* career was coming to an end.

From the beginning, Jackson had felt nothing but chilly disrespect from Arledge. Even before the season began, when ABC organized a publicity tour for *Monday Night Football*, Arledge had sent Cosell, Meredith, Chet Forte, and even NFL star O. J. Simpson on the road. Jackson had stayed home. Arledge seldom spoke to him during the games he produced. When he did, it was usually to remind him of how minimal his role was supposed to be.

Early in November, Jackson heard from a friend at CBS that Arledge intended to add a new name to *Monday Night Football* in its second season. It was a name never far from Arledge's mind—Frank Gifford.

When Jackson quietly checked out the rumor at ABC, he learned that Arledge was indeed in the process of putting together a deal with Gifford. And he didn't need a decoder to figure out where the new man was going to fit in. The Meredith-Cosell act was all anyone was talking about. There was no way Arledge was going to break up that combination.

The news hit Jackson hard. It was the cruelest blow in a season filled with slaps to his ego.

Keith Jackson had sat nondescriptly behind the mike while his partners became overnight American icons. They had made embarrassing mistakes, thrown up on the air, staged childish tantrums; he had performed with flawless professionalism. While Meredith was charming the nation that night in Dallas with his heartfelt empathy for the Cowboys, Jackson had worked through a series of plays with his pants leg on fire, thanks to a cigarette dropped by Cosell that ignited a pile of debris under the announcing table. He had fallen in a mudhole in Pittsburgh and had his topcoat stolen in Philadelphia.

After tracking down the rumors, Jackson went to Cosell. "I've had it, Howard," Jackson said. "I'm not going back next season anyway." A self-styled "tough son of a bitch," Jackson could not abide being so coldly taken for granted.

He realized there was only one thing he could do to get that message across to Arledge. He thought: *I will make his decision as hard as I can.*

4.

TAKING A
GIANT STEP

"Roone felt Frank was the greatest thing in the world. . . . Roone really was almost like a guy falling in love."—CHUCK HOWARD

In April 1971, Keith Jackson was on the road again, plowing through another assignment—a bowling event in the tiny town of Lake Geneva, Wisconsin. He had spent much of the winter running between events for *Wide World* and play-by-play assignments on ABC's NBA package. He had been too busy to think about his future on *Monday Night Football*

Jackson finished up the bowling on a Friday night and stayed over in Lake Geneva. Early the next morning he drove his rental car the thirty-five miles up to Milwaukee, site of a first-round NBA playoff game he was assigned to cover that night. As he checked into the Downtowner Inn, the clerk behind the desk told him that he had some phone messages.

Jackson waited as the clerk went for the messages. He came back with a stack as high as a double-decker sandwich. Jackson held his breath for a second, thinking of his family, before he started flipping through them. A moment later, he realized what was going on. All the messages were from newspaper reporters. They had called in from all over the country. Jackson didn't need to call back to know what the story was about. At that moment, Keith Jackson knew he'd been dumped from *Monday Night Football.*

He had heard nothing from Arledge, or from anyone else at ABC, official or otherwise. Jackson wondered if ABC had held a press conference in New York. He went to his room and dug through the messages again: not one from ABC.

Jackson returned just one call—to the television reporter of the New York *Daily News,* Kay Gardella. The *News* had broken the story the day before, with a report by Val Adams that had been picked up by the wire services and sent around the country. It said that Frank Gifford was expected to leave CBS to join ABC as the play-by-play announcer on *Monday Night Football.* It also said that Keith Jackson was not expected to be back.

On the phone with Gardella, Jackson was blunt. He told her that he had expected the change, but made a point of saying that he had not heard from Arledge. "I did not appreciate having to read it in the papers first," he said. "I have yet to hear from Roone Arledge, and while I realize he's a busy man, it doesn't make you proud." He was upset at the way the switch was handled, he said. "I'd be a darn fool and a liar to say otherwise."

His rage was directed squarely at Arledge, who he knew was the person—virtually the only person—who didn't believe he had done an outstanding play-by-play job in the first year of *Monday Night Football.* Of course, Arledge was also the only person who counted.

Jackson, professional to his core, got through his NBA assignment without boiling over. He flew home to Los Angeles and holed up with his family. He did not call New York and ask for an explanation. It was their move, not his.

Arledge called him Monday and got a frosty reception. He wanted Jackson to come to New York—they had to talk. Jackson told Arledge he would be in the following weekend on assignment, and they could talk then.

While Keith Jackson was stewing in Milwaukee, Roone Arledge and Frank Gifford were contemplating a bright future together in Augusta, Georgia, home of the Masters golf tournament.

CBS had the rights to the Masters, but Arledge wanted them. That was reason enough for him to fly down with Gifford, who was the host of the tournament for CBS. Gifford came on at the opening of each day's coverage and delivered what Arledge called "the benediction," a solemn announcement that there would be a minimum of commercial interruptions in this grand event.

Gifford had told Arledge that before their deal was announced, he wanted to break the news to the CBS network president, Bob Wood, a good friend since their days together at USC. Wood always attended the Masters, so Gifford decided to talk to him there.

Gifford's switch had been in the works for months. After the *Monday Night* season ended, Arledge hinted to Chuck Howard, his vice-president in charge of production, that he was contemplating a change. "Keith is not a prime-time player," he said.

Cosell heard the news in January, on a flight to California with Arledge. He did not object to Gifford, though he did speak up in Jackson's favor. He figured it was Arledge's call to make.

In February, at an NCAA meeting at the Breakers Hotel in Palm Beach, Florida, Arledge gathered with his brain trust and dropped the bomb—Gifford was coming in for Jackson.

The opposition was immediate—and unanimous. Chuck Howard, Jim Spence, who was then Arledge's second-in-command, and Arledge's young aide Dick Ebersol voiced objections. They said hiring Gifford away from CBS made sense, but they opposed the idea of using him on play-by-play.

The conversation was surprisingly direct.

"I think Frank has reached the end of the road at CBS, Roone," one aide said. "He could stay there, but he's not about to get a huge offer. I think he's manipulating you."

Arledge denied that. "He's my friend," Arledge said. "He's helping me through a hard time in my life and I'm helping him through a hard time in his."

They knew what Arledge was talking about. He was going through a painful and expensive divorce from his wife, Joan. At the same time, Gifford was having family problems of his own. The two men were spending lots of time together, drinking at P. J. Clarke's or having dinner in Manhattan.

"Fine," the staffer said, sticking his neck out further. "Well, you guys can continue to help each other out; let's just not do it on Monday nights at nine o'clock."

Arledge listened without rancor. He was thick-skinned when criticism came from those he respected. Besides, he thought, some of the opposition was probably a reaction to his effort to keep Spence and Howard, whom he considered the "meat-and-potatoes, hard-core sports guys," away from *Monday Night Football*. Now, given a chance to express their opinions, they were outspoken.

Arledge responded by spelling out a long list of reasons for hiring Gifford, none of which had anything to do with their friendship.

Frank, he said, could add the technical expertise that *Monday Night Football* lacked, since Meredith had shown no interest in preparing to be an expert analyst. Even as a play-by-play man, Frank could bring up questions of strategy for discussion.

Frank is a team player, he went on, with the kind of ego that will allow him to work in the same booth with Cosell and Meredith. He's like a brother to Don, and might be a good influence on him, might even make him work a little harder. And Frank has a good relationship with Howard and great respect for his abilities.

Then there are Frank's ties to the NFL establishment, he continued. ABC had made its statement of independence with Cosell, so Frank could serve as a bridge to the league. Arledge knew, after all, that ABC needed a strong schedule from the NFL. And Rozelle's people already had been dropping hints about how some teams might not want to play on Monday nights if Cosell was going to say terrible things about them. Frank could help overcome that. He is as admired as anyone who has ever played in the NFL, and Rozelle is his friend.

Finally, Arledge said, Frank is well known and well liked. "He would add stature to the games," and to ABC Sports, he said.

The aide listened patiently to all of Arledge's arguments. "But how is it going to look?" he asked. "Won't a lot of people misconstrue this?"

"Well, that's a price I'll have to pay if they do," Arledge said.

*   *   *

Roone Arledge hated to deliver bad news. Often, he would delay a negative decision for as long as possible and then order a lieutenant, usually Howard or Spence, to do the job. He had put off the announcement of the *Monday Night* change because Gifford was still under contract to CBS, but during the wait, he never got around to telling Jackson. Now Jackson was in his office.

Arledge had worked out his consolation prizes for Jackson— the lead role in the NCAA broadcasts, replacing Schenkel, as well as continued work with *Wide World* and the NBA, and lots more money. It was, he thought, a generous deal under the circumstances.

Arledge greeted Jackson somewhat sheepishly, aware that the announcer had every right to be upset. But he was going to make it up to him.

"You probably won't believe this," Arledge said, "but out of all this you're going to emerge as a major figure in TV sports."

Then Arledge apologized for the way Jackson had heard the news. "I tried to call you, Keith," Arledge said.

Jackson had been waiting for that line. He shoved his hand inside his jacket pocket and pulled out the stack of phone messages from the Milwaukee Downtowner Inn. He tossed them on the desk in front of Arledge.

"Find it!" he said.

Keith Jackson, the first *Monday Night* player to exit the stage, did not go quietly to Saturday afternoons. In several interviews, Jackson poured out his feelings. He told a reporter the Monday night show would become either a "soaring success or a bastion of buffoonery." To another reporter, he said, "I had deep misgivings last year. I felt like Charlie Anonymous in that booth."

Jackson said that he became close to Cosell and Meredith, but that Cosell was "on an ego trip" and Meredith was "all bullshit and a mile wide."

The comments did nothing to patch things up with Arledge, but the leathernecked Jackson had no interest in doing that. He did come to acknowledge, though, that, however unintentionally, Arledge had helped his career by sloughing him off to college football. Arledge had predicted Jackson would be seen as a martyr—and he was. ABC was deluged with mail and newspaper columns supporting Jackson. Belatedly, Arledge realized that some viewers had appreciated the solid voice amid the craziness of that first season.

Despite some bitterness, what Keith Jackson remembered most about his *Monday Night Football* experience was that he walked away with his head held high—and his pockets full.

His turned out to be one of the series' more upbeat departures.

When Frank Gifford was finally introduced as the new play-by-play voice of *Monday Night Football,* he handled himself with his ever-present grace. He acknowledged that his hiring amounted to a roll of the dice for ABC. "It won't be easy replacing Keith Jackson," Gifford told a reporter. "He's a very fine announcer. If I fall on my face, well, everything's a gamble."

Gifford was moving from color analyst to play-by-play man, from the sports ghetto of Sunday afternoons to the unforgiving glare of prime time, from CBS's old-school approach to the seat between Howard Cosell and Don Meredith on ABC's razzle-dazzle mix of action, drama, soap opera, and farce. Surely this ranked as the biggest gamble of his career, which up to then had been built on the carefully plotted exploitation of his status as New York's favorite football hero.

The summer he joined ABC, Frank Gifford was healthy, handsome, famous, and forty-one—a beautifully groomed, impeccably mannered, tautly built idol of millions. It was easy to conclude that he had lived a charmed life. But, as much as Gifford was liked—and for a time he was among the most-liked men in America—he inspired an undercurrent of resentment in those who just could not see how he had parlayed so little talent into so much success after his playing days were over. "We're not talking about anybody here who's either good at being a sports reporter or good at being an entertainer," said one of Gifford's ABC associates. "His success is one of the true miracles of the latter half of the twentieth century."

He grew up not as a pampered California beach boy, a tag sometimes affixed to him because he had played football at USC, but as the shy son of a transient roughneck on oil-drilling rigs.

Born in 1930, in Santa Monica, California, Gifford had no real roots as a child. Before high school, he had moved all over California and West Texas, never completing even a single grade in one school. In one year he attended seven schools as his father moved from rig to rig.

The one constant in his life was athletics. Gifford learned very early that he could, as he put it, "run faster and jump higher than most other kids, and look better doing it, too." Sports became his roots.

USC recruited him in football and basketball, but Gifford, who never liked school, failed to meet the academic entrance requirements. "No one in my family had ever thought about going to college," he said. He spent a semester at a junior college, then was admitted to USC, where he took night courses to make up for deficiencies in English. He also took speech courses to overcome the overpowering shyness he felt in the presence of strangers and drama courses after some Hollywood producers took note of the golden-boy looks that went along with his all-American moves.

Gifford displayed those moves in abundance. On offense, he was a slashing, gliding halfback, quick to find a hole and a breakaway threat on the sweep. On defense, he was smart and tenacious. He was named to All-America teams on offense and defense during his senior season in 1951—a remarkable feat.

By then, Gifford was the prototypical college-football hero, Mr. Touchdown USA, at a time when that image stood for physical and moral—and American—splendor. He was as much a symbol as a person, a figure, in the eyes of those who idolized him, made not of flesh and blood but of bronze. The image was so powerful that author Frederick Exley made art out of his hero-worship of Gifford in *A Fan's Notes*, his novel published in 1968.

"Frank Gifford was an All-American at USC, and I know of no way of describing this phenomenon short of equating it with being the Pope in the Vatican," Exley wrote. He described Gifford's USC publicity shot as "a head and shoulder print showing him the apparently proud possessor of long, black, perfectly ambrosial locks that came down to caress an alabaster, colossally beauteous face."

Gifford headed for New York in 1952 as the first-round draft choice of the Giants, who gave him a $250 signing bonus and a rookie salary of $8,000—good money in those days. He began as a defensive back and played both ways in 1953. So great was his ability that he made All-Pro on defense. Later, he made All-Pro as a running back four times, becoming the only NFL player ever to be All-Pro on offense and defense.

But Vince Lombardi, who became the Giants' offensive coach in 1954, put a stop to that double-duty. For the next seven seasons, Gifford became the heart and soul—and feet, and occasionally arm, since Lombardi had installed the halfback pass expressly for Gifford—of the Giants' offense.

It was a time for legends in New York sports. Joe DiMaggio was retired, but Mickey Mantle and Willie Mays had just arrived. Whitey Ford pitched for the Yankees; Yogi Berra caught him. And Jackie Robinson was in Brooklyn, with the boys of summer.

The football Giants carved out a special identity. Gifford, Rote, Conerly, Huff, and Robustelli were a shared experience for the fans of New York, who were falling in love with pro football. The team enjoyed a rare camaraderie, with Gifford leading the offense on and off the field. "He was the number-one guy," said Alex Webster, the Giant fullback.

The Giants lived together in the Concourse Plaza Hotel near Yankee Stadium during the season. After the games they would all go back to Gifford's or Charlie Conerly's place. They would eat and drink together at Toots Shor's and Mike Manuche's and P. J. Clarke's. "We were New York," Gifford said. If there was a note of discord, it came only from the defensive men, who stuck together and sometimes scorned Gifford and his crowd as glamour boys.

Gifford was well paid by the Giants, but he quickly perceived that he could do much better financially if he took advantage of the magic effect he seemed to have on people.

"People have always looked for things in me they'd like to see in themselves," he said, adding somewhat disingenuously, "I've never known what to think of it."

Gifford may not have known what to think of it, but he did know what to make of it—associations, opportunities, and, most of all, money.

"When I was getting done with football practice," he said, "I was putting on a suit and tie so I could meet someone who might be able to help me in the off-season."

First Gifford pursued a Hollywood career, trading on his matinee-idol looks and contacts from USC, but also throwing himself into acting classes. He signed a contract with Warner Bros. in 1957 and, during the off-season, had bit parts in two movies and starred in pilots for television series, including a show about the New Jersey state police called *Turnpike*, which was his personal favorite. Gifford played a trooper whose job was to keep the Jersey Turnpike safe for good citizens.

When Gifford's Hollywood career stalled, he concluded that he was being "jerked around" and Giant owner Jack Mara helped buy him out of his contract with Warners. But he continued to dabble in acting, and he was convinced he could drop everything else and succeed at it if he ever decided to.

Besides, Gifford thought, his training in acting came in handy when he was faced with situations that made him uncomfortable. "A lot of times you don't like to be where you are; so you can perform there," he said.

Gifford began performing as a broadcaster in 1958, on a Giants pregame show with Chris Schenkel. He was hampered by some voice problems and struggled with pronunciation— *Pittsburgh* always came out as "Pissburgh," a risky situation when the Giants played the Steelers. Gifford's solution, as always, was hard work. He took voice and speech lessons and corrected the problems.

Still, at first Gifford was a disaster behind the mike, "from nervousness and inexperience," he said. "The audiences kind of forgave me because they liked me." There were those who would say that was the story of Gifford's life.

His broadcasting career got an unexpected boost from the devastating Bednarik hit in 1960. Gifford became a full-time radio sportscaster in 1961 and kept the job when he returned as a player the following season.

The Maras raised his salary to a team-high $35,000 when he returned, but he was making more than twice that sum from his off-the-field activities.

By 1962, beyond his sportscasting work, Gifford could be seen endorsing hair tonic, swimming trunks, sweaters, shaving cream, slacks, belts, and cigarettes. He appeared in an episode of the television comedy *Hazel* and made speeches all over the country. He had developed a taste for the good life, as evidenced by the comment of a Giants executive who said, "Not many athletes live in the style that Frank does. When we fly, say, into Chicago on an afternoon, the players are given $6 for dinner that night. Many of the boys will buy four hamburgers and a Coke and pocket what's left. But Gifford is apt to drop in at the Pump Room of the Ambassador East and eat a good dinner for $12."

Gifford retired from football in 1964, ending what was, by any measure, a Hall of Fame career. He finished with 3,704 yards rushing, 5,434 yards pass-receiving, and 78 touchdowns—the last two are still Giants records.

He glided smoothly into network television, announcing on the day of his retirement that he was signing a deal with CBS to be the analyst on Giants games. Before long, he was getting the top assignments to NFL championship games and to the 1967 Super Bowl. His low-key, traditional approach to the game fit the CBS image perfectly.

Seven years after retiring from football, as the new star of Arledge's championship team at ABC, Gifford's future seemed secure. He had settled in the exclusive New York suburb of Mamaroneck, where he and Maxine, the campus homecoming queen he had married at USC, were raising their three children—Jeff, eighteen, named after his coach at USC; Kyle, fifteen, named after his Giants teammate Kyle Rote; and twelve-year-old Vicki. The rough-edged son of an oil driller had come a long way, and if he still felt uptight in public or uncomfortable around strangers, he rarely let it show. Gifford was enjoying the success he had worked so hard to achieve.

"Frank likes to be number one," said Alex Webster, his friend and former teammate. "There are a lot of guys around who are number two and number three, but how many are number one?"

Gifford was going to be number one at ABC, at least in Arledge's mind, although Gifford was not at all sure he liked ABC's new style of NFL coverage. To Gifford, a traditionalist to the core, the grand game of football was supreme; no fancy packaging was needed. "I feel strongly about commentators becoming the show," he said. "The game of football is the event. We're strictly there to report." He stood by his the-game-is-the-thing line all through the years, even when evidence to the contrary was flying around his head every Monday night.

Frank Gifford, a football hero of the old school, brought the values of the gilded age of the 1950s to the most revolutionary sports program ever hatched. It would be an odd mix, at best. The combination of Gifford and Cosell, an antihero of no school but his own and a product of the turbulent 1960s, ought to have been explosive—an anachronism meeting an anarchist.

That it wasn't, at least not for some time, was entirely the result of Frank Gifford's surpassing ability to carry the ball— determinedly, tirelessly, bloodlessly.

Arledge worked closely with Gifford in the months leading up to his first ABC football assignment, the Hall of Fame Game in Canton, Ohio, which was added to ABC's NFL package in 1971. Gifford needed some special attention, Arledge thought, because he was about to enter "a cauldron," surrounded by Meredith, the instant Emmy winner, and Cosell, who was "now in orbit, the darling of Hollywood," with appearances on sitcoms and variety shows.

The Hall of Fame Game was a good place to start. A mid-August exhibition game, the contest was ignored by all but the most fanatic fans. "It's a good chance for you to get to know the other guys and break in on the air," Arledge told Gifford. Still, Gifford was a little apprehensive, especially since he was new to play-by-play, and the preseason rosters were packed with dozens of unfamiliar names and numbers.

The night before the game, Gifford suddenly had a lot more to worry about. He was told that part of his premiere assignment would be to interview the president of the United States.

It was a break for Gifford in one sense: He considered Richard Nixon an old friend. They had met at a football game in Washington in the 1950s when Nixon, then vice-president, yelled to Gifford from his box at Griffith's Stadium; Gifford went over to introduce himself. When Nixon ran for president in 1960, Gifford endorsed him. Several years later, when Nixon moved to New York to practice law, Gifford regularly got him tickets to Giants home games. After the games, Nixon loved to drop over at Gifford's place to meet the players and talk football.

As much as Gifford might have felt at home then with Nixon, he was now being asked to question the president in a slightly more formal setting—inside a sealed-off building with cameras rolling and spotlights shining, under the scrutiny of producers, technicians, presidential aides, Secret Service personnel, and a national television audience.

Gifford, Arledge, and Dennis Lewin, who was now co-producing the series with Forte, were ushered into the Hall of Fame and locked up early in the afternoon. Gifford, who was conscious of his need to prepare for the upcoming game, could do nothing but wait for the president.

Nixon arrived an hour later and greeted Gifford warmly. He then shook hands with Arledge, assuring him that he really did know Frank Gifford, that he really had attended parties at Gifford's apartment. Arledge could not believe what he was hearing: "Here was the president of the United States trying to impress people because he knew Frank Gifford—and because Frank Gifford knew *him*!"

For ten minutes or so, Frank Gifford and President Nixon talked football. Nixon was worried about the Washington Redskins and their off-season trades. He impressed Gifford with his knowledge. "He knew the names of all the players involved," Gifford said. Nixon even suggested a candidate for the Hall of Fame, a player from the fifties named Gene Brito, who had died of a rare, crippling disease.

Finally, they did the on-air interview. They talked about Nixon's plans to go to China. Gifford was surprisingly relaxed, and Arledge told him afterward that he had done a great job.

Gifford did not get through the rest of the preseason so smoothly. The telecast of a Jets-Chiefs game was ragged and slightly out of control. Meredith and Cosell, trying to help Gifford, talked incessantly, to the point where Arledge ordered them to back off. Gifford acknowledged he was doing badly, blowing a lot of names and numbers. The ghost of Keith Jackson haunted the early reviews.

By the time the *Monday Night* team arrived in Detroit for the opening game of the 1971 season, Gifford was as nervous as he had ever been. The booth was not like the football field, a place where his natural gifts were unquestioned. This was a place where talents would be tested that no one, not even

Frank Gifford himself, was sure he possessed. In the press, Cosell called Gifford "a tense young man who is aware that he is performing before millions in prime time, something he has never done before." He also told one reporter that he thought ABC had made a mistake substituting Gifford for Jackson.

Gifford tried to compensate for inexperience with what one ABC executive called "a work ethic that could kill you." He began a routine that he would maintain throughout his *Monday Night Football* career, watching game films during the week, watching more NFL games on Sunday, attending practices, talking to players and coaches, and spending much of the weekend poring over names, numbers, and background data. He committed some information to index cards, and condensed as much as possible onto a board that sat in front of him at all times during games. Some people admired his diligence, but others thought the routine was obsessive. "Frank had a way of taking an hour's worth of preparation and turning it into four," one producer said. "He's a worrywart."

Gifford was sure that the effort paid off. "There's nothing wrong with a little preparation," he said. "And there's a whole lot to be said for a whole bunch of preparation."

The production plan for the second season was designed to ease Gifford into the flow. The plan, according to one staffer, was to "put the fucking blinders on Frank. Don't look at Don or Howard. When the ball was dead Frank was supposed to shut up."

On Sunday afternoon in Detroit, they taped an opening for the show. Gifford began by calling Detroit cornerback Lem Barney "Mel Barney."

That night, Gifford could not sleep. His nervous system was on overload. In just a few hours, he would be on television trying to remember numbers and keep up with Cosell and Meredith. And the whole world would be watching.

If Gifford was an anxious newcomer, Cosell and Meredith were starting their second season on a roll. They were telling the world how much they admired, respected, even loved each other. The act was back—this time in near Day-Glo bright-yellow blazers that Arledge had conceived as the new ABC Sports uniform. Maroon just hadn't been eye-catching enough.

Meredith was in mid-season form for the opener in Detroit. Just before airtime, with tension in the booth at the cracking point, he grinned and said, "Peace, flowers, and love, everybody." Gifford put up his fingers in a V-sign—he didn't cross them—and the booth manager counted him down into the opening.

Gifford committed two fumbles in his first game as the quarterback of *Monday Night Football*, but neither proved costly. First, he mistakenly announced that backup quarterback Norm Snead had entered the game to replace starter Gary Cuozzo. The information had been passed to him by Meredith—not the most reliable of spotters, as he had proved the year before. When Gifford announced the switch, Cosell shook his head violently. Meredith, recognizing his error at once, jumped in to apologize and try to take the heat off Gifford.

Then, early in the second quarter, a production assistant, trying to plan ahead, put a card in front of Gifford that gave him the exact wording to use at the halftime break. But Gifford grabbed the card and at that moment announced the end of the first half—ten minutes too early.

Yet considering all that he had been asked to do—set the lineups, call the plays, get the telecast into commercials, work in the incessant promotional announcements, and avoid stepping on his two mates in the booth—Gifford could be forgiven a mistake or two. Down on his stool in the A-truck, Arledge was elated. "Frank is getting better by the minute," he announced buoyantly. "No matter what all those other guys think, this thing is going to work!"

Meredith still had the old charm. He cringed after the Vikings' Carl Eller whacked the Detroit quarterback with a stiff forearm. "Ah, be nice to those boys, Carl," he said. "They've got mothers, just like you." When the camera zoomed in on stone-faced coach Bud Grant, Meredith broke into a few bars of "You Are My Sunshine."

After the game, Gifford was relieved. He even managed to say, "It was a lot of fun."

Not all the reviewers agreed. Jack Craig in *The Boston Globe* cited the game's "mixture of errors of fact and judgement plus contradictions." In the *San Francisco Chronicle*, Glenn Dickey said, "I much preferred Keith Jackson, who had everything necessary to be a good play-by-play man for the show except the one absolute essential: the friendship of Roone Arledge." Stan Isaacs of *Newsday* called Gifford "a walking mannequin" and said, "Gifford moved into a spot with Cosell because he's producer Arledge's buddy. Gifford is a nice guy; it's nice he has a friend like Arledge."

But there was still praise for Forte and his camera work and imaginative use of replays. A reviewer in the Houston *Post* called the game "a smashing success . . . the opening show was platinum smooth."

Overall, it sounded like a plus to ABC. The ratings were strong, the phenomenon was holding, even building. Gifford could withstand being called a mannequin—he would get plenty of experience withstanding it in years to come.

Gifford's arrival altered the chemistry of the *Monday Night Football* broadcast booth, though the changes were barely noticed at the time.

During the early games of the season, Meredith made every effort to help his pal Frank shine as much as possible. That was a logical move for Meredith, given the debt he owed Gifford for getting him the job, but it also made sense for the show, which had so much riding on Gifford's performance.

Meredith's approach did not sit well with Cosell. He felt left out, the outsider on his own show. After Game Three in Cleveland, Cosell went back to his hotel suite to have a few drinks with his friend Herb Granath and Dick Wozniak, an ABC account executive in Detroit. He began to complain about the way things were going in the booth. That night, Cosell had made a comment and solicited a reaction from Meredith, only to have Meredith pass it on to Gifford. He accused the two ex-jocks of deliberately shutting him out of the commentary—a charge that was to have an indefinite statute of limitations.

Cosell, overreacting as always, got so worked up he decided on the spot that he needed official representation. Because of his unswerving fealty to the company, Cosell had never before used an agent. Now he grabbed the phone and called Bob

Schulman, his attorney in New York, and asked him to take on the responsibility of representing him immediately. The groggy Shulman agreed. It was one-thirty A.M.

When the show arrived in Dallas for Game Four, Cosell had some fun at the expense of both his partners. The Cowboys and the Giants, their former teams, were engaged in a poorly played, fumble-filled comedy of errors.

"Well, gentlemen," Cosell said, "neither of your respective teams is showing me much this evening."

"Well, Howard," Meredith replied, seizing the opening, "at least we do have respective teams."

In the truck, Forte, looking out for his own buddy, provided Cosell with an even better comeback. He suggested that Cosell ask Gifford and Meredith if they knew who held the NFL record for the most fumbles in a game.

Cosell then announced that the ignominious record-holder was none other than the Danderoo, whereupon Forte switched on the camera in the booth to catch Meredith's reaction.

"Aw, I didn't do that, did I, Howard?" he said, winningly as usual.

The Dallas game also proved to Forte and Dennis Lewin just how unworkable their co-producing arrangement could be.

Forte had decided to use the Goodyear blimp on the telecast to capture the atmosphere of the Texas State Fair outside the Cotton Bowl. Standard practice called for the producer to pass the word that the blimp was being used back to ABC, so that the sales staff could make any necessary adjustments. Bitter rivals Goodyear and Firestone then sponsored alternate weeks of *Monday Night Football*.

But with neither man clearly in charge of the broadcast, Forte and Lewin both had failed to make the necessary call from Dallas, because each thought the other man was responsible for it. Because the game was so sloppy, Forte used the blimp early and often, frequently breaking from a commercial to a shot of the blimp flying high overhead. Gifford, of course, noted its presence: "And there's the Goodyear blimp on this beautiful evening in Dallas." Meredith, bored with the telecast, grabbed a publicity package supplied by Goodyear and delivered a lesson on the blimp's history and construction to the audience.

When the game ended, Lewin got a call in the truck. It was

Granath, from Sports sales, with a clipped question: "The blimp, why did you use it?"

Lewin said something about the nice view of the fair.

"Yeah, nice view," Granath said. "But Firestone was a sponsor on the show and you guys came out of every single Firestone commercial with a shot of the Goodyear blimp!"

Firestone threatened to pull out of the series over the incident. "They were absolutely convinced that there was a payoff, that somebody was on the take," said Granath.

It took him most of a year to smooth things over.

Game Six in Baltimore featured a classic Cosell encounter of the political kind.

Before the game, Cosell strolled through the Colts locker room casually needling players in his facetious way. He spied Colt owner Carroll Rosenbloom talking in a corner with Spiro T. Agnew, the once-obscure Maryland governor who went on to become vice-president of the United States. In 1971, Agnew was at the peak of his fame as Nixon's conservative hatchet voice.

Cosell sauntered over. "Do you know this man, Mr. Vice-president?" Rosenbloom asked.

"Of course," said Agnew. "Howard and I have worked the banquet circuit together."

"Absolutely true, Mr. Vice-president," Cosell replied, "but presently irrelevant. Tell me, sir, what is your position on Jewish ownership?" Rosenbloom grimaced in mock pain.

"There's no statute that bans them, Howard," Agnew said, no slouch at the game.

Cosell then walked with Agnew toward the lockers of four of the Colts' black players, including star tight end John Mackey. He then pronounced, in his booming tones, "Then it's your position, Mr. Vice-president, that this team is saddled with too many blacks?"

Again Agnew didn't flinch. "I didn't put it that way, Howard. What I said was there ought to be an intelligent reexamination of the quota."

Cosell had so much fun with Agnew that, without consulting the producers, he invited him to be his guest on the opening of the show. He brought Agnew up to the booth and introduced

Meredith, who was decked out in his canary-yellow ABC blazer, red tie, boots, and suede cowboy hat.

"Agnew? Here?" Meredith bellowed. "Well, hello, Mr. Vice-president. I luv ya, but I didn't vote for ya. But here's someone who luvs ya and probably did, Frank Gifford."

Gifford and Agnew shook hands as Meredith ran down the seating arrangement for the vice-president, who observed it all and said the booth housed "a veritable plethora of talent."

"Whooeeeeee!" Meredith yelped. "Did you hear that, Howard?"

Off to the side, Gifford merely mumbled, "Just fantastic."

Agnew turned back to Meredith with a suggestion. "The next time a player is complaining to a referee about a call, why don't you say that he's keening?"

Meredith shook his head. "I'll tell you what. If you tell me what it means, I'll use it."

In the opening, Cosell reminisced with Agnew about the great Colt teams of the past, with Agnew recalling that he bought his first season ticket in 1947.

"For you, sir," Cosell said with a flourish, "we wish the Colts a victory. As for us in the booth, absolute objectivity!"

As always, Cosell concluded his part of the opening by throwing it to Meredith. Meredith was ready. He remembered that Spiro Agnew wristwatches were the rage. "I hope you all noticed," he said, "that the vice-president was wearing a Howard Cosell wristwatch."

Once Gifford became more comfortable in the booth, Arledge traveled to fewer games. He was a man for conceiving and launching things, not for sustaining them. He watched the show, of course, and called in each week with comments, suggestions, and demands, if only to let the troops know he was paying attention. He would tell Forte to turn up the crowd noise, or to flash the score more often. Still, Arledge's absence was a sign that the show was on solid ground.

The show's success brought out the arrogance of the young hotshots on the production team. Forte loved to boast about *Monday Night Football*. He was telling people he found it "incredible" that CBS had won an Emmy for its football coverage.

Don Ohlmeyer, who had just joined the show as replay director, also shot off his mouth. "I'll put any one of our *Monday Night* telecasts up against either NBC or CBS's coverage of the Super Bowl to date," he said.

None of this endeared ABC Sports to the competition. In what was surely the best evidence of the show's impact, the sports divisions of CBS and NBC began to denigrate *Monday Night Football* publicly.

Bill MacPhail of CBS Sports, who had tried to hire Don Meredith, was now putting him down. "I wince with embarrassment when those guys do a funny. Meredith is like a buffoon, waiting to be cute. Cosell's style is good for a 15-minute show, but not for an action game," MacPhail said. "On CBS the game is the star. ABC has lost sight of the fact that pro football is a game, not a show for three TV stars. What should we do, follow them with a team of Don Rickles, Milton Berle, and Mickey Rooney?"

Carl Lindemann of NBC said, "Don and Howard are amusing for a while, but they become an intrusion. We don't subscribe to ABC's show-biz approach to pro football. Our sports department is in the news division, and we try to present football in a journalistic way. The novelty of ABC's approach is rapidly wearing thin."

Privately, the campaign took other forms. Neither CBS nor NBC executives were at all sure that the ABC approach would wear thin, so they complained to the NFL about the *Monday Night* schedule. Bob Wood, president of the CBS Television Network, sent a three-page letter to Pete Rozelle, complaining in great detail about the attractive matchups that the league was giving to ABC. Rozelle saw the complaints for what they were— "professional jealousy"—but the NFL did placate the other two networks a bit with the next schedule.

It would make little difference. *Monday Night Football* had become the starship of television, a fast-moving monolith that swept enemies aside in its wake. The ratings soared during the second season, to a 20.8 average with a resounding 36 share. *Mayberry R.F.D.* was canceled. Carol Burnett was moved to Saturdays for her own protection. NBC started buying the rights to bigger, more blockbuster-type movies to run on Monday nights.

Frank Gifford had proven that he was more than a mannequin with friends in high places. He was becoming one of the
most popular personalities on television—just as Keith Jackson
was on his way to becoming the answer to a *Monday Night
Football* trivia question.

Critics of Roone Arledge inevitably came back to the same
theme: Sports was all show business on ABC. The charge was
not entirely unfair. After all, Arledge's college-football memo, his
manifesto of sports television, had promised to "add show
business to sports." And Arledge ultimately did view sports
merely as raw material, unformed clay that needed to be
shaped, embellished, and packaged for popular consumption.

But the implication of the charge was that Arledge himself
was nothing more than a creature of show business, a man who
lacked seriousness. His detractors portrayed him as spendthrift
and splashy, but not substantial.

The rebukes bothered Arledge, who cared deeply about his
reputation. As much as he enjoyed his success at ABC Sports
and the financial rewards it brought him, Arledge also craved
legitimacy. He wanted to be seen as someone who mattered, not
just as the casting director who matched Howard Cosell with
Don Meredith.

Arledge became someone who mattered in September 1972.
He responded forcefully to his critics—and enhanced his own
reputation—by producing a stunning series of words and
pictures beamed from the blood-stained arena of Munich, West
Germany.

Arledge and his men seized the attention of the nation for
one tragic day in Munich, as Arab terrorists raided the living
quarters of the Israeli Olympic team. Their resourcefulness in
covering the story was amazing. Nothing quite like their live
up-close-and-personal coverage of a life-and-death story had
ever before been done in the history of television journalism.

Arledge was at the center, of course, sitting in the ABC
control room, orchestrating reports from the Olympic Village—
most of them from Cosell and Peter Jennings—with the brilliant
anchor coverage of Jim McKay in the studio. Munich changed
the image of Roone Arledge, changed the image of ABC Sports,

changed television itself. From then on, whenever a catastrophe struck, viewers no longer were content to wait for film at eleven; they expected television to afford them a chance to be eyewitnesses to history.

The rest of the '72 Olympics were marked by chaos and controversy, especially for the American team—and ABC documented all of it. Cosell confronted the American track coach who had failed to get his sprinters to the stadium in time for a heat, and managed to generate some heat of his own, as viewers complained that his interrogation was too harsh. Cosell also sorted out the debacle of the basketball finals, in which the American team was robbed of a gold medal—and in the process rescued Gifford, who had been assigned to the event but was overwhelmed by it.

He put the entire Olympiad in typical Cosellian perspective with his description of Avery Brundage, the chairman of the International Olympic Committee and a man Cosell saw as an ancient fount of Olympic hooey. "There was a time for Avery Brundage," Cosell said, pausing for dramatic effect, ". . . that of William of Orange."

There was one small piece of fallout from Munich that directly affected *Monday Night Football:* Don Meredith did not appear as an ABC commentator during the games. No one thought much of it at the time—except Meredith, who had made it clear that he wanted to be included in ABC's plans.

The snub turned into a burr that buried itself deep under Meredith's saddle.

As *Monday Night Football* began the 1972 season, just being Howard Cosell had become an event. Everywhere he went, he was mobbed by well-wishers and hooted at by ill-wishers. The first week of October, he graced the cover of *Newsweek*—the first and, to date, the last sportscaster to appear there.

That same week, the Giants beat the Eagles, 27–12, in Philadelphia, and Cosell decided to ride back to New York after the game rather than stay over. After his experience two years earlier, Philadelphia was not his favorite city.

ABC had arranged for a limousine to take Cosell home. With him was Emmy—Cosell had it written into his contract that his wife could accompany him whenever she wanted, at ABC expense—and his pal Herb Granath.

Cosell had a drink in the owner's box while waiting for the parking lots to clear and all the fans to go home. The stadium had gone dark and quiet by the time Cosell and his party walked out to the parking lot. Across the way in the darkness a shout went up: "It's Cosell!" Cosell and the others looked around and saw a convertible, with its top down, filled with a bunch of young fans. Beer cars were strewn nearby.

Granath sensed at once that they were the sort of "drunken crazies" who could be a problem. He hustled Howard and Emmy into the back of the limo and told the driver to take off—fast. The limo shot through the parking lot and headed for the expressway. Granath turned and looked through the back window.

"Shit, they're following us," Granath said. "Get moving," he told the driver. Cosell, sitting next to him, was getting edgy.

The driver wheeled the car skillfully through the streets until he hit the expressway. Then he gunned it up to seventy miles an hour. The convertible was close behind.

The limo flew to the entrance to the New Jersey Turnpike and got through before the convertible could catch up. Then they were on the turnpike, flying north in the thin traffic in the early hours of Tuesday morning.

They looked back again. The headlights of the convertible beamed into their eyes.

Inside the limo, the concern was building. What were these lunatics going to do if they caught up?

"Here they come," the driver said, and they could feel the rush of the flying convertible as it pulled out from behind them and moved alongside in the left lane. Granath's heart raced. He pushed himself deeper into the backseat. Cosell said nothing.

The convertible passed them doing at least eighty, and began to cut in and out in front of the limo. Granath thought of how easily the drunken kid behind the wheel could spin out of control. But suddenly the convertible slowed down, until the limo pulled even with it, and they were careening along side by side. The crazies inside the convertible were holding up beer cans and yelling wildly; inside the limo the passengers were holding their breath.

Then, in the backseat of the convertible, one of the young rowdies pushed himself to his feet, rocking wildly with the speed of the hurtling car. With herky-jerky exaggeration he spun himself around, bent at the waist—and dropped his pants.

"My God!" Cosell said in horror. "That man is exposing himself!"

"Howard," Granath said, suddenly relieved, "he's mooning you."

ABC's schedule of Monday night games looked weak in 1972. Many of the games involved lesser teams, and several appeared to be potential mismatches. Game Four, when the mighty Oakland Raiders traveled to Houston to play the woeful Oilers, turned into a rout.

Cosell believed it was the worst football game he had ever witnessed. Oakland was stumbling badly, but still annihilating the Oilers. At one point Cosell said, "I think we should get some game films of this, Giff, and take it around to the local high schools to encourage the youngsters. There's no way they can be this futile."

The score mounted to 34–0. It was the worst scenario for ABC, a blowout with the home team on the short end. The Astrodome was emptying as though a bomb threat had been phoned in.

In the truck, Forte, who became frustrated and angry when the games got dull, saw that one of his cameramen had spotted a curious sight. In an almost-deserted section of the stadium was a man asleep—the perfect image to convey a dreadful night in Houston.

Forte called for a long shot. There was the man on national television, sleeping in an empty section. Forte milked the shot—Cosell called it "a vivid picturization of the excitement attendant upon this game"—and then zoomed in for a close-up. Just then, the fan's eyes popped open into a take-this leer and he lifted the middle finger of his left hand.

The booth erupted. "Oh, ho!" Cosell cried. At that moment in the truck, Lewin hit the key to Meredith's earpiece: "It means we're number one!" he shouted.

"They're number one in the nation," Meredith said, the

comment timed perfectly as the initial raucous reaction died down.

The line made its way instantly into the collected folklore of Don Meredith. It would be years before he admitted that one of his best _Monday Night Football_ lines was the product of a ghostwriter.

"Cyril Pinder, up the middle! Power and speed at play!"

Howard Cosell turned his voice up to full throttle, pounding out the words like a vocal jackhammer. Halftime highlights soon became a full-blown phenomenon.

Everyone at ABC was amazed by the mania surrounding the highlights. Conceived by Arledge as a way to hold on to viewers between halves, the highlights had become so popular that advertisers lined up to sponsor them at premium rates. Fans talked about them as avidly as they discussed the games.

The clips, supplied by NFL Films, were thrillingly shot and tightly edited. But Cosell's narration turned the highlights into a prime-time event. O. J. Simpson was always "The Juice," Ken Anderson was always from "tiny Augustana College," and every star receiver was "that man."

Cosell would perform his weekly theatrics on Monday afternoon, using only a few notes drafted by a production assistant. No one else in broadcasting could have transformed a batch of football clips into such compelling entertainment.

Nor could anyone else have provoked the frenzy over the highlights that gripped some fans.

By 1972, the highlights were attracting more mail than any other aspect of _Monday Night Football_. Fans wrote to complain when their favorite team had been snubbed by Cosell.

The protests often were fanned by local radio and television reporters, who would seize the fact that their team had been left out one week as evidence of ABC's—and Cosell's—dislike for their team and city. The highlights were such an issue with Pittsburgh Steeler fans that the Pennsylvania state legislature passed a resolution censuring Cosell and ABC for keeping the Sunday Steelers' games out of the highlights. Cosell cited the resolution for years as proof that sports were out of whack in America—as well as proof of his own impact.

The highlights lunacy reached its peak in Miami in 1972. The Dolphins were in the midst of an undefeated season, so their fans believed every win deserved a place in the highlights. When a game was excluded, the mail would pour into Cosell's office, much of it vicious. One letter was sufficiently threatening that Cosell turned it over to the FBI.

By the time the ABC crew arrived in Miami, the papers were running stories about ABC's anti-Dolphins bias. What appalled Cosell and the others, however, was that the campaign was being led by the sports anchor at ABC's affiliated station in Miami.

To try to stem the tide of ill feelings, Forte and Cosell did interviews with the sportscaster, spelling out to him the limitations of halftime highlights. In the six minutes allotted, fewer than half of Sunday's games could be included. When games of the nation's bigger market teams—particularly the Giants—were blacked out at home, they usually were included. But the bottom line was that Cosell had nothing to do with picking the highlights. That was co-producer Dennis Lewin's job.

The interviews ran on Miami television that Sunday night. But the anchorman had a hot thing going and he intended to ride it. He announced, on the air, that Howard Cosell and Chet Forte were staying at the Sonesta Beach Hotel in Key Biscayne.

Forte and Cosell were deluged with nasty calls. Cosell had to travel to the game with a special security detail.

It wouldn't be the last time.

The Cosell-Gifford relationship turned testy and unpredictable in 1972. Cosell's designation of Gifford as "Faultless Frank," in the alliterative triumvirate that included "Dandy Don" and "Humble Howard," contained the same convoluted mixture of friendship, jealousy, and contempt that marked Cosell's deepest feelings about Gifford.

Gifford was indeed a friend. Cosell told the world this repeatedly in those years, one time even telling a magazine writer that Gifford was "nonpareil, the best friend I have in life." Both men joked about the time one of Cosell's daughters wet through her diaper while sitting in Gifford's lap.

Yet Cosell resented the all-too-obvious Gifford image: the football hero, the nice guy, the most likable man in any room. Frank Gifford was everything Cosell was not. And millions of fans did see Gifford's work as faultless, although Cosell knew firsthand how absurd that was. Gifford, still new to play-by-play, made errors and misstatements every week that drove Cosell to disgust, all the more so because he often seemed to be the only person in America who noticed them.

Cosell's conflicted feelings surfaced often.

In Game Six, when the Bears beat the Vikings in Chicago, Gifford said on several occasions that Mike Eischeid of the Vikings was back to punt. This was fine when he was punting for the team that employed him, the Vikings, but Gifford also had him punting for the Bears. When Cosell told him afterward that he had Eischeid punting for both teams, Gifford tried to turn it into a joke: "Why not, Howard? The guy's a hell of a kicker." Cosell treated Gifford kindly when he told the story in his first book. But when his feelings shifted, Cosell would use the story to ridicule Gifford and steal the punchline for himself.

For the most part, Cosell had nothing but nice things to say about Gifford in public. He praised him for his hard work and dedication, and even exempted Gifford from his frequent attacks on the "jockocracy"—a favorite term he borrowed from the writer Robert Lipsyte and used to describe the folly of taking athletes straight off the field and into the broadcast booth.

Privately, though, Cosell could be scornful of Gifford's talents.

The twin emotions that Cosell felt toward Gifford came together during the last two weeks of the 1972 season. On the first of the last two Mondays, Mayor Joseph Alioto of San Francisco hosted a typically garish *Monday Night Football* lunch at the St. Francis Hotel. The room was packed with local dignitaries and the press, including a *San Francisco Chronicle* columnist named Glenn Dickey. Dickey was not a fan of *Monday Night Football* and said so in that morning's *Chronicle*. He particularly opened up on Gifford, who was, in Dickey's opinion, "the worst play-by-play man in the business," an announcer incapable of criticizing athletes and coaches.

At the lunch, Cosell took the keys to the city from Alioto on behalf of his partners, then introduced Meredith, who did a few minutes of shtick. Finally Cosell called on Gifford. Nobody expected Gifford to mention the column, but that was all he could talk about. He had been rattled by Dickey's attack, and as he attempted to defend himself, he all but broke down.

Cosell, seeing Gifford's distress, ushered him off and took over the microphone himself. He had, of course, seen the column, which also contained a slap at him, namely that he was becoming an "establishment" announcer. Now Cosell set out to avenge both wounds. "Is Glenn Dickey in attendance here today? Because he has attacked my colleague and now he will endure my wrath!"

Cosell, at the height of his powers, could extemporize as well as any man alive. He tore into Dickey that afternoon with his own uniquely engaging brand of venom. When he was finished, the room rose in a standing ovation and Gifford and Meredith approached him with pride. The "coach," as they fondly called him, had done them all proud.

A week later, the team was in Oakland for the season-ending game matching the Raiders and the Jets. In the middle of the game, Gifford suddenly announced that Oakland receiver Warren Wells was flanked wide to the right. Wells, in fact, was in prison. The onetime star receiver had been arrested and imprisoned on rape charges the year before.

Cosell, who had a "cough key" on his microphone so he could go off air when he felt the urge to cough, switched himself off and turned to the young gofer working the booth. Cosell mouthed the words: "Can you fucking believe that?"

When Cosell turned back, Meredith leaned in and whispered: "Did Frank just say Wells was flanked out wide?"

"He sure did," Cosell whispered back. "He's flanked out wide all right; he's all the way out in San Quentin!"

Meredith would come to label the game "The Great Escape."

After the game, Cosell called aside the twenty-five-dollar-a-day gofer, a college sophomore named Dorrance Smith to whom he had taken a liking. "You've got to ride back with me in the car," Cosell said to the stunned Smith. "Because I'm going to tell you something and you're the only person that will know."

Smith, believing he was onto the scoop of a lifetime, naturally went along. After a suspenseful buildup, Cosell told him: "Kid, I'm never going to work another *Monday Night Football* game again. You've heard it here first."

Cosell blamed it all on Gifford. He complained about him and his mistakes all the way back to San Francisco from the Oakland stadium. He brought the Eischeid game back up again. And now tonight. "Could you believe that Frank would have Wells in the game? I'm calling Arledge tomorrow and I just wanted you to be the first to know. What do you think?"

What else could a twenty-year-old gofer think? He told Howard he was "absolutely right."

Cosell, of course, had no intention of quitting. And Arledge knew it. So, when the call came, Arledge did what he always did when Cosell threatened to quit—nothing at all. Cosell, he knew, needed "constant reassurance."

"His security blanket was Roone Arledge," said an ABC executive. Another said: "I think Howard needed Roone just to be on the other end of the line saying, 'You're right, Howard.' "

Cosell's calls to Arledge often came at six A.M., when Cosell, the early riser, was getting up—and Arledge, the late-nighter, might be just getting to bed. The calls became so frequent that Arledge took out the private line in his apartment and installed an answering service. After that, Cosell called Chet Forte, Herb Granath, Dick Ebersol, Don Ohlmeyer, or whomever else he could find to listen, and urged him to pass his complaints along to Arledge.

Arledge let slide most of what Cosell said about Gifford, realizing that "what might be vindictive in another person was just normal behavior for Howard."

But it was not an easy balancing act, because when Arledge saw Gifford, for golf or whatever, he heard the other side. And Gifford, Arledge learned, was being driven "crazy" by Cosell's harping on his mistakes.

Cosell was just getting warmed up, and Gifford's resentment was just starting to build. Arledge would be caught in the crossfire for years.

Despite a weak schedule and aggressive competition, *Monday Night Football* maintained its ratings strength in 1972. More important, the show was making money.

In the third year of its contract with the NFL, ABC was still paying $8.5 million a year for the rights to the games. That was the best bargain in sports television. With ad rates rising, *Monday Night Football* returned more than $20 million in revenues in 1972, nearly half of which flowed through to the network's bottom line.

The contribution was significant. ABC announced that in 1972 the network had turned a profit for the first time in ten years.

*P*ete Rozelle (left) and Roone Arledge after sealing the deal
to bring football to prime-time television, 1969

*F*rank Gifford
with his first wife,
Maxine, 1958

Keith Jackson, the original play-by-play man, 1970

Capital Cities/ABC, Inc.

Chet Forte, the director of *Monday Night Football* from 1970 to 1986

Capital Cities/ABC, Inc.

*D*andy Don Meredith

Dennis Lewin, producer of *Monday Night Football*'s replay unit in 1970, went on to become full producer of the show from 1977 to 1979.

President Richard M. Nixon, with Arledge and Gifford, before Gifford's first appearance on *Monday Night Football*, 1971

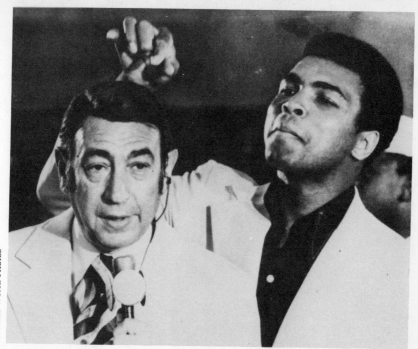

The Cosell and Ali act, 1972;
the champ threatens to lift the lid on Howard.

Monday Night Football at its best: Meredith looking askance,
Cosell waxing eloquent, and Gifford keeping his eye on the field

Don Ohlmeyer, *Monday Night Football* producer from 1973 to 1976

Fred Williamson, the first *Monday Night* flop, 1974

Alex Karras with
Cosell shortly after
Karras joined the
team, 1974

Cosell, kicking off the publicity for another
Monday Night Football season, with Karras and Gifford, 1975

Arledge in the
ABC control room,
calling the shots

Cosell appropriated Ed Sullivan's theater
—temporarily—for his variety show in 1975.

5.

AMERICA'S TEAM

"Someone once asked me: What was the best course you took in college to prepare you for what you're doing today? I said: 'Child Psychology.' "—DON OHLMEYER, producer of Monday Night Football

Against the slate-gray sky of a bitter-cold Saturday in late December 1972, two teams of proud, determined men stood face-to-face with destiny in an arena whose every rafter housed a host of gridiron ghosts.

The place: Yankee Stadium. The teams: ABC's *Monday Night Football* crew and ABC's NCAA football men. The game: touch football. The line: *Monday Night Football* by ten. The stakes: bragging rights inside ABC Sports—and a winners' share of one hundred dollars a man. Losers share: minus one hundred dollars a man.

The fierce rivalry between the casts and crews of ABC's two football packages was played out on the same field of battle where that other momentous pigskin clash, between a team from Baltimore and a team from New York, had been waged on a frigid afternoon fourteen Decembers earlier. The only difference: The hitting may have been slightly harder in 1972.

At least that's how the only participant in both games felt

after the very first play. Frank Gifford set up to go out for a pass and somebody knocked him down. "Touch football turned into a war," he said.

The hard hitting reflected the hard feelings between the two factions of ABC football. The NCAA faction, led by producer Chuck Howard, took great pride in its achievements. They had been the first to apply Arledge's style of sports television to football, giving viewers tight shots of players, reaction shots of coaches, and the sounds and colors of Saturday afternoons on campus. But Chet Forte's *Monday Night* bunch was getting all the glory, and they were not about to relinquish any to the college boys.

The rivalry was partly personal. Forte and Howard were longtime competitors for Arledge's favor, and they couldn't stand each other. When they worked together, which was seldom, they would play "top this" in every conceivable way.

"If Chet suddenly turned around and told you to get him a pizza," one production assistant said, "Chuck would suddenly want fried chicken. So you'd move heaven and earth to get it there fast. Then the stuff would arrive and neither one of them would eat it."

Sometimes the bad blood affected the telecasts. Forte would do as little as possible to promote Saturday college telecasts on Monday nights. "Why should I help that son of a bitch?" he would say. "He never mentions our games on Saturday."

The NCAA crew took the game so seriously, they ordered team shirts and held practices. On the day of the game, Howard arranged for a chartered jet to pick up ABC's college-football announcer, Bud Wilkinson, the legendary Oklahoma football coach who was going to quarterback the NCAA side. The charter picked up Wilkinson in Oklahoma City and flew him to Dallas so that he could fly to New York for the kickoff.

The *Monday Night*ers didn't bother with preparation. They didn't expect to have any trouble, not with an NFL All-Pro in Gifford; Bob Goodrich, who had played in the Cotton Bowl for SMU only five years earlier; and a basketball All-American in Forte—though his forty-three-year-old body was fueled mostly by pizza, junk food, and cigarettes. They had another big man on the squad, the six-foot-three, 220-pound Don Ohlmeyer, who was to take over as producer the following season. Don Mere-

dith, who didn't have a shred of interest in grudge touch
football, did not fly in for the game.

Gifford pulled some strings with the Giants and the Yankee
Stadium ground crew to secure the field. ABC provided a
camera crew to record the game. Howard Katz, a *Monday Night*
production assistant, got the play-by-play assignment. Beano
Cook, NCAA publicity man, provided the color.

There were a handful of spectators, including Ethel Kennedy, a friend of Gifford. Roone Arledge was not in attendance.

The game went back and forth—"changing tides, ebb and
flow," Cosell might have intoned, had he been there.

At halftime, Cook brought on his special guest for an
interview: Ethel.

In the second half, the hitting remained ferocious. Dennis
Lewin went down hard and dislocated a shoulder.

When it ended, with dusk creeping over the hallowed façade
of the House That Ruth Built, the *Monday Night*ers had hung on
to win, 21–18, upholding their place of honor as the men behind
America's favorite football telecast.

"But they didn't cover," Cook announced.

With Don Ohlmeyer running the show, *Monday Night
Football* was in the hands of a quarterback who would take
command of the team.

He was creative, tough, and almost obsessively dedicated. As
one of his contemporaries put it, "He was a brute for work."

Everything about Ohlmeyer was outsized: his talent, his
physical presence, his ambition, his ego, and his will to succeed.
In 1973, he was twenty-eight years old, married, and a father,
though hardly settled. He was unmistakably a leader.

"O. J. Simpson was born to run with a football and Don
Ohlmeyer was born to work in television. It was just something
predestined," said Dick Buffinton, a production staffer who
worked dozens of shows with Ohlmeyer.

Born in Cottonport, Louisiana, Ohlmeyer grew up in Glen-
view, Illinois. He hooked up with ABC in 1966, over a pool table
in a dank little bar called Joers in South Bend, Indiana.
Ohlmeyer, then a senior at Notre Dame, hustled twenty dollars
out of an ABC crew member who was in town for a football

game. He also signed on as a gofer for the telecast—and found a calling. Here was a business you could bull your way into and brass your way up in. For all Ohlmeyer's talent, his hole card was his limitless store of bull and brass.

His rise at ABC was rocket-propelled, but he started in an out-of-the-way place—the tape room. A fast and creative tape editor, he did some of his best work on the tape-delayed broadcasts of the Indianapolis 500 in the late 1960s. The word went out: In the edit room there was a big kid who had verve and guts; he could seize command of a situation. That got Arledge's attention.

Ohlmeyer enjoyed another advantage over other would-be producers at ABC Sports—he was a skilled director. He had directed the replay unit on *Monday Night Football* in 1971 and studio portions of the Munich Olympics.

By then, Ohlmeyer was a leader of the ABC Sports wrecking crew, a group of young staffers who lived fast and played hard. He was known as a "cocky, ballsy kid"—and he took every opportunity to embellish that reputation.

Ohlmeyer loved to tell the story of a college game he produced in Texas with Forte. The game was lousy, and he and Forte were bored. In the third quarter, Forte, who was directing, turned to him and said, "I'm going shopping." There was a shopping mall across the street from the stadium. Forte dropped his headset and took off.

Ohlmeyer picked up the headset and started directing the coverage. Several series later, Forte returned. He was beaming. He had brought back three pairs of pants and a chocolate malt. "They've got a great sale on pants across the street," the director said, taking up the headset again.

That was enough for Ohlmeyer. He left the truck, went to the mall, bought some pants, a couple of shirts, and a chocolate bar and was back in time to finish the fourth quarter. "Nobody at home would have known the difference," Ohlmeyer said, "unless we showed them the pants we bought."

He got the *Monday Night* assignment after the 1972 season. By then, Arledge had decided that the co-producing arrangement between Forte and Lewin was clearly unworkable; the series needed one producer.

Arledge's decision meant that Forte would lose his

co-producer title and, more important, the power that went with it. The producer always had on-site authority for the telecast at ABC Sports. What else could be expected from a division with a boss who was a producer down to his soul?

The new *Monday Night* producer needed to be strong enough to deal with Forte's entrenched power, yet sensitive enough to work with him or around him but not against him. No one at ABC Sports was better equipped to do that than Ohlmeyer.

Chuck Howard labeled him—critically, but with a touch of awe—"one of the great political animals of all time."

His political instincts, plus his talents in the truck, would make Ohlmeyer the first, last, and only real producer *Monday Night Football* ever had.

On the eve of the 1973 season, few people had more reason to be delighted by the success of *Monday Night Football* than Pete Rozelle. Rozelle still considered the series his brainchild, especially when he remembered how much resistance he had overcome to get the NFL into prime time. His instincts, when it came to television, were rarely wrong.

The *Monday Night* games had been a boon to the NFL. The more the series grew as a phenomenon, the more casual fans tuned in to see what the noise was all about. Husbands persuaded their wives to watch, and women became more interested in the games. NFL ratings climbed on all the networks. "Because it was on prime time, it really enlarged our base of followers," Rozelle said.

Grateful as he was for the exposure, Rozelle recognized that the original $8.5-million-a-year package had turned out to be a bargain. He knew ABC now could be induced to pay much more for the games.

As Rozelle made the rounds of the networks during the summer of 1973, the negotiations went smoothly. The NFL was thriving on all the networks, so none resisted higher prices. "We felt we knew what the games were worth," Rozelle said. "It wasn't overkill."

CBS agreed to pay $88 million over the next four years, a 20 percent increase over its existing deal. CBS had always paid the highest rights fee, because its package of NFC games covered the biggest television markets. NBC agreed to pay $74 million for the AFC package, an increase of 51 percent.

As for ABC, *Monday Night Football* did not look like such a steal anymore. ABC signed a new contract for $72 million, more than double the $34 million it had paid during the previous four years.

None of the networks saw any reason not to give Rozelle what he wanted. They weren't going to pay the increases anyway; the advertisers were. And enough advertisers were lined up to get into the games so that if a few dropped out, selling their spots would be no problem.

Once the contract took effect, Herb Granath would hit the streets with $100,000 minutes to sell in *Monday Night Football*. They were the most expensive minutes you could buy anywhere on ABC.

Ohlmeyer fondly called the show "Brother Love's Traveling Freak Show." The line was borrowed from a Neil Diamond song, and it was really Meredith who applied it to *Monday Night Football*, but Ohlmeyer had no qualms about appropriating it. During his tenure, the description certainly fit.

"We were all nuts," Ohlmeyer said. "There were times I felt like I was really losing it. A lot of pressure, a lot of focus, and it was constantly wacky."

One key to Ohlmeyer's success in dealing with Forte was his ability to be just as wacky, profane, intense, and volatile as the director—on the surface, that is. Underneath, Ohlmeyer had the ability to calculate his every move. He gave Forte the impression that the director had free rein without ever removing his own hands from the controls, and carefully managed his relationships with all three announcers, maintaining their respect without kowtowing to them.

Ohlmeyer's first major decision was to drop the second unit. He could call the replays himself while producing the game. Nobody at ABC would mind cutting back the expense of two trucks.

When Ohlmeyer moved into the A-unit, he and Forte became soul mates in temperament; they were all but certifiable. Ohlmeyer reacted to the perpetually excitable Forte by matching him scream for scream. If Forte's camera guys failed to isolate on the player the producer had asked for, Ohlmeyer would yell into his ear: "Chet, you didn't isolate on that linebacker, for Christ's sake!"

Forte, never taking his eyes off the monitors and the action taking place in front of him, would jump back down Ohlmeyer's throat: "Goddammit—take one—you can't talk to me—take three—like that, you goofy motherfucker!"

Ohlmeyer, his own concentration unbroken, would scream back: "You cocksucker, Chet—set up one—you don't know what the fuck you're doing."

"Fuck you, asshole—take six—you're giving me the camera calls too late."

In the midst of all this, Forte, in his own words, would "eat like a pig." Surrounded by bags of M&M's, boxes of candy bars, and cold slices of pizza, Forte would munch maniacally throughout a telecast. It was not unusual for him to devour up to ten candy bars in a single game, washed down with sloshes of Coke. During an intense game, Forte never left the truck, not even to go to the bathroom; he'd grab the nearest empty cup.

He and Ohlmeyer also would frantically light cigarettes, take a few drags, put them down, and light up again. In a three-hour telecast, they would knock off an entire carton.

Nor were junk food and cigarettes their only vices. Into this smoke-filled, candy-wrapper-strewn den of profanity, Forte and Ohlmeyer began to usher a string of sensational-looking young women. The producer became Forte's frequent partner in an outlandish mating dance. With Arledge now almost never on the scene, Forte felt secure about bringing his dates into the truck. If he arrived in a city without prospects, he would be constantly on the prowl for companionship.

Upon setting up at the stadium, Forte often would fix on a stunning female with spectacular dimensions and an attachment to the home team—a cheerleader, a waitress at the stadium club and, on one occasion, the host of a local television show. Forte would introduce himself, describe his glamorous and exciting job, and ask his new acquaintance if she would like to sit in the truck to watch the *Monday Night* telecast. If he had not found a date by game time, he would often have one of the

sideline cameramen proposition a cheerleader before the opening kickoff.

"Tell her who I am," Forte would entreat in the camera
operator's earphones. "Tell her I'm rich. Ask her if she'd like to
be on national television."

The approach would be made: Would she like to be on the
air tonight? Because it could be arranged. Later she'd be
brought around to meet Forte. The so-called honey shots—
those tight close-ups of a beauty in the stands or on the
sidelines—often held special meaning on *Monday Night
Football*.

Ohlmeyer was generally more discreet. Together with Forte,
for example, he helped make a national phenomenon of the
Dallas Cowboy Cheerleaders. "It was very helpful *after* the
telecasts," Ohlmeyer said. "I mean, they were so fucking
good-looking."

Others watched in awe. Buffinton said, "You just hung
around and hoped maybe there'd be one girl too many."

Like so much else about *Monday Night Football* at its height,
the locker-room mentality was taken to extremes. The cast and
crew amounted to an exclusive male club. Women were rarely
hired as anything but gofers. Some younger, low-echelon crew
members were taken aback by the brazenly macho atmosphere;
they would never bring their own girlfriends around for fear of
what they might inadvertently witness.

Arledge was not unaware of the X-rated activities taking
place on the ABC caravan. He understood the pressures of
working on the show, and believed in allowing creative talents
some leeway. He liked the "swashbuckling" atmosphere surrounding *Monday Night Football*: "That's what made the show
what it was," he said.

But he was not fully aware of the level the swashbuckling
had reached until Game Two of the 1973 season in Dallas.

By then, Arledge rarely traveled to Monday night games,
though a suite was always booked for him in case he decided to
attend. A production assistant would check with his office on
Monday to see if he was coming, but Arledge often did not make
up his mind until the last minute.

No word had reached Dallas about Arledge's plans, so it was
assumed he would not be coming. Arledge had flown to Miami

that day to make a speech. When he finished, unbeknownst to his crew, he boarded a plane to Dallas.

At the Cotton Bowl, Ohlmeyer and Forte had ushered their dates into the truck, where they were perched on stools in the back, the best vantage point to watch these two hugely important men put a nationally celebrated television show on the air.

Forte was about two minutes away from his countdown to the opening when the door to the truck opened and a familiar face appeared in the doorway. Forte looked up. "Oh, hi, Roone," he said casually.

Ohlmeyer froze in shock.

Forte saw Arledge's head turn slowly and take in the scene at the back of the truck. Without saying a word, Arledge stepped back, slowly closed the door, and disappeared.

"Jesus Christ, that was Roone!" Forte bellowed at Ohlmeyer, who knew exactly who that was. "Get the fucking girls out of here!" Forte yelled. "Where the hell did he go?"

With less than a minute until the opening, Forte could not do anything but wait for the countdown. Ohlmeyer frantically shooed the two girls out. He poked his head outside, but Arledge was nowhere to be seen.

"Where the fuck is he?" Forte cried. The show was starting. He couldn't think about Arledge—until the first commercial. Then he sent a gofer to find the boss and bring him back.

The gofer was gone for much of the first quarter. When he returned he had a grim report: Arledge had taken a limo straight to the stadium from the airport. After his brief encounter at the truck, he had gotten back into the limo, driven back to the airport, and flown back to New York.

"We're dead men," Forte said.

When Forte got back to New York, he decided to go see Arledge before Arledge came to see him. He found the boss occupied with some paperwork on his desk.

"Roone, about the other night in Dallas," Forte said.

Arledge didn't look up.

"Roone, you should have stayed for the game. Why did you leave, Roone? You could have come back to the truck and done the game with us. Why didn't you come back to the truck?"

Arledge looked up slowly. Without changing his blank expression in the slightest, he said: "There was no place for me to sit."

Forte returned to his own office to give Ohlméyer the news. It was a typical Arledge dressing down: no hard words, no raised voice—just stone-cold reprobation. Forte felt run over, but at least he had his job.

The next week there were no girls in the truck.

In two weeks they returned. "You can never change your bad habits," Forte concluded.

For all their freewheeling personal habits, Forte and Ohlmeyer made a dynamic professional team. Ohlmeyer had once served as Forte's production assistant; he knew the director's philosophy and he shared it. In essence, it was the gospel according to Arledge, and Ohlmeyer, like so many at ABC Sports, revered the boss and swore by his ideas. Of course, he figured the boss would take note of the depth of his faith. But that didn't make the faith any less genuine.

With Forte's support, Ohlmeyer constantly pounded the message home to the announcers: "Give the fan information that allows him reason to root. Tell him where the players are from. Tell them where they went to college. Tell them interesting sidebar stories about these guys. Give them a reason to like them. Give them a reason to hate them."

Ohlmeyer and Forte were impressed by what they saw coming out of NFL Films and kept aiming for that approach— lower angles, tighter close-ups, anything to bring the players' faces closer and capture more of their emotions.

Before one game, Ohlmeyer and Forte were struck by the devastating good looks of a Dallas wide receiver named Golden Richards. Meredith was going to talk about Richards at the top of the show, so they recorded a still picture of him on tape.

On the Cowboys' first drive, Richards caught a long pass. They were now using the same tape for replays that they had used for the opening. When the operator rewound the tape, the replay stopped just short of the end of the thirty-second-long tape and ran right into the close-up of Richards.

"Gimme the face!" Ohlmeyer said. With the close-up on the

screen, Meredith went on about how that Richards really was a good-lookin' fella.

Ohlmeyer and Forte had a brainstorm. They were so taken with the idea of following up a replay with a player's picture that they began cutting the replays short to allow time for head shots. That led directly to the development of a device to make the technique easier. The device, called the still store, went into general use.

Both men were demanding and uncompromising. Ohlmeyer would order up hundreds of features and interviews for use during games in the event of technical difficulties or unexpected delays in the action. Only a handful of these ever aired.

After a game, Ohlmeyer and Forte would sit in the truck, drained, for more than forty minutes, trying to figure out why the telecast had not been perfect, why it fell short of their demands, and how they could do it differently the next week.

"It was all Chet and I would talk about all week," Ohlmeyer said. "What can we do better? What was wrong? If we just move this camera . . . It was like surfing and trying to catch the perfect wave and knowing you're probably never going to find it. But the real fun is looking for it."

Ohlmeyer was the one producer of *Monday Night Football* whom every announcer seemed to like. Even Cosell.

Ohlmeyer had a special touch with Cosell that no other producer—other than Arledge—came close to matching. He could play up to him and stand up to him; he could even challenge Cosell to do better, a daring gambit given Cosell's conviction that he alone was the master of his greatness.

Ohlmeyer would sit in the truck and listen to Cosell lay down the audio track on the halftime highlights. Invariably, when he finished, Cosell would say, "All right. That was great."

Usually he was right. But Ohlmeyer would know when he wasn't; and when he wasn't, Ohlmeyer would disagree.

"Howard, I'll buy that if you want. But I know you could do it better."

Cosell, offended, would say, "You want me to do it again, huh?"

"Hey, Howard," Ohlmeyer would reply, "it's average and,

you know, nobody will really know the difference. . . . But we will."

Cosell would let that sink in for only a moment before he would restoke his energy and say, "Okay, let's go again."

During the game, Ohlmeyer adhered to Forte's philosophy of talent management. It was a simple approach—give everything to Cosell. "I couldn't interrupt Gifford; he had his troubles and I didn't want to bother him," Forte said. "Meredith, I think it would have gone in one ear and out the other, because Don didn't really care. I knew if I gave my information to Howard, he would come up with something."

Ohlmeyer liked the feed-Howard system because it helped provoke the creative tension in the booth. If he had a funny line, he'd feed it to Meredith. But the information they gleaned from coaches or insights they had about players they would feed to Cosell.

In a game involving the Washington Redskins, Ohlmeyer gave Cosell some of his best information ever. Ohlmeyer had learned from the Redskin coaches that if Washington had a first down inside the 10-yard line but outside the 5-yard line, the Skins would go with a play-action pass to the tight end, Jerry Smith. The situation came up at a key moment.

In the booth, Gifford was talking about the difficulty of scoring from that position on the field. Ohlmeyer hit his key to the line connected with Cosell. "Howard," he said, "talk about how the ideal play here is a pass to Smith off play-action."

On the air, Cosell said, "Well, you know, Giff, this is the ideal situation for the play-action pass to the talented tight end, Jerry Smith."

The ball was snapped. Pass to Smith. Touchdown. Down in the truck, Ohlmeyer could see in his mind's eye a picture of Cosell rocking back in his chair, taking a long, satisfied puff on his cigar.

In the same game, Redskin kicker Mark Moseley was injured, forcing Washington to use punter Mike Bragg on place-kicks. As the Redskins lined up near the end of the half for a long field-goal try, Ohlmeyer jumped in again to Cosell: "There's no fucking way Bragg can kick the ball that far, number one. And number two, Theismann is the holder and he can run like hell. I think it's a fake."

"Well, Giffer," Cosell interrupted as the play was about to start, "in reality you must recognize Bragg's utter inability to kick a ball this distance, and the fact that Theismann, with his elusive speed, as evidenced during his years in the Canadian Football League, is always a threat to run."

Joe Theismann took the snap, Bragg faked the kick, and Theismann took off around the end for a long gain and a first down.

This time Ohlmeyer could all but hear the chair squeak as Cosell rocked back to blow the cigar smoke up into the air.

After the game, Cosell climbed into a limousine with Ohlmeyer, heading for the airport and a flight back to New York. Cosell's spirits were aflight already.

"Did you hear me tonight, kid?" he said to Ohlmeyer. "On the Jerry Smith play, I called it ahead of time. On the Theismann fake field goal, I had the play cold."

Ohlmeyer shook his head in disbelief. "Howard," he said, "this will work on somebody else. But you know it sounds to me like you're starting to think that fucking thing in your ear is your brain. Don't start feeding back to me how you were ahead of the game on those plays that I gave you!"

Unshakable as always, Cosell just looked back at Ohlmeyer. "That's right," he said. "Thanks, kid."

Monday Night Football had made headlines for three years, but that wasn't enough for Ohlmeyer and Co. There was a swagger to the show now, an arrogance built on the conviction that the *Monday Night* men could do anything, say anything, and the nation would laugh, applaud, or recoil in shock.

Ohlmeyer and Forte set out to feed the *Monday Night* frenzy at every opportunity. They were once given a story in a small-town paper about a bowling league that had rescheduled its Monday night games to avoid a conflict with *Monday Night Football*. That was all they needed to hear. For weeks, they would announce during interviews that bowling leagues all across the country were canceling on Monday nights. Ohlmeyer figured that anyone who "still bowled on Monday nights would feel like: Are we chumps? Are we the only league left that bowls on Mondays?"

After reading a few stories about restaurants that served fewer customers on Monday nights, Ohlmeyer and Forte would feed the information to the press: Restaurants across the country are down 25 percent on Monday nights.

"We were like Joe McCarthy running around the country," Ohlmeyer said. "I have in my pocket a list of seven thousand restaurants . . ."

Some bars and restaurants did capitalize on the *Monday Night* phenomenon. A bar in Costa Mesa, California, doubled its Monday business after installing a large screen, putting its waitresses in football jerseys, and serving hot dogs and peanuts with the beer. The Los Angeles Playboy Club converted its Playroom into a ministadium on Monday nights. And another Los Angeles restaurant started bringing TV sets to the tables on Monday nights along with meals.

The *Monday Night* madness made itself felt in other ways too:

The auto industry reported a major change. Its worst sick-out day became Tuesday instead of Monday. The suspicion—workers on the early shift stayed up late watching *Monday Night Football.*

Process servers in some states were advised that the best time to corner defendants in lawsuits was Monday nights—they seemed to be home watching football.

The police, to their delight, made the same discovery. A New York study revealed that arrests were down 16 percent on Monday nights. "Men congregate in groups to watch football on Monday nights," one police official said, so there were fewer men on the streets committing crimes.

However, one crime—gambling—was being committed more often. The Monday night game was an unqualified hit with the bookmakers of America, as millions of bettors who took a beating on Sunday afternoons tried to get even on Mondays. One bookie reportedly joked: "The people at ABC are the best friends our industry has this side of the Jersey City Police."

Other businesses took advantage of the mania too. A bank in Redding, California, tried to attract young executives as clients by throwing *Monday Night Football* parties in a motel conference room.

A batch of theater chains tried to attract football widows by offering reduced ticket prices on Monday nights, along with free coffee and doughnuts. Business picked up for a while, then tapered off.

Arledge contended that on Monday nights the women need not have felt abandoned. For some *Monday Night* games, women made up more than 40 percent of the audience.

Unarguably, the audience was growing. Ratings exceeded previous highs, regularly reaching a 36 share, according to Nielsen.

The actual audience was larger. Nielsen didn't measure viewing in bars, so J. Walter Thompson, the advertising agency for Ford, *Monday Night*'s biggest sponsor, commissioned its own survey. The agency reported that the show was watched in 92 percent of the bars visited in six cities. The average number of viewers per establishment—28. The conclusion—*Monday Night Football* was seen by at least 1.8 million people uncounted by Nielsen. Add those viewers to the Nielsen numbers and the ratings rose another 9 percent, to the levels occupied by the most-watched shows on television.

No wonder Arledge kept demanding more and better graphics. He wanted the folks at the bar to enjoy the game.

Herb Granath knew the numbers inside out—the Nielsens, J. Walter Thompson's surveys, the male demographics, the prices the other networks were charging, and, most important, the new $72-million rights deal signed by ABC—but no matter how he massaged them, they didn't add up.

To make any real money on the games, ABC had to charge a lot more than anyone else, more, even, than the ratings could justify. The price of a single sixty-second ad was approaching $100,000, more than ABC was charging for its top-rated prime-time series. On a cost-per-thousand basis, which was the way most ads were sold, *Monday Night Football* didn't make much sense.

Granath had to sell the sizzle as well as the steak. In network meetings, he called it "on-site merchandising." In plain English, Granath enlisted the help of the attractive young women who staffed ABC's client-services department to crisscross the country with the *Monday Night* crew and throw a party in every city where the traveling freak show set down. They were not ordinary parties, but splashy, star-studded, high-flying bashes that were the envy of the other networks. "It was," Granath said, "the ultimate in business entertainment."

Game tickets were part of the appeal. ABC had to buy them from NFL, which hurt, especially after shelling out $72 million for broadcast rights, and most of the tickets were pretty bad. One salesman recalled climbing what seemed like a thousand stairs with a client on the way to the very last row of the Orange Bowl. Still, people were grateful just to get into a game in cities where sellouts were the rule.

Typically, the parties would either be at the stadium or at a nearby hotel. Details were handled by the women from client services, sometimes dubbed "the Roonettes." They saw to it that only the finest food, wines, and liquors were served, and on occasion they pulled out all the stops. In San Francisco, partygoers enjoyed their pregame cocktails on a cruise ship that deposited them near Candlestick Park.

Often there were gifts for clients—seat cushions, helmets, jerseys, autographed footballs for the high rollers. All the trinkets were manufactured by NFL Properties, another Rozelle creation. Rozelle was always willing to help, as were the owners and coaches, who would show up at ABC events.

Gifford and Meredith occasionally were helpful, especially if they were paid for their time. By the late 1970s, Gifford was getting five thousand dollars for showing up and making a few remarks at a client lunch on game day. But Gifford and Meredith skipped most parties.

Granath's best weapon was Cosell, who almost always went to the parties. He was drawn by his loyalty to Granath and ABC, by the chance to schmooze with corporate bigwigs, and by the knowledge that he would show up and instantly be the center of attention. He would work the room like a politician, shaking hands, bestowing kisses on the women, and often remembering the names of people he'd met years ago.

"Howard was the best friend of the sales department. He could always be counted on," said John Lazarus, Granath's top aide. Once, in Dallas, Cosell really turned on the charm at a party with John Roach, chairman of Tandy Corp., and his wife, who was the object of a stream of Cosellian flattery. By the end of the evening, they were practically embracing. "Howard had a way of making people feel incredibly comfortable," said one ABC salesman. "He'd have them hypnotized, mesmerized. They'd eat out of his hand."

Eventually, the parties grew so big that they were used by all of ABC Sales to entertain clients. Since the other networks weren't keeping pace, advertisers looked favorably on ABC. "Guys looked for a way to do business with ABC," said Jerry Solomon, an ABC salesman. "That's when you get business when you don't really earn it on the merits of your ratings."

To his surprise, Granath found advertisers willing to absorb higher and higher prices as long as they could remain in the package. Arledge's $72-million rights deal was beginning to look like another bargain for ABC.

Halftime on *Monday Night Football* had become the 1970s equivalent of sitting in the audience during the old *Ed Sullivan Show*—the place to take a bow on national TV.

One night in late November 1973, the *Monday Night* team settled into Candlestick Park in San Francisco. As the half approached, Gifford heard some commotion in the back of the booth and turned around to check it out. The scene looked like something out of the demented fantasy of a political cartoonist.

There was Ronald Reagan, the governor of California, ramrod straight and blue-suited, standing with his arm draped around the shoulders of the straggly haired, bearded figure of John Lennon. Reagan was in the process of explaining American football to the apparently fascinated ex-Beatle.

The nonplussed Gifford shook his head and said to himself, "Holy cow!"

Gifford became accustomed to welcoming just about anyone to the *Monday Night* booth. Celebrity visits were used to hype ABC shows and lend glamour to the scene.

ABC used the halftime platform shamelessly. Arledge would issue *Monday Night* invitations to stars of ABC Sports events, such as skater Dorothy Hamill, and to friends who might have an upcoming network special, such as John Denver. It added to the *Monday Night* aura when Ted Kennedy or Henry Kissinger or Burt Reynolds made an appearance in the booth. None of those people was turning up on CBS to talk with Pat Summerall on Sundays. Nor, on the other hand, was Mike Douglas or Olivia Newton-John, who also elbowed their way into the *Monday Night* booth.

Usually, Cosell would do the pro forma interview. He never needed a briefing on who the visitor was or what to ask.

Of course, when two visitors appeared, as they did in San Francisco, Cosell might get a little help from Gifford. That night, Gifford interviewed Reagan; Cosell interviewed Lennon. Man-for-man coverage.

Once the celebrity parade started, Arledge wanted somebody in the booth each week. "I wanted to make it as much a happening as possible," he said. "That's also the reason we started shooting all those banners."

The banners. That flourish of the phenomenon began to unfurl one night when Forte was trying to enliven a boring game. He saw a funny banner draped across a stadium railing, and turned a camera on it.

Within weeks, every stadium was dotted with bed sheets when the *Monday Night* team arrived. Forte called for more and more shots, some with obvious self-promotional advantages; at least one banner a week had the initials *ABC* weaved into the text. But Ohlmeyer and Forte frequently were impressed by the cleverness of some fans. One all-time favorite—WILL ROGERS NEVER MET COSELL.

Some people accused the *Monday Night* team of putting up their own banners, especially the ones celebrating the glory of ABC and Howard Cosell. Ohlmeyer always denied it. "Sure we promoted it by shooting them," he said. "That just hyped the people in the next city to bring more out. But we never hung a banner. The more we denied it, the more they printed it. The newspapers had gotten onto Watergate; this was Bannergate."

Whatever its roots, banner hanging became another craze attached to the *Monday Night* carnival. In Atlanta for Game Ten of 1973, a reporter counted 113 banners hung on the upper deck alone, with at least that many on each of the two lower tiers.

The fans were no different from Ted Kennedy and Burt Reynolds. They wanted to get their faces on *Monday Night Football* too.

*   *   *

Howard Cosell adored being famous—most of the time.

He was everywhere—in television sitcoms like *The Odd Couple*, on the lecture circuit, and on college campuses. With his face and name recognition climbing to the stratosphere, Cosell floated a trial balloon the size of the *Hindenburg* by declaring his interest in running for the U.S. Senate seat from New York held by James Buckley. His friends did what they could to keep that display of hubris under control.

On the road with *Monday Night Football*, Cosell was the first one out of bed and the only star down in the hotel lobby in the morning—reading the papers, greeting people who recognized him.

One time in San Francisco, Cosell and Joe Aceti were having drinks with Woody Allen, Warren Beatty, and Julie Christie. "Woody," Cosell said, "how can you stand it? These people never stop bothering you. I can't take it. I never get a minute of peace."

Aceti, an ABC Sports director and longtime Cosell pal, was not about to let him get away with that. "You sit in the fucking lobby, where they can see you, you ever think of that? In a yellow coat that looks like a fucking canary? And you tell me that you don't want to be noticed? The day you're not noticed is the day you'll be very unhappy. The day nobody says, 'Hey, Cosell, you asshole,' you'll be very unhappy." Cosell didn't say anything.

Cosell would walk down a Manhattan street and be stopped a dozen times within a few blocks by people calling out his name, shaking his hand, or honking the horn of a car. To a first-timer sharing the reaction, Cosell would swagger noticeably and bray: "Do you witness the adulation?"

In those feverish days, there were even—against all odds—Cosell groupies. Cosell experienced an avalanche of female attention the likes of which he had never known before. He revelled in it.

Sometimes he would tease a couple in a hotel or restaurant with a stock line: "My dear, it is so obvious you've married beneath yourself." Women he encountered, including some female reporters, were treated to sloppy, wet kisses after he informed them that they were driving him crazy with their "succulent lower lip."

Forte witnessed the dance more often than anyone, and he knew just how it would play out. At the hotel bar after a game, Cosell often would draw a crowd of female admirers.

"What would happen," Forte said, "is the girl would come over and Howard would kid around and he'd smooch with the girl and it would get kind of disgusting, to be very honest with you. That's when I'd get up and leave."

Then Cosell would have some fun. At some point, he would give the woman a room number: "Room 411," he'd say. "In about an hour." Then he'd duck out and go upstairs.

An hour later there would be a knock at the door of room 411. "Howard? Howard?" the sweet voice would call out—and Chet Forte would open the door.

"He'd give out my room number," Forte said. "So in the restaurant I would think at some point, let me get out of here now. He's bombed, she's bombed; it would be about an hour. So let me go up and lather and take a shower and get set for this. I'd be all set and have my routine down: 'Oh, Howard's not here, but why don't you come in? Howard will be right along shortly. I'm Chet Forte, I'm the director on *Monday Night Football*. . . .' And you know what? I made out pretty good that way."

Cosell, of course, did nothing but play at the game. His Emmy, his bride, as he told one and all with unassailable sincerity, was his life.

Cosell also was getting plenty of attention from the press, some of it favorable. His old enemies among the sportswriters still attacked him, but he was featured in *Playboy* and *The New York Times Magazine*, and he put his book, *Cosell*, onto the best-seller lists for six months. Everywhere he went, he granted audiences to the reporters who wanted them.

To Gifford and Meredith, Cosell's eagerness to make himself constantly, consumingly available to the public was symptomatic of his neurotic need for recognition. For the two of them, who had been recognized for most of their adult lives, there was no thrill at all in witnessing the adulation. They not only failed to pursue it, they hid from it, taking meals in their rooms or ducking out for a quiet game of tennis when Gifford wasn't busy studying his cards.

"I don't think Howard probably read about himself until he was in his fifties," Gifford said. "He never had anyone critique him. Then, all of a sudden, the whole world was critiquing him. At least Don and I were prepared for it. Howard never understood that. He never understood that the pomposity could irritate people, and he blamed it all on the writers. He thought America loved him. Hell, all he had to do was read the mail to know they didn't."

Cosell read the mail; he read everything. And as soon as he had finished reading the paper, any paper, the phone would ring back in New York in the apartment of some production staffer he felt was on his side, up in Ohlmeyer's or Forte's room, somewhere.

"The morning after a *Monday Night* game he'd call me up," Forte said, "and he'd say: 'Did you see the Dubuque *Courier*?' I'd say: 'What the fuck is a Dubuque *Courier*?' Or it was the Wichita *Sun*. I'd say, 'What are you *talking* about?' "

With the mail he was even worse. Forte said, "Hate letters tore him up. Every nasty sign draped over a stadium wall cut him to the bone."

That was the dark side: the abhorrence that went with the adulation. It went well beyond a few drunken rowdies dropping their pants.

Bars in two states raffled off the chance to do violence to Cosell. In Colorado and New Jersey, the winners got to throw a brick through a television screen when Cosell's face appeared.

Meredith saw the mob enmity up close. "To walk through a crowd with Howard, man, people shout all *kinds* of things at him. And they're not kidding around. I heard curse words yelled at him, we had bomb threats. People can be very violent toward Howard."

In Game Seven of 1973, the first *Monday Night* game ever in Buffalo, Cosell performed under the protection of the FBI. The week before the game, a postcard postmarked in Buffalo arrived at the ABC building in New York. It was intercepted before it got to Cosell, and brought to the attention of the FBI. The postcard read:

"Howard Cosell—the MOUTH—why don't you drop dead. There's a bomb in Rich Stadium. It will blow you up at 10 Monday."

Cosell arrived in Buffalo with Emmy and was met by an FBI detail. They remained with him throughout the weekend.

Three agents were posted inside the booth. Cosell enjoyed their company, but everyone else spent the game quaking. The tension particularly got to Meredith, who downed a quart of vodka straight from the bottle during the game. Ohlmeyer was appalled that Meredith would be openly swigging from a vodka bottle in full view of the reporters in the adjacent press box.

The only one who seemed to notice was one of the FBI guys, who gaped in amazement at Meredith. "Does he do that all the time?" he asked Emmy. She said he was just nervous.

When a firecracker went off somewhere near the booth, Gifford and Meredith hit the floor. Cosell just stood there, staring blankly down at the field.

The blank stare was a well-honed defense mechanism. If Cosell had looked around, really looked around, he would have seen how many of those hundreds of banners contained messages of hate directed at him. Typical example: HOWARD IS ABC'S DEEP THROAT—HE SUCKS.

In San Francisco for Game Eleven, Cosell was plagued by a persistent antagonist. One fan, sitting in the deck just above the press box, had fashioned his own campaign to harass Cosell. He brought along a fishing pole and at unpredictable moments would drop his line in front of the ABC booth. The bait: nasty signs about Cosell.

For three seasons the signs had appeared, dangling from the pole, each message more vile than the next. Cosell would sit, seemingly oblivious, as Gifford and his statistician, Terry O'Neil, would lean out over the lower deck to try to rip down the signs before Cosell could see them.

Several times security details were supposedly sent out to find the offender. The signs would disappear for a while. But then they'd be back: HOWARD IS A HEMORRHOID, and other immortal bons mots. The most graphic of the signs depicted the face of Cosell with a penis thrust into his mouth.

Finally, in the 1973 game, Emmy caught sight of one sign and swung into action. She left the booth, walked up to the section above, spotted the culprit, and found a security guard to throw him out of the stadium.

That night in San Francisco, Cosell met Dick Buffinton in his room in the Fairmont Hotel. He was worn and exhausted; for the first time in his life, Buffinton saw Cosell without his toupee. Bald and bowed, cradling a vodka in his fingers, Cosell looked old and vulnerable.

"Buffer," Cosell said softly. "I don't know how I can continue to do this. These people are vicious."

The glare surrounding *Monday Night Football* in 1973 would have made anyone wince and squint. It made Don Meredith want to turn his back and walk away.

All season long, the question was not how Meredith would perform; it was, would he show up in the booth at all? He was, to most observers, including one production staffer, "a very unhappy man."

Meredith's problems were not limited to *Monday Night Football*, though he talked openly of his discontent with the "carnival atmosphere" of the program. "You can get tired of going to the carnival," he said.

He had been through a failed marriage. He was seeking custody of his son. The restlessness that dogged his final football days was back. He felt more and more unfulfilled, and longed for a new outlet, a new start.

Hollywood again beckoned. Meredith saw acting as a way to expand himself, challenge himself, give vent to the creative urgings that had pushed him twice to start work on a novel and later try painting in oils. As the season began, he was into a period of intense, almost agonized self-scrutiny.

And he was sick to death of "Dandy Don."

The alter ego, that happy-go-lucky country performer who crooned "Turn out the lights, the party's over" to the nation, had become for Meredith a buffoon. The public reaction seemed to confirm it. While people usually steered clear of Gifford and his icy perfection, they invariably slapped Meredith on the back, expecting Dandy to do his cowboy funnies for them. Dandy Don seemed to have taken over his life.

Meredith started talking about Dandy Don as if he were a totally detached person. "I take Dandy Don and send him into another room," he would tell people, "and he charms everybody. He's a hell of a guy, but that's not me."

Meredith consulted a sports philosopher-guru on the West Coast who was helping him sort through his personal confusion and his mixed feelings about football. He had met Susan Dullea, the estranged wife of actor Keir Dullea, and she helped him explore his feelings as well.

And all this introspection was being fed by his increasing use of marijuana. On the road, he would smoke joints with friends in his room as a way of relaxing after games. Arledge believed he was occasionally smoking before games as well. It never became a serious personal or professional problem for Meredith, and he did not smoke pot during the telecasts.

But some observers, including Arledge, believed the drug use was contributing to his mood of disaffection. Don seemed to be looking at the world in a different way. Smoking pot seemed to give Meredith an "artificial sense of introspection," one of Arledge's aides said.

Never a dedicated worker, Meredith's approach was more laid-back than ever. Given his role on the telecast as the spontaneous gag man, this was not a critical problem, but it further separated Meredith from football, the sport he was supposed to be analyzing as an expert.

His celebrated devil-may-care attitude now extended to his work, and to the weekly production meetings, where a peculiar ritual developed:

Up in his hotel room, Ohlmeyer would call the meeting to order. Meredith would get up, pick up this three-deep charts of players, and go sit on the john with the door open. He'd take part in the meeting from there.

After a few weeks, Ohlmeyer got fed up. "Don, am I like Ex-Lax or something?" Ohlmeyer called out to him. "Every time you see me you go take a shit."

Ohlmeyer had been forewarned about Meredith's alienation. He was always checking to make sure Meredith had shown up for the game, and to make sure he was all right.

In Game Two in Dallas, Ohlmeyer checked and found Meredith in the booth, where he was supposed to be. Deep into the first quarter, though, Ohlmeyer had not heard anything from him. So, after asking Forte for a close shot of Dallas quarterback

Roger Staubach, he hit the key to Meredith and told him, "Don, here comes a shot of Staubach for you."

Ohlmeyer expected to hear the familiar twang and some pleasantry about the Cowboy star. Instead he heard the voice of Gifford: "And there's Roger Staubach, just waiting to get his hands back on the ball. . . ."

Ohlmeyer shook his head. But he quickly set up a replay for Meredith to comment on. "This is for you, Don." Instead, Cosell's voice came booming back: "As you can observe on this play . . ."

Ohlmeyer turned to Forte: "Are we in another of these things where Don is pouting?"

"Who the fuck cares?" Forte replied.

They went to a commercial and Ohlmeyer decided to press the issue. He hit the key to Gifford: "Is there anything wrong with Don?"

"Nope," Gifford said.

Ohlmeyer hit the line to Meredith: "Don? What's the problem?"

Silence. Ohlmeyer lost his patience. "Frank, what's going on up there?"

"I'll tell you later," Frank said.

"Bullshit. What is going *on* up there? Where the fuck is Don?"

"He's not here."

"What do you mean he's not there? We're fifteen minutes into the telecast and he's not there? Where did he go?"

"I'll tell you later."

The commercial ended and Ohlmeyer kept right on talking, knowing he was running the risk of totally disrupting Gifford's concentration. Gifford started to spot the play, "New Orleans takes over on its own twenty . . ." At the same time, Ohlmeyer was muttering in his earphone: "I can't wait to hear where Don is."

This went on for another series of plays, and then, out of nowhere, Meredith's voice came across the air. "Well, Frank, the Cowboys are fer sure looking strong tonight."

Ohlmeyer let out a long sigh. Meredith had not caught a plane for Hollywood after all. After the game, when he pressed the issue, he learned that Meredith, whose loyalty to friends was as legendary as Gifford's, had been called away at the start of the game. His old buddy Pete Gent, Mr. *North Dallas Forty* himself, who was not the most popular guy ever to appear at a Cowboy game, had been picked up for being rowdy and was being held under the stadium. A friend who had accompanied Gent to the game realized that Meredith might be the only man in Dallas able to spring Gent loose. So he'd climbed up to the booth and summoned him. Meredith, after vouching for Gent and getting him released, returned immediately to the booth.

Ohlmeyer was more than relieved; he was reminded that Don Meredith really was a good guy, and that it was probably worth putting up with some of his unpredictability.

The following week, in the production meeting before a game in Detroit between the Lions and the Falcons, Meredith quit *Monday Night Football*.

Ohlmeyer had been trying to get his people up after two lopsided games sapped everyone's energy level. Meredith interrupted his speech to announce: "I shouldn't even be here. I shouldn't have started this season. I'm talked out. I haven't got anything to say about football anymore." He said he wasn't going on that night.

Ohlmeyer tried to placate him. So did Gifford, Cosell, and Forte. Finally Meredith sat through the meeting. But he still told Ohlmeyer he wanted to quit.

After the meeting, the producer called Arledge in New York and related Meredith's announcement. "What should I do, Roone?" Ohlmeyer said. "Tell him not to quit," Arledge said. "Gee, thanks, Roone," Ohlmeyer said.

Arledge called Meredith himself later and, with some effort, smoothed things over—for the moment.

In Denver for Game Six, Meredith made a rare visit to the client party before the telecast. His spirits, with the help of some artificial stimulation, were soaring.

There had been a major traffic tie-up outside the stadium that night, and there was no time for the announcers to rehearse the opening. Following Cosell's introduction, Gifford did his spot analyzing the Raiders. Meredith was supposed to do the Broncos.

The camera settled on Meredith. Before he even spoke, Ohlmeyer looked at him in the monitor and thought his eyes looked like a "Rand McNally road map." Meredith, beaming goofily, said:

"Welcome to the Mile-High City—and I really am!"

Ohlmeyer all but jumped through the truck roof. "Get off of him!" he shouted. "Get the fuck off of him! Take it, Frank! Take it, Frank! Lead to commercial!"

Gifford, the camera suddenly jerked back to him, said placidly, "We'll be right back after these messages."

The following week, Meredith was drinking a bottle of vodka openly in the press box in Buffalo.

On the air, Meredith had survived his turmoil blithely. His image was so entrenched by then that every excess only sounded to the public like more hijinks from the irrepressible Dandy.

The night of Game Eight in Pittsburgh, he staggered over the line. During the game between the Steelers and the Redskins, President Nixon's favorite team, Meredith suggested on the air that Washington might do better if they consulted "Tricky Dick" about some plays.

In the truck, Ohlmeyer and Forte were in the midst of a profane screaming match. Neither heard the line. But within seconds the phone rang. Arledge was livid: "What the hell did Meredith just say?" Ohlmeyer had no idea, so he asked Forte, who didn't know either.

Arledge told them what he'd said, and advised them to let Meredith know he had better start framing an apology.

When Ohlmeyer confronted him after the game, Meredith didn't know whether he wanted to apologize. He asked for Gifford's advice. "Do what you want to do," Gifford told him. "You've already done it."

By the time Meredith came on the next week in Kansas City, he had decided, under pressure from Arledge, to make a public apology. But he hemmed and stammered, finally turning to Gifford and saying, "Help, Frank." To which Gifford replied, kiddingly, "You got yourself into this."

Meredith knew fer sure that he wanted to get himself out of it.

Meredith stopped exulting to the world about how wonderful Cosell was as a partner and what a delight he was as a person. He no longer announced that he loved the "coach."

Terry O'Neil, Gifford's statistician and a comer at ABC Sports, had helped edit Cosell's first book. He approached Meredith and asked him if he'd had a chance to read it.

Meredith looked at O'Neil as though he were from the moon.

"Read it?" he said derisively. "I had to live it. Why would I want to read it?"

Their banter on the air was taking on a harsh edge. At first, Cosell was stunned by the change. He had become genuinely fond of Meredith. Later, he grew more sensitive to Meredith's barbs, wondering whether they were meant in good fun or were part of a Meredith trait he came to call "Texas cruel."

What finally pushed Meredith over the edge was Cosell's incessant harping on the fluffs he alleged were being committed by Meredith's soul mate, Gifford. To Meredith, "It was like somebody's picking on my brother. Look out."

Meredith, who had never much cared about getting his share of time to talk, was now berating Cosell after each telecast for "dominating the game."

Everyone assumed that Meredith was reacting at least partly to Cosell's gargantuan celebrity. "Howard had transcended Don," Arledge said. Cosell, of course, felt the same way, and said so.

In earlier years, the announcers had all shared a limo to and from the stadium for the games. But starting in 1973, Cosell decided he deserved his own limo. Ohlmeyer and Forte would take turns riding either in Cosell's limo or with Gifford and Meredith. The night of Game Eleven in San Francisco, Ohlmeyer was riding with Gifford and Meredith.

As rocky as the season had been in terms of managing Cosell and Meredith, Ohlmeyer took solace in the steadiness of Gifford. Frank, he thought, was the "pillar of strength . . . the bastion of sanity." But as they left the Fairmont Hotel, Ohlmeyer sensed that Frank was not his usual self.

As the limo slowed in the traffic heading for Candlestick Park, Gifford turned to Ohlmeyer and said: "We're not going to talk to him tonight."

"What?" Ohlmeyer said, immediately panicked.

"We're not talking to him tonight," Gifford repeated. Meredith, grinning, added a triumphant "Yeah!"

Ohlmeyer could feel himself starting to sweat. "Frank, you're about to go on national television, forty-five million people watching, and you're going to tell me you're not going to talk to him tonight?"

Gifford said, "He's been bad-mouthing us to the press. This business about jocks in the booth."

Ohlmeyer wondered if they were serious. They seemed hurt more than angry, as though they felt they had to protest in some way, to do something. He decided they meant what they said.

"You've got to talk to him," Ohlmeyer said.

"We're not talking to him," Gifford said resolutely.

"Yeah!" Meredith added again, joyous at Frank taking this stand with him.

"Well, what if he asks you a question?" Ohlmeyer tried.

"We're not answering."

Suddenly Ohlmeyer was grateful for the traffic jam. He used the extra twenty minutes or so to work on them, pleading with them not to expose the strain between them and Cosell. He could see his career flash before his eyes.

Finally he wore them down. They agreed to talk to Cosell.

The next week there were three limos. Ohlmeyer and Forte had commandeered one of their own. "These three guys really are fucking wild," Forte told Ohlmeyer. "Let's go out and get drunk, or let's go out and get some broads, because they're completely off the wall."

Though he showed up every week and never attacked Cosell on the air, Meredith seethed all year. Forte finally got so fed up with Meredith's moaning that he went to Ohlmeyer.

"We've got a big problem here, Don," Forte told the producer, who didn't have to be told. "I'm not gonna get involved in it. I don't think we can handle it ourselves. Can you handle it?"

"No," Ohlmeyer said.

"Okay," Forte said. "So let's get the boss in here and see what he can do."

Ohlmeyer called Arledge and told him a disaster was brewing; he had to intercede, call a meeting, get the thing aired out, or Meredith was either going to walk out or do something crazy on the air.

Arledge flew in from New York on a Monday morning for an emergency meeting. The announcers, Forte, and Ohlmeyer gathered in Arledge's room. As always, Arledge served as a calming influence; his authority was unquestioned.

"Okay," Arledge began, "I understand that there are some problems, Don. What's going on?"

Meredith, expressionless, replied, "There's no problem, Roone. What do you mean?"

That was too much for Forte. He couldn't control himself, even in the presence of Arledge. "What the fuck?" he exploded. "Are you crazy? You do nothing but complain to me about Howard's talking too much, you're unhappy, you're going to quit. We fly Roone out here to sit down and try to work this thing out and you're going to sit there and say there's no problem?"

Arledge turned to Forte and started laughing. "I can't believe these guys," he said.

Within a few months, Arledge would not think Meredith's problems with *Monday Night Football* were the least bit funny.

6.

A DANDY
DEFECTION

"There's an athlete's mentality that you gotta get what you can while you can get it because next year they can cut you and the rest of your life you'll be pumping gas someplace."—ROONE ARLEDGE

Roone Arledge sat on a plane somewhere over the middle of America, convinced that he still had a shot at keeping Don Meredith on *Monday Night Football.*

It was the last week of February 1974, and all the evidence suggested that Meredith was heading elsewhere—to NBC. Rumors had been circulating for weeks, ever since Meredith hired E. Gregory Hookstratten, a high-profile agent with close ties to NBC. Howard Cosell had heard the news directly from the head of NBC Sports, Carl Lindemann, who had called him to brag that NBC had landed Meredith.

Now Arledge was flying to Los Angeles to see Meredith. He believed that the deal was not yet final. Until he had used up all his plays, Arledge was never willing to concede defeat.

He was prepared to match any offer NBC had made. He also had an argument he was sure would be persuasive—NBC football on Sundays was not only a step down from the glitter of prime time, it was two steps down because CBS dominated

Sunday afternoons. Arledge intended to argue that by going to NBC, Meredith would be taking his act to Palookaville.

Arledge understood the broader game being played by his friends at NBC. The wooing of Don Meredith was not motivated solely by the desire of NBC Sports to add his wit and football expertise to its afternoon lineup of AFC games. Nor was NBC's entertainment division exactly clamoring for Meredith.

Somewhere in the master planning of the great minds at NBC, Arledge knew, was the notion that depriving *Monday Night Football* of its jolly cowboy might just wreck what had become a powerful force in prime-time television—three solid hours of hit programming on Monday nights. The defensive maneuver of stealing a key performer from the competition had been around since the 1940s, when CBS patriarch William Paley had raided NBC Radio for names like Jack Benny and Burns and Allen.

Arledge knew that in an earlier foray against *Monday Night Football,* Herbert Schlosser, NBC's president, had tried to seduce Cosell with talk of his own variety show on NBC. Cosell, with all his passion for show business, was tempted by the offer, but he felt too much loyalty to ABC to accept it.

But Meredith, who was loyal to people, not institutions, proved to be a more approachable target. Certainly he wasn't awash in loyalty to ABC—the memory of the snub during the Munich Olympics ran too deep for that.

On a personal level, Arledge had ambivalent feelings about Meredith. Don could be a great guy, he thought, but he was unreliable. Despite Meredith's closeness to Gifford, who was probably Arledge's best friend, Don had never attached himself to the Arledge crowd at ABC.

That winter, Arledge had seen Meredith at a golf tournament and at the Super Bowl. On neither occasion did Meredith drop any hints about leaving. As rumors heated up, Arledge called him. Again Meredith breezily assured the boss that he was coming back to *Monday Night Football.* Only after Cosell heard the news directly from Lindemann did Arledge start to worry. Once more he called Meredith, but this time Don offered no assurances. Arledge told Meredith that they had to meet right away.

Whatever his personal feelings, Arledge felt Don was a vital part of the *Monday Night* formula. Subtracting the Meredith factor, he believed, could undo the chemical reaction that had turned *Monday Night Football* into the most successful franchise in the history of sports television.

For the sake of that franchise, Arledge was willing to drop everything and jump on the next plane to L.A.

At that point, Don Meredith had no intention of staying on *Monday Night Football*. When he approached Ed Hookstratten a few weeks earlier, he had told the agent that he was unhappy with ABC and authorized him to begin negotiations with NBC. Divorced from his wife, Cheryl, Meredith was newly married to Susan Dullea, a strong, shrewd, capable woman who knew something about the backstage business of Hollywood from her previous marriage. She was urging him to make a change in his life.

After his season of discontent, change seemed not only desirable but necessary. Meredith was enchanted with the idea of being an actor. He had appeared as a guest star on the NBC anthology series *Police Story* and enjoyed it immensely. His work was well received.

In conversations with producers in Hollywood, Meredith learned that his announcing career could be an impediment. "If I really truly was seriously interested in pursuing an acting career," Meredith said, "the phenomenon of *Monday Night Football* was influencing the public perception of my persona. . . . Maybe I should get a little lower profile in the sports world and concentrate on the acting."

In other words, if he wanted to be a television cop on Tuesday night, it wasn't too smart to be Dandy Don, the wisecracking football expert on Monday night.

In the deal NBC was offering, sports seemed secondary. Meredith would work a schedule of Sunday afternoon games for NBC—not even every week. He would do the Rose Bowl and the Super Bowl. On the entertainment side, Meredith would star in television movies, make pilots for series, and do guest roles. NBC also dangled the possibility of hosting the *Tonight* show on Johnny Carson's nights off.

Against this, Arledge and ABC were making vague promises. They mentioned a minor role in a miniseries about Eisenhower.

Hookstratten told Meredith that ABC didn't seem interested in using him as an actor.

The money stacked on the table by both networks towered over the salary he'd taken in the previous four years, even as *Monday Night Football* flourished. The 10 percent annual raise he had squeezed out of Arledge at their lunch at Toots Shor's in 1970 now seemed puny. He'd barely topped out at $40,000 a year. Now NBC was offering $200,000, and Arledge had matched it. Even taking into account all the fringe income he had been able to amass because of his *Monday Night* celebrity, the new contract promised to take Don Meredith to a new financial plateau.

Through all this, Meredith cast himself as a passive participant in the high-powered financial negotiations swirling around him. Some people saw him differently. "He's not the country boy he wants everybody to think he is," said one network executive who knew Meredith. This executive thought Meredith had already worked out a deal with NBC and now was stringing ABC along: "That's really been Meredith's M.O. for as long as I've known him."

Meredith denied any duplicity. Years later, though, he acknowledged that the hassle over his departure had permanently soured his relationship with Arledge.

When he arrived in Los Angeles, Arledge took a cab to the Beverly Wilshire Hotel. His plan was to unpack, freshen up, and take off immediately for Meredith's house. But when he entered the lobby, Don and Susan Meredith were waiting there for him. Arledge left his bags with the bellman and accompanied them to the bar.

They drank the afternoon away in the bar, then left for the Meredith home in Beverly Hills. There Arledge stayed up all night with Meredith, cajoling him, laughing with him, talking man-to-man with him, using every bit of his considerable charm. Meredith remained noncommittal, though he clearly enjoyed the attention.

"He was probably flattered that Arledge was coming to him," Hookstratten said later. "It was probably attractive to his ego. But, in the grand scheme of things, Gifford came number one,

Cosell came number two, and Meredith came number three in Arledge's mind." Hookstratten was sure Meredith believed he always ranked third with Arledge.

The next morning, Meredith invited Arledge to play squash at a health club in Century City. Arledge agreed. He was proving his commitment to Don. Meredith, however, still would not commit to Arledge, even after he had been assured that ABC would match anything NBC offered, point for point.

After squash, Irwin Weiner, Arledge's new vice-president for administration, joined them for more formal negotiations at ABC's Century City offices. Nothing changed. Weiner and Arledge met later with Hookstratten back at the Beverly Wilshire. Hookstratten kept emphasizing that NBC had made entertainment guarantees that he didn't see coming from ABC.

No final word was spoken, but when Arledge and Weiner got back on a plane to New York, they both knew Meredith had made it about as clear as he could that he was leaving *Monday Night Football.*

Weiner thought Meredith had been pulling their chain all along. Arledge, profoundly unhappy, wasn't so sure. He believed that he had almost turned Meredith around during their marathon encounter. In the final analysis, though, Arledge concluded that it had been impossible to turn Don around because Hookstratten had promised him to NBC. The entire trip had been a waste.

The following week, when NBC made it official, Arledge called Meredith one more time. He serenaded Don with a Kris Kristofferson lyric: "The game is over, nobody won."

Out from under ABC, Meredith began to talk publicly about his discomfort during his last season on *Monday Night Football.* He called it "the *Monday Night* freak show," a phrase that now sounded more pejorative than playful. He admitted that he was tired of being called "Dandy Don" and "the Danderoo," and implied that nobody announcing football games on NBC would be calling him anything but Don.

Though he never apologized to Cosell, Meredith conceded that there had been a harsh edge to his on-air banter, reflecting his animus toward his *Monday Night* role. "I was pretty snippy to Howard," he said. "I don't know why I did that. I like Howard. I really do. I mean he's very weird but I respect him. It was pure frustration on my part."

Cosell was generous in his comments about Meredith, saying he still loved him. "Deep inside," Cosell said, "Don feels he can be a latter-day Will Rogers. Maybe he can."

Gifford, naturally, praised his friend extravagantly. "I'll miss Don," he said. "Nobody can do the same things for us that Don did." Gifford added, characteristically, that *Monday Night Football* would be fine because they still had "the product."

Meredith compared his defection to NBC to his experience as a teenager when he left the womb of little Mount Vernon for SMU. "It's a big spooky world out there," he said. "I'm scared to death."

Long before Meredith's departure became official, Arledge had a replacement in mind—Joe Namath, the most celebrated quarterback of his era and the on-the-field star of *Monday Night Football*'s debut. Ahead of everybody, as usual, Arledge had sounded out Namath about his intentions during the prior season. At their meeting, which was arranged by Cosell, Namath said he intended to remain active as a player.

Now Arledge put together an offer anyway, meeting with Namath's lawyer, agent, and chief worshiper, Jimmy Walsh. Walsh, who had attended Alabama with Namath, devoted his life to nurturing Namath's career and celebrity. His proposal to ABC was too absurd for rational consideration . . . almost.

Walsh wanted Arledge and ABC to do for Namath what Sonny Werblin and the New York Jets had done for him eleven years earlier—make Namath an offer so big that it would change an industry. Namath wanted a huge salary, long-term low-interest loans, even a piece of ABC Sports. Arledge found it all preposterous, but he didn't say a flat-out no.

Walsh had more bad news: He could not persuade Namath to retire. Undaunted, Arledge called NFL commissioner Rozelle with a question: What would the league think of having an active player work the games on television Monday night after playing on Sunday?

To everyone's surprise, Rozelle said that he would not object but that the player's owner would have to agree to the scheme.

The Jets' ownership opposed the idea emphatically. Arledge, over the protestations of Walsh, backed off.

That Rozelle would have sanctioned so risky a concept was entirely out of character. Had Namath been allowed to spend Sundays on the field and Mondays in the booth, every football writer in America would have attacked the league and ABC. But Rozelle was willing to let ABC use Namath, or hire almost anyone else, as long as the network steered clear of a man who was high on Arledge's list—Alex Karras. He was the last man Pete Rozelle wanted to be part of the most conspicuous presentation of the National Football League.

Arledge had already brought Karras to New York to meet his staff. The former All-Pro defensive tackle of the Detroit Lions had begun to establish an identity in Hollywood, notably in the hit movie *Blazing Saddles*. Playing a mean cuss named Mongo, Karras had stolen the film with a scene in which he literally punched out a horse.

There were times when Karras felt like administering the same treatment to Rozelle. The two men had been bitter enemies since Rozelle suspended Karras for the 1963 season, at the peak of his career, after he admitted to betting on NFL games. Karras was enraged by the punishment, and by Rozelle's handling of the case, which included a degrading episode with a lie-detector test. His bitterness grew when the commissioner insisted that he sell his interest in a Detroit bar before he could be readmitted to the league.

Karras wasn't the type of man to hide his feelings. He refused to speak to Rozelle. One time, when the commissioner was handing out trophies at a dinner before the Pro Bowl, Karras turned his back on him and refused to shake his hand. After being cut by the Lions in 1971, Karras often mocked Rozelle's corporate style and perpetual tan. And he never expressed remorse for his supposed sins.

The Karras-Rozelle feud troubled Arledge. Rozelle had no formal power to interfere with the choice of an announcer, but, for once, Arledge yielded to the commissioner. "I allowed myself to be influenced by Pete," he said. "I thought he had a case, in a way, with the whole question of the image of the game."

Arledge had other reasons to be concerned about Karras. Reports on his performance as an announcer for the Canadian

Football League were mixed. And Karras seemed to be thumbing his nose at the football establishment again by allowing his name to be used in a football betting sheet called "Pro in the Know"; a column about how to bet *Monday Night Football* ran under Karras's byline.

Arledge dropped Karras's name from his list. With Cosell at his side, he reviewed a parade of possibilities that came to include almost every prominent ex-football player in the land.

Cosell, ever the foe of the so-called jockocracy, made a case for two big names from show business—Burt Reynolds and Bill Cosby. Neither was seriously considered. "It would have been too violent a change from the way things had been done," Arledge said. He was not always a revolutionary.

Three other former NFL greats were considered—Jimmy Brown, Dick Butkus, and Paul Hornung. Only Hornung got close, but Arledge had seen some of the ex-Packer's broadcast work and it seemed leaden. Hornung's name was scratched.

Unexpectedly, the name of O. J. Simpson entered the picture. Simpson, then embroiled in a prolonged contract dispute with the Buffalo Bills, called Arledge to see if there would be room for him in the *Monday Night* booth if he decided to quit football. Arledge assured him that he could have the job, but encouraged him to reconsider. Giving up football in the midst of a brilliant career made no sense, Arledge told him.

Simpson had a new contract from the Bills within a week.

With the first preseason game less than two months away, Arledge felt his options were exhausted. He went to lunch with Rozelle and told him the wheel had come around again to Karras.

Rozelle took it personally. He told Arledge that naming Karras would mean trouble with the owners and pleaded for one last shot at finding someone more palatable. A short time later, Rozelle turned up with a new list of candidates, all ex-players with ties to broadcasting or entertainment.

Most of the names did nothing for Arledge, but his eye stopped at one possibility—a former Kansas City Chiefs defensive back named Fred Williamson.

Fred "The Hammer" Williamson was wearing two enormous gold chains around his neck when he shook hands for the first time with Roone Arledge. From one hung a clenched black fist. From the other, a well-defined solid-gold penis.

Arledge hired him anyway. He thought Williamson showed a lot of "attitude," and he liked that. That was the best reason anybody could come up with for hiring him.

There were numerous reasons not to hire him. He had almost no broadcasting experience. His popularity as a movie star was limited to black audiences, since he had taken to starring in lurid "blaxploitation" movies. He had been a brutal football player whom nobody, neither teammates nor writers, could stand. And his personality was so aggressively hostile that he and Cosell amounted to an ego-wreck waiting to happen.

But Arledge was not the type to weigh the pluses and minuses carefully when evaluating talent. He relied on his instincts, which had always served him well.

Moving fast, Arledge checked out Williamson. He went to Cosell, and together they listened to an interview that Cosell had done with Williamson for his radio show. They watched _Three the Hard Way_, a movie starring Williamson and Jim Brown. Then Arledge dispatched his personal assistant, Dick Ebersol, to Los Angeles to spend the weekend with The Hammer. Ebersol had a blast, and came back enthusiastic.

Because of his movie schedule, Williamson needed a decision right away from ABC. Arledge brought him to New York, set up a dinner, and asked Cosell and Gifford to come along.

They ate at Alfredo's, not far from Arledge's apartment on Central Park South. Williamson came across winningly. He was brash, irreverent, articulate, and full of himself.

One appeal of the Meredith-Cosell act, Arledge knew, was having someone in the booth who could "prick Howard's balloon." Even after it got nasty, the put-down humor was thought to be a key to the _Monday Night_ magic. Williamson, with all his style, intelligence, and self-confidence, showed promise of being able to joust with Cosell.

When the meal ended, Arledge suggested they drop by his place for a few drinks and a game of pool.

As they were setting up, Arledge called Ohlmeyer, who was in his usual haunt, the edit room at the ABC studios on Sixty-eighth Street. Arledge told him to come by the apartment.

Then Arledge picked up his pool cue and set up teams: he

and Cosell against Williamson and Gifford. With Williamson running the table, he and Gifford quickly wiped up Arledge and Cosell in two games of twenty-five balls each. Arledge told Cosell and Gifford to play their own game while he had a private chat with Williamson.

By the time the game was over, Arledge and Williamson emerged smiling from the next room. Williamson was a member of the ABC team. The other announcers shook his hand enthusiastically. Cosell in particular seemed high on the new man.

Ohlmeyer arrived a few moments later. As soon as he entered the room, Arledge said, "I want you to meet the new analyst on *Monday Night Football,* Fred Williamson."

Ohlmeyer looked at the striking black figure extending his hand—and had no idea who he was. He was in shock. He was also hurt. The job had been filled and he, the producer, had not even been consulted. Not until someone referred to Williamson as "The Hammer" did Ohlmeyer remember the name. *The Hammer: Oh, that guy,* he said to himself.

When he had a chance, Ohlmeyer pulled Arledge aside. "Are you fucking kidding me, Roone?" he said. "Fred Fucking Williamson!"

Arledge assured him The Hammer was going to be great.

Fred Williamson christened himself The Hammer after his distinctive technique for bringing down pass catchers. Huge for a cornerback, at six feet three inches and 220 pounds, Williamson would hold out a massive forearm—his hammer—and coldcock an unsuspecting receiver whose eye was on the ball.

He displayed his "attitude" by announcing to the world that he hated opposing players, the better, he said, to maintain his competitive edge. "There were not many passes thrown at me," he said. "The only way I could stay involved was to make other people dislike me. Otherwise, I could be standing the whole goddamn game with my finger in my ass."

No one could tell with Williamson where the put-on began. His whole career, he admitted, was based on braggadocio. He once labeled himself "the Muhammad Ali of football."

Had Williamson not been so intelligent, the bombast and ostentation would have played like comical ravings. But he was smart and shrewd; The Hammer was his role in a carefully calculated act.

Born in 1938, Williamson, the son of a welder, grew up in Gary, Indiana. He won a track scholarship to Northwestern, a school he chose for its architecture program.

As a pro, he starred in the mid-1960s for the rugged, take-no-prisoners Oakland Raiders, where his bruising brand of play fit in perfectly. In a typical burst of self-congratulation, he claimed to have invented the "bump and run" style of pass coverage, which consisted of belting a receiver at the line of scrimmage to knock him off-balance, then running with him—if the opponent could run at all at that point.

Oakland shipped him to Kansas City in time for the first Super Bowl, an ideal stage for The Hammer's special talent for outrage. Williamson hired a chauffeur to drive him around, and showed up for practice in a tuxedo. He bragged all week about how his hammer would devastate the Packer receivers.

Near the end of the easy Packer victory, Williamson was knocked over by a wall of blockers on a sweep and had to be carried off the field, semiconscious. Later, he said he was faking.

Williamson left the NFL in 1968, played a year in Canada, and briefly owned an architecture firm in Montreal. But The Hammer longed to perform on another stage. He went to Hollywood, where he bluffed his way onto the television series *Julia* by telling the producers that he had acting experience. He soon met Robert Altman, who cast him in *M*A*S*H*.

Handsome and macho, Williamson had the perfect profile to star in the blaxploitation movies that thrived in the early 1970s. He starred in such epics as *Black Caesar, Hell Up in Harlem,* and *The Legend of Nigger Charley.* He was grinding out five movies a year when ABC hired him.

Williamson was in top form at a press conference in New York announcing his appointment. He told the world, "I am a star and I will continue to be a star." Williamson also explained how he planned to prepare for his Monday night duties: "I'll go home and swim a lot in my pool, go to the latest discotheque in Los Angeles and brush up on my dancing, dress real pretty and show up."

Arledge, grinning contentedly, told the press about ABC's

exhaustive search for a new analyst. "It took a while," he said, "to select whom we consider the perfect person."

Cosell and Gifford were buoyant too. "He's a real person," Gifford said. "He comes on with no airs. I think we have a real champion."

The one overt stab at humor attempted by Williamson that day should have tripped somebody's alarm system. "At least," he quipped, "I'll bring some color to the show."

On Monday night, August 19, 1974, Fred Williamson went on the air cold. By the end of the evening, he'd iced over completely.

There were no dry-run practices for The Hammer. Mr. Self-confidence told ABC he didn't need anything like that. The ABC people, full of their own brand of arrogance, went along. Arledge had picked him, hadn't he? Williamson arrived in Minnesota for the preseason game with his "gift of rap and wit," ready to make the nation forget Don Meredith.

He didn't turn up with a tie, however. ABC had a standard-issue canary-yellow blazer for him, but Williamson refused to conceal his trademark chains-and-bare-chest look behind a tie. "I wear your ABC yellow jacket," he said. "I ain't wearing no fucking tie."

The new star of the trinity was given a wide-open opportunity to deliver his introductory remarks. Cosell brought him on by referring to him as someone who was " already a movie star," clearly a little dig at Meredith and his California dreaming.

Williamson came on all breezy and self-assured, admitting, "I'm a movie star. I don't know anything about broadcasting football." For Williamson, this passed for irreverence. It set the tone for his work. He did color commentary the same way he played football: bluntly, brutally, without a shred of subtlety. It was bump and run in the booth too. When in doubt, use the hammer.

He piled cliché onto cliché, then directed his most memorable line of the evening at Cosell: "Even an old cripple like you could have made yardage through that hole, Howard." This was not likely to ignite a round of sparkling repartee.

It became Williamson's defensive position that Cosell let him down on the air by refusing to talk to him. Cosell was afraid of him, Williamson said, particularly after he had shown him up during a publicity tour that summer.

No one else believed that. But Williamson had a point in saying he was not well served, if not by Cosell, then by the *Monday Night* establishment.

Forte, who stood by his man Cosell in those days, never liked Williamson. "The minute you put the light on, Freddie Williamson was nothing," he said. He kept up a steady yap in Williamson's ear, most of it critical. Arledge and Ohlmeyer, perhaps seduced by the new recruit's bravado, did nothing to break him in or help him play off Cosell. They could only point to the fun everyone had when Meredith jabbed at Cosell.

There was no way, though, that The Hammer could play the role of Dandy Don. Meredith, for one thing, was charming and likable. For another, he didn't instigate the fun but played the counterpuncher to Cosell. Williamson's nature forced him to be the aggressor. All of a sudden, ABC had two black hats in the booth, and the results were disastrous.

After the first game, Arledge called in Ohlmeyer to talk it over. "What do you think?" he asked the producer. Ohlmeyer didn't say a word. Finally, he said, "What do you think, Roone?" Arledge was silent. Ohlmeyer burst out laughing. "Oh, my God, here we go," he said.

The reviews were savage. "Sportscasting," said one, "had sunk to new depths."

Williamson survived two more exhibition games. By that time, the chemistry had turned explosive. Still trying to be funny, Williamson was telling Cosell that he was talking too much and getting boring. He even suggested that Cosell did not know football because he "never played the game." Nothing was more likely to enrage Cosell.

Arledge knew that Williamson just didn't get it—didn't understand the essence of *Monday Night Football.* "No matter how much you didn't want Howard to control things," Arledge said, "as a practical matter, if Howard wasn't going to get along with the person, it's not going to work."

He told Ohlmeyer, "If they did a hundred games together, it wouldn't get any better."

Williamson's contract was paid off. It had called for Williamson to star in television movies and was worth well into six figures. ABC said he would still make the movies, but Williamson never again appeared on the network.

He did appear, however, in Cosell's second book, *Like It Is*, which had gone to press before the season began and was released that fall. Cosell devoted Chapter Two—"Say Hello to The Hammer"—to the coming of Fred Williamson, whom he welcomed with unfettered enthusiasm.

It was nobody's favorite chapter of *Monday Night Football*.

Alex Karras had given up on *Monday Night Football*. He had never been dying for the job, anyway. Karras was already having some success as an actor, and he had seen the *Monday Night* job merely as a way to advance his acting carer and make some money.

But Roone Arledge had not given up on Karras. He had Dick Ebersol stay in touch with Tom Vance, Karras's friend and agent. As Williamson's shortcomings became more evident, Ebersol's calls became more frequent. Karras, in the meantime, had been offered a job as an announcer with the new World Football League.

Once Ebersol called from Europe, awakening Vance at two A.M., just to be sure Karras was still available. "We're trying to work things out to get Alex," Ebersol said. "Please don't sign anything yet." Vance agreed, just so he could go back to sleep. The week before the regular-season opener, Karras and Vance flew to New York for a lunch with Arledge and Cosell.

Cosell was immediately enthusiastic about Karras, but Arledge held back, trying to feel him out, to get a sense of how he might approach the games. What do you think you could contribute to *Monday Night Football*? Arledge wanted to know.

"Entertainment," Karras replied. "It's show biz." He went on to explain that, while the football is important, "you've got to have fun with it." It was exactly what Arledge wanted to hear. Monday nights hadn't been much fun lately.

Next, Arledge said, there's the problem of Rozelle. Alex had to take his name off the tout sheet. Karras agreed, though he thought it was hypocritical. The NFL and ABC both knew that gambling only fueled the pro-football boom.

Arledge was still proceeding with caution. He did not want to make another long-term commitment. If nothing else, in order to avoid a battle with Rozelle, he wanted to announce Karras as a temporary replacement.

Sounding almost apologetic, Arledge told Karras that he wanted to start him on a week-to-week basis.

"That's okay," replied Karras, "because I might not like you either."

Alex Karras had not always been a good talker. When he reported to the Detroit Lions in 1958 as a rookie defensive lineman, he was a beer-guzzling, fun-loving blue-collar guy, painfully shy and rough around the edges. He had spent more time partying than studying in Iowa, where he had fought constantly with the coach. Karras was a jock's jock, not the type who would be likely to end up in a jacket-and-tie job analyzing football.

Born in 1935, he grew up in an ethnic neighborhood in Gary, Indiana. His father, a working-class doctor, died when Alex was thirteen, leaving a large close-knit family behind. He was not, by nature, an aggressive kid, but he was big and strong and drawn to sports. "Football," he said, "was what was going to get me out of Gary." It got his older brother, Teddy, to Indiana University, and it got Alex a free ride to Iowa.

Karras played football with great intensity and brute force. He was the top draft choice of the Lions, and he became the premier pass rusher of his day, a player capable of terrorizing offensive linemen. For a big game, Karras would work himself into a frenzy.

One Sunday, in a game against the hated Chicago Bears, Karras was manhandling the opposing guard so thoroughly that George Halas sent in a sub. Karras squinted—he never saw well on the field without his thick glasses—and vowed to destroy the newcomer. On the first play, he belted the guy in the jaw. The next play, he landed a knee to the groin. That brought a scream from the fallen Bear. "Dammit, Alex, stop," said the enemy lineman. It was his brother, Ted.

Karras once got so worked up that he threw a helmet at his teammate Milt Plum after the Lions' quarterback threw a dumb interception that cost the team a crucial game. Usually, though, he saved his best shots for opposing quarterbacks. "I hate every quarterback in the league," he'd say. "They're nothing but blond, blue-eyed milk drinkers."

Maybe quarterbacks represented authority to Karras. The free-spirited lineman instinctively rebelled against authority— the coach and the administration at Iowa, the management of the Lions, and, most of all, Rozelle and his minions at the NFL. He was a bull-headed man.

What saved him from unredeemed obnoxiousness was his sense of humor. He could even laugh about his suspension, as he did the first time he trotted out to midfield as the new co-captain of the Lions in 1964.

"Mr. Karras, do you call heads or tails?" asked the referee.

"I'm sorry," replied Karras, "I'm not allowed to gamble."

Karras got his first taste of show business when he played himself in the movie *Paper Lion*. After the Lions cut him, he turned to performing full-time. He was able to earn a living from a steady schedule of sportscasting, acting in commercials, talk-show appearances, and roles in such movies as *The 500 Pound Jerk*. Still, there weren't a lot of parts for a six-foot-two-inch, 250-pounder with a wobbly gait and a pudgy nose— especially since Karras took pains to avoid being typecast as a buffoon or a heavy.

Cautiously, he kept his home in the Detroit suburb of Bloomfield Hills, where he lived with his wife, Joan, whom he met at Iowa, and their five children. "I don't want to uproot anyone until I establish myself," he said. But he never doubted that he could make it as a television or movie star.

Monday Night Football now became crucial to his game plan.

Karras had one thing in common with Fred Williamson. He did not like the ABC blazer. The one he wore for his debut on the night of September 16, 1974, was the biggest ABC had on hand, but it still did not fit comfortably over Karras's odd shape. He had to struggle to squeeze his thick arms into the sleeves. And that wasn't the only problem with his appearance: His glasses slipped down his nose; his hair was a mess. Don

Ohlmeyer made sure the sequence was all captured on tape, then played it at the top of the show.

Then, as Mongo, Karras flattened the horse.

So went the introduction of the new man in the *Monday Night Football* booth, who had two significant advantages over his predecessor.

He was not replacing Don Meredith.

He was replacing Fred Williamson.

Karras had another advantage too: Even on days when he didn't have anything especially funny to say, he looked funny. The largest of shirt collars tugged at his neck. His arms flapped. He waddled.

To Ohlmeyer and Forte, those were all assets. Karras was cast as a working-class Joe, the guy you'd invite over to share a six-pack and watch the action. If Karras managed to get off a few quips during a game, so much the better.

The ABC people eventually concluded that each week Karras came prepared with a few gag lines that he would try to work into the game. Karras claimed that his humor was unrehearsed. Certainly his most famous line was spontaneous. He delivered it during the first regular-season game of 1974, between the Oakland Raiders and Buffalo Bills.

During a timeout, one of Forte's nine cameras captured a vivid close-up of one of the Raiders, a hulking defensive lineman with a menacing sneer and a shaved head that glinted in the stadium lights.

"That's Otis Sistrunk," Karras said, pondering the other-worldly image on his monitor. "He's from the University of Mars."

In the truck, Arledge and Ohlmeyer cracked up. "It was an incredible line," Arledge said. Sistrunk always believed that the quip made him a lot of money in commercials and movies. Years later, he said, "What Karras said that night left me with a trademark that will probably be with me the rest of my life." It proved once more the impact of *Monday Night Football*.

The line did a lot for Karras too. Arledge and Ohlmeyer decided that night that he had marketable talent, though he had to appear twice more as a "temporary" replacement before his appointment was made official. This time, there was no news conference. ABC simply issued a press release admitting Karras to the royal triumvirate of *Monday Night Football.*

Alex Karras perceived the minefields that awaited him on *Monday Night Football.* He had heard about Meredith's divisive discontent and he had seen the Williamson debacle unfold. Karras was no diplomat, but he was smart enough to realize that, as the new kid on the show, he ought to steer clear of any conflicts with the *Monday Night* power structure.

Ohlmeyer and Forte presented no problems. Both were happy to be rid of Williamson and prepared to like Karras, as long as he did his job. Ohlmeyer was also the first to see that Karras's appearance could be put to comedic use.

"People look at Alex Karras and think: big, dumb lineman," Ohlmeyer said. "Alex isn't dumb at all. He's a very, very bright guy and has a good comedic sense." Because people's expectations were low, they tended to laugh even when Karras's gags were just ordinary. He became known as a wit, and friends would suggest one-liners to him. Not all the humor clicked, but Karras was clearly trying.

His efforts helped to appease Gifford. Of all the *Monday Nighter*s, Gifford was the least inclined to welcome the new man. "I really didn't think much of Alex before he came on the show," he said. Karras's sins, in Gifford's eyes, were that he had been critical of the NFL and rude to Rozelle. But Gifford's first loyalty was to Arledge. He was also a team player down to his cleats. He could learn to accept Karras, and maybe even learn to like him.

Cosell, in contrast, embraced Karras—at first. He enjoyed Karras's irreverence and respected his work as an entertainer. Most important, he knew Karras was no threat—not as a broadcaster, not as a personality, and certainly not as a competitor for airtime.

Karras, said one production staffer, was the "right fit for that era. Howard had a lot to say, Frank necessarily had a lot to say doing play-by-play, and Alex was content with a line every four plays. Which was okay."

Everyone on the show realized that Karras saw the *Monday Night* job as a stopover on his way to Hollywood. "I was an outsider," Karras said. "I knew there was no way in the world that I could do that for a living. Frankly, I was not that good."

Karras's weakness was that he had never studied football. He knew line play, of course, and knew some of the men on the field, but he was not well versed on offensive or defensive strategy. "He didn't have a clue and didn't care much about what was going on," Gifford said. Everyone assumed Karras would improve with time. Football expertise had never been a prerequisite for the job.

Karras also had a curious habit of upsetting the show's biggest advertiser, Ford, by making an Edsel joke or noting that a star player drove a Cadillac. Ohlmeyer and Forte would remind him to be more careful—"Well, that's good," they'd say into his ear, "because Ford gives us eighteen billion dollars a year and here you are with your Cadillacs"—but the comments were not entirely happenstance. Karras still harbored some bitterness toward the Lions, a team owned by William Clay Ford.

Still, for a season or two, a relative calm settled over the *Monday Night* scene. Cosell was businesslike, if not content. Gifford was placid as always. Karras was easygoing too—until provoked.

In November 1974, after a game in San Francisco, three men with knives came after Cosell, Gifford, and Karras in the stadium parking lot. The *Monday Night* men fortunately had a couple of off-duty cops with them. Karras was the only one of the trio to join with the cops in subduing the attackers, who were threatening Cosell. "I became one of Howard's bodyguards," Karras said. "I thought somebody had to do it."

The following year in Washington, Karras and Gifford were leaving a game when they were approached by a crowd. Most of the people were friendly, but when the announcers stopped signing autographs and got into their limo, one man said something nasty to Karras. "Boy, Alex came out of the car," Gifford said, "and the guy leaped away from him and fell over something and rolled over and over." Karras said he never laid a hand on the man.

The next time they visited Washington, Karras was handed a sheaf of court papers. "Jesus," he thought, "one of my friends is playing some kind of practical joke." It was no joke—a man had sued Karras and ABC for $5.3 million, claiming that in the incident the previous fall, Karras had slammed him on the hood of a car and caused him head, body, and back injuries. ABC was sued for hiring "a man of vicious temperament and uncontrolled or uncontrollable temper."

Network lawyers settled out of court to avoid further publicity. Karras was furious, but the network people told him that the facts of the case were less important than protecting everyone's reputation. Typically, he thought that was "bullshit," and, typically, he told them so.

But Karras had no desire to invite controversy. He knew he had a good thing going: all the exposure; a five-thousand-dollar-a-game paycheck, which doubled his best salary as a player; and a job that was far from taxing.

Yet Karras also knew he was not meant to be a broadcaster. He found it difficult to do three hours of live prime-time television. He much preferred working in movies, where there were always opportunities for retakes.

Karras began spending more and more time thinking about movies, and less and less thinking about football. Midway through 1975, he began work on a television movie called *Babe* that would soon lead him out of football altogether.

If Alex Karras and Fred Williamson never felt comfortable in their blazers, there were two other men in the booth whose chests swelled with pride every time they wore the yellow jackets with the ABC patch.

Steve Bozeka and Jerry Klein were so proud of their association with ABC that they paid for the blazers themselves.

Bozeka was Gifford's spotter, and Klein was his statistician. They were the fourth and fifth men in the *Monday Night* booth, men under strict orders to keep the lowest of profiles—literally. "Hit the deck," Forte would scream as he was about to call for a shot of the stars in the booth. Bozeka and Klein would obligingly dive to the floor.

"It became a joke that an air-raid drill could strike at any moment," said Klein. "It was three gods being shown to the nationwide audience. They all were the kings and we were serfs."

Serfs or not, Bozeka and Klein felt honored to be part of

Monday Night Football. They traveled everywhere, stayed in the same hotels as the stars, and played important supporting roles during the telecasts.

Bozeka, then forty-seven, was hired in 1973. A carpet salesman at a Sears, Roebuck store in Canton, Ohio, he had done some spotting for a local television station that broadcast high school games. When ABC came to Canton for the Hall of Fame Game, Bozeka seized the opportunity to work as Gifford's spotter. The experience encouraged him to go after the regular-season job. "I wrote to Frank, I called him, I hounded him, but I never heard a word," Bozeka said. Four days before the season began, Gifford told him to fly to Green Bay for the opener. Bozeka was hired on the spot for fifty dollars a game, plus expenses. With the exception of one game when a snowstorm hit Canton, he worked every *Monday Night* game for the next thirteen seasons.

During games, Bozeka would stand behind Gifford's right shoulder—at five feet five he was too short to sit down and still see the field—and manage the spotter board, which lay flat on the table in front of them. Gifford made up the board himself, and it was an elaborate production—listing the names and numbers of every player on both teams, by position, with the home team's defensive unit at the top and the visiting team's offensive unit at the bottom. On the opposite side of the board were listed the home team's offense and the visitors' defense. Gifford also would use the board to note, in meticulous penmanship, relevant facts about key players, such as where they went to college or the year they were drafted.

Bozeka and Gifford understood the board, but others found it indecipherable. "It looked like the hydrogen-bomb formula," Klein said.

Bozeka's job was twofold. First, he kept track of all the players entering and leaving the game, moving colored pins around the board to indicate who was in the game for each play. That task alone required full concentration, especially as the game got more specialized and players were shuttled in and out on nearly every play. Second, Bozeka, using the eraser end of a Sears pencil, would point during each play to the names of the ball carrier and the tackler. He never spoke. If he needed Gifford's attention, he'd scrawl him a note or use hand signals:

Five fingers held aloft, for example, meant that a team was employing the nickel defense.

Klein was hired in 1975 and stayed for seven years. Then twenty-eight, Klein had done statistics for college teams and for the NCAA. He would help prepare graphics before a game, then would try during the contest to be alert for record-breaking performances or statistical anomalies. If a quarterback completed five passes in a row, or a star rusher was being held to less than twenty yards, Klein would tell Gifford or the production assistants in graphics. Like Bozeka, Klein worked on a per-game basis for ABC.

Both men admired Gifford. Klein, who worked with almost every announcer at ABC, said "There is not a nicer, more congenial, or friendly man than Frank Gifford." His only regret, he said, is that "all those years I worked I never had a meal with Frank."

The two men were grateful for whatever attention they got. After Bozeka's first game, in Green Bay, Gifford invited him to join the *Monday Night* crew for a few drinks at the hotel. With Gifford, Cosell, and Meredith were O. J. Simpson, who had flown in to appear at halftime, and Paul Hornung, who had done the game on radio for the Packers. People recognized the ex-players and wanted autographs from everyone, including Bozeka. "I'm a nobody," he protested.

The ever-gracious Gifford didn't like the sound of that. "Steve," he said, "everybody's a somebody. Give the kid your autograph." Bozeka never forgot the gesture.

Gifford used to thank Bozeka and Klein near the end of the telecasts, but he occasionally forgot. When he did, Karras made a point of reminding him. One night, when Gifford thanked Bozeka, Karras was ready with a comeback. "Yeah, Frank," he said, "behind every good announcer is a Greek spotter." Gifford replied, "I won't touch that one with a ten-foot pole."

Over the years, Bozeka became a minor celebrity in Canton. People would come up to him in restaurants, seeking gossip about the *Monday Night* scene. "I tried to keep everything in perspective," he said. "When I got off that plane at the Akron-Canton airport, I was getting back to my rugs. Back to my carpets." In the years to come, Bozeka was sometimes relieved to get back to the carpet section and away from the *Monday Night* complaint department.

By 1974, CBS and NBC realized that the best way to counter *Monday Night Football* was with programs that appealed to women. CBS tended to rely on weekly series, while NBC turned to movies and miniseries. But both networks figured that, with a growing number of families owning more than one television set, they could reach women even when men were committed *Monday Night Football* fans.

CBS intended to reach the entire nation on the night of October 28, 1974, with a special episode of *Rhoda,* a new series created that fall and positioned against *Monday Night Football.* In the much-hyped hour-long show, Rhoda finally found a husband. The stunt worked, as Rhoda was the top-rated show for the week. Shortly after ten P.M., Cosell joked over the air that he had not been invited to the nuptials and welcomed everyone back to the game.

The next fall, CBS sent its own New York loudmouth—Archie Bunker—into battle against Cosell. *All in the Family,* which was then the top-rated show on television, moved from Saturdays at eight to Mondays at nine, right up against the opening kickoff. Before the season, experts speculated that Archie would be the weapon to kill ABC. As it turned out, the switch helped CBS to remain strong on Mondays, but it did not damage the games' ratings.

NBC saved its blockbuster movies for Mondays. Two of the most popular movies ever made, *The Godfather* and *Gone With the Wind*—which cost advertisers a record-breaking $225,000 a minute—were scheduled against football in 1976. Both did well, but the games held their own. And the fans came back after each blockbuster.

Monday Night's ratings, in fact, grew slightly after a dip following Meredith's departure. Prices for commercials rose too, surpassing the $100,000-a-minute barrier, and they were about to climb even higher—thanks to a beer company, an ad agency, and a new brew called Lite.

*   *   *

John A. Murphy, the chairman of the Miller Brewing Company, was a man with a mission—to make Miller the number-one brewer in America. If he ever forgot what stood in the way, he had only to look down. Under his desk was a foot rug bearing the eagle symbol of archrival Anheuser-Busch, Inc.

Murphy was about to walk all over A-B. He set out to become the exclusive beer advertiser on dozens of sporting events on network television, then to blitz the viewers with Miller ads unlike anything the beer industry had ever seen, and to do it all before the people at A-B knew what hit them. One of Murphy's first targets: *Monday Night Football.*

Already, Murphy and his hotshot advertising agency, McCann-Erickson, had transformed Miller from a sleepy regional company to America's fastest-growing brewery. Now Miller had a new product to sell—a low-calorie beer, Lite. Instead of pitching the beer as a drink for dieters or sissies, McCann-Erickson came up with an inspired campaign built around a parade of beefy ex-jocks who testified that they could drink Lite all night long and not get filled up. Lite, declared Dick Butkus, Bubba Smith, and Deacon Jones, was "everything you always wanted in a beer—and less." What better place to hammer that message home than on *Monday Night Football,* with its huge male audience, in particular those 1.8 million viewers in bars?

The plan to seize the sports audience for Miller had been hatched by Steve Leff, who was in charge of buying media for McCann-Erickson. The Miller people had figured out something that no one else in the beer industry yet knew—people who drink beer also tend to watch lots of sports on network television. Before then, brewers would advertise on local stations, going to warm-weather markets and concentrating on the summer months. It was wasteful, they thought, to buy time on a nationally televised football game in November.

Leff disagreed. He thought national spots were worth buying. "If you believe that people are watching something, and they're really caught up in it, they're going to view the commercials with equal intensity," he said. "Sports is open-ended. You have a chance to root on many levels. That's the real value of sports. And *Monday Night Football* took that to a new high."

Leff went to see Herb Granath at ABC Sales. How much

would it take, he wondered, to lock up the beer category on Monday nights?

At the same time, Leff was buying college football on ABC, NFL games and basketball on CBS, and baseball on NBC. But Anheuser-Busch was such a dominant player in the beer industry that the networks felt obligated to let the Busch people know what was going on.

The networks had nothing to lose. The sports advertising market had softened a little in 1975. Granath figured he could let Miller become the exclusive *Monday Night* beer for about $5 million—provided that A-B was not interested.

They were not. Schlitz also got a shot at Monday nights, but turned it down as well. Neither could see the logic of blowing all that money on a network show, and one that ran in fall, no less.

"By the time anybody had woken up, we had essentially cornered the market," Leff said. "There was a period of two, three years when we totally dominated the market."

Now on Monday nights, people stuck around to watch the ads—Bubba Smith ripping the top off a can of Lite, Rodney Dangerfield in a joint so tough that "the hatcheck girl is named Dominick." Miller couldn't make enough Lite to satisfy consumer demand. Back in Milwaukee, Murphy smiled with satisfaction when he watched the games—and every time he glanced down at his rug.

At Anheuser-Busch, the ads were no laughing matter. August A. Busch III, who had just taken over the company from his father, Gussie, knew someone had made a colossal mistake. A-B never realized just how many beer drinkers were also big fans of *Monday Night Football.* "That's where we missed the boat," he said. "We were unsmarted." Busch had no intention of watching from the sidelines. A-B wanted a piece of *Monday Night Football.*

As an actor, Alex Karras achieved a breakthrough in *Babe,* a good but not exceptional television movie. He played George Zaharias, the wrestler and promoter who was married to golfer and track star Babe Didrickson. Both Karras and Zaharias were big men, and both were of Greek descent. And Karras had performed briefly as a pro wrestler many years earlier.

But Karras was untested in a dramatic role. On-screen and

off, he was thought of as a funny man. He fought for the role in *Babe,* realizing that with a strong performance he could prove himself as an actor. The role demanded that he be rough, affectionate, and sensitive. During the final scenes, when his wife was dying of cancer, he cried. The reviews were excellent.

Karras had no problem with the love scenes. He was falling for his co-star, Susan Clark, an emerging actress who played Didrickson. A month after the movie completed production in June 1975, Karras separated from his wife of eighteen years. She filed for divorce the following spring. By then, Karras had moved to Los Angeles.

Monday Night Football held less and less interest for him. He was bored with the games, quieter than ever during the telecasts. His mind was on other things. When he had to turn down several acting jobs because of his ABC schedule, he resented the Monday night obligations. "The first year was a lot of fun for Alex, the second year was okay, and the third year it became 'Oh my God, I've got another game,'" said one close friend.

His lack of interest showed. Karras had never been a diligent worker, but now he did even less preparation. Ohlmeyer and Arledge had hoped his performance would improve as he grew more comfortable in the booth, but they were disappointed. Karras and Cosell never developed a way of relating to each other on the air. Arledge said Karras's first game "turned out probably to be the high point . . . he was good after that, but he never was quite as good."

Others were less charitable. By 1976, Karras's third season on the show, production staffers thought he was coasting. "He was sort of distant," one said. "He would show up, do the job, and go home."

"Karras was indifferent," Cosell said. "He just didn't care about the quality of his work." Tensions between them grew after Cosell criticized Karras's work habits.

During a game that fall, Karras observed that a linebacker on the Pittsburgh Steelers had great range and pursuit. Trouble was, the player he was referring to was a defensive tackle. When the error was pointed out, Karras chuckled and said, "Everybody knows that." No one in the truck found that funny.

Some of the criticism found its way into print. Word spread around the league that Karras was going to be dumped if Joe Namath, then on the verge of retiring, became available. Karras was not looking forward to another season, but he had no plans to quit.

Namath signed with the Rams for a final, ill-fated season as a player. It didn't matter. Karras's *Monday Night* career was over.

7.

OTHER NIGHTS TO CONQUER

"My deepest fear is that one day I'm going to find out that this is all there is to life, and it won't be enough."—DON MEREDITH

Howard Cosell stood stiffly in his tuxedo at the corner of Broadway and Fifty-second Street, haunted by one overriding concern—"I just don't want to make an ass of myself."

Ten minutes before the debut of *Saturday Night Live with Howard Cosell*, the star of the show was scared to death.

It was Saturday, September 20, 1975. Cosell's live variety show was ABC's latest prime-time experiment as well as the most hyped new program of the 1975–76 television season. That night, a crowd had gathered on the sidewalk behind the police barricades. Onlookers stared into the blinding klieg lights arrayed along the avenue, wondering what was about to happen.

Cosell wondered about something else: Could he translate the popularity he had built in the world of sports to the world of show business, a world in which he longed for acceptance?

He knew that in the control room Roone Arledge had taken charge in his confident, unflappable way. It was a comforting thought. If anyone could manage the challenge they had set for themselves—to create a show so exciting and unpredictable that America would be afraid to miss it—Arledge could.

Cosell also took pride in the guest lineup they had been able to arrange, even if it didn't—couldn't—quite live up to the promises he had made to the press all summer, topped by his pledge that "the pope will be on sooner or later."

At this point, it looked as if His Holiness had stood up His Humbleness.

But the pontiff would not be missed this week, not with the Chairman of the Board on hand. How much bigger could a show get than to land Sinatra? He had agreed to make an appearance, loyally repaying a debt he owed to Arledge and Cosell for helping him stage an ABC special the previous year.

Arledge, through his close association with the Kennedy clan, had also secured Ted Kennedy for a cameo. John Denver, another Arledge friend, was going to perform. And Jimmy Connors, the tennis star, was going to sing a number called "Super Girl, You Turn Me On"—that, at least, qualified as unpredictable.

They would be taking viewers live by satellite to London and Las Vegas. And the opening! What an opening! Cosell started to feel a surge of energy. ABC was counting on him to carry an hour of prime time. What better proof that Howard Cosell was a force in show business, that His Humbleness was a star.

The stage manager gave the signal and Cosell was on the air, introducing the show and himself, saying, "Tonight on our stage, you'll be seeing _other_ great faces, plus the unexpected, because this is live!"

The music came up and the cameras swung out into the middle of Broadway, where the cast of the musical _The Wiz_ began high-stepping their way uptown to the show-stopping tune "Ease On Down the Road."

The air was suddenly electric. The show shot off sparks. Maybe, Cosell thought, this was _Monday Night Football_ all over again—taking a risk, defying the critics, nerves and tension and pressure followed by success and fame and another show becoming a coast-to-coast phenomenon.

Cosell felt better. Maybe he wouldn't make an ass of himself after all.

*   *   *

The *Monday Night* institution had been up and running for five years, and the inmates were getting restless.

Howard Cosell had been telling the world that he wanted off the *Monday Night Football* thrill ride almost from the moment he climbed on. "Do you think," he asked a reporter from *Newsweek* back in 1972, "that I, at 52 years of age, and at the peak of my intellectual prowess, am going to spend the rest of my days worrying whether Roger Staubach's shoulder will heal in time for the Washington game?"

The implication was clear: Sports was beneath him. Cosell had long held ambiguous, even contradictory feelings about sports. He poured his life into them, cared deeply about some of the people in sports, and could be wildly excited by a title fight or an exciting Monday night matchup. Yet he felt that the contests lacked real importance. So long as he continued to be identified only with sports, Cosell had concluded, he would never be accorded his proper due.

He turned to Hollywood. His fame made him a sought-after guest on talk shows, variety shows, and situation comedies, and he was flattered when Woody Allen gave him a role in two of his movies, *Bananas* and *Sleeper*. Like Arledge, Cosell enjoyed the company of celebrities. He began to look forward to his trips to the West Coast, where the stroking of big egos is a highly refined art. "I always felt most comfortable in Hollywood," he said without a trace of self-consciousness, "where I was taken for granted as a superstar and paid homage to by the greatest stars in show business."

Arledge too was eager for new adventures. It had been some time since he had created anything. The Olympics were always a challenge, but they came only every four years. And, although he would never say so in public, Arledge was growing bored with sports. "Roone," said Don Ohlmeyer, "had done everything he wanted to do in sports. He changed an industry." When Arledge's friends at ABC got together, the conversation often came around to an intriguing question: What is Roone going to do next?

Periodically, when ABC's entertainment shows slumped in the ratings, there was talk that the network might ask Arledge to take over all of prime time. He had dabbled in show business. The Sinatra special in 1974, broadcast from Madison Square Garden and called "The Main Event," was an explicit effort to apply the techniques of sports television to a prime-time entertainment show. The show was live, and Arledge's cameras caught the arriving throng, zoomed in for intimate close-ups of Sinatra, then panned the crowd for reactions. Cosell delivered an effusive introduction, the ratings were strong, and the experience was a heady one for all.

Saturday Night Live with Howard Cosell was the next step. Arledge and his friend Fred Pierce, who had become president of the network in 1974, dreamed up the idea during one of their early-evening bull sessions. The two men often unwound after work in Pierce's office, talking about the company and its problems over a couple of drinks. Cosell and his needs were a frequent topic, as was Arledge's future with ABC. Arledge's contract was about to expire in August 1975, and he expressed a desire to try something new. One night, Pierce put two and two together. "Hey," he said, partly in jest, "maybe Cosell could become the next Ed Sullivan!"

The more Pierce considered the idea, the more it made sense. "We were having trouble on Saturday night anyway," he said, "so why not give it a shot?" Even if the show failed, Arledge and Cosell would get a chance to flex their muscles and make some money. Cosell's company, Jillary Productions (named after his daughters, Jill and Hillary), would own the show and Arledge would be paid a fee as executive producer. Pierce saw the venture as a way to "put a little bread on the water with very little risk for ABC." And it just might help keep two of his biggest stars, Arledge and Cosell, in the fold.

Saturday Night Live with Howard Cosell would mix traditional variety acts with the satellite technology used in sports and news, enabling Arledge and Cosell to cover entertainment events around the world. They all agreed that there could be no better place to recapture the magic of variety television than the Ed Sullivan Theater, so that was the stage they rented. They would throw in a troupe of comedians, a few sports celebrities, maybe some names in the news, and, if all went well, the results would be dramatic, surprising, and occasionally controversial— not unlike *Monday Night Football.* "We felt we might be able to build a variety series into the kinds of unpredictable weekly events that the football games are," said Pierce.

If *The Mary Tyler Moore Show* could spin off *Rhoda*, why couldn't *Monday Night Football* spin off *Saturday Night Live with Howard Cosell*?

The show was promoted heavily for weeks. Inside ABC, Pierce was rooting for it to succeed, but Fred Silverman, the programming wunderkind who had just been hired away from CBS to take charge of ABC's prime time, was unenthusiastic.

Everyone spent months planning the premiere. Cosell had even tried to reunite The Beatles on the same stage where they had made their American television debut, but he got no further than a brief meeting with John Lennon. Instead, Don Ohlmeyer was dispatched to London to produce a concert by a Scottish rock group called The Bay City Rollers, who, in a fit of hyperbole, were billed as "the next Beatles" by Cosell. Viewers wound up seeing frenzied fans rush the stage and bang the group's lead singer on the head, knocking him cold.

The rest of the evening was no knockout. Sinatra's walk-on was the biggest moment, but he didn't sing. Instead, he joked to Cosell, "This show will be a millstone on American TV." Connors did sing, but shouldn't have been allowed to. His duet with Paul Anka was an embarrassment. Otherwise, the parade of singers and comics had a stagy, mechanical flavor, not unlike the Sullivan show in its waning days. Cosell himself was nervous and subdued. Arledge had realized that something was amiss when Cosell, who never used cue cards, had wanted them for backup.

Just a few days before the opening night, Cosell had sounded an alarm during a walk over to the theater with the show's director, Don Mischer. "The most important thing we have to do in this show," he said, "is to be honest." The young director, not knowing what Cosell was driving at, found the remark rather odd. Cosell went on to say that while people often disagreed with him, they always expected him to tell the truth as he saw it, to tell it like it is. "We have to protect my integrity," Cosell said. Again, Mischer did not see how that would be a problem.

It became a huge problem. The moment he walked onstage, Cosell fell into standard variety-show banter. Every vocalist was a superstar, every new comedian a brilliant talent. The lame

Jimmy Connors–Paul Anka duet was described by Cosell as "a great magical moment in musical history." Shirley Bassey, he said that same night, was "the greatest singing star on the international scene." He was not about to stop and ask her, "Shirley, they say you can't hit the high notes anymore. True or not true?"

John J. O'Connor, the television critic of *The New York Times*, observed that "the Horrible Howard monster is now being marketed as the Cozy Cosell doll." The reliance on cue cards drained the show of its spontaneity. It became obvious that the man who always promised to tell it like it is was having it written for him before he told it.

What most surprised Cosell-watchers was the way he shied away from controversy. On the second show, the pop group LaBelle got into a flap with Arledge. They had come on with a promise that they would have time to do two songs, but after a segment with Evel Knievel ran long, Patti LaBelle, the lead singer, was informed they could do just one. She walked.

Arledge did not panic. Instead, he told Cosell to go out and blast them for their unprofessional conduct. Cosell's response shocked him. He said he was worried about being sued. Arledge told him not to worry—blast them anyway. Cosell said nothing about LaBelle, and killed the time by wandering into the audience.

All the next week, the producers kept coming back to the incident. They all agreed that they had missed an opportunity to generate some ink and get people talking about the show. No one, though, could figure out how to loosen up Cosell. No one had realized how desperately he wanted to be welcomed into the world of show business.

"Howard was unwilling to really be Howard. He tried to be a nice guy all the time," Arledge said. "The thing that made him Howard on *Monday Night Football* was his fearless, outspoken, brash, opinionated approach to things. And on this program he was being just the opposite."

If Cosell was unwilling to be Cosell, Arledge was unable to be anything but Arledge. He was as disorganized as ever, and just as hard to reach. That was not a problem at first; they had months to plan the opening show. But, after the premiere, Arledge spent less and less time at the show's production offices. He would show up for a production meeting on Monday or Tuesday, then disappear until Friday. In between, everything was on hold—the sets, the lighting, the music, the dance numbers, the comedy. Everyone was waiting for Arledge.

Arledge was simply unaccustomed to dealing with a blank stage every Saturday night. Mischer explained with an analogy: "When covering a sports event," he said, "that game happens whether ABC television is there or not. The players are costumed, the referees are there, there's an audience, and they start the game. They hike the ball, they throw the pass, and you have drama unfolding. So you go there as a television producer, and your job is to capture that drama. No one has ever done that better than Roone and ABC Sports."

The variety show demanded not only that coverage be produced but that the event itself be created. "It was as if we had to find the stadium, cast the players, rehearse the plays, put them in the right costumes, light it, and so forth," Mischer said. "Unless we booked somebody to stand there and sing, selected the music, got the orchestration, wrote the comedy, built the set, rehearsed the comedians, and whatever, nothing was going to happen. We were always flying by the seat of our pants."

Arledge thrived under deadline pressure. One Saturday evening, after the dress rehearsal, he was thumbing through the newspaper and said, to no one in particular, "I'm wondering what big bands are in town." Silently, the rest of the production team prayed that there were no big bands to be found anywhere east of Cleveland. But Arledge discovered that Lionel Hampton was playing in midtown, and that he wasn't due to start his set until after nine P.M. Arledge tracked him down, booked him for the show, and somehow a producer got a set of vibes to Fifty-second Street in time for the jazzman to play—and play well. It proved that you could sometimes rearrange things at the last minute and make it work. But not often.

Before long, Arledge began to lose control over the show. The ratings were largely responsible for that. Had the premiere been a big success, top management probably would have left him alone. But the show opened to modest ratings, and the numbers then took a dive. Now everyone at ABC, it seemed, had ideas for saving *Saturday Night Live with Howard Cosell.*

One Saturday afternoon several weeks into the season, Fred

Silverman slipped unnoticed into the back of the control room as a comedy troupe hired for the show was rehearsing a skit. When the skit ended, Arledge and Mischer agreed that it wasn't bad at all. Silverman, scowling, spoke up for the first time. "It was awful," he bellowed.

Arledge looked around, surprised, then recovered quickly. "Oh, yeah, I guess, Fred, you're right," he said. "It does need a little work." They went off to a closed-door meeting for one more discussion on how to save the show.

Arledge had begun to doubt himself. Jim Feeney, who had come over from Sports to work on the variety show, noticed the change. "Roone was not the Roone I had seen in Sports—quiet, authoritative, sure of what his next move would be," he said. "He seemed to be a guy who lost his confidence."

Arledge set aside his own instincts. Years later, in a published interview, he said, "When the research people with little scraps of paper in their hands told me children and old people want Kate Smith and tigers jumping through hoops, I went along with them. And it was all downhill from there." At the bottom of the hill, television viewers were subjected to Cosell and Barbara Walters singing a duet of "Anything You Can Do, I Can Do Better." Except sing—neither of them could do that.

By Thanksgiving, *Saturday Night Live with Howard Cosell* was a dead turkey, although final services were put off until early January.

Arledge, for the first time in all his years at ABC, had to admit failure. His reputation was only slightly tarnished, since most new entertainment shows fail. Saturday had been a terrible night for the network, and it would be 1982 before ABC found a hit on Saturdays at eight, with *T. J. Hooker.*

What Arledge regretted more than losing was losing control. He had failed on someone else's terms. The next time he made a move—and he was always thinking ahead to his next move—he would insist on controlling his own destiny.

Cosell was not thinking ahead. He was wondering why everything had turned out so badly. "Howard, to some degree, felt humiliated," said Ohlmeyer. "Howard was very irritable—but we all understood it."

The greatest damage was done to the friendship between Arledge and Cosell. In crises, Arledge could still be counted on to rush to Cosell's defense. But they had not had any fun together on Saturday nights. The feeling would soon spill over to Mondays.

David Gerber, a producer at Columbia Pictures Television, paid close attention to the screen test. The more he watched, the more enthused he became about the face on the screen. Don Meredith was ad-libbing as—what else?—a cowboy.

Gerber was impressed, and he said so to Dick Clayton, the agent who was shopping Meredith around Hollywood. "He's a big kid and all, and he's got nice rugged looks," Gerber said. "He's a natural, a fun guy. If we can capture that attitude, that feeling . . . he'll be fine."

Clayton felt the same way. A veteran agent who had handled such actors as James Dean, Tab Hunter, and Nick Nolte, he prided himself on his ability to spot young talent. Burt Reynolds, another client, brought him Meredith. Don, he thought, had the makings of a star.

Gerber found a role for Meredith right away. He cast him as a detective on *Police Story*, an anthology series created by cop-turned-novelist Joseph Wambaugh that Gerber was producing for NBC. Meredith attracted good notices. "He hit well," Gerber said.

So well, in fact, that NBC wanted to develop a series around the cop played by Meredith and his partner, played by Tony Lo Bianco. Neither actor, however, wanted to commit to the grind of a weekly television series. "You wind up playing the same guy every time out," Meredith explained. "I mean, how many different ways can you say 'You're under arrest.'"

That Meredith possessed acting talent was never in doubt during his years in Hollywood. "He had a natural gift," said John J. McMahon, the executive who ran NBC's West Coast entertainment operations.

But Meredith did not really want to work at acting. Clayton tried unsuccessfully to persuade him to take acting lessons. "I don't think his heart was really in it," he said. "You have to want it, badly, to succeed in this town, and Don really didn't want it."

"If he has a flaw," said Ed Hookstratten, Meredith's business agent, "it's that he's laid-back and has a tendency to be lazy."

Meredith admitted that. "I more or less laid back and expected things to come my way," he said.

The same qualities that made Meredith so much fun to be around—his lack of aggressiveness, his easygoing personality, his hunger for new experiences—did not serve him well as an actor. One friend saw his passivity as a "security blanket." If Don never pursued anything, the friend thought, he would never have to feel rejected.

Meredith's last project for NBC was typical. Gerber cast him as the lead in a television movie called *Banjo Hackett: Roamin' Free*, about an itinerant cowhand, part hero and part con man, who traveled the West with his son. Gerber envisioned the movie as a pilot for a series, but Meredith would not make a long-term commitment to the show. NBC passed on it.

To Meredith, Hollywood was never about riches or fame or the day-to-day grind of building a career. Instead, he saw acting as a way to express himself, just as he had dabbled in painting and talked about writing a novel. Gerber called the mid-1970s Don's "Hamlet period"—a phrase that could easily have applied to most of Meredith's adult life.

Football still paid most of the bills, though Meredith now did his talking on NBC. He was teamed with the veteran Curt Gowdy, who managed to persuade him to prepare for the games.

One afternoon before an NBC game in New York, Chet Forte ran into Meredith, who was holding a thick loose-leaf binder under his arm. "What the hell are you doing with that book?" Forte asked in a state of near-shock. "My homework," grinned Meredith.

To Forte, the idea of Meredith studying before a game was ludicrous. "I don't care who he was working with in the booth," Forte said. "This wasn't Don."

Others felt the preparation paid off. "When he put that effort in, he was really good—and he knew it," Gowdy said. Susan Meredith told Gowdy, "You're the only one who was ever able to give him hell about work."

Still, Meredith's work went largely unnoticed on Sunday afternoons. People would approach Meredith and say, "Hey, you're not doing *Monday Night Football* anymore. What're you doing?" Meredith would reply, casually, that he was "doing a game or two," and the fans would often seem surprised.

He had, in effect, disappeared.

Meredith came to the conclusion that he could act in movies for any network. But, so long as he was going to do football, there was no reason to stay at NBC.

"To me, there was only one showcase to do football," he said. "That was on Monday night." He put in a call to his old buddy Frank Gifford. It was time to hitch up his wagon again to the traveling freak show.

Palm Beach Company, makers of men's clothing, surveyed thirty-five thousand men, testing their reactions to such celebrities as Alan Alda, Bruce Jenner, Robert Redford, and O. J. Simpson. Even in that crowd, one man stood out—Frank Gifford. His very name projected style, class, and clean living. "Gifford scored among the highest with men of all ages and lifestyles," said a Palm Beach executive. "These men identify with Gifford, understand him, believe in him."

Frank Gifford's success after football was almost as simple as that. People liked him. They believed in him. They admired and respected him. At the ceremonies marking Gifford's induction into the Pro Football Hall of Fame, Wellington Mara, the president of the New York Giants, said, "For twenty-five years, Frank Gifford has personified the son all of us dream of."

The fame that went along with *Monday Night Football* had paid off for all the men in the booth. Meredith was featured in print ads for Munsingwear sportswear and Cessna Pilot Centers in addition to his famous television spots for Lipton Tea. Even Cosell, who was too controversial to suit most merchandisers, landed a deal, selling underwear for Fruit of the Loom.

But Gifford turned his golden-boy image into an industry. He made hundreds of speeches and endorsed products from swimsuits to sherry. In 1976, Gifford made his most lucrative business connection with a company called Standard Brands and its new president, H. Ross Johnson.

Johnson was a serious weekend golfer and gung-ho sports fan. He put Gifford on the payroll, as the corporate equivalent of a multipurpose back. Gifford spoke at company meetings, narrated motivational videos, and served as an all-around goodwill ambassador. Johnson and Gifford became good friends; each was best man at the other's wedding.

Standard Brands merged with Nabisco, then was swallowed up by R. J. Reynolds to form RJR/Nabisco. Johnson rode to the top after each merger. By then, Gifford and hockey player Bobby Orr, who was also hired by Nabisco, had assembled a dream team of athletes, called Team Nabisco, to represent the company. They appeared at company sales meetings, Nabisco-sponsored sports events, even charity dinners favored by Johnson. Nabisco's most important customers—top executives of the major grocery chains—loved to get up close and personal with the star athletes.

Gifford was virtually the general manager of Team Nabisco. He signed up Don Meredith, who sold Oreos on television. He drafted O. J. Simpson and golfer Dave Marr from ABC as well as ex-Giants Alex Webster and Tucker Fredrickson. "The difficult part," Gifford said, "is finding the right people. You can get a lot of jerks."

Of all the *Monday Night* men, Gifford seemed most content with his lot. He loved ABC. He loved football. He loved the money he was making. He didn't need a variety show.

Roone Arledge cast a vast shadow over ABC Sports—so vast that it hid even the six-foot-three, 220-pound frame of his favorite producer, Don Ohlmeyer. When Ohlmeyer wanted to leave ABC, Arledge offered him money, power, promotions, practically anything to keep him. But Arledge couldn't erase his own shadow.

Ohlmeyer had directed two Olympics and produced four phenomenal years of *Monday Night Football* by the time he turned thirty-one in 1977, when NBC approached him to produce the 1980 Moscow Olympics. They were envisioned as a showcase for the entire network—and the Sports division's chance to forget an embarrassing performance in Sapporo in 1972. Before committing to Moscow, however, big advertisers wanted to know who was going to produce these Olympics. If NBC couldn't get Arledge, Ohlmeyer was its best hope.

Ohlmeyer idolized Arledge. Not since Dick Ebersol had any of the Young Turks at ABC grown so close to the boss. "Nobody had more impact on me," Ohlmeyer said. "He was like a father to me. He knew I loved him." As Ohlmeyer weighed his options, he spent hours talking with Arledge.

Arledge matched every offer that NBC put on the table, even when the numbers began to approach $500,000 a year—a previously unheard-of salary for a producer.

It wasn't enough. "This decision has nothing to do with money or position or power or anything," Ohlmeyer finally told Arledge. "What it really has to do with is that I've got to find out whether I'm any good, or just good here because I work for you and Chet and with Howard, and these other guys who are terrific. It's really a little like leaving the womb. That's what it comes down to."

Arledge understood. He was grappling with similar feelings, wondering if he could work his own magic beyond sports.

Monday Night Football had lost its star play-caller. The huddle would become a very unruly place.

Shortly after New Year's Day, 1976, Arledge and Geoff Mason, another of the bright young men who were drawn to ABC Sports, went aloft in a helicopter to get a bird's-eye view of Innsbruck, Austria, where the Winter Olympics would begin in four weeks. The Games were shaping up as a programming disaster for ABC.

The 1972 Winter Games, telecast by NBC from Sapporo, had been an unalloyed failure, proof to many in the television industry that winter sports had little appeal to Americans. Hundreds of athletes would journey to Innsbruck, but none was a household name. Even the American figure skater Dorothy Hamill was known only to loyal viewers of *Wide World*.

Fred Silverman, meanwhile, had been working his prime-time magic for ABC. Thanks to such hits as *Happy Days* and *Starsky and Hutch*, Silverman had moved ABC ahead by quantum leaps in the weekly Nielsens. Now he was saying that the Olympics would destroy all the momentum he had created.

With the Cosell variety-show debacle still fresh in everyone's mind, the last thing Arledge needed was another embarrassing failure in prime time.

Arledge and Mason surveyed the town and the surrounding

mountains, saying nothing. There was no point trying to talk above the din of the helicopter blades. Finally, they touched down, and Arledge had his plan.

"We've got to send a postcard back to America. We'll do *The Sound of Music*," he said. "If the Olympics fit in, fine." The model, of course, was *Wide World*. Mason went to work, producing hours and hours of tape with, as Arledge put it, "a lot of *gemütlichkeit* and pretty singing."

On ABC, the Games began the same way each night: Viewers watched breathtaking views of the Tyrol Alps, created by airborne cameras that seemed to swoop over the mountains like powerful birds, and they listened to the stirring tones of the "Olympic fanfare" that had been made famous by ABC Sports, all before the first words were spoken by Jim McKay. The competition was highlighted by Franz Klammer's thrilling victory in downhill skiing, covered by fifteen ABC cameras and called by Frank Gifford, who for years afterward would say it was the most dramatic event he had ever witnessed in sports. Luck also entered ABC's equation—the weather was good, and the United States won eight medals in the first nine days.

Innsbruck was an artistic and a financial triumph. The ratings surpassed even the impressive numbers generated in the weeks before by Silverman. And five months later, ABC Sports delivered another standout performance in Montreal. The Summer Games were a seventy-three-hour showcase for Arledge, who manned the control room for more than two weeks and brought such stars as Bruce Jenner, Sugar Ray Leonard, and Nadia Comaneci into America's living rooms. Montreal made a one-million-dollar profit for ABC, and the ratings were good enough to propel the network to victory in the year-long Nielsens—its first ever.

Never had Arledge's stock been higher. And never had he enjoyed more leverage at ABC. He had been working without a contract since August 1975, and that was no accident. He knew there were a lot of people in the television industry who wanted to make him rich, and he was in no hurry to commit himself.

Arledge was making good money at ABC—reportedly one million dollars a year. But several Hollywood entrepreneurs were willing to pay him much more to become an independent producer. NBC, meanwhile, wanted him to take charge of its sports division—for the second time. They had made a run at Arledge in 1964, but he had stayed at ABC for more money and a better title. Now NBC put together a better offer, a lucrative package that included a deal to produce entertainment shows. "They offered almost a blank check," Arledge said. It looked as if NBC president Herb Schlosser—who had hired Meredith, was about to hire Ohlmeyer, and had made overtures to Cosell—was trying to rebuild his network at the expense of ABC and *Monday Night Football.*

Word of the offers to Arledge reached his superiors at ABC. Arledge made sure of that by giving an interview to the New York *Daily News,* saying that he could make "unlimited money" by leaving the company to start his own production company. But, he added, money "isn't the only consideration. I would much rather have it on my tombstone that I did something important."

Fred Pierce came up with a solution, just as he had dreamed up the Cosell show a year or so earlier. Pierce and Arledge were having a long, late liquid dinner one night when the talk turned to ABC News. News was the last big problem facing ABC, which had earned respectability first in sports, then in daytime, and now in prime time. Would Arledge, Pierce wanted to know, be interested in taking a shot at News?

The more they talked, the more intrigued they became by the idea, even though both men knew Pierce, as president of the network, did not have the News job to offer. News reported to Elton Rule, who was president of ABC Inc. What's more, the job of News president was not then vacant.

The next morning, Arledge called Pierce and raised the subject again. "Were you serious about that?" he wanted to know.

The reply was disappointing. "It was mostly booze talk," Pierce said. But Arledge was not about to drop the subject. Before long, Pierce was trying to convince Rule and Leonard Goldenson that Arledge was the man to solve ABC's problems in News.

Pierce needed to use all the persuasive skills that had once made him the company's top salesman. "I had a lot of resistance," he said. Arledge, to begin with, had not come up through News; network news divisions had almost always been entrusted only to news veterans. While Arledge's talents were widely recognized, he also remained a controversial figure. His critics blamed him for all the evils that television brought to sports: the commercial timeout, the made-for-TV starting times, extended seasons and interminable playoffs, and the ever-increasing sums of money that flowed to owners and athletes. Not to mention Howard Cosell.

Goldenson and Rule had another problem. They didn't think Arledge—or anyone else, for that matter—could run both News and Sports, yet Arledge was unwilling to give up Sports. "Elton and I felt that was a mistake," Goldenson said. "It would encompass too much. But Fred was very insistent." Pierce warned them that if they said no, Arledge would leave ABC.

Arledge had kept his hands clean, but, first through the press and now through Pierce, he had skillfully maneuvered himself into a position to become the most powerful executive in television. Arledge was offered the News job at an ABC meeting in Hawaii in November 1976. On his way home, he stopped in Los Angeles to see his old protégé, Dick Ebersol. The two men talked all night, as Arledge tried to sort out his conflicting emotions.

"This is my chance, as head of News, to be a player," he said. ABC News was important, maybe important enough to be carved on a tombstone. Arledge knew that his college friends Dick Wald, who was running NBC News, and Max Frankel, who had won a Pulitzer Prize at *The New York Times*, were already playing in the big leagues.

"On the other hand," he told Ebersol, "I could be financially secure for the rest of my life." The money was no small matter. Arledge was financing a very expensive divorce from Joan, his first wife. He had three daughters and a son to put through college. And he had by then married his second wife, Ann Fowler, a former Miss Alabama. He was also maintaining a pair of expensive homes, one on Park Avenue and the other a weekend place in Sagaponack, Long Island. Still, as morning neared, Arledge said he was leaning toward News. The challenge of tackling ABC News, with all its problems, was irresistible.

Ebersol agreed. Roone, he knew, was not really cut out for show business. "He might like to meet a movie star," Ebersol thought, "but he'd much rather sit and talk to Dick Nixon or George Shultz. That's the kind of mind he has."

Not everyone saw it that way. When Arledge's appointment was announced in May 1977, skepticism abounded in the press and at ABC News. *The New York Times* reported the story beneath the headline ARLEDGE WILL HEAD ABC NEWS; DISCLAIMS THEATRICAL FLOURISHES and described Arledge as "one of television's leading showmen." The harshest critics raised the specter of *Network*, the Paddy Chayefsky movie about a crass programmer with show-business values who corrupts a fictional network news division. And columnist Robert Lipsyte, who once worked for Arledge, handed down a scathing indictment in The *New York Post*, saying the news could "easily be delivered by an anchorteam of John Denver, Mason Reese and Farrah Fawcett-Majors."

More often, the columnists indulged in terrified speculation that Howard Cosell would end up in an anchorman's chair. Arledge's frequent denials did nothing to stop the columns, but they did get under Cosell's skin. He would have gladly followed his boss over to News.

Inside ABC News, meanwhile, resistance was building. Some producers worried that they would be displaced by the Young Turks from Sports. Bill Lord, a respected veteran, was delegated to meet with Pierce and warn against wholesale changes. One executive summed up the prevailing attitude—"Roone is all glitz. Roone is all replays. Roone is all slo-mo. Roone is all Olympics."

It didn't help when word got around that Arledge was belittling ABC News. ABC News, he said, was "not competitive, it was not well regarded, it was not anything." He had arrived with a strong bias against the veterans, and had cast himself in one of his favorite roles—the savior, the lonely hero, fighting against all odds for the glory of ABC. As well as the glory of Roone Arledge.

The truth was that the News division was neither as bad as Arledge made it out to be nor as good as the veterans thought it was. ABC News had some strong producers and correspondents—among them Peter Jennings, Ted Koppel, Sam Donaldson, and Steve Bell—but it lacked creativity, aggressive leadership, and, most of all, money. Its evening newscast was not only poorly rated but anchored by Harry Reasoner and Barbara Walters, who barely spoke to each other off-screen. And, when big stories broke, ABC would not interrupt entertainment programming; to Donaldson's lifelong embarrassment, he was unable to get airtime to report the Saturday Night Massacre during the Watergate era.

The veterans met Arledge face-to-face for the first time at a resort in Montauk, Long Island, where about a hundred News staffers gathered for a weekend of meetings with their new boss. The limousines and helicopters that deposited the journalists at the Montauk Yacht Club also delivered a message—money, for the first time, was going to flow to ABC News. Some staffers felt the symbolism was a little overdone.

The meetings themselves were marked by diplomatic dancing around. Arledge was taking the measure of his new staff, and they were monitoring his every word, suspicious of anything that hinted of show-business values. Both sides did their best to say just the right things.

That Sunday night at the bar, Jeff Gralnick, a fiery young field producer, ran into Arledge. Tired of mincing words, Gralnick said the problems with ABC News were simple: "We pay third-rate salaries, we have third-rate equipment, and we have a third-rate mentality at the top." Then he added: "Why do I want to work for you?"

"You want to work for me," Arledge replied coolly, "because I'll make you work harder than you ever worked and you'll be better than you ever thought you could be." Gralnick's salary, he said, would be taken care of too.

Gralnick had recently asked his boss to round off his salary from about $39,900 to an even $40,000 a year, but was refused. On Monday morning, with everyone back in New York, an Arledge aide called Gralnick to say that he was getting a raise to $70,000.

The money was there to spend. Before taking on News, Arledge extracted a commitment from Elton Rule to increase the budget by 25 percent.

More than money was needed to win over the veterans. And Arledge took some embarrassing missteps that summer. By far the biggest story in New York at the time was the "Son of Sam" lovers-lane killings, so when suspect David Berkowitz was captured, Arledge was determined to go all-out. He arrived at police headquarters at three A.M. to supervise the coverage, much of it provided by the charismatic, controversial Geraldo Rivera. The next morning, Arledge shocked the old-timers by saying that the story "could be our whole show." They persuaded him to save a few minutes for the rest of the world; even so, the broadcast reeked of sensationalism. Dressed in jeans and a T-shirt, Rivera called the suspect a "fiend" and a "murderer." Some ABC Washington reporters and producers sent Arledge a letter of protest, which soon made its way into print.

Caught up in the excitement of hiring newcomers like Carl Bernstein of Watergate fame, Arledge slighted some incumbents. Ted Koppel, who was then anchoring the Saturday night news, returned from a vacation to find out that his producer had been removed from the program to make room for a new hire. Koppel suspected he was about to be forced off himself, and submitted his resignation to Arledge. Arledge eventually patched things up with Koppel, but the incident left a bad taste around the News division.

Still, ABC News felt like a different place by summer's end. There was, for the first time, what one producer called "a lot of creative messing around." Producers were encouraged to experiment with new ways of presenting the news, and all the most up-to-date technical equipment was brought over from Sports.

To the evening news, Arledge brought new graphics and an innovation borrowed from his Olympics coverage, called the whip-around, which enabled correspondents to introduce each other's reports. And now, when big stories broke, ABC News mobilized rapidly and entertainment time was cleared. Forty-six ABC reporters and technicians—more than any other network dispatched—converged on Tennessee when James Earl Ray, the convicted killer of Martin Luther King, Jr., escaped from prison. Prime time was preempted for a special report on the New York city blackout, though some saw that as more New York provincialism.

By the time football weather arrived, Arledge was certain of two things: The first was that the problems facing him at News were greater than even he had imagined they would be; the second was that he had made the right decision.

Becoming competitive in news was tougher than creating a sports division or improving the ratings in prime time. While Arledge was prepared for a long uphill battle against CBS and NBC, he had not planned to fight a rear-guard action within ABC. Nor had he expected such opposition from the press. Some television critics persisted in calling him a "hype artist" or the "Barnum from sports."

Yet Arledge had not been so excited in years, except, perhaps, when working such big events as the Olympics. "He just loved News, more than he thought he was going to," said David Burke, Arledge's top aide in News and one of his closest friends. Now every day at the office brought unexpected challenges. Arledge was intellectually engaged. He was drawing on all of his instincts for television. And his competitive juices were flowing.

He was also incredibly busy. Running News was more than a full-time job, and so was running Sports. Arledge was trying to do both.

One day, Arledge had to review cassettes from prospective news correspondents, run a meeting on the World Series with his Sports people, have lunch with an unhappy Harry Reasoner, plan for news coverage of an upcoming space-shuttle flight, and supervise the evening news broadcast. Phone messages, as always, piled up unanswered.

How, he was asked by a reporter, does he decide what to do? "It depends on where the fire is," he said.

On *Monday Night Football*, there were no fires. Not yet. So Arledge paid less and less attention, at a time when the show needed his guiding hand more than ever.

Commissioner Pete Rozelle negotiated a new contract with the networks in 1977. It was not only the biggest deal in the history of the NFL—it was the biggest programming deal in the history of television.

The contract was also a monument to the success of *Monday Night Football*.

In 1970, ABC had agreed to pay $34.5 million for four years of *Monday Night Football*. In 1974, ABC had agreed to pay $72 million for the package. This new deal was going to cost $232 million. The rights fees had multiplied almost seven times in seven years.

As the last network to get a piece of the NFL, ABC paid less for television rights than either of its rivals in the first two deals. Now ABC was going to pay substantially more than CBS and NBC, which were paying $192 million and $168 million, respectively.

Yet Pete Rozelle was not an unreasonable man. He was, this time around, giving the networks more for their money—two more regular-season games for everyone, as the league expanded to a sixteen-game schedule, and four additional games for ABC, in the form of "special" prime-time contests to be scheduled on Sundays and Thursdays.

The fans were getting more too—more aggravation, as the allowable commercial time in the telecasts was expanded from twenty to twenty-two minutes, again to help the networks recoup those higher rights fees.

Arledge and Pierce, who negotiated the deal for ABC, were pleased to expand the *Monday Night* schedule to sixteen games, but they were not enthused about the plan to add the four special games to the package. They were persuaded to buy the Sunday and Thursday games only after Rozelle indicated that if they didn't, he would offer them to the other networks. "We felt we shouldn't give up on the prime-time franchise," Pierce said. "If there was prime-time football, it should be on ABC." Pierce also had confidence in his Sports sales force; they had always been able to squeeze enough out of the advertisers to cover the higher rights fees.

Rozelle's only concession to ABC was to limit the Sunday and Thursday package to four games. Under the contract, the NFL had the option to schedule up to six of the extra prime-time games each season, at a cost to ABC of $3 million a game. By scheduling four games instead of six, the league gave up $6 million in each of the four years of the rights deal. Later, whenever Rozelle was concerned about his image as a greedy rights-holder who always got the better of the networks, he would point to those games as proof that the NFL was not simply out to gouge the networks any way it could. That was $24 million left on the table, Rozelle and his NFL spokesmen would say.

But the extra games were instantly a flop. The Monday night

magic was not transferable to other nights of the week—not even after ABC labeled some of the games as the "special Thursday night edition of *Monday Night Football.*"

Irwin Weiner was Arledge's money guy. He haggled over dollars with the sharpest of the talent agents, ensured that *i*'s were dotted and *t*'s crossed on all contracts, held the accountants from ABC corporate at bay, and kept a wary eye on expense accounts to make sure abuses didn't get out of hand. Nevertheless, Weiner had a lot of friends in ABC Sports.

He also had perhaps the most bizarre idea ever to be spawned by *Monday Night Football.* Weiner wanted to turn the show into a Saturday morning cartoon, featuring animated versions of Cosell, Meredith, and Gifford. They would supply their own voices, and the humorous stories of their exploits inside and outside the broadcast booth—excluding, presumably, some of the wilder tales not suited for the kiddies. Weiner was as promotion-minded as everyone at ABC, and he figured the Monday night games could be used to promote the Saturday morning cartoon, and vice versa.

"*Monday Night Football:* The Cartoon" was not an entirely outrageous idea. CBS had sold a lot of sneakers a few years earlier with a Saturday morning show based on the Harlem Globetrotters basketball team. So no one laughed when Weiner shopped his concept around the office. Some thought it had real possibilities. But he was told that the first person he had to sell it to was Cosell.

Weiner had never met Cosell. He called ahead, arranged an appointment, arrived at Cosell's office, and introduced himself. He began to explain the idea but didn't get very far.

"Young man," Cosell declaimed in his most Cosellian tone, "do you know whom you're speaking to? I am the biggest name in show business today. And you want to make a cartoon character out of me!"

Weiner, aware that his idea was dead, left his next thought unspoken. *Howard,* he said to himself, *you already are a cartoon character.*

8.

SCRAMBLING UNDER PRESSURE

"I've lost my sense of humor until January."—ROBBIE COWEN,
production assistant on Monday Night Football

Ned Simon squashed his foot down onto the accelerator like
a man trying to annihilate a bug—or a director.

As his rental car flew down the highway in a desolate section
of the Florida Everglades, Simon stared blankly ahead like a
robot. The speedometer climbed toward eighty miles an hour.

Simon was going nowhere; he wanted to be nowhere. All he
wanted was escape—and rest. Never had he felt so physically
and mentally exhausted.

Eight months into his job as a $280-a-week production
assistant for ABC Sports, Simon, at twenty-three, felt angry and
depressed. He had always wanted to work in sports television;
now he wondered whether he had made a terrible mistake.

Everything had come to a head the night before during a
Monday Night Football game in Miami. Simon was nearing the
end of a grueling eight-day marathon—a Monday night game in
Washington, two baseball playoff games in Philadelphia, two
more baseball games in Los Angeles, and then the Monday night
game between the Dolphins and the Cincinnati Bengals at the
Orange Bowl, all on about four hours of sleep per night. In

Miami he had performed his usual duties—generating graphics, writing the notes for Cosell's halftime highlights, making sure the limousines for the stars got to the airport on time and the suites in the hotel were suitably plush. By the time he arrived at the Orange Bowl, all he wanted to do was get through the game and then get a good night's sleep.

Instead, he got a torrent of abuse. It began after the Dolphins had scored their second unanswered touchdown, putting everyone in a sour mood. One-sided games always had that effect.

Simon was responsible for keeping the scoreboard graphic up to date. But after Miami kicked the extra point, he forgot to tack on the additional digit, leaving the score on the card at 13–0. That was the score that flashed on the screen when Chet Forte punched up the graphic leading into a commercial.

For the next sixty seconds, Simon's eardrums all but melted under the blast of rage from Forte and producer Dennis Lewin.

"Wake up!" Lewin yelled.

"What the fuck's the matter with you?" Forte screamed, even louder. "You fuckin' jerk!"

Simon sat silently, feeling humiliated. Forte and Lewin had found a target, as they did just about every week, pouring their own frustrations onto the hapless victim. This week, it was Simon's turn.

For the rest of the game, Forte and Lewin took every opportunity to excoriate the shell-shocked Simon. With the Dolphins rolling to an easy, and thuddingly dull, 21–0 win, Forte and Lewin had nothing better to do.

Simon hit rock bottom when he woke up the next morning. He hadn't slept well. He was so down, after working so hard only to be treated so thanklessly, that he simply got into his rental car and drove south, into the wastes of the Everglades.

He had no one to abuse, so he abused the car's engine, forcing it up to ninety miles an hour. *These guys don't appreciate anything I've done*, he thought. *All I'm doing is getting shit poured on me.*

Finally, he eased off the accelerator and pulled over, left the car in a deserted spot, and wandered onto a boardwalk extending into the swamp.

Simon was not the only one feeling stressed. Lewin and Forte were older, better-paid, and more experienced, but they too were putting in brutal hours under constant pressure. Lewin had produced all the baseball playoffs as well as *Monday Night Football,* and Forte had been on duty almost nonstop for weeks. This was also ABC's first season of Sunday and Thursday night football, which nobody liked—not the ABC salespeople, not the advertisers, not the production staff, and especially not the announcers. The extra games meant that everyone had to spend more time in planes and rush through preparations each week.

Roone Arledge wanted to be sympathetic, but the pressures building on *Monday Night Football* were the least of his worries. Arledge was thoroughly wrapped up in News—he was experimenting with a three-anchor team for the evening news and trying to launch *20/20,* among other things—and he never wanted the extra games, anyway. The Sunday and Thursday package was the brainchild of Pete Rozelle, whose owners wanted him to come up with more money from the networks. Rozelle had done so well that the typical NFL team was now making more money from television than it was collecting at the gate.

So much was riding on *Monday Night Football.* The owners pressured Rozelle, who pressured the networks, who pressured their salespeople, who pressured their advertisers. Arledge pressured Lewin and Forte, who were already feeling pressure from their stars, notably Cosell. They took out their frustrations on Simon. With no one to pressure, he ended up in the Everglades.

Simon decided that morning that the only way to survive the season was to become more hardened to the abuse. He was never going to change his bosses. *You can't let these guys get to you,* he told himself. Simon drove back to Miami—under the speed limit—and boarded a plane for New York. It was time to begin work on the following week's game.

Don Meredith had never been a scrambling quarterback, but now that his playing days were over, he was proving that he could change direction as well as anyone. Especially when contract time came around.

It came around next in the spring of 1977. As Meredith's

three-year deal with NBC was about to expire, word filtered back to Arledge that he might be available. Irwin Weiner called him. Yes, Don said, he'd like to come back. He missed Monday nights, he missed Frank, he even missed Cosell. He told Weiner that Susan, his wife, would be representing him.

When Arledge and an assistant, Jeff Ruhe, went to Los Angeles in May for an affiliates meeting, they spent a pleasant evening drinking wine with the Merediths at their home in Beverly Hills. Soon afterward, Weiner worked out a deal with Susan over the phone. He was so pleased, he went down the hall to deliver the good news to his boss.

Arledge said that was terrific. He called Fred Pierce and Elton Rule to let them know that Don was, indeed, back in the fold. They were all delighted.

The celebration was premature, as they should have expected. Meredith, after all, broke a moral commitment to CBS when he first signed with ABC in 1970. Four years later, Meredith was negotiating with Arledge and Weiner at the same time that his agent, Ed Hookstratten, was arranging to deliver him to NBC.

Sure enough, a week or so later, a telegram arrived from Al Rush, a top NBC executive, accusing ABC of tampering with Meredith while he was still under contract. The telegram also said that Meredith had agreed to renew his deal with NBC, and warned that NBC would sue if he left.

By then, Arledge was enjoying a yachting vacation in the south of France. He ordered Weiner and Ruhe to fly to Los Angeles to confront Meredith. They were to report back over a ship-to-shore phone—speaking in code. Arledge apparently thought NBC had spies everywhere.

Meredith appeared at the door of his home in his tennis togs. He was as friendly as ever, greeting Weiner and Ruhe like old buddies as he ushered them into the kitchen, where Susan was waiting.

Weiner was in no mood for chitchat. "Don," he said simply, "we had a deal."

"Well, Irwin," Meredith began slowly, "let me tell you what I'm thinking." Weiner thought to himself, _Here comes the country-boy bullshit._

Meredith explained that he just wanted the fellows from

ABC to consider things from his point of view. He had never liked being thought of as a buffoon, but his image as a regular guy was important to him. He was worried about what a lawsuit from NBC might do to his reputation. Think of the publicity, he said. The last thing he wanted was to come across to the public as a star with a Hollywood-sized contract, the kind of star who would play one network against another.

"I got this persona," he said, "and I really don't want people to know what I make. NBC is really uptight about this thing and they're going to sue me."

Weiner was unsympathetic. "So you're reneging, right?" he said coldly.

"Well, they're going to sue me," came the reply.

"Hey, Don," Weiner said firmly, "it's too late for that. I went into Roone's office. I told him we had a deal. Roone called whoever he called and said we had a deal. So I tell you what. If you go to NBC, I'm going to sue your fucking ass."

Weiner noticed that everyone was staring at him, slightly shocked. He was ordinarily the calmest of men, soft-spoken and polite.

He stood up to leave and repeated his threat: "We're going to sue your fucking ass." He and Ruhe said good-bye to the Merediths, went to a phone, and called Arledge.

They broke out the code. Arledge wanted a report on the meeting.

"With Number Seventeen?" said Ruhe.

"Yeah, the cowboy," said Arledge.

"He wants to come back to us," Ruhe reported, "but the peacock is giving him a hard time."

Arledge indicated he was disgusted with Number 17.

Ruhe had a thought. Meredith had become a wine lover. To smooth over the tensions, Ruhe suggested sending him a case of wine.

"Great idea," Arledge said, straining to be heard over the transatlantic static. "Get a case of the finest wines available and have it delivered to the cowboy's house."

Ruhe and Weiner composed a friendly note—"Good seeing you. Hope you make the right decision."—and sent it over with an assortment of French wines.

Ed Hookstratten, meanwhile, was trying to figure out what

had gone wrong. He had verbally renewed Meredith's deal with NBC in April, and everyone seemed happy. Meredith would be paid $400,000 a year—one of the top salaries in sports television—and he had a commitment from the entertainment division that guaranteed him starring roles in two movies a year.

"Al Rush made an offer to extend Meredith's contract. Don said okay. We shook hands," Hookstratten said later.

Meredith and Susan had then left for Europe, where they joined Frank Gifford and his new wife, Astrid, on their honeymoon. There Meredith had second thoughts.

When he got back to Los Angeles, Meredith was ready to deal with ABC. Hookstratten was furious. He told Meredith to find himself a new agent. "Life's too short to have the reputation of bouncing back and forth," Hookstratten said. "Your handshake has got to be your word." He couldn't blame NBC for threatening to sue.

Meredith asked Herb Barness, a friend and former neighbor of his in Bucks County, Pennsylvania, to help straighten out the mess. A real-estate tycoon who once owned a third of the Philadelphia Eagles, Barness flew Weiner up to his estate in Bucks County to negotiate a new deal with ABC and somehow keep NBC from suing. Since NBC had the right to renew its existing contract with Meredith, as long as it matched any new offers, there seemed to be no way out. Finally, they drafted an ABC contract that guaranteed Meredith the opportunity to do *prime-time* football. "That particular idea," Meredith explained, "came from Roone Arledge himself."

No one sued. Talent wars between the networks were then at their peak, and NBC had just spirited O. J. Simpson away from ABC. They claimed they had gotten the better deal.

Years later, Weiner admitted that ABC would never have gone to court against Meredith. "There was no way you could win," Weiner said. "He hadn't signed anything."

Nor did anyone at ABC hold the episode against him. They liked Don, even if they didn't entirely trust him.

"He's a quarterback," said Weiner. "If there's any way he could see an opening in the line, he's going to take it. And if he called a play, one great thing about quarterbacks is that they can always call an audible. This was an audible."

Meredith had always liked calling his own plays.

*   *   *

No one was thrilled when Dennis Lewin was named the new producer of *Monday Night Football* on the eve of the 1977 season. Not even Dennis Lewin.

"I wasn't sitting around pining for *Monday Night Football*," he said. That wasn't his style. Self-effacing in public and a dedicated company man, Lewin claimed that he never once went after an assignment during all his years at ABC. He did what he was told. Now Roone Arledge was telling him to produce *Monday Night Football.*

There really weren't any other candidates. Chuck Howard, who had produced college football for years, could have done the job, but he was a bitter rival of Forte. Besides, Howard wasn't interested. He wanted to spend Sundays with his family.

Lewin, at thirty-two, was an ABC veteran. A New Yorker, he had grown up in a sports-minded family in Forest Hills; one uncle was a sportswriter, another played pro baseball. Lewin wasn't much of an athlete, so he looked for another way to get into sports. He picked up a degree in communications at Michigan State, worked briefly as an NBC page, then joined ABC in 1966.

He was a solid, thoroughly dependable producer. Lewin had toiled for more than a decade on *Wide World*, rising to the post of coordinating producer. It was a tough job—he had to mold the show, schedule the coverage, and fit in all the events—and it matched his skills well. He was hard-working, organized, and good at details. As proof, he won a batch of Emmys for *Wide World*, several for ABC's sparkling presentations of gymnastics and figure skating.

Lewin also was behind an ABC invention known as the Roone phone—a dialless red phone, one of which was eventually placed in every production truck and studio, reserved exclusively for incoming calls from Arledge. Lewin came up with the idea one night when Arledge tried to call him and all the lines to the truck were busy.

But Lewin did not have much in common with most of the men who rose through the ranks of ABC in the late 1960s and early 1970s. Arledge, Forte, Howard, and Ohlmeyer fit a certain mold—they were mavericks, risk-takers, men of forceful personalities. Lewin was more cautious and less creative. "Denny is a great sports aficionado," said a top ABC Sports executive. "But he's not a showman." Nor was he a dynamic leader. "Dennis is a real nice guy," said another Arledge aide, "but he's as interesting as white bread. No, the bread leaves a taste. This guy's next original idea will be his first one."

Arledge was not unaware of Lewin's shortcomings. Still, he thought Lewin was the logical choice for Monday nights. The show was well established. It did not need creativity as much as a producer who could keep the personalities in line. Lewin had co-produced the show for two seasons, so he knew the drill, and he had worked extensively with Forte, Cosell, and Gifford.

"He gets along well with people," Arledge said. "A large part of that job is refereeing."

Lewin would try to referee *Monday Night Football* for the next three seasons. It was an assignment that would test any man. It overwhelmed Lewin.

Roone Arledge labeled the return of Don Meredith "a great leap backwards." But there was no way to turn the clock back to what everyone recalled, with selective memories, as the glory days of *Monday Night Football.*

For a while, they all tried. Meredith's return buoyed Gifford, and briefly sparked Cosell. "We were right back where we were," said Lewin. "It was like the good old days."

But not for long. Lewin soon realized that it would be impossible to recapture the chemistry of the early years. So much had changed since then.

The first time around, Meredith had been a novice and Cosell was experiencing true fame for the first time. Each man owed some of his success to the other, and both knew it. "Egos were involved," Lewin said, "but they weren't totally involved yet. There was still insecurity. Everybody was feeling their way, and everybody was having fun. And the stardom was growing."

Now Meredith considered himself a star in his own right. Cosell obviously felt the same way. Lewin discovered that "each had his own way of doing things, and they were both fairly set in their convictions."

Meredith had come back from NBC a different man—more

experienced in the booth, more self-assured, hoping to be taken seriously as an actor, and determined not to be pigeonholed as the old Dandy Don. "When he came back, Don was different," said Frank Gifford. "He had been a movie star. He had won an Emmy. He had received a doctoral degree from some university." Not that he didn't deserve it, Gifford was quick to add.

To Forte's amazement, Meredith carried a briefcase to production meetings. "Maybe he wanted to prove to himself that he wasn't a buffoon," the director thought. Forte wasn't convinced. He ridiculed the idea of Meredith studying depth charts.

Meredith did work a little harder, though not much. He could not take football seriously enough to spend time with coaches and players, seeking insight into their strategies. Once, a reporter asked him whether he had ever mastered the rule for pass interference that he had stumbled over years ago. "I don't think I have it yet," he replied. "Good Lord, there's no excuse for me not to know those things. Except I can't get interested." It sounded like a joke, but it wasn't.

Cosell expected the same old Dandy, and he wasn't the least bit impressed by Don's record in Hollywood. If anything, Cosell felt that Meredith should have been chastened by his frustrations with NBC. He should be grateful to ABC for readmitting him to the *Monday Night* pantheon. The last three years had proven to Cosell that he had been correct all along—he was the star and Meredith *needed* him. Meredith could not have disagreed more.

On the air, they really had no choice but to try to revive their act. *Monday Night Football* had become a soap opera, and the characters were locked into their roles by the viewers' expectations. Cosell still wore the black hat, Meredith the white, and they were expected to clash—all in good fun—every week.

But an edge crept into their needling, just as it had before Meredith's departure. Only this time the unpleasantness was double-edged. The change in tone was subtle, but unmistakable to insiders. Said Gifford: "What had been funny was now cutting."

It was not so much what they said but how they said it. Cosell told a long story one time about Conrad Dobler, the outspoken offensive lineman of the St. Louis Cardinals, and concluded, with a flourish, by informing viewers that Dobler "was talking to Dandy Don Meredith one day and he said, 'Don, before I'm done, they'll know me better than you.'"

Meredith was not in the mood for that game. "How you do carry on," he said, with a touch of disdain. "I've never met him."

Cosell, for his part, would refer to Meredith as "the extraordinary quarterback of yesteryear who always failed to win the title game." That was a needle that was sure to reopen an old wound.

Lewin often intervened, trying to get either Cosell or Meredith to loosen up. "I spent a good part of my time telling both of them that it was not necessarily funny. They each thought that the other was the problem," he said. "The chemistry wasn't there anymore. Because what made the chemistry the first time around was that they worked off each other and had fun with it. Neither one of them was having fun with it anymore." Before long, he said, "neither one of them was *close* to having fun with it anymore."

Occasionally, Meredith let his feelings slip in public. He told one reporter that, yes, the testiness that viewers detected on Monday nights was sometimes the real thing. "There are three fairly large egos involved," he said. And he began to rewrite history. Meredith himself had told the story of Cosell coming to his assistance in the bar of the Warwick Hotel when he was down and ready to quit during the very first season of *Monday Night Football.* Cosell had told the story too, taking more and more of the credit for Meredith's success. Now Meredith said, "The story that he saved my career after the first game is not true."

Meredith's complaints weren't limited to Cosell. He was unhappy with the people of ABC Entertainment. They had turned down several of his ideas, including one that was dear to him, a movie in which he would play Charlie Roswell, a blind golfer. "The movie stuff was not going well," Meredith said. He renegotiated his deal with ABC so that he would have the right to act on any network.

When the *Monday Night* package expanded from fourteen games to twenty in 1978, his second year back, Meredith wanted no part of the added games. Gifford agreed to do them, and so did Cosell. But Meredith told anyone who asked that his contract called for him to appear on fourteen games, so he would appear on fourteen games.

Sometimes Meredith felt like it was all he could do to drag himself out to that many.

Finding excuses for Frank Gifford's mistakes had become increasingly difficult by the late 1970s. Gifford had been a professional broadcaster for nearly twenty years. He worked harder than most, and he was teamed with the best producers and directors in sports television. But the mistakes kept coming, so predictably that you could bet on them—and some *Monday Night Football* crew members did.

Every play-by-play man makes mistakes, of course. With 150 plays to call in each game and 80 players shuttling on and off the field in countless combinations, errors are inevitable. Some of Gifford's supporters said they would watch Sunday afternoon games and hear widely respected play-by-play men make one error after another.

Besides, few viewers even noticed the mistakes. "Frank has the most important quality—people liked him," said Don Ohlmeyer. "Frank could make fifty mistakes and nobody cared." Another ABC executive said, "He's a guy who America has wanted in its living room for twenty years. That's the best and most pertinent thing about him."

Roone Arledge always claimed that Gifford had the toughest job in sports television—coping with Cosell and Meredith. "Howard would sulk a lot of times, and not say anything for a whole quarter. If Don couldn't think of anything funny to say, he just didn't say anything," Arledge said. "Meantime, Frank had to keep some sanity. He'd do everything: play-by-play, all the promos, all the commercial lead-ins and station breaks, everything!" Meanwhile, "he also had Howard pointing out every damn mistake he ever made."

Put any other play-by-play man in that cauldron, said Arledge, and "it'd just be a nightmare."

What Arledge's analysis didn't take into account was the peculiar character of Gifford's errors. Gifford made his share of run-of-the-mill mistakes—missing the yard line, getting the down wrong, misidentifying a player. Critics said he made more than his share. But Gifford was best known for those mind-boggling blunders that became part of the lore of *Monday*

Night, passed down through the years to legions of young production assistants. The Great Escape game and Eischeid's double-duty punting were early classics of the genre.

Perhaps the most embarrassing of Gifford's flubs involved not only the wrong player and the wrong team but the wrong sport. It happened in Cleveland early in the 1979 season, when defensive back Dennis Thurman of the Dallas Cowboys brought down one of the Cleveland Browns. Steve Bozeka, Gifford's spotter, pointed at the name on the spotter board, whereupon Gifford announced that the tackle had been made by "Thurman Munson." Munson was the New York Yankee catcher who had died in a plane crash near his hometown of Canton, Ohio, several months earlier. Meredith turned to Bozeka with a horrified look that could only mean, "Did he say what I thought he said?" Bozeka nodded silently.

A week later, as everyone waited for the Monday morning production meeting to begin, Cosell had a question for Bozeka. Gifford had not yet arrived.

"Steve," Cosell began, "you're from Canton, Ohio, right?" Bozeka, who had no idea what he was getting into, said that he was.

"Steve," Cosell continued, "you knew Thurman Munson, right?" Yes, Bozeka said, he sure did. Matter of fact, Munson's mother worked with him at Sears.

"Now," Cosell declared, warming to the task, "have you been out to see Thurman Munson's grave?" Bozeka, still the unsuspecting straight man, said he had.

"And," Cosell boomed, now sounding like a prosecutor about to trap a crucial witness, "he's still buried there, is he not?" This time, Bozeka only nodded.

By now, the room was quiet. Some people could not believe what they were hearing. Cosell plowed ahead.

"Then how in the hell," he declared, "can he go out there and make all those tackles for the Cowboys!"

Gifford arrived a few minutes later; no one let him in on the joke, at least not then.

Gifford also had trouble with the name of Leeman Bennett, then the coach of the Atlanta Falcons. Whenever Atlanta played on Mondays, Gifford could not help, at some point during the telecast, referring to him as "Leeman Beeman." It became a running gag among the production assistants, so much so that they set up a betting pool. Staff members would wager five dollars and guess the time and the quarter in which the gaffe would occur, with the best guess winning the pot.

Gifford's mind always seemed to be playing tricks on him. Once, he had a punt-return man signaling for a "cair fatch." Another time, a staff member swears, Gifford opened the show by saying, "Hi Frank, I'm everybody." For a while Gifford used cue cards for his introduction, but that had risks too. One time, the words came out in the right order—"Hello, everyone, I'm Frank"—but a long pause followed before he spoke the word "Gifford." The production assistants had made the mistake of writing *Frank* on one card and *Gifford* on another.

"He was not a clear-thinking person," said John Coulter, a production assistant for three seasons. "Things were muddled." More than one staff member wondered whether Gifford had taken too many blows to the head during his playing days.

Few were aware of all the pressures on Gifford. For one thing, the mistakes, and the criticism they brought on, really troubled him. Gifford was accustomed to excelling at everything he tried. "Frank has great pride," said Arledge. "He does not like to be embarrassed."

Gifford also had more serious worries. His first wife, Maxine, who had multiple sclerosis, was confined to a wheelchair. Gifford told friends that she had become bitter and difficult to live with. He hated going home, but agonized for years before he left her. They agreed to divorce.

Gifford married Astrid Naesse Lindley, a half-Norwegian, half-English, Swiss-educated aerobics teacher, in March 1977. Astrid was a striking woman who stayed in shape by swimming and running each day. They had known each other for five years. "Frank and I had parted ways and then we discovered we couldn't live without each other," she said. That spring, she and Frank took a honeymoon tour of Europe, where they were joined by the Merediths; that was when Don had decided to return to ABC.

Gifford's toughest trial began about a year later. He had always been especially close to his middle son, Kyle. He never missed a Scarsdale High School football game when the boy played, and sometimes he managed to announce the Scarsdale score on Monday night games. On the night of March 1, 1978,

Kyle was nearly killed when the car he was riding in was involved in a serious accident. His father was devastated. Kyle lay in a coma for months at a New York hospital, where Frank visited him every day.

Through it all, Gifford carried on bravely. He kept his worries to himself, and worked as hard as ever. Only on occasion did the pressure get to him. One Monday night in Pittsburgh, Gifford lost his cool and punched Bozeka in the stomach when the spotter caused him to misidentify a player. Afterward Gifford apologized. He told Bozeka that he felt terrible but was under a lot of stress. Bozeka, ever loyal, said he understood.

Others were not as forgiving. Gifford had to shoulder much of the blame for one public foul-up that nearly landed ABC in court. The incident involved his beloved Giants, who went to Washington to play the Redskins in September 1979.

The Giants were having a dismal season, and Cosell could not have been more delighted. He had never forgiven the Maras for moving the team out to the New Jersey Meadowlands. Before the game, Cosell laid into the Giants in an interview with *Newsday.* "Nobody gives a damn about the Giants except the 70,000 imbeciles who go to that stadium each week," Cosell said. Neither Arledge nor Gifford was happy to read that—not as Giants fans, and certainly not as men who wanted the Monday night game to be a success for ABC.

When the hapless Giants fell behind, Cosell and Gifford heaped some of the blame on New York's offensive right tackle, number 78, Gordon Gravelle. The announcers reminded viewers that Gravelle had been fined $15,300 for reporting six weeks late to camp, implying that he might not be ready to play. A Washington sack late in the game sparked this exchange.

"I tell you," Cosell said, "the Giant linemen look like statues."

"There they go around Gravelle again," agreed Gifford.

"He may take another fine and go home now," said Cosell.

There was just one problem. That wasn't Gravelle wearing number 78. The Giants tackle who was getting beaten so often was a man named Gus Coppens. It said so, in big white letters, right there on the back of his jersey—and on the printed roster provided to all members of the media.

Gifford wasn't relying on the roster. He was reading the names off his spotter board, put together as always by Steve Bozeka.

Bozeka was home in Canton several days later when the phone rang. "Steve," said Gifford, trying to sound calm, "have you got the spot card?"

What was wrong now, Bozeka wondered as he went off to find his scrawlings. "Who do we have as number seventy-eight?" Gifford asked. The answer, of course, was Gravelle.

Bozeka had obtained his names and numbers as he always did, from a public-relations man representing the home team. Because of a communications mix-up in the noisy press room, Gravelle's name had landed on the board in place of Coppens.

Then Gifford delivered another blow. "Howard is being sued by Mrs. Gravelle," he said.

Gravelle had talked to reporters. His wife, he said, had been "hysterical" after the game. "Cosell," Gravelle declared, "is a pompous senile idiot." ABC's tapes showed, however, that only Gifford had actually named Gravelle. He was designated to straighten out the mess.

The next week, Gifford apologized over the air to Gravelle's wife, Molly, who had sent a letter of complaint to Cosell. He also went quietly to the Giants' management, who prevailed on Gravelle not to sue. But Cosell could not let the matter lie there. He had to reply to Mrs. Gravelle's letter.

"The mistake was Mr. Gifford's," he wrote. "My one reference to No. 78 was a throwaway line offered in jest—and jest was needed because the Giants performance was so shoddy as to produce an all-time record low for *Monday Night Football*. The damage done by the Giants to the NFL through its terrible performance is inestimable."

Cosell went on to say that he personally regretted the fact that "Mr. Gifford was in error."

Cosell had come a long way from the days when he would rush to the defense of a man he once called "the best friend I have in life."

Cosell loved to hand out nicknames. His first set of names for the *Monday Night* crew may have been coined with fond intentions, but eventually they began to sound like put-downs. Gifford was "Faultless Frank"; Meredith was "Danderoo"; and Lewin was "Dendoo."

By the late 1970s, Cosell came up with a new set of labels for the trio. Gifford was "the mannequin"; Meredith was "the imbecile"; and Lewin was "the boy producer." Now there was no mistaking Cosell's intentions.

Dealing with Cosell was never easy, but it was getting harder every year. It was especially hard now because Cosell was nagged by the feeling that somehow he had been left behind. Here he was, climbing onto the *Monday Night* merry-go-round for one more season—worrying, yes, about whether Roger Staubach's shoulder was going to heal in time for the Washington game—while two ABC associates whom he most respected, Arledge and Ohlmeyer, had moved on to bigger things.

His relationship with Arledge was no longer a calming influence. They had drifted apart after the variety show, and now, inevitably, they drifted farther apart as Arledge focused on News. No longer could Cosell count on the boss to lend a sympathetic ear.

Cosell felt both neglected and rejected. He had always yearned to cover world and national events. Now he thought he deserved the opportunity. He wanted to join Arledge at News, and he wasn't thinking about an entry-level position. He wanted to anchor *World News Tonight*.

Arledge thought that was a terrible idea. He had to persuade everyone of his seriousness to shed his image as the ringmaster of sports. Hiring Cosell would be a step backward. The press would kill him, and besides, one of the pleasures of running News was knowing that he no longer had to listen to Cosell complain every day.

One night in Los Angeles, Cosell and Herb Granath ran into Arledge in the Beverly Wilshire Hotel. They had a few drinks, and Arledge began discussing the frustrations in News. ABC needed a big story, he said, a breakthrough, to prove that it could compete.

Cosell spied an opening. "Why don't you end your troubles?" he said grandly. "Make Jim McKay and me co-anchormen, and your rating problems will be over."

The last thing Arledge wanted was to provoke an argument with Cosell. Not then, not anytime. He did his best to brush the subject aside. "Don't think I haven't thought of that, Howard," he said. "I'm not through with that idea yet."

Cosell never forgot the conversation. Arledge, he felt, had virtually promised him the anchor job and had never come through. Cosell began to proclaim that Arledge had no business trying to run News and Sports at the same time.

With each passing Monday night, Ohlmeyer's departure had an increasing impact on Cosell. He liked Lewin all right as a person, but he felt nothing but scorn for his abilities. In Cosell's mind, the idea that Lewin could run *Monday Night Football* was an affront.

He complained nonstop to almost everyone about Lewin. "I don't know how he ever got the job," Cosell would say. Lewin had no creativity, he said, nothing to offer. It reached the point that when Lewin addressed him at a production meeting, Cosell would either ignore him or interrupt him until he drowned him out. Lewin usually took the snubs silently.

Midway through the 1978 season, Cosell made a speech at a production meeting that stunned some staff members because it sounded like a direct attack on Lewin. "Changes need to be made," Cosell said. "We need more creativity. We need a new approach to these games." Lewin, again, said nothing.

Cosell's favorite targets, though, remained Gifford and Meredith. "Howard was *Monday Night Football*," Forte said. "Once he realized he was *Monday Night Football*, he didn't want to take any shit from anybody."

Now Cosell felt he was taking altogether too much, especially from the jocks in the booth. When he railed against the jockocracy, he no longer made exceptions of Gifford and Meredith. Sometimes he made a point of including them, telling people that they had no business starring in prime time.

"That fucking Gifford," he'd say to Forte in a disgusted tone of voice. "Did you ever stop to count his mistakes? He is pathetic."

Then he'd harp on Meredith. "Don't you think Meredith is needling me a little too much?" he'd ask.

The more time Gifford and Meredith spent with each other, the more they inflamed the paranoid streak in Cosell. He began to believe they were ganging up on him, each working hard to make the other look good at his expense. If Meredith complimented Gifford on the air, or vice versa, Cosell felt slighted. Everywhere, he saw signs of conspiracy.

Cosell turned for support, more and more, to the production assistants, or "p.a.'s" young men just out of college getting started in sports television. At least they could be counted on to listen to his woes. They had no choice.

One morning, Cosell was the last of the stars to arrive at the hotel dining room for breakfast. Gifford and Meredith were eating together. Lewin was sitting at a table by himself. So was Forte. Cosell ignored them all and sat down with Jack Graham, a newly hired p.a. "Jake," he said, pausing for emphasis, "you're the only one I'll eat breakfast with."

Yet, on another occasion, Robbie Beiner, a young associate director with a gentle manner, was leaving the show. He took a few minutes before a production meeting to say how much he had appreciated everyone's help and enjoyed working Monday nights. The next sound heard was the nasty rasp of Cosell: "Well, isn't that a bunch of bullshit."

Cosell's moaning was at its worst when Emmy stayed home. She was a soothing presence, and her absence left him morose. He missed her terribly. "I'm tired," he would say. "I miss my wife. I miss my grandchildren." Cosell had great reserves of energy to draw on when his adrenaline got pumping, but more often he appeared worn out. He had turned sixty in 1978. Some nights, his body bent over as he trudged slowly out of the stadium and into the darkness, he looked like an old man.

He had begun to drink during games again, pouring from his own bottle of vodka. One production assistant whose duties included supplying the liquor to Cosell said Cosell would "take an extra drink or two" if a game became dull. The debacle of Philadelphia was never repeated, but everyone felt the alcohol made him more belligerent, less likely than ever to yield the floor to Gifford or Meredith.

One time in Washington in 1979, Cosell had been socializing at a cocktail party. He was visibly disoriented during the rehearsal before game time. Lewin told him over the headset to drink a few gallons of coffee before going on the air. "You knew when he was really shit-faced because he'd drop out of sight. He had nothing to say," said Mark Wolff, a gofer who worked in the booth.

Even when he wasn't drinking, Cosell would often just sulk. If Lewin or Forte said something that displeased him, he would say nothing, sometimes staying silent for as long as ten minutes. Once, on a cold and rainy night in Green Bay, where the broadcast booth is exposed to the outside air, Cosell kept up a stream of complaints about the weather. Lewin, fed up, finally told him to stuff it. Cosell was infuriated. He pulled off his headset and stormed out of the booth. "Let the jocks handle it," he declared.

Once in a while, though, Cosell displayed his old vitality. He enjoyed visiting cities where he had friends—Miami, where he loved to spend time with Don Shula; Los Angeles, when his pal Don Klosterman was the GM of the Rams; Oakland, as he became closer to Raider owner Al Davis; and, of course, Washington, where he liked to mingle with the news types and politicians who came to the games.

A great game could also get his juices flowing. Perhaps the most exciting *Monday Night* game ever played unfolded in Houston on November 20, 1978, when the Oilers, led by their rookie running back, Earl Campbell, won a seesaw 35–30 victory over the Miami Dolphins before a crazed throng in the Astrodome. Campbell put on a tremendous show, rushing for 199 yards and 4 touchdowns.

Cosell was caught up in the emotions of the night as the crowd rocked the arena, sang the Oilers' fight song, and turned the stands into a sea of blue-and-white pompons.

"Oh, boy!" he declared after a Campbell touchdown run. "What a game! What a performance by this whole Houston team! The offensive line! Earl Campbell! Pastorini! Mike Barber! Rick Caster! The whole team! And the crowd is beside itself, on their feet as one, the pom-poms going!" And that was early in the third quarter. By the final minutes, Cosell and Gifford, who worked the game without Meredith, were so caught up in the excitement that they often spoke at the same time. Afterward, everyone was exhausted but happy. Cosell and Gifford even seemed to like their chemistry as a twosome.

It was a momentary reminder of the way things were supposed to be on Monday nights.

Honeydew melon came to stand for all the things that had gone wrong with *Monday Night Football*. Dennis Lewin, who had a craving for honeydew, demanded a supply of melon at every production meeting. "We used to get in huge trouble," said one p.a., "if we didn't have melon, or if it didn't get to the meeting on time." And pity the poor p.a. who tried to serve honeydew that was not ripe. Lewin could get really worked up over his honeydew.

Lewin's tensions were visible to all by 1979. He had never been able to take command of *Monday Night Football*, and now the show was out of control. Forte ran the operation during the games. Cosell resisted Lewin's every move. And the squabbling among all three announcers was worse than ever.

Lewin got the show on and off the air, and took care of all the details, meeting with team officials and NFL representatives, but he had little impact on the way the games were being presented. He began production meetings on a lame note, asking each announcer if he had anything he wanted to say during the game. Gifford might make a remark or two and Cosell often had ideas, but Forte would inevitably take charge. He'd decide how to open the show and what story lines to follow, perhaps point to a key matchup. Then, rubbing it in a little, he'd say, "What do you think about that, Denny?"

The situation was untenable. "In Roone's scheme of things, the producer was the boss," Forte said. "But that was nonsense on *Monday Night Football*, because the producer wasn't the boss. I was the boss."

No one doubted that. Forte had become more abusive than ever. Some of the p.a.'s thought it was his only way of getting up for the games after nearly ten years on the show. "There weren't many games when he didn't start lambasting somebody," said Jack Graham. It seemed like Forte needed a whipping boy every week, so the p.a.'s began to root for one of the cameramen to screw up so it would take the heat off them.

Even Lewin felt his wrath. One night in Cleveland in 1979, ABC had a blimp on the scene, the crowd was going wild, and fireworks were exploding. Forte was revved up too, calling for one camera, then another, to capture the mood. When Lewin spoke up, telling him to take a different shot, Forte erupted. Don't you ever, he warned Lewin, tell me which camera to take. "He yelled and screamed at him like he was some gofer," said Graham, who witnessed the incident.

Trying to argue with Forte was deadly, but the p.a.'s did come up with one safe way to get back at him. They would flash an insulting graphic on a screen that never went over the air—"Chet, you suck" was a favorite—and then pull it off so fast that no one could be sure he had seen it.

Lewin had no such outlet. He was, in his own words, "physically and mentally drained." The conflicts were eating away at him.

"You've got to get off the show," Forte once told him. "If you don't get off, you're going to be in an insane asylum." Lewin glumly agreed that he needed a change.

Lewin began to lash out at others, though he was not, by nature, mean-spirited. Soon after joining the show, Robbie Beiner was mugged outside Texas Stadium in Dallas and hospitalized with a concussion. Lewin barely knew him, but he went to the hospital in the middle of the night and sat with Beiner. "Dennis showed me a lot of class with that gesture," Beiner said.

But Lewin's unpleasant side surfaced when he began to obsess about the melon, and the limos, and the hotel suites, and all the other accoutrements of the good life that had become fixtures on the *Monday Night* scene. "It was grinding on him so much that he ground on us more," said one p.a.

By ABC standards, the perks weren't excessive. Staffers at ABC Sports had lived well since the early 1960s, when Arledge led small groups to Europe to acquire events for *Wide World*. Later, perks were used to motivate people. Arledge was so sparing with his praise, and gave so little emotionally to those who worked for him, that limos, first-class travel, and other amenities were a way to provide "extra gratification," said Irwin Weiner.

Lewin, though, sometimes seemed more fixated on the perks than on the product. On a rainy night in Foxboro, Massachusetts, Lewin spent much of the second half trying to decide whether to go back to New York via Boston or via Providence, and wondering which bags were in which limo. "This is amazing," thought one of the p.a.'s. "We've got a game going on and they're debating the traffic patterns."

"Your job was in jeopardy if a limo wasn't there," said Bob Rosburg, Jr., another p.a. Ned Simon remembered going to

Lewin for a review of his performance, confident that he had done a good job on the show. Lewin disagreed, telling him, "You were a step behind. You have a problem with limos. You had a problem with hotels."

The perks came to be seen as status symbols. Once in Washington, the Watergate Hotel gave Jack Graham a free upgrade to a suite. When Forte saw the room list, he immediately called Graham, who was already out working at RFK Stadium.

"Who the hell do you think you are with a room like that," Forte yelled. "You're just a p.a." Graham explained the circumstances, but it made no difference to Forte. Graham had to return to the hotel and inform the desk clerk that his boss was forcing him to change rooms—even though the bigger room wasn't costing ABC an extra dime.

Eventually, everyone who lasted on the show learned how to dodge bullets from Lewin and Forte—when they could.

One time in Minnesota, Simon decided to give the only available suites to Cosell and Forte. He had to put Lewin in a pair of connecting rooms. When Lewin discovered the situation, he was livid. Simon and Graham were called in for a scolding. "I'm the producer of the show," he told them. "I should get a suite."

As the two p.a.'s left the room, Graham, shaking his head, said to Simon, "I don't believe that."

"I don't either," Simon replied. "But Jack—if you had two suites, and had to choose from the three people, wouldn't you give them to Chet and Howard?"

"Absolutely," Graham agreed.

No more proof was needed of the pecking order on the show.

If Dennis Lewin ever felt the need for spiritual sustenance during his unhappy tenure as the producer of *Monday Night Football,* he could have found it at a tavern called 1129 in Santa Barbara, California.

In that holiest of shrines, *Monday Night Football* became a religion. Officially. A local advertising man and a couple of his pals formed the Church of Monday Night Football, incorporated the name, and began selling memberships. For five dollars, worshipers got a *Monday Night* schedule, a decal, and a sacred scroll of "the six commandments and the commandment after."

Among them: "Thou shalt keep Monday night holy . . . and tune in early"; "Honor thy point spread . . . for it is right on"; and "Thou shalt not covet thy neighbor's beer." The church attracted national attention and hundreds of members.

Secular confirmation that *Monday Night Football* remained a force could be found at the other end of the country, where a group of would-be fans, most of them women, gathered on Mondays at Miami-Dade Community College for a course called Understanding and Appreciating *Monday Night Football*. Students paid fourteen dollars for a six-week class that was designed to explain the game and, the instructor said, help women "overcome the psychological barrier of being on the outside of the football circle."

Naturally, classes were dismissed at 8:40 P.M. so that everyone could get home in time for the opening kickoff.

Meanwhile, in the late 1970s, CBS, armed with the rights to the radio coverage of *Monday Night Football*—rights that had become valuable only because of the enormous popularity of Cosell & Co.—mounted a drive to get viewers to listen to CBS's radio voices, Jack Buck and Hank Stram, while they watched ABC's coverage. The campaign got a boost from some Cosell-bashers in the press, notably Gary Deeb, the vitriolic television critic of the Chicago *Tribune*. Deeb wrote several columns about how people were turning off the sound on their television sets to eliminate "the gross excesses of Howard Cosell." But none of the claims that Deeb or CBS made about the defections to radio were well documented, and the campaign faded.

More substantive evidence that the *Monday Night* phenomenon was alive and well was provided by the people in Sports sales, who were still getting rich by selling commercial time for Monday night games.

Herb Granath had moved up to become vice-president of ABC Inc. In 1975, the department was turned over to his protégé, John Lazarus. Lazarus, then thirty-five, was a gregarious, hard-driving executive who took Sports sales to its greatest heights.

By the late 1970s, Lazarus led an aggressive sales force, a close-knit group of mostly young men who loved sports and traveled the country first class. They felt like a family and, in fact, spent more time with each other than with their wives and children. They seemed able to sell any sports program at any price, so much so that Arledge and ABC management felt confident as they paid higher and higher rights fees for events.

For *Monday Night Football*, the crunch came when the new rights deal took effect in 1978. Lazarus had more games to sell and more commercial minutes to fill in each game, and still he had to raise prices from $124,000 to $170,000 a minute. No matter how you packaged the ads—and now they were being sold in thirty-second spots, for $85,000 a spot—that came to a 37 percent price hike.

The timing, at least, was right for ABC. Lazarus went into the marketplace after 1977, the year of Meredith's return, when *Monday Night Football* achieved a record-high 21.5 rating and 37 share. Even so, he said, the higher prices could not be justified by the ratings.

Ford, the show's first and biggest advertiser, choked on the increase and dropped out. That was no problem for Lazarus. Steve Leff of McCann-Erickson, who handled the Buick division of General Motors, had been lobbying for several years to get into *Monday Night Football*. Buick took half of each game, and Toyota took the other half. GM's Chevrolet division was also interested, but they didn't move quickly enough.

Miller Brewing renewed quickly too, much to the dismay of Anheuser-Busch. August Busch III was so determined to break Miller's lock on the show that he invited Lazarus, Jake Keever, the head of ABC Sales, and Jim Duffy, president of the network, to St. Louis. With an unmistakable edge to his voice, Busch declared that A-B would pay whatever it took to get into the show. The ABC men could not be encouraging. They were committed, they said, to Miller as the incumbent.

Firestone and Goodyear also hung in, despite the price hike, and Lazarus brought in IBM and Boeing. By August, *Monday Night Football* was almost sold out and well on its way to another profitable season.

If all the buyers were paying more, they were getting more too. Miller, in particular, used the *Monday Night* stars, especially

Gifford, to romance their distributors and key customers at weekly luncheons on game days. Miller gained on A-B and passed Schlitz in 1978 to become the number-two brewer in America.

The *Monday Night* parties grew more elaborate. By getting the local people who sell beer and cars and tires out to the games, Lazarus was able to put grass-roots pressure on the advertisers to renew. He needed all the pressure he could generate as the rates climbed toward the sky.

Dennis Lewin was always a little surprised that viewers seemed unaware of the tensions plaguing *Monday Night Football.* "The chemistry had just totally disintegrated," Lewin said, but "the audience perception wasn't the same as mine. Maybe I was too close to it. Maybe I knew what was going on, and the guy at home didn't."

Some viewers were turning away. After the gains sparked by Meredith's return, the ratings slid—down 6 percent in 1978, down another 3 percent in 1979. The Sunday and Thursday ratings were edging toward embarrassment. No one was about to form a Church of Thursday Night Football.

Even as Roone Arledge drifted away from Sports, he could not ignore the *Monday Night* problems. The ratings were a worry, but he was more concerned by the reports he kept getting about turmoil on the show. Cosell was always on the phone to New York, complaining about Lewin or his booth-mates to one ABC executive or another, and Arledge spent enough time with Gifford to know that Frank and Don were disgruntled. Besides, he could see the games for himself, though increasingly he didn't want to.

Arledge now concluded that Lewin was incapable of running the show. Lewin's woes were common knowledge around the Sports division, where speculation had begun about who would be the next producer sent into the *Monday Night* maelstrom. Chuck Howard expressed the prevailing view, saying, "Dennis was just along for the ride. He was holding on to the wing and Forte was flying the plane." And Forte was a reckless pilot.

Midway through the 1979 season, Lewin called a meeting to clear the air. It was time, he thought, for some face-to-face discussion instead of "everybody sniping at everybody behind their backs."

Arledge, who flew out to Los Angeles for the session, began by calling on anyone who had a problem to lay it on the table so it could be addressed.

Gifford and Meredith took the offensive. Gifford said that Cosell seemed angry in the booth—his temper tantrum in Green Bay was fresh in everyone's mind—and that his attitude made everyone uncomfortable. Meredith said he did not have enough time to make his points during the telecast. He said Cosell kept getting in his way.

Cosell was enraged. He defended himself, reminding his mates in the booth that he was the heart of the package, the only one capable of shaping the presentation. He didn't dare go after Gifford in front of Arledge, but he did argue that Meredith had more than enough time to speak. The implication and, not a very subtle one, was that Meredith had nothing much to say.

Forte straddled the fence. That had become his standard operating procedure. He would tell whomever he was talking to whatever he wanted to hear. He especially didn't want to take sides in front of Arledge. Cosell was bitter about that too. He had counted on Forte as an ally.

Lewin tried to play mediator. He urged everyone to work together as a team, for the good of all. It was an absurd hope. "Everyone thought everyone had ganged up on everyone else," he said later.

Through it all, Arledge said very little. Nerves were too raw, he thought. He had often tried, as gently as possible, to get Cosell to tone down his act. "One of the basic maxims of sports," he would say, "is that if something great happens, don't say anything." Cosell had an annoying habit of overpowering such moments, often to pat himself on the back for predicting whatever had just happened. He would also overpower his partners with his stentorian imprimatur—"Exactly right!"—and then go on to make a point of his own. Arledge was tempted to say something to Cosell, but this was no time to provoke him. Best to let things lie, and somehow get through the rest of the season.

That night, Arledge knew the meeting had been a waste. He flew back to New York with Cosell, who now felt free to vent his fury. Gifford and Meredith, he charged, wanted him off the show. They were ganging up on him, just as they did in the booth. They were ungrateful for everything he had done for them, and now he, Howard, would give them what they wanted.

He was quitting *Monday Night Football.*

Not again, thought Arledge. News was a picnic compared to this.

Cosell didn't quit, of course, though he never forgot what happened in Los Angeles. Years later, he would say that the meeting "seared [his] soul."

There was, however, one casualty in 1979. Lewin went to Arledge and told him that he'd had enough. Arledge was relieved. He had wanted to make a change anyway.

The time had come to bring on someone with the muscle to straighten out the *Monday Night* mess.

November 10, 1975, was not a banner night for Cosell in Dallas; he had irritated the Cowboy fans with comments made about Number 44, running back Robert Newhouse.

*H*oward in his prime in the mid-seventies

*A*lways an inviting target for hostile fans,
Cosell literally became a punching bag in Boston in a promotion set up
by an author hawking a book called *Stop Howard Cosell*.

*T*erry O'Neil, the producer
who never made it past the 1980
exhibition season

The *Monday Night Football* triangle

Bob Goodrich,
the producer of
Monday Night Football
from 1980 to 1985

Capital Cities/ABC, Inc.

Gifford at work
in his ABC office

Capital Cities/ABC, Inc.

Jim Lampley,
the half-time highlights
specialist for 1984

Capital Cities/ABC, Inc.

Capital Cities/ABC, Inc.

*O.*J. Simpson and Joe Namath in the booth during
their first game together, the Hall of Fame Game, August 1985

John Martin, who turned down
Arledge's offer in 1983 to become
president of ABC Sports

Arledge in front of the controls in his biggest year,
the double Olympics year of 1984

Dennis Swanson, the marine in charge of ABC Sports, 1986

The first two-man team to announce *Monday Night Football*: Al Michaels (left) and Frank Gifford, 1986

*D*ennis Lewin, now senior vice-president
of production, at Calgary, 1988

A trio again: Dan Dierdorf joins Gifford
and Michaels as the announcing team in 1987

9.

FORCED TO
PUNT

"If the price for a new creative approach was going to be bedlam, we just couldn't do that."—ROONE ARLEDGE

As Terry O'Neil sat outside Roone Arledge's office on an afternoon in March 1980, he went over in his mind all the things he believed a producer would have to do to regain control of *Monday Night Football*. He knew that Arledge wanted the new producer of the series to be tough, and he was willing, even eager, to be tough.

He was also ready to sell Arledge on his conviction that *Monday Night Football* had degenerated into something that was "a mile wide and an inch deep." O'Neil had observed the chaos of the preceding year as both a viewer and an insider who heard the tales of the backstabbing that was going on. He had witnessed the spectacle of Cosell standing in the lobby of the ABC building on Tuesday morning "recounting verbatim to everybody who walked through on their way to the elevators all the mistakes Frank had made the night before."

O'Neil was prepared to tell Arledge that he believed the series had become too distanced from the action on the field. *Monday Night Football*, he thought, was not "saying or communicating anything interesting about the players and coaches during the three hours of the telecast, either visually or in the commentary."

O'Neil figured he could state his position diplomatically—and would have to, since the man sitting next to him, about to go into the meeting with him, was Chet Forte, the last person likely to accept radical changes on *Monday Night*. O'Neil planned to argue that more football could be brought into the telecast without compromising the ntertaining approach that had made the series so popular.

By the time the secretary told them to go in, O'Neil had worked out carefully what he would say and how he would say it.

He never had to say anything. Arledge said it all for him.

"The series is in total disarray," Arledge said grimly, after he had greeted O'Neil and Forte. "Howard is completely out of control. The other guys on the series are so resentful of him and so unhappy with him that most of what I do on the series is just listen to people bitch on the phone. And I don't want to do it anymore. The antipathy that they all feel for each other is so palpable it's obvious on the air. It's the subject of everybody's gossip. It's threatening to destroy the series.

"Howard is openly drinking on the air and before the telecasts," Arledge went on. O'Neil had heard that too. Arledge said Cosell was ripping Gifford and Meredith in the press, and that they were now ripping him back.

Frank and Don, Arledge said, "don't feel the production side has exercised any kind of even hand on who gets what pieces of the show. And they're right about that."

The only thing that surprised O'Neil about this message was how bluntly Arledge was putting it, right in front of Forte—and that Chet was sitting there calmly, nodding in agreement.

"Somebody's got to take control," Arledge said. "Somebody has to come in from the outside, untainted, who has a reputation for being tough enough to get the job done, because they won't believe it coming from Lewin. Besides everything else that's wrong with the show, it's no fun watching it. It's bad television."

Arledge had reached that conclusion by watching the show, which he usually did on Monday nights in his news office while working late. He would use the Roone phone to call Lewin to make suggestions, deliver a message to one of the announcers, or order an extra promo for *Nightline*.

One night, sitting with his assistant, Jeff Ruhe, Arledge watched the opening of an important game and was annoyed to see nothing but tight shots of the announcers in the booth. He was on the Roone phone immediately. "I want to see people screaming in the stadium," he said, paraphrasing his twenty-year-old memo on how to produce football games. "This is an event!"

More often, Arledge was bored. "I can't watch this stuff anymore," he would say to Ruhe. "I don't understand how my people don't see it."

Monday Night Football, he thought, had stagnated. "There was a sameness to it," he said. "The creative spark that had made the program really good had gone out of it."

Arledge himself was partly to blame. He was preoccupied with News, unwilling to commit his energies to Sports, yet reluctant to relinquish his authority over the division. He left the production to his lieutenants—Chuck Howard, Chet Forte, and Dennis Lewin. They were the men who had built ABC Sports for the past two decades, but they no longer saw innovation as a priority. They would say, again and again, that ABC Sports is number one, as if saying it alone could make it true. A close Arledge aide said, "His lieutenants were very good at carrying out his instructions, just not good at adding to them." The Young Turks of the 1960s were becoming the establishment of the 1980s. Now the Young Turks of the 1980s were hungry for an opportunity to show what they could do.

Inside the ABC production shop, the younger producers had long resented the trio of Howard, Forte, and Lewin for hogging all the key assignments. By 1980, Arledge was ready to acknowledge that ABC Sports needed a shot of young blood. He wanted a producer who would revitalize *Monday Night Football*.

That was where O'Neil came in. The slightly built, curly haired young man with horn-rimmed glasses had it all: the experience, the creative reputation, the solid journalism credentials, along with the familiar ABC Sports blend of consuming ambition and outspoken arrogance.

When he left Arledge's office, O'Neil was sure he could handle the most important production job at ABC Sports.

*　　　*　　　*

Terry O'Neil always had a plan for his life; from a young age, he always wanted to be a big-league journalist, which he pursued with single-minded devotion. He never doubted his ability to reach that goal.

O'Neil grew up in Pittsburgh. He saw sports reporting as a good way to break into serious journalism, and he was good enough at it to win a Grantland Rice sportswriting scholarship to Vanderbilt. Instead, he chose Notre Dame.

Like many Notre Dame students, including Ohlmeyer, O'Neil took advantage of the national attention focused on the football program. He became sports editor of the college paper early in his freshman year, and as a junior he wrote and produced a slick magazine about the 1969 Notre Dame season.

When ABC began sniffing around the country for hot young sports talents who could assemble a background book about the athletes likely to star in the 1972 Olympics in Munich, O'Neil's name turned up—in boldface. By then he had been accepted at the Columbia School of Journalism. With the offer to work at ABC, he put off Columbia until after the Olympics.

Though technically only a research assistant, O'Neil impressed everyone at ABC Sports with his journalistic and production skills in Munich. Cosell used him as a legman, and decided he was brilliant.

O'Neil could have gone to work full-time for ABC after the Olympics, but he decided to go on to Columbia. To support himself, and to keep his hand in at ABC, he accepted a part-time job as Gifford's stat man. He spent three seasons in the booth beginning in 1972—the era when the *Monday Night* phenomenon was at its peak.

O'Neil's carefully laid plans did not include the discovery of thyroid cancer at age twenty-five. Typically, he didn't waste time while recuperating. He was hired by Rocky Bleier, the Steeler and ex-Notre Dame running back, to write the story of Bleier's battle to make it in the NFL after a harrowing tour in Vietnam. The book, *Fighting Back*, was a huge success, as was the ABC-TV movie that grew out of it.

Fully recovered, O'Neil finally joined ABC in 1976 as an associate producer, a job usually reserved for more experienced hands. "I arrogantly told them I was beyond just being a trainee," O'Neil said. It rankled some of his contemporaries when he skipped the traditional scut work as production assistant, but O'Neil didn't mind leaving the impression that he was special.

O'Neil took on a wide range of assignments, including a well-regarded magazine show with Cosell and specials that previewed the Kentucky Derby. Those specials helped advance O'Neil's growing reputation for slickness and style as well as extravagance.

"O'Neil was even more fiscally irresponsible than Arledge," said Chuck Howard, who tried to supervise him. "He was the most fiscally irresponsible person that I think ever worked at ABC." O'Neil got such a reputation for bingeing—spending thousands of dollars on music groups for a feature or other nonessentials—that "you had to put a guy with him almost joined to the hip," Howard said.

O'Neil's free spending, combined with a personality that could be grating, managed to alienate some important people at ABC. Irwin Weiner, Arledge's chief money manager, was at the top of that list. "When people would say ABC Sports was arrogant," Weiner said, "they were talking about Terry O'Neil."

Arledge thought that O'Neil was "very aggressive, young, and kind of cocky," and that he had a "lot of ability." O'Neil had also proved to Arledge that he could perform under pressure during the 1980 Winter Olympics when he produced a preview special that got the games off to a rousing start. Arledge, who almost never handed out compliments, called O'Neil the next day and was effusive in his praise.

That was in February 1980. Nothing official had been said to O'Neil about *Monday Night Football*, but the plan to bring him on was coming together. Late in 1979, with the chaos at its height under Lewin, Chet Forte had called O'Neil and told him: "Howard and I really think you're the right person to produce next year. And we've told Roone so. Don't be surprised if you hear from Roone."

O'Neil was fully aware, then and later, of how significant the opinions of Howard Cosell and Chet Forte could be.

*   *   *

Terry O'Neil, then thirty-one, went into the 1980 season of *Monday Night Football* all fired up. Arledge had given him a mandate. He wanted O'Neil to end the hostilities in the *Monday Night* booth and to restore the creative edge that had been missing since Don Ohlmeyer left. Arledge had made O'Neil his quarterback, with the hope that this highly touted recruit could move the team forward.

This new offensive strategy had one significant drawback: Nobody but Arledge and O'Neil knew he had been authorized to introduce a fresh approach. Forte had more or less heard the same thing from Arledge, but he did not come away with the same impression that O'Neil did.

O'Neil did not go in with a confrontational attitude; he had worked enough with Cosell to realize how easily he could be antagonized. As for Forte, no one at ABC was unaware of the director's volatile nature. Everyone knew that he considered himself the real producer of *Monday Night Football*, and that he had walked all over Lewin.

Though the ratings had eroded only slightly, and the press remained generally favorable, the view inside ABC Sports was that the show was deteriorating. "The more they were directly confrontational with each other in the booth about anything, any topic, the worse it was going to be," O'Neil said. "They were in such an isolated state; isolated from the game, isolated from each other, sitting around brooding in their hotel rooms about how's he going to try to fuck me on the air tomorrow night, that it was inevitable when they came on the air they'd do the bad, bad shtick that they were doing. They were trying to couch it in humor and they were the worst comedians in the world at that point."

As if that wasn't enough of a problem, O'Neil also suspected that Forte was no longer the director he used to be. Others agreed. Robbie Beiner, an associate director, said, "As great as Chet could be in making a good game great and a great game greater, if there was an average game, he would bring it down a level. And, if it was a bad game, he would bring it down even more."

Still, O'Neil felt the problems could be corrected if everyone focused on the game. As he observed it, "The commentators and production guys flew into the city on Sunday night, holed up in their rooms Sunday night and Monday, never spoke to or saw anyone connected with either team, marched into the booth and truck Monday night and did the game. And I thought it looked and sounded like that."

O'Neil, most of all, wanted to get the commentators talking to the players and coaches again. "I thought the best thing that Howard and Don ever did was exploit—in a good way—the personalities of the players." He felt that Meredith had grown more and more distant from the players as his contemporaries retired and that Cosell, with his profile now as big as the skyline of Manhattan, worked almost exclusively with his sources among the league owners and general managers.

O'Neil decided to try to initiate contact between the announcers and the teams. He wanted to open up a suite in the hotel with hors d'oeuvres and beer, inviting key players and coaches for the visiting team to drop by. Howard, Don, and Frank could just wander through and chat, O'Neil thought. "And then they'd be ready to go on the air with the kind of anecdotal material that's fresh and firsthand and not something we could read in the media guide."

O'Neil planned to work his changes in gently. For one thing, though he believed that Cosell's drinking had become a "debilitating factor" in the broadcasts, he saw no reason to confront that issue right away. "Trying to wean Howard from his vodka during games was like priority seventy at that point," O'Neil said.

Before he began work on the first preseason game, O'Neil sought out Cosell. "Howard, I'm new at this," O'Neil said. "I'd love to have your opinion about how I should proceed. I want to accommodate your interests in every way."

Cosell expected nothing less. Certainly he didn't see any need for drastic changes in a series that had become a national phenomenon. Forte was on the same wavelength as Cosell, even after listening to Arledge's critique of the show.

But even as he assured Cosell and Forte that he intended to consult with them before any change was made, O'Neil was quietly setting in motion alterations that led them to suspect that he wanted to put his stamp on the broadcast. He had his production assistants develop a new opening for the series. He had even ordered literal alterations—in the width of the lapels on the announcers' taxi-cab-yellow jackets. To Forte, that had the ring of a call to arms for a palace revolution.

Before the Hall of Fame Game in August, O'Neil took the first small step toward adding substance to the coverage. The San Diego Chargers, who were playing, had become famous for their wide-open, intricate passing attack. O'Neil got Joe Gibbs, the architect of their passing game, and a few players to agree to a meeting to discuss their offense.

O'Neil called around the hotel to the commentators and Forte to see if they'd like to join him in chatting with Gibbs. The Chargers' hotel was about two minutes away. O'Neil even told them they could just stop by and, if they wanted to leave, he would play the diplomat.

No one had the slightest interest. Forte reacted with utter disdain. "Terry," he said, "if you want to go watch coach's film to get ready for a game, that's fine with me. Go ahead and have a good time."

O'Neil went, realizing how tough it was going to be to get these guys—especially Forte—to change. But they'd change; he'd see to that. He had a mandate, after all.

The Hall of Fame Game was never a joy to cover, with both teams using hundred-man rosters and nobody caring who won; it turned particularly ragged in 1980. Midway through the fourth quarter on a steamy day in Canton, Ohio, thick clouds rolled in, shooting lightning across the sky and pouring water onto the field in torrents. The game was meaningless, so it was stopped and never resumed.

For *Monday Night Football*, the tumult in the heavens was a preview of things to come.

After just one game, Chet Forte did not like what he was seeing from the new producer. O'Neil's arrogance was singeing Forte's thin skin; O'Neil lacked the political skills that had enabled Ohlmeyer to work so dynamically with Forte. At the same time, O'Neil had too much Pittsburgh steel in his spine to be intimidated into doing everything Chet's way, as Lewin had been.

"Terry had this attitude problem that would just grate on your nerves," said Bob Crivelli, the technical unit manager in

1980. "He took seriously that he wanted to be the producer on the show. He was trying to tell Chet how to do it. . . . And you just don't do that."

O'Neil was intensely disliked, not just by Forte but by most of the members of the technical staff. O'Neil treated them like underlings; he could be aloof and snooty, and he made demands that crew members found unreasonable. One thing they all despised was O'Neil's habit of calling the tech guys "Daddy" or "Bub." Crivelli said, "I felt like I was on *My Three Sons*, for Christ's sake."

Before the next preseason game, with the Steelers playing the Falcons in Atlanta, O'Neil took another misstep. As a Pittsburgh native and a friend of Rocky Bleier, O'Neil knew the Steelers like an insider. So he gathered a raft of information from the players and coaches, and relayed it to the commentators.

They accepted it well, O'Neil thought. Certainly Gifford was responding; he loved emphasizing the game. Meredith took the exhibition season off, but O'Neil expected him to cooperate. As for Cosell, O'Neil saw no problems there either.

Cosell, in fact, was insulted. That this kid would presume to tell him about the Steelers was astonishing. These were the Steelers, the team Cosell had adopted as his own. The very word *Steeler* would trigger one of Cosell's stock lines—"They were my kids."

Later, Cosell related the incident to Forte. "I thought Chet was gonna go through the sky," he said.

In the truck that night, Forte and O'Neil didn't speak to each other. "When Chet was upset he'd sit in that truck and he wouldn't say shit," said Crivelli. "And he'd wait and he'd wait, and he was thinking out what was going to happen."

Almost any incident could have sparked the fuse.

That summer the New England Patriots faced a crisis. Four of their most important players, Mike Haynes, Sam Cunningham, Richard Bishop, and Tom Owen, all represented by one agent, Howard Slusher, were holding out for new contracts. Their absence threatened to devastate a potential Super Bowl team.

With *Monday Night Football* on its way to New England for its final preseason game, O'Neil considered the holdouts a major story. Cosell could hardly have disagreed under the circumstances, but the circumstances were special—and personal—for Cosell.

The owner of the Patriots, Billy Sullivan, had been a friend to Howard and Emmy Cosell for more than twenty-five years. As Cosell well knew, the holdout by the four Patriots threatened not only the future of the franchise but also the economic survival of the Sullivan family. "Billy didn't have a goddamn dime," Cosell said.

Cosell began work on Monday by interviewing Chuck Sullivan, the Patriots' executive vice-president and son of his friend Billy. In mid-week, O'Neil called Cosell at his home in Westhampton Beach, Long Island to set up an interview with Slusher. "Jesus, I'm out here with Emmy and the grandchildren," Cosell protested.

O'Neil was insistent. He promised to fly Slusher to New York from Los Angeles, and, to make things easy for Cosell, he arranged for a helicopter to pick him up in Westhampton and a limo to drive him to ABC from the Manhattan heliport. As usual, O'Neil spared no expense.

Cosell did the interview with Slusher—skillfully, as always. O'Neil told Cosell they would add to the Patriots' side of the story when they got to New England.

On Saturday morning, Cosell again talked with Chuck Sullivan. Then Cosell left to spend the rest of the day on Cape Cod with Billy Sullivan. By the time he got back, he had some reservations about the holdout story.

O'Neil had called a meeting for that night to upbraid the new booth manager for showing Cosell special treatment during the first two games; O'Neil was determined to have an evenhanded policy in all things.

When Cosell turned up in the hallway outside the meeting room, O'Neil told him, "Howard, I don't want you in on this meeting."

"What?" Cosell bellowed in disbelief as O'Neil shut the door. A veteran crew member needled Cosell: "Hey, Howard. You just got thrown out of the meeting!"

Cosell turned to him in chilly anger. "That little goddamn shit can't throw me out," Cosell said. "He'll learn who I am."

When he caught up with the producer the next morning, Cosell demanded a meeting about the holdout story. He wanted to screen the version O'Neil had edited to air at halftime that afternoon. Forte came along.

After they watched the tape, Cosell exploded. It was slanted, he told O'Neil. The piece would screw Billy Sullivan.

O'Neil tried to argue that it only seemed slanted because Slusher was a more effective advocate than Chuck Sullivan.

Cosell considered Chuck Sullivan a "fucking moron," but he said the feature, as edited by O'Neil, was dominated by the players.

The argument quickly deteriorated.

O'Neil became convinced that Billy Sullivan had spent the previous day at the Cape filling Cosell with "Irish piss and vinegar" and beating him over the head with the claim that Slusher's demands would ruin the family.

Cosell ignored O'Neil's points, because he had a bigger one to make. The issue was becoming control. Who was going to control the series, he asked, you or me?

O'Neil tried to stick to the holdout story, but it was no use.

"Terry, I don't want to offend you," Cosell said, "but you're a child." O'Neil, he thought, was out of his league. "There's a difference between here's the way you hit the tight end in the seam in the middle and really knowing what goes on in sports," he said.

The ultimate confrontation was at hand. "I won't do that piece, Terry," Cosell said.

Forte jumped right in. "Terry, Howard's dead right," he said quietly but menacingly. "I won't do that fucking piece either. And you can go fuck yourself."

O'Neil refused to back down. He told them the piece was as fair as he could make it. But if Cosell felt so damn strongly, O'Neil said, he could have an extra minute at the end to make a personal comment. They would label it "Commentary," and Cosell was free to say anything he pleased.

That got the piece on the air. Cosell and O'Neil agreed that it ended up a fair, balanced piece, but each contended that was only because he had won the battle against the other.

Cosell used his extra minute mostly to restate the issue, but he did emphasize that the Sullivans had suffered through "struggle and turmoil" to reacquire the franchise. Cosell also called Slusher a "very effective attorney and agent who is doing his job as he sees it." Then he expressed sympathy for the fans of New England.

Still, as the game was played, an undercurrent of venom was transmitted through the production earphones. During one break, Cosell spat out a message to O'Neil: "This show is not big enough for both of us. We'll see who survives."

Unafraid, O'Neil shot back: "When we get back, there's going to be a meeting about this."

Cosell's clipped reply: "There will be no meeting."

Forte said nothing. He had been waiting for the right moment to move against O'Neil. The Atlanta game had convinced him that O'Neil wanted to produce the show without him.

After the game in Atlanta, Forte had conferred with Cosell about the O'Neil problem. "You gonna back me if I go to Roone?" Forte asked. Cosell said he didn't have anything against the kid other than "he's kind of a pain in the ass." But after the New England game, Forte and Cosell agreed—Terry O'Neil had to go.

Forte decided to play the heavy and went to see Arledge. Arledge had just supervised ABC News's coverage of two political conventions that summer—coverage which Forte, in his first foray into the news side, had directed—and was deep into his planning for the 1980 presidential election. He could scarcely believe the petty demons of *Monday Night Football* were rising up to haunt him again.

Forte didn't mince words. "You've got to get that kid out of there, Roone," he said. "You're not even going to be able to get on the air. Howard detests him. He's making problems for everybody. His attitude is not one that's going to be conducive to getting this show on and off the air."

Arledge heard the same message from his most trusted administrative aide in Sports, John Martin, who was unofficially delegated to take the howls-of-rage calls from Cosell. Martin felt compelled to call Arledge and tell him the new producer just wasn't working out—even though he felt the situation tilted unfairly against O'Neil.

Finally, in utter disgust, Arledge called Cosell. "This is bullshit," Arledge said. "Every year there's a new crisis with *Monday Night Football*. The goddamn thing—it never fails."

Cosell said it was Forte who couldn't possibly work with this kid. "And you know, Roone," Cosell said, "Chester is the key man."

What Arledge knew was that he had two key men who went back to the beginning of *Monday Night Football*, ten years earlier, standing against the young producer he had picked to rejuvenate the series.

"Basically there was no choice," Martin said. "I hate to say it, but Howard was going to win that battle."

Arledge, typically, avoided delivering the bad news. He delegated Martin and Jim Spence to tell O'Neil he was being taken off the show.

In the meantime, he needed another producer, with only one week to go before the opening game that would mark the tenth anniversary of *Monday Night Football*.

The priorities had changed. "Now the priorities were that you've got these characters who've got to get on the air every week," Arledge said. "It was at a point where every week we would have a rebellion. I mean, literally having to solve World War Three before we could get on the air." Any hopes of reigniting the creative spark that had set the show apart in 1970 were abandoned.

Arledge asked for suggestions for producer and one name emerged—Bob Goodrich, the steady-Eddie producer of the B-games on college football. "Bobby's strength," Arledge said, "was that he was likable and calm and not identified with anybody in particular."

The likable, calm, nonpartisan new quarterback would not be expected to move the team, only to take the signals from the sidelines—and punt.

As for the guy with the big arm and the big expectations, he was dispatched to the bench. The few plays he had tried ended up as incompletions. Before he left the field, he looked around frantically for the coach on the sidelines; but he was nowhere to be found.

Arledge never contacted Terry O'Neil to explain how fragile mandates can sometimes turn out to be.

On a sweltering Labor Day, Bob Goodrich met Chet Forte in the otherwise empty ABC building. They sat there all day with no air conditioning, going over every detail of *Monday Night Football*. Forte was generous to Goodrich in every way; he was openly relieved to be rid of O'Neil.

Forte asked Goodrich if he would like to change anything about the telecast, but Goodrich had no intention of bucking him.

Forte did want to get Goodrich's approval of one recent change. He had created the job of "stage manager" and filled it with an attractive young woman. Forte described it as a ploy to try to keep Cosell under control. "Howard is less likely to turn around and say, 'You dumb mother-fucking asshole' with a girl up there," Forte said. Goodrich thought it was a great idea.

Bob Goodrich, then thirty-five, was not considered one of the top young producers at ABC Sports, but he had done well in the nine years since he had worked as a p.a. on *Monday Night Football*. Goodrich had a football past; he'd played tight end for SMU, long after the Dandy Don era. He was the forgotten receiver on a team whose star was split end Jerry LeVias.

A native Texan, Goodrich was the son of a successful Dallas preacher who had his own television show. He got his first taste of the television business hanging around the studio before his father's sermons.

Goodrich had been a premed student at SMU, but after graduation he dropped the idea of becoming a doctor. He was sick of school. He was working part-time at a Dallas television production company when, on a whim, he picked up the phone, called ABC in New York, and got the address of the network's headquarters. He got on a plane, flew to New York, and took himself up to 1330 Sixth Avenue in search of a new career.

But Goodrich got no farther than a secretary in the Sports division. He took down some names, returned to the airport, and flew back to Dallas.

He called and badgered for months before he connected with John Martin, then a young producer, who agreed to use him as a gofer when ABC got to Dallas for a golf tournament. That led to a meeting with Terry Jastrow, the college-football director, and more gofer assignments. Finally he was offered a production assistant's slot. He jumped at it.

As a producer, Goodrich mostly worked regional college-football telecasts. He did various golf and *Wide World* assignments, none especially high-profile. Goodrich established a reputation early for being solid, durable, and dependable—a genuine tight end of a producer.

He was not considered creative. "Goodrich was not the kind of guy who would pick up the ball and run with it," said one announcer who worked with him often. "The highest value in Bob's life is punctuality. If you come to the eight o'clock meeting at eight-oh-three, you have no credibility whatsoever with him."

But Goodrich worked well with Forte. He knew football better than any other producer at ABC, except for Chuck Howard. Most important, he had an amiable personality and a subdued ego; no one ever called him arrogant. As Arledge now conceded, *Monday Night Football* needed a peacemaker—not a playmaker.

Roone Arledge loved the Washington power scene, but he was not looking forward to his trip to the nation's capital for the 1980 regular season opener of *Monday Night Football*.

He had called yet another meeting of the *Monday Night* crew, this time at the urging of John Martin. "Roone, this is bullshit," Martin told him. "You've got to go down there."

But Arledge was fed up to his aviator glasses with the feuding. It was starting to remind him of the Harry Reasoner–Barbara Walters debacle on *World News Tonight*, a pairing of anchors that produced such overt tension, Arledge felt it was making viewers uncomfortable. It certainly made him feel that way.

He could not tolerate another season of trench warfare. "It was very disconcerting if you were a viewer," Arledge said. "You tune in to be entertained by a football game. You don't want to have people fighting all the time."

Arledge had to intervene. He told his assistant, Jeff Ruhe, that he was going to Washington to conduct a "head-knocking session."

They met in Arledge's suite at the Watergate Hotel—Cosell, Gifford, Meredith, Forte, Ruhe, and a nervous Bob Goodrich. With Arledge on the scene, every hint of rebelliousness disappeared. Even if no one else did, Arledge commanded everyone's respect.

"Look," Arledge began, softly but seriously, "everybody in this room is who we are as a result of our mutual success on *Monday Night Football*. This show has been good to everybody. Everybody has benefited. Everybody has made a lot of money. This is a multimillion-dollar project."

Then he delivered his message, as firmly as he could. "All this bickering and pettiness has got to stop." If it did not, he warned, "you're going to destroy this thing."

Again and again, Arledge made the point. They had all become richer and more important because of *Monday Night Football*. Their reputations had been secured chiefly by this show. He explicitly included himself.

Now, flushed with that success, they were allowing themselves to get all worked up over "little things that are really totally insignificant."

"I don't want any more bullshit from you guys," Arledge concluded ominously. "This nonsense has got to stop."

The room went silent. It sounded to Ruhe like a "collective 'Yessir!' "

Arledge left the meeting reasonably satisfied. He believed they'd all taken it well—though he was never sure about Cosell.

Bob Goodrich left in a panic. "Holy shit!" he said to himself as he wandered off to his room. He realized that a big part of the responsibility for keeping this overinflated balloon afloat fell directly on him.

As he prepared for his debut, a debut to be supervised by Roone Arledge, Goodrich was very tense. He later said, "One big mistake and I'd be gone like Terry O'Neil was. If I fucked up *Monday Night Football*, I was gonna be out of there."

The opening show came off smoothly, without a whisper of conflict. In the booth, the announcers, chastened by Arledge, managed to exude energy, if not enthusiasm. In the truck, Goodrich controlled his panic and slid unobtrusively into the flow of the telecast. The game itself made for dull viewing as Dallas crushed Washington, 17–3.

Despite the lack of suspense, the telecast attracted a massive audience—a 23.4 rating and a 40 share, the largest opening numbers in the history of the franchise. The matchup was too appealing, the hype surrounding the tenth anniversary too powerful, to be undone by either a lackluster game or a quiet little civil war raging behind the scenes.

Immediately after the telecast, Arledge had disappeared with the stars without saying a word to Goodrich. Goodrich hung around the truck with Forte, unwinding, and then made his way back to the Watergate, wondering what Roone had thought of his performance.

As Goodrich and Forte walked through the lobby of the hotel, they spotted Arledge sitting with Cosell, Gifford, Meredith, and Jeff Ruhe, off in a corner having drinks. Forte would never enter a social situation that featured Arledge, so he headed upstairs to his suite. Goodrich somewhat sheepishly stopped by where they were sitting, just to be polite. Again, Arledge said nothing about his performance. Goodrich felt too awkward to join them.

Don Ohlmeyer would have flopped down and thrown himself into the conversation. Dennis Lewin would have sat in, though he might not have said much. O'Neil would have found something intelligent to add. Goodrich, an entirely different sort of producer, moved on.

He went up to Forte's room where the two of them, sitting in a two-hundred-dollar-a-night suite in the Watergate Hotel, sent out for pizza.

About an hour later, Goodrich went to his own room to call it a night. He was finally feeling relieved; there were no indications that it had been anything but a solid opening show. Just as he was about to fall asleep, the phone rang. It was Jeff Ruhe.

"Bob," Ruhe said, "I just want you to know that Roone really thought you did a good job tonight. He's happy he made the move to you. He knows it was the right thing to do and he wishes he'd done it in the first place."

It was secondhand, and not exactly a mandate, but it was enough for Bob Goodrich. He slept well.

The tenth anniversary of *Monday Night Football* was deemed an event of such historical significance by ABC that it was commemorated with an hour-long special.

With the three stars relaxing on a living-room couch, watching clips and reminiscing amiably about the good old days, Gifford took pains to dispel all those nasty rumors about personality conflicts in the booth.

"I've heard people say we don't get along," he said. "Don's fighting with Howard. Howard's fighting with me. Howard's fighting with all of us. That's simply not true."

So much for telling it like it is.

The 1980 *Monday Night Football* season did not remain dull. The show careened between comedy and tragedy, delivering shocking news and making a few headlines of its own.

At Game Three in New England, the fan violence at Monday night games, directly tied to drunkenness, reached a deadly height. One fan was killed and forty-five people were arrested outside the stadium in Foxboro, Massachusetts, during a traffic crush after the game. The Foxboro Board of Selectmen, hoping to give the fans less time to drink before the games, subsequently asked that Monday night games begin at eight P.M. instead of nine P.M. The request was later dropped.

Game Four in Chicago, where the Bears beat Tampa Bay, 23–0, ranked as one of the all-time worst games on a Monday night. Tampa coach John McKay said his team "set back *Monday Night Football* a thousand years."

The League of Women Voters put presidential politics on a collision course with pro football by scheduling two debates between Jimmy Carter and Ronald Reagan for Monday nights. When fans of the other league objected, the politicians retreated. The one debate that eventually took place was held on a Tuesday.

Game Thirteen in Oakland turned into a civic protest meeting. Thousands of Raider fans boycotted the game for five minutes so that they could attend a rally outside the stadium opposing owner Al Davis's plans to move the team to Los Angeles. Cosell, whose close ties to league rebel Davis contributed to his growing alienation from—and opposition to—the NFL power structure, dismissed the late-arriving crowd as the result of a "traffic jam."

The following week, fans of the hapless New Orleans Saints made themselves a memorable part of the show by wearing paper bags over their heads and renaming the team the "Aints." Forte went to the bags early and often as New Orleans succumbed to the Rams, 27–7.

In the middle of Game Fifteen in Miami, Cosell broke into the commentary with a news bulletin. He had just taken a call from Arledge in New York. "Howard, I know you can handle this," Arledge had said. "The country doesn't even know. They just shot John Lennon."

Cosell, his voice soft but full of power, revealed first that Lennon, the former Beatle and rock-music legend, had been shot in front of his apartment building in Manhattan. A short while later, Cosell interrupted again to announce that Lennon was dead. Then he tried to put John Lennon's life and career into perspective. He spoke sensitively of having met and liked Lennon. He questioned whether a football game could still be enjoyed under the circumstances. And, as only he would, he dared to quote from poetry, Keats's "Ode to a Nightingale," behind the scene of bodies crashing in the night: " 'My heart aches,' " Cosell intoned, " 'and a drowsy numbness pains my sense.' "

Monday Night Football's next creative advance was initiated by Bob Goodrich, the producer written off as lacking creativity. It was the simplest of gimmicks.

For years, Forte had thought about putting a camera on the far side of the field, to deliver a replay view of plays that could not be seen by any of the cameras on the press-box side. Goodrich undertook the project, going around to the stadiums they would visit in 1981 to find locations for the extra camera.

It was an expensive experiment. Most stadiums required that ABC spend up to eighteen thousand dollars to construct an extra camera platform. In some locations, no platform could be built, so Goodrich had to arrange for a ladder tower. One time, he had to hang a temporary position out from the upper deck.

But by Game Two of 1981, the device was in place. Goodrich gave it a catchy name—reverse-angle replay—that was flashed on the screen every time the camera was used.

The reverse angle became an instant hit and a *Monday Night* trademark. Forte and Goodrich played with it a lot in the early games, often to no real purpose. But the extra camera sometimes delivered a useful new perspective on the action.

Occasionally, that perspective became invaluable. In a game between the Giants and the Redskins in 1985, the reverse-angle-replay camera captured in gut-wrenching detail the sack by the Giants' Lawrence Taylor that snapped the leg of Redskin quarterback Joe Theismann. "We never would have had it without the reverse angle," Goodrich said. "Boy, that was gruesome; but it was a great shot."

Roone Arledge's best efforts were not good enough to resolve the conflicts in the *Monday Night* booth, especially since everyone knew that before long Arledge would again be wrapped up in News. Arledge's head-knocking had the least effect on Meredith, who was never all that impressed when the boss flew into town.

As usual, Meredith was unhappy with ABC. Some of his discontent went back to yet another bad experience at the Olympics. At Lake Placid, Meredith had made sure he got an assignment, but his work as a roving feature reporter was disappointing. Few of his stories were used.

He was frustrated; Arledge was displeased. Arledge's assistant, Jeff Ruhe, said, "You came out of it with the feeling that Don's good old country-boy act was starting to wear out."

On Monday nights, Meredith's preparation had become a joke. He didn't want to ruin his spontaneity, he would say, by cluttering up his brain with facts. He clowned his way through the production meetings, poking fun at any serious comments, especially when they came from Cosell.

In truth, Meredith cared little about the games, and everyone knew it. "Don followed the game," said p.a. Jack Graham, "but the longer he was away from it, the more it got away from him."

Yet Meredith remained popular with the crew; he was always the best liked of the men in the booth. Meredith would play tennis with the p.a.'s or take them to lunch. "He was buddies with everyone down to the thirty-five-dollar-a-day runners," Jerry Klein, Gifford's statistician, said. "He was a human being. He had sensitivity." The p.a.'s in the truck would cheer on Meredith when he'd zing Cosell.

Meredith seemed to have made an uneasy peace with himself. He was no longer battling the demons in Green Bay jerseys, no longer soul-searching or dreaming about what might be over the next hill. His wife, Susan, traveled with him, and he started taking more literally his self-styled role as "America's guest."

In the booth, like Cosell, Meredith sometimes would enjoy a few drinks during the game. Cosell didn't give a damn; he half admired Meredith's refusal to take football seriously.

But Gifford, not surprisingly, was troubled by his friend's cavalier attitude. Gifford worked as hard as ever, cared about the football, and cared even more about making the show a success each week. He sometimes bristled when Meredith goofed off during the production meetings. In the booth, Gifford was too focused on the contest to worry about the cocktail-hour atmosphere around him, but he made a point of never touching a drop of alcohol until the clock ran out. Then, and only then, a gofer would bring him a drink.

Gifford still loved Meredith, but America's love affair with the cowboy was cooling off. After the 1981 season, ABC's research department did a study of viewer attitudes toward *Monday Night Football*. One conclusion—Don Meredith's appeal was fading.

Six times a year, Meredith was replaced by someone far more dedicated, if far less well liked: Fran Tarkenton.

Tarkenton was assigned to the least-important games, and his impact on the package was never more than marginal. If he was remembered for anything, it was his hard-hitting style. He slammed the players more than any other announcer in the package's history, even Cosell.

This didn't surprise anyone who knew Tarkenton well; as a player he had a reputation for being egotistical and demanding. When he came across the same way in the booth, nailing quarterbacks for making bad decisions or receivers for missing catchable balls, he ran afoul of the players—and of Gifford, their most ardent advocate on the telecasts.

"Somebody must have told him to be harsh, because Fran basically is not that way," Gifford said. "He was critical to the point where he overdid it. There was a redundancy. He would hark back to what he thought was a bad call by an official maybe four, five plays later." Viewers, Gifford thought, did not tune in to hear an announcer continuously knocking the officials or the players. "You can be critical and all," he said, "but there comes a point where you say, okay, that's it."

Tarkenton played eighteen seasons in the NFL with the Vikings and the Giants before retiring in 1978. His scrambling style excited the fans but displeased his offensive linemen, who complained that he exhausted them and forced them to hold blocks for too long. Tarkenton's career statistics were spectacular— 47,003 yards passing, 3,686 completions, 342 touchdown passes, all of them NFL records, as he never failed to point out.

"When they talk about home-run records, they talk about Babe Ruth and Hank Aaron," he once told a reporter. "I'm in that category in football passes but you don't often hear my name."

On nights when Tarkenton was added to the *Monday Night* equation, the balance shifted, with Cosell and Tarkenton allied against Gifford. Cosell professed admiration for Tarkenton's work, and Tarkenton, in the few games he worked on *Monday Night Football* over four seasons, was shrewd enough to realize that the best way to shine was to feed off Cosell.

The price was a certain subservience, but Tarkenton was willing to put up with that. Besides, he had to side with Cosell; at the other end of the booth sat Gifford, who had harbored negative feelings about Tarkenton since his ill-fated days as quarterback of the Giants. "The Giants were very down on Fran when they traded him," Arledge said, "and Frank went along with that."

Tarkenton came to be a symbol for the "modern player," the one out more for himself than for his team. Gifford was a totally dedicated team man. But only occasionally did the differences between them surface on the air.

During one game Tarkenton made a strong point about a player's inadequacy, then repeated it after a replay. "You've made that point, Fran," Gifford said, cutting him off. Tarkenton reacted as though he might go after Gifford physically, right there on the air.

Tarkenton's work was respected, if not highly regarded. Everyone conceded that he worked at it.

In a game in Minnesota in 1981, Tarkenton arrived in the booth suffering from an infection in his right arm. It had swollen to almost twice its size and Tarkenton was in intense pain. The unit manager, Bob Crivelli, sent out for bags of ice, which were then tied to the arm. Tarkenton got through it, according to Crivelli, "like a champ. . . . He had a job to do and he did it. That had to impress you." As soon as the game ended Tarkenton was rushed to the hospital.

But overall the substitution of Tarkenton for Meredith wasn't playing. It was too harsh a transition.

Somehow Frank Gifford managed to tolerate Howard Cosell. It could not have been easy.

"After a while," Gifford said, "Howard, to me, was more of a joke than anything else."

The feeling was mutual.

Cosell never apologized for the ridicule he heaped on Gifford. "By my precepts I was never cruel to Frank," Cosell said.

He did admit to poking fun at Gifford's mistakes, though. "Well, you had to keep your sanity," he said. "You had to treat it with humor."

Not everyone was laughing. "It drove Frank nuts," said Arledge.

Still, week after week, Gifford would turn up in the booth, put on his professional face and voice, and treat Cosell with unfailing courtesy on the air.

One *Monday Night* staffer was amazed at "the way Frank swallowed it and never once said a word. [He] defended Howard, even set him up for lines on the air. . . . In this regard Frank is the classiest guy who ever lived."

Gifford tried not to take the criticism personally. "The only thing that saved me," he said, "is that he bitched and moaned about everybody else. I certainly didn't have a franchise on it."

Yet Gifford remained the primary target, if only because he still supplied plenty of material for Cosell's put-downs. At least once in all three games in 1980 and 1981 involving the Cowboys, Gifford called Dennis Thurman "Thurman Munson." Like "Leeman Beeman," it had become a mental block for him. Gifford would go into a game trying to will himself not to repeat the errors, an approach that would serve only to plant the misstatements in his mind; they would pop out as the occasion arose.

Goodrich quickly became aware that Gifford tended to stumble jarringly over names and facts. But he felt insiders made far too much of the fluffs. "The audience was not aware of it," Goodrich said. "Frank was easy to listen to and obviously knew the game. And people liked him. Did he make a few mistakes? Yeah. But as far as I'm concerned it wasn't disastrous."

Out of range of the public and the press, Gifford's struggles with segments taped in advance were dreaded by the production crew.

In a game in New England, Gifford did the opening because Cosell was away. He was supposed to say something along the line of "We're here tonight in Foxboro, Massachusetts . . ." But he couldn't get past the word *Massachusetts*. No matter how slowly he tried to say it, it kept coming out "Masschusis," or "Mattashusis." This went on for thirty to forty takes. Finally a crew member suggested that Frank just say "Foxboro, Mass." But Gifford would have none of that. He kept at it until he got it right.

Though Gifford came to believe he was capable of any assignment, whenever he was designated to narrate the halftime highlights in Cosell's absence, the crew members would be overcome by a feeling of "here we go again"—and again and again and again. They started yet another Gifford pool, this one for the closest guess to the number of takes Gifford would drag everyone through before the highlights were backed with an acceptable narration. Forte, driven batty by Frank's mistakes, would rage at the p.a.'s, warning them not to be heard giggling or making derisive remarks for fear it would upset Gifford and extend the session even longer. He threatened them with grievous bodily injury if Frank got wind of the retakes pool.

Forte entered the pool himself, of course. He just didn't want Gifford unduly distracted.

The winning entry was usually somewhere between forty and fifty takes.

By the early 1980s, Howard Cosell was starting to feel like he had created his own Frankenstein.

Or, as he confessed before the start of the 1980 season, "[there is] a certain moral ambiguity about what I do."

The problem was obvious. Cosell could—and did—boast that without him _Monday Night Football_ would have been just another game. His unique ability to inject drama, pathos, comedy, and controversy turned the football game into a weekly television event. His work had helped to exalt sports; his presence at an event signaled its importance.

Yet Cosell, after touting his accomplishments, would in the next breath declare that sports had been elevated to a position of inflated importance in America. He was tired of explaining how to isolate a running back on a linebacker, he would tell the world—from the students in his seminar at Yale to any sports-writer who dared to solicit his opinion on a pedestrian sports matter.

He was so conflicted that it was becoming next to impossible for him to do what had made him famous, what he did best— be Howard Cosell, full of equal parts of righteous anger and fun. The anger had taken over completely.

Cosell told one reporter: "Do you think I actually _like_ doing this? You think I actually look forward to another year of _Monday Night Football_? Another year in the booth with Dandy Don and Faultless Frank? You think I actually take any of this seriously?"

It was the plaintive cry of a man protesting too much. The truth was that a part of Cosell certainly _did_ look forward to another season in the booth. That's why his endless threats to quit the show always rang hollow. Cosell clearly thrived on the recognition that _Monday Night Football_ had brought him. Where else was he going to get that level of fame? Where else could he find so enormous an audience for the sound of his voice?

The fame made Cosell's blood pump faster; he reveled in the effect he had on people; he loved to show off. Those who saw him in action could tell dozens of stories about Cosell getting a kick out of just being Cosell.

One famous incident took place in 1981, when Cosell and Al Michaels, his young play-by-play partner on baseball games, were in Kansas City. After dining together, they were riding back to their hotel in a limo when they found themselves in a rundown neighborhood on the fringe of downtown. A young woman named Peggy, their regular Kansas City driver, was behind the wheel.

Cosell was puffing contently on a large cigar when he turned and spotted something out the window. "Drive over there!" he commanded the driver, pointing left. She abruptly turned the car in that direction.

As Michaels looked out the window, he saw two strapping, menacing-looking black men, about seventeen to twenty years old, engaged in what looked like a half-joking, half-serious fistfight on the corner. The car pulled up toward them and Cosell barked out: "Stop this car!"

The driver did as ordered, though she looked back at Michaels and Cosell in distress. Cosell never saw her. He had the door open and was bounding out, waving his arms as he dashed toward the scene.

Michaels watched in horror, wondering if he was about to witness the end of Howard Cosell. He had already made up his mind—any sign of trouble and he was ordering the car to take off, Cosell or no Cosell. Michaels couldn't see risking his neck over a bizarre incident like this.

The two guys had stopped in mid-swing as they saw the limo pull up. Now they seemed bewildered as this hulking figure in a yellow sports coat, with a cigar dangling from his lips, ambled toward them.

"Okay, okay," Cosell announced in his best play-by-play style. "You, young man, you obviously don't have a left hand; and *you*, my friend over here, you obviously do not have the stamina to continue. This fight is over *now*!"

The combatants were too astonished to speak. Then a glimmer of recognition swept over one's face. "Hey!" he yelled. "It Howodd Co-*sell*!"

Cosell shook hands with each, draped his arms briefly around their shoulders, and then waved them off to fight no more. He returned to the limo flushed with triumph.

"Drive on!" Cosell ordered as he flopped back into his seat.

As she took off, the limo driver turned to Cosell and said, "I can't believe what I've just seen."

Cosell, blowing out a mouthful of smoke, replied: "Peg! You've got to understand. I know *exactly* who I am!"

* * *

It may have been a product of the conflicts in his soul. It may have sprung from pure boredom with the sameness of his weekly assignments. Or it may have been because he knew the rules didn't apply to him.

Whatever the explanation, Cosell began to pour more vodkas for himself before and during games.

The booth assistants were under instructions to try to rein him in, but there was no way to deny Cosell if he really wanted something.

In Pittsburgh for Game Seven in 1981, Goodrich became concerned about Cosell's escalating belligerence during the game. He phoned the booth and told the runners, according to one who was there, to "cut him off the booze." The runners found the command ludicrous. They had supplied Cosell with the bottle. "How do you cut him off if he wants to get a drink for himself?" said one runner who worked the booth. "What do you do, go over and stop him?"

That night, the runner said he poured Cosell "about six drinks, vodka, straight up. . . . He was just obviously in the bag."

The telecast went so badly that the moment it ended the phone rang in the booth. It was Arledge.

No one heard Cosell say much of anything during the conversation.

For most of a decade, everyone on _Monday Night Football_ made fun of the brand of football produced by NBC and CBS. The announcers were dull, the camera work was uninspired, the attitude was suitably respectful.

That changed overnight at NBC in 1977 with the arrival of Don Ohlmeyer. He never produced his Olympics for NBC, but he did recast NBC Sports in ABC's image. Ohlmeyer brought his showman's instincts to the once-staid peacock network. The words _story line_ were seared into the brains of every producer, director, and announcer at NBC Sports.

Ohlmeyer appropriated Arledge's three-man-team concept for NBC's college-basketball coverage when he assigned Al McGuire and Billy Packer to work with play-by-play man Dick

Enberg. This time the three-men-in-a-booth act was widely praised.

His most inventive bit of gimmickery was also inspired by Arledge. Late in the 1980 NFL season, Ohlmeyer announced that NBC would telecast a game between the Dolphins and the Jets without any announcers. He instantly turned a meaningless game between two mediocre teams into a minor media sensation.

The presentation overwhelmed the game; eliminating the announcers gave viewers a reason to watch, just as adding a highly entertaining extra announcer had given them reason to watch on Mondays. Ohlmeyer miked the field for all the smacks and hits, ordered up special graphics, and brought a lot of curious viewers to NBC—and a lot of attention to Don Ohlmeyer.

Ohlmeyer also took the junk-sports craze, which he had popularized at ABC with *Battle of the Network Stars*, into prime time on NBC with a show called *Games People Play*. The games included belly-flop diving, tugs of war between overweight union members, hot-dog–eating contests, demolition derbies for taxicabs, valet-parking competitions, and, most memorably, barroom bouncers throwing stuntmen for distance and accuracy.

None of this was quite what Arledge had in mind when he talked about spanning the globe for the human drama of athletic competition.

The ABC revolution hit CBS in 1981 with the arrival of a new, aggressive executive producer for NFL coverage. He had been given a mandate for change; his name was Terry O'Neil. He was hired by the new president of CBS Sports, Van Gordon Sauter, who told him to "bring some of the ABC trade secrets along."

O'Neil did more than that. He brought an influx of ABC people, particularly the young production people he thought were neglected by the Old Guard at ABC. He also brought along his ABC-bred arrogance, which helped him to make a core of instant enemies at CBS Sports.

But O'Neil didn't care about making friends or enemies; he cared about making a reputation. CBS's football needed fixing; he thought the producers and directors were lazy. One director shocked him by flying in to do a playoff game the morning the game was to be played.

O'Neil was also shocked to find a major talent buried deep in the pecking order of CBS announcers. He resolved immediately to make John Madden his first star.

O'Neil's plan for CBS's NFL coverage was the one he had drafted for Monday nights. He dictated everything from camera placements to the requirement that his announcers meet with players and coaches before every game.

He also introduced the Telestrator, a graphic device that enabled an analyst to diagram a replay on the screen. O'Neil called it "the CBS chalkboard," and made it Madden's personal toy. Madden demonstrated his expansive football knowledge with it immediately, and soon was using it for gags as well, drawing lines all over the screen to accompany his sometimes zany commentary.

As Ohlmeyer and O'Neil went head-to-head in their efforts to out-ABC ABC at the other two networks, the excess that had always been a side effect of Arledge's quest for innovation began to take over sports television. O'Neil's profligate spending peaked at the Super Bowl in 1982. He spent two million dollars to produce the game, using equipment valued at ten million dollars. The event was documented by a record twenty-three cameras.

To Gene Klein, the owner of the San Diego Chargers and a member of the NFL's television committee, selling football to the networks was like "selling candy to a baby." The networks craved pro football so desperately, Klein thought, that they had no choice but to pay the prices set by the NFL. "What are they going to do," he'd say, "buy bowling?"

Klein had invited Pete Rozelle and Art Modell out to his home in Rancho Santa Fe, California, after the Super Bowl in 1982 to figure out how much money to seek from the networks. They tossed around some breathtaking numbers—$2 billion, maybe $2.5 billion, over the next five years.

While Rozelle was a skilled negotiator, he was also coming to the networks at a perfect time. The 1981 season had been the best ever for the NFL on television, as CBS and ABC set ratings records. CBS's Super Bowl in 1982 between San Francisco and Cincinnati was seen by more people than any other sports event in television history. The NFL also knew that the networks had made record profits on football in 1981.

Rozelle began at ABC with a big lure: the Super Bowl. Over lunch at the ABC executive dining room, Rozelle told Roone Arledge and Fred Pierce that this contract, unlike the previous ones, would be a five-year deal so that ABC could join the Super Bowl rotation. The network's first Super Bowl would come after the 1984 season and climax a big year for ABC Sports. "I knew Roone," Rozelle said. "When I offered him, in the Olympic year, a chance at the Super Bowl, I knew that would pique his interest. That would create a tremendous year for them."

The price was tremendous too: $650 million for five years of *Monday Night Football* and the extra prime-time games, plus $17 million more for the Super Bowl. Pierce and Arledge were hesitant; although they had always come out ahead in the past, projecting the market for advertising that far into the future was risky. Despite their image as big spenders, Pierce said, they were not reckless.

"The image of 'damn the cost, full speed ahead' was a lot of bullshit," Pierce said. They played with the numbers for a few days, assuming the high inflation rate would continue. "While it was a lot of money at the time," Pierce said, "there was no doubt in my mind that we'd make money on the NFL." Arledge agreed, but they both wanted to persuade Rozelle to bring down his price.

The commissioner didn't budge. Eight days after their first lunch, Arledge and Pierce met again with Rozelle and made the deal. By then, they had secured Leonard Goldenson's support, since the contract needed the approval of ABC's board.

Rozelle moved on to NBC, which agreed without much argument to pay $590 million. But he ran into resistance at CBS. CBS executives told Rozelle that the NFL's asking price of $720 million was outrageous. "We thought the others were stupid," said Gene Jankowski, the president of the CBS Broadcast Group. "If there was any kind of economic downturn, we'd all be in big trouble with football."

That sent Rozelle back to Arledge. He was, he said, having trouble with CBS. There was even a chance that they might not make a deal. In that case, Rozelle wanted to know, how would

ABC feel about adding Sunday football to the *Monday Night* package?

Arledge said that that sounded terrific. This time, ABC was being used as the Rozelle hammer against CBS.

Two days later, on a Saturday afternoon at Rozelle's home in Westchester County, Jankowski and Neal Pilson, the president of CBS Sports, made their deal. They compromised on a $665-million price tag for the package, not including postseason games.

Jankowski had been swayed by the very real threat that the NFL would take pro football off CBS. ABC was in strong enough financial shape to expand to Sundays, he thought, "and Roone Arledge was ruling the roost in the sports world." Still, Jankowski felt that CBS had done well, shaving $55 million off the league's original demand.

When Rozelle delivered the package to NFL owners at their winter meetings in Phoenix, they were jubilant. They had reason to be. At the time, the average cost of running an NFL team was $11 million a year. The new $2.1-billion contract would pay each club about $14 million a year. So most owners were guaranteed a profit before they made a dime from ticket sales, parking, or concessions.

Some owners, Klein among them, had paid less than $14 million for their franchises.

As the owners celebrated, Madison Avenue was stunned. Media buyers called the rights fees outrageous. Others predicted advertiser defections.

The advertisers were already braced for price increases tied to the new contract, expecting the usual ripple effect. Now a tidal wave was building.

It would wash away all the old assumptions about how no one could lose money telecasting pro football.

10.

THE COACH
BOWS OUT

"I was utterly bored with the games, utterly bored with the players, utterly bored with the jockocracy. Utterly."—HOWARD COSELL

Howard Cosell stepped into a hotel elevator in Minneapolis, on his way to yet another production meeting, in preparation for yet another football game, early in yet another year of *Monday Night Football*. He no longer even pretended to find meaning in the exercise.

Leaning against the back wall of the elevator car, Tony Tortorici, a twenty-three-year-old production assistant who had just joined the crew, beamed as Cosell stepped in and the doors closed behind him. It was his first opportunity to speak to the legend.

"So, Howard," Tortorici piped up, his excitement all but bursting the buttons on his shirt, "what do you think about the game tonight?"

Cosell turned his head slowly toward him, the massive cigar in his mouth confronting Tortorici like the point of a saber, the chill of his reaction immediately apparent from his forbidding glare.

"Young man," Cosell snarled, his voice dripping with equal

parts disgust and contempt, "the Russians have shot down a Korean jetliner, taking hundreds of lives. Fighting is raging in the streets of Beirut. Death squads are terrorizing the innocent in El Salvador. The world is gripped by political crises. And you ask me about a *football* game. What does a football game mean against all of that?"

The elevator doors opened and Cosell lumbered out, leaving Tortorici stunned and speechless. All he wanted to say was, "Sorry I asked."

On the day before the opening game of the 1982 *Monday Night* season, Don Meredith was refusing to report for duty. With the game to be played in Dallas, Meredith's absence was bound to be noticed by the viewers.

He didn't care. His message to ABC was blunt: no contract, no work.

Meredith had been negotiating a new three-year contract with the network since February. On the Friday before the opener, Irwin Weiner thought they finally had everything wrapped up. ABC had put the details into a telegram and sent it to Meredith, who was supposed to fly to Dallas on Saturday.

First, Meredith said he didn't get the telegram. Then, he wanted changes in the contract. They were minor changes, involving his acting work and payments in the event that *Monday Night Football* was switched to cable—as if that was about to happen. Meredith said his lawyer would be in touch. On Sunday afternoon, Meredith was still sitting at home in Beverly Hills.

Weiner was on the road, driving his family to a wedding in New Jersey, but stopping frequently at gas stations along the way to call Meredith's lawyer. Weiner, Meredith, and the lawyer spent the whole day going back and forth on the telephone until they finally closed the deal on Sunday night.

Meredith needed to rush to Dallas. He had not done a game in months, so his preparation figured to be below even his own substandard level. He left right away—in a jet chartered by ABC.

Don Meredith did not go on strike in 1982, but the NFL players did—stopping the action for fifty-seven days and chopping the *Monday Night* season from twenty-one games to twelve.

For the ABC crew, the season peaked during Game Two, just hours before the strike was declared. With a couple of blackouts at Giants Stadium serving as an omen of the darkness about to descend on the season, Cosell and the production team had an outstanding night, coming through under duress with a performance reminiscent of their old-time flair.

Forced to fill two long interruptions in the game when the lights went out, Forte and Goodrich improvised resourcefully. They threw an expanded package of highlights into the breach, forcing Cosell to do a live narration. He pulled it off brilliantly, proving to some doubters on the scene that when he needed it, he could still summon up the old magic.

Meanwhile, Cosell the journalist threw himself into the coverage of the strike, interviewing representatives from both sides. Following the Dallas opener, an exciting game that had set another ratings record for season starters, Game Two provided evidence that the *Monday Night* crew members might be regaining their royal status.

But at the stroke of midnight the strike intervened, knocking them out of their glass slippers for nine long weeks.

ABC filled the gap with television movies, none of which played up to the ratings standards of *Monday Night Football*. The strike shattered the momentum of the record-setting 1981 season. Millions of fans who found their football turned off in 1982 felt no urgency to turn it on again when play resumed.

The timing could not have been worse for the networks. They were facing four more years of spiraling rights fees at a time when their business was growing tougher.

Cable television was emerging as a serious competitor for viewers' time and advertisers' dollars. Videocassette recorders were coming down in price, so more and more people could stay home and program their own evening's entertainment. Meanwhile, the end to years of steady double-digit inflation added to the woes on Broadcast Row.

Still, *Monday Night Football* made a healthy profit in 1982. Before the strike-interrupted season began, John Lazarus and his men in Sports sales had persuaded advertisers to absorb a 20 percent increase in the price of commercials—with a nudge from Fred Pierce and the help, once again, of their friends in the beer industry.

Anheuser-Busch, still determined to break Miller's lock on Monday nights, had hired a media buyer named Jerry Solomon, who had worked at ABC for nearly twenty years and was close to Pierce. The moment Solomon heard about the new NFL rights deal, he saw opportunity and brought a no-lose proposition to ABC.

At that time, Miller was spending about $12 million a year on *Monday Night* ads. Solomon proposed that the beer category be expanded to $18 million, with each brewer paying half and taking half the games. If Miller refused the split, he said, A-B would swallow the whole category.

Surprisingly, ABC's sales people resisted at first. "They had a tremendous allegiance to Miller, and they didn't want to hear about it," Solomon said. He went to Pierce, who told the sales staff to maximize their revenue, one way or the other. Miller agreed to the split; its six-year exclusive hold on *Monday Night Football* was over.

With thirty-second spots going for $150,000 in 1982, every category was splintered; no sponsor could afford exclusivity. Datsun, Chevrolet, and Buick shared the auto segment; even the new, fast-growing computer-games segment was split between Mattel and Atari. Lazarus was forced to include as many buyers as he could, so he could no longer charge anyone a premium for shutting out the competition. The best he could do was persuade buyers to sign two- or three-year deals, at prices that grew each year.

That approach helped as sales began for the 1983 season. Dismissing the strike year as an aberration, ABC's sales people used the lofty ratings of 1981 to set their prices and project their audience levels. But everyone knew they faced an ominous downside if the games underperformed.

Roone Arledge made one move that he hoped would regenerate interest. He dumped Fran Tarkenton, and replaced him with a star who was far more popular with football fans, television viewers, and the other men in the ABC booth.

Into the 1983 lineup, Arledge wrote a name that occupied a storied place in the NFL's past—and a place in the story of *Monday Night Football*'s past—O. J. Simpson.

*   *   *

O. J. Simpson always knew he would wind up on *Monday Night Football*. He had been a part of the favored crowd at ABC ever since Arledge took the unusual step of hiring him during his senior year at USC. Arledge knew a star when he saw one, and he knew Simpson's star shone just as brightly out of uniform.

Simpson electrified the nation as a collegian, running the ball with such power, speed, and abandon that he seemed to tower over the mortals on the field. He was a runaway winner of the Heisman Trophy in 1968.

He was also a spectacular physical specimen: a chocolate-brown Adonis. His physique belonged on a pedestal in front of a Greek temple. His face, dominated by two elevated, chiseled cheekbones, was strikingly handsome.

With his talent and his looks, Simpson could have been a daunting figure. Instead, he was a delightful one. O.J. was instantly, inescapably likable.

Born in 1947, he grew up poor in San Francisco. He was always a boy with a purpose, hustling tickets to 49er games or catching fish in the bay that he sold for a few dollars in the projects. He grew into a kid with a fullback's size and world-class sprinter's speed. His athletic ability, he knew, would be his escape route to a better life.

His name added to his aura—the initials stuck in the memory the first time the ability caught the eye. Surely he would have gained fame and fortune as Orenthal James, but it might have taken slightly longer than it did as "O.J." or "The Juice," nicknames he picked up in the black ghetto of Potrero Hill in San Francisco.

Simpson came out of USC in 1969 in a position of such singular power that he could have tested the NFL's draft system—and won. He certainly had the motivation; he wanted to play in Los Angeles or San Francisco. Instead, he was picked first by the Buffalo Bills, the NFL's worst team, which played in the league's smallest media market and in the city with the least appealing climate. Simpson considered trying to break the draft, but after landing the record-setting $600,000 contract he demanded, he agreed to play for Buffalo.

He became one of the greatest players in NFL history. In

1973, Simpson set his most illustrious record when he rushed for 2,003 yards, becoming the first man ever to break the 2,000-yard barrier. He set numerous other league records, including most rushing yards gained in a single game (273), most career 200-yard games (6), most consecutive 100-yard games (7), and most touchdowns in a season (23).

But Simpson performed in undeserved obscurity. The Bills did not play in a Monday night game until 1973, and when they did, he recalled, "we were sky-high. It was, like, we finally made it."

Simpson single-handedly carried Buffalo to respectability, but no further. The Bills made the playoffs only once with him, as a wild-card team in 1974, but they were eliminated in the first round by Pittsburgh. Surely O. J. Simpson is the greatest football player never to play in a championship game; he is arguably the greatest professional athlete never to make it into the ultimate contest of his sport.

Simpson had to settle for stardom on Monday nights, on the field and in the booth. He traveled with the *Monday Night* crew on their preseason publicity tour in 1970, frequently visited the booth, and briefly flirted with the idea of taking the analyst's job during his holdout in 1974. In the meantime, he was working events for ABC during the off-seasons, analyzing track and co-hosting a Sunday edition of *Wide World*. As his broadcasting career progressed, Cosell, who was always fond of The Juice, became his mentor. "Howard was one of my very best friends in broadcasting," Simpson said.

When he retired from football in 1979, after recurring knee injuries and a disappointing two-year stint with San Francisco, Simpson was no longer available to ABC. NBC had lured him away with a contract to produce and star in television movies— the kinds of entertainment guarantees Arledge could never match. By then, Simpson had starred in several theatrical films, including *The Towering Inferno*. He hoped for a major movie career.

He didn't find it at NBC. He made a high-profile television movie, *Goldie and the Boxer*, and did some sportscasting for his old ABC friend Don Ohlmeyer, who was then running NBC Sports. None of it had much impact. By the time Simpson's NBC deal expired in 1983, he had no reason to stay.

Fully aware that Simpson was a free agent, Arledge called

with a question: Would O.J. be interested in *Monday Night Football?*

For Simpson, it was more than a job offer—it was an opportunity he had been anticipating eagerly most of his professional life.

As the 1983 season began, another new talent arrived in the truck—a specialized computer called the Dubner that could generate high-tech graphics. ABC bought the Dubner, which was named for the company in New Jersey that developed it, to replace the existing Chyron graphics machine—and to do much, much more.

In the early years of *Monday Night Football*, the graphics had been absurdly primitive. Numbers and names were posted on a black screen in white letters, then held up in front of a camera by a p.a. wearing black gloves so that his hands wouldn't be seen.

The Chyron took graphics a step further, generating names, numbers, and statistics by computer. The Dubner, with its ability to create animation as well as elaborate lettering, ushered ABC into a new era of visual pyrotechnics.

Using the Dubner, ABC opened the show with an animated display of words and pictures that could spin and fly, pulling the viewer inside and through the three-dimensional letters of *Monday Night Football* to see an image on the other side. During the games, p.a.'s used the Dubner to create charts and bar graphs in all their multicolored glory. The Dubner was, in the words of Tortorici, who was one of the first p.a.'s to use it on Monday nights, "the Cadillac of graphics."

The show would soon have more information than ever along for the luxurious ride, thanks to the arrival of Steve Hirdt of the Elias Sports Bureau, the source of some of the most original statistical information on sports.

Over the years, *Monday Night Football* had pioneered numerous statistics. In the early 1980s, Robbie Cowen, a p.a., and Jerry Klein, the booth statistician, dreamed up the "turnover and result" graphic, showing what a team did after a turnover. Soon everyone covering football started using it.

Hirdt, who had contributed to ABC's baseball coverage since

1976, was persuaded by Forte to work *Monday Night Football* in 1982. Unlike the booth statistician, who simply kept track of game statistics, Hirdt massaged and manipulated his numbers to put them in context, always trying to relate the numbers to winning and losing. He also devised new stats that provided insight into teams and players.

After the frustrating strike season, Hirdt approached the announcers with new ways of looking at the reams of stats ground out by the NFL. He found them eager listeners, though Gifford seemed to think it was weird that someone could make his living fooling around with numbers. He took to calling Hirdt "Mr. Univac," which Hirdt found a little weird himself since that brand of computer had become an industry dinosaur.

Hirdt worked out formulas for measuring individual and team excellence that departed from such traditional yardsticks as 100-yard games by rushers and 300-yard games by passers. Instead, he tracked the correlation between yards gained and points scored—which teams used their yardage most effectively. The resulting stat, called "points per 100 yards," was complicated, but Cosell liked it and tried to explain it on the air.

As he grew more comfortable in the job, Hirdt also began to have fun with the personalities, working in offbeat breakdowns of their NFL careers. Once, on Gifford's birthday, he threw on a graphic of other famous people with that birthdate, including Madonna and Menachem Begin.

Hirdt's arrival and the coming of the Dubner proved that *Monday Night Football* was still trying to move forward, at least when it came to statistics and graphics. Those were areas where ABC's football coverage maintained a clear edge over the other networks. Those were also areas where changes could be made without stepping on the feelings of the show's entrenched personalities.

The opening game of 1983 was everything ABC wanted in a football game—and less.

The game, set in the din of RFK Stadium in Washington, was exciting, suspenseful, full of big plays and points. In the ABC blueprint for a comeback by *Monday Night Football*, no game could have fit the bill better. Dallas staged a stirring comeback of its own, rallying from a 23–3 halftime deficit to beat Washington, 31–30.

But no one on the ABC team could enjoy the excitement. By halftime, Cosell was engulfed by new controversy, perhaps the most distasteful one of his long career.

Late in the second quarter, Joe Theismann fired a pass to Alvin Garrett, one of the small, quick Redskin pass receivers being celebrated as the "Smurfs" by Washington writers. These Smurfs were black, not blue.

Garrett had been cut by two teams, but he was starring in Washington coach Joe Gibbs's passing offense. Cosell, who perked up when a game captured his interest, could not restrain his enthusiasm. He blurted out: "Gibbs wanted to get this kid and that little monkey gets loose, doesn't he?"

Cosell meant to praise Garrett, not degrade him, though obviously any reference to monkeys could carry the vilest sort of racist implications. Some people did interpret the remark as a racial slur, which proved two things: First, those people were unaware of Cosell's unassailable record on racial issues; and second, they would use any pretext to attack Howard Cosell.

In the truck, Goodrich and Forte heard Cosell characterize Garrett as a "little monkey." They thought nothing of it. But a short time later, Irv Brodsky, the head of publicity for ABC Sports, arrived at the truck with bad news: "The guys in the press box are all bullshit about what Howard said."

Goodrich didn't know what Brodsky was talking about. "What the hell did Howard say?"

"The 'little monkey' thing," Brodsky said. He explained that the AP wire in the press box had a story reporting that the Reverend Joseph Lowery of the Southern Christian Leadership Conference had fired off a telegram of protest to Cosell.

Goodrich barely remembered the remark. But he and Forte decided to tell Cosell what was going on. Goodrich hit the line into Cosell's earphones to tell him about the telegram from Lowery and that the press wanted a statement.

"I didn't say that," Cosell said, sounding more upset than angry.

"Yeah, I think you did, Howard," Goodrich said. "I wouldn't swear on a Bible, but I think I remember you saying it."

Cosell thought it was absurd. He denied making the remark.

Even if he had made it, he could not believe that anyone would construe it as racist.

Early in the second half, Cosell went on the air with his explanation: "According to the reporters, they were told I called Alvin Garrett a little monkey. Nothing of the sort and you fellows know it. No man respects Alvin Garrett more than I do. I talked about the man's ability to be so elusive despite the smallness of his size."

Gifford, always the man to stand tall by his teammates in a crisis, backed up Cosell. "I don't know who they were listening to," he said on the air. Off the air, he thought the furor was ridiculous, if typical of the clamor surrounding Cosell. Gifford had never been more estranged from Cosell, but he knew the man well enough to reach one unshakable conclusion—"One thing Howard is not, my God, is a racist."

Those who knew Cosell found it mind-boggling that Lowery, and all the newspaper writers who chose to run with the story, could accuse him of racism after Cosell's unflagging campaign on behalf of Muhammad Ali, his incessant hymn of praise for his "closest friend in life, Jackie Roosevelt Robinson," his support of Curt Flood's battle with the baseball establishment, and his calls for black managers in baseball and black coaches in football. Polls showed that among black viewers, Cosell was the most popular sports announcer in America.

Reverend Lowery evidently had another agenda. He used the controversy to make sweeping statements about the absence of blacks on TV sports crews. He even threatened to picket Monday night games if Cosell did not offer an apology.

Cosell still could not believe that he, of all people, would have to defend himself on a racial charge—but defend himself he did, with all the formidable energy and influential allies he could muster. He overreacted, entreating black friends such as tennis star Arthur Ashe, whom he called at six-thirty the next morning, to come to his defense.

He didn't suffer for defenders. Arledge issued the official ABC line, citing Cosell's "superlative and continuing record of promoting harmonious race relationships." Rachel Robinson, Jackie's widow, agreed to issue her own press release under the letterhead of the Jackie Robinson Foundation.

Even Garrett took his side. The Redskin receiver, told of the remark after the game, reacted by saying, "I think Cosell looks like a monkey." But, in an official statement issued by the team the next day, Garrett said, "Howard Cosell is just great. And I do not take exception to what he said about me on the broadcast last night. Matter of fact, I'm pleased he singled me out for such favorable attention."

Eventually, Cosell got the public support of leading black figures from Bill Cosby to Jesse Jackson.

But the incident cut Cosell to his marrow. He was weary of the battle. Alienated from his boothmates, at odds with the NFL, disillusioned with Arledge, Cosell's mood grew darker. As he looked ahead, he could see twenty more football games looming in the 1983 season.

A drowsy numbness pained his sense.

O. J. Simpson walked into the *Monday Night Football* booth ready to roll, party, and do it up right. He remembered the old days, the excitement when *Monday Night Football* hit town, the sense that the whole sports world was watching—jealously.

But as soon as he took a look around in 1983, he realized that those days were gone. "The bud was off the flower," Simpson said.

The problem wasn't just Cosell. What Simpson detected from everyone was that the all-time high-times television sports vehicle had turned into a commuter train—people climbed aboard cheerlessly and went to work.

This wasn't what Simpson expected. It was starting to look like a job, and even if he was going to be well paid, O.J. wanted to have some fun, not simply work at a job.

He had been told nothing by the ABC Sports hierarchy—nothing about the shadow that Cosell's black moods cast over the series, nothing about the bitterness between Cosell and Gifford, nothing about Meredith's disaffection.

What negatives Simpson had heard he put down to the usual grumbling about Cosell. Simpson never worried about that; he knew he had a special relationship with the coach. Whenever he came into New York he would call the Cosells. They would all go to dinner. Simpson had celebrated Howard and Emmy's thirty-fifth wedding anniversary with them. He expected the friendship to carry over into the booth.

For a time it did. Cosell was the only member of the ABC team to help Simpson during his early games. There were no practice sessions for O.J. The production team assumed that, with all his media experience, he could step right in.

He couldn't. The format threw him at first. Gifford would have his say, Cosell would have his say, and Simpson was left to try to squeeze something in edgewise. For a while, he depended on Cosell to lead him in. That got him through some of his early worries about when to talk.

But Simpson had another, more basic problem. He was having difficulty getting his sentences out coherently. Cosell advised him to slow down his thoughts, to concentrate on making one point at a time, but he continued to stumble.

Simpson worked on his delivery. His agent, Ed Hookstratten, lined him up with a speech therapist in Los Angeles who analyzed a tape of his work every Tuesday. Simpson practiced diligently.

Hookstratten thought the problem stemmed from the pressures of live performance. "When the red light went on, he was back on the streets of San Francisco as a kid, rather than being the polished person he is," he said.

Still, Simpson had that winning personality. He got some complimentary reviews, headed by a column in *Sports Illustrated* in which Bill Taaffe, the TV-sports reporter, called him the cheerful note in an otherwise dismal 1983 season. Taaffe said O.J. came across as "warm, sincere and enthusiastic," projecting "an intensity and radiance that help compensate for his lack of language skill."

Taaffe also managed to compare Simpson's presence favorably with Cosell's; he suggested that Cosell would not be missed if he disappeared.

It was one of several columns Cosell saw—and fumed over—that both praised Simpson and denigrated his own work. Cosell was irked even more when Simpson said publicly that he had to instruct Howard on the nuances of football.

Simpson had been saying the same thing for years. It was his standard method of kidding his pal. "Howard is helping me with my diction, and I'm helping him with his knowledge of the game, because Howard doesn't know what the hell is going on," O.J. would say.

But Simpson didn't realize how the years in the media shooting gallery had left Cosell's notoriously thin skin full of holes.

When *Monday Night Football* arrived in Buffalo in the fifth week of the season, Cosell was feeling more hostility toward Simpson than he had ever felt before. This was to be a showcase for O.J., his homecoming as a television star to the town where he had starred as a player. Not that Simpson was all that thrilled to be back in Buffalo—he checked into the hotel and asked for a "room without a view."

Buffalo did make a fuss over its most celebrated football alumnus. At a luncheon on the day of the game, Simpson was the star attraction. Naturally, the talk got around to Cosell, so Simpson used his old line about giving Howard some lessons in the game. He also detailed his affection for Cosell. But the press—and Cosell—took note only of the barbs.

The game matched the Bills with the Jets, another of Cosell's least favorite teams. He thought Joe Walton, their coach, was incompetent. The franchise had secured a place in his hall of infamy by announcing plans to abandon New York and follow the Giants to the New Jersey Meadowlands.

As the game began, Cosell had the Jets in his sights and was firing at will. He got so hostile during one commercial break that Gifford felt he had to remind Cosell that his comments about Walton, supposedly off the air, were still going out over satellite and might be picked up and reported in print. Cosell, as usual, had no use for anything Gifford tried to tell him.

The Jets led, 7–0, in the second quarter. Cosell assessed the situation and said: "If the Bills can get anything going, they'll be right back in this thing."

Simpson, still looking for spots to kid good-naturedly with the coach, couldn't let this one go by. "Howard," he said, "you've proved once again you have a tremendous grasp of the obvious—to use one of your lines."

"Fine! Okay," Cosell snapped back, on the air, while leveling a look at Simpson that made him flinch. Simpson instantly felt a wall of ice go up between him and Cosell. They hardly spoke the rest of the night, but Simpson was sure he could smooth things over in time.

Cosell missed the next two games to do the World Series, so Simpson filled in. Early the following week, with the crew set to go to Dallas for a Sunday night game, Simpson got the word that he had been assigned to replace Cosell on that game as well. He also heard a rumor that it might not be the only game Cosell would miss. The word was Cosell might not be coming back at all.

Simpson was shocked—though only by the suddenness of the news. Cosell had been muttering all season about not being long for *Monday Night Football.* Simpson believed him, but thought he'd probably work at least through ABC's first Super Bowl, in January 1985.

Simpson was genuinely concerned, both for the show and for the man he still considered his closest friend at ABC. He decided to put himself on the line, to try to give Howard a pep talk.

Simpson called Cosell at his apartment. The pep talk didn't get far.

Simpson tried to tell Cosell he couldn't quit because the show would be nothing without him. Cosell cut him off. He described his dismay at the things O.J. had been saying about him in print, the knocks about his lack of knowledge of the game. Simpson tried to explain the comments, saying that they had been taken out of context and that they were just what he always said about Howard in an affectionate, kidding way.

Cosell didn't buy any of it. He was brusque and cold. He told Simpson acidly that he wasn't his friend anymore.

Simpson was rocked, and deeply hurt. He wound up talking to Emmy, who spoke to him briefly before hanging up. Simpson called back, tried to explain, and professed his friendship again. Cosell, now more depressed than angry, got on again and only told him they would have to talk another time.

It was an intensely emotional conversation. A sensitive, surprisingly vulnerable man, Simpson hung up in anguish. He felt as if he had been through a terrible fight within his own family.

Howard Cosell, in the autumn of his discontent, was in a state of virtual professional isolation. He was disgusted with the NFL. He was thoroughly fed up with Gifford and Meredith. He was distant from old friends Forte and Simpson. And some of the scorn he felt for his colleagues was getting personal.

When Cosell's spirits sagged during *Monday Night*'s first year, Pete Rozelle was a reassuring presence. Now the two men were barely speaking. In Cosell's eyes, the NFL—greedy, arrogant, openly defiant of the public interest—had become his own version of the evil empire, the symbol of all that was wrong with American sports. "Howard really honestly felt that we should dedicate three and a half hours on Monday nights to the ills of the NFL," said John Martin, an ABC Sports executive.

Cosell and Rozelle parted ways irrevocably over the issue of Al Davis and his legal challenge to the NFL, which tried to block him from moving his Oakland Raiders to Los Angeles. The former Brooklyn lawyer explained his support for Davis strictly as a matter of law—the NFL, by telling Davis that he could not move his team without the support of three fourths of the owners, was engaged in a clear restraint of trade.

Rozelle and most of the owners interpreted Cosell's vigorous defense of Davis as a direct assault on the league whose games had made him famous. They accused him of playing favorites because of his close friendship with Davis. And they called him a hypocrite, pointing to his violent opposition to previous moves by sports franchises.

Cosell was also downgrading the NFL's product. He had no compunction about declaring a game a farce before the ball had even been kicked off. In 1983, Cosell dismissed a matchup between the Rams and the Falcons from the beginning as such a mockery, such a mismatch, that an NFL official watching that night wondered why Cosell did not just urge the viewers to change channels. (Cosell had pegged the game right—the Rams routed the Falcons, 36–13.)

Cosell's belittling of the product reached a point where NFL officials called Arledge, who was sympathetic to them. Arledge had never wanted Cosell to shill for the NFL house, but he did not want him to be a plague on the NFL house, either. "You don't have to come on and plead with people not to watch," Arledge said. "There's a difference between being honest and being destructive."

In the booth, Cosell's affability with Gifford and Meredith was entirely phony. They were saying things at each other, not to each other. Cosell knew the interplay was a charade.

He was convinced that Gifford and Meredith were still plotting against him. He focused on a suggestion they made several times that Cosell might be better off working out of the studio in New York if he so hated going on the road: Proof, Cosell concluded, that they were out to get him.

His paranoia was reined in by Emmy. Her presence made him feel more secure. When Howard would fly into one of his wilder rants, she would interrupt with a dose of reality, urging him to try to be reasonable. Everyone noticed the difference she made. "When Howard was with Emmy, he was fine," Gifford said. "But when he was alone, he was a bastard."

Cosell unchained saw enemies everywhere. Even the warm smile of O. J. Simpson had started to sprout fangs. And when he looked at Forte, he no longer saw his oldest buddy at ABC Sports.

Professionally, they had drifted apart. Cosell was devoting more of his energies to *SportsBeat*, the obscure but award-winning magazine show that he proclaimed as his legacy. Forte, the consummate live director, was not part of that news- and issue-oriented program. Cosell and Forte had once traveled the world together, playing gin rummy and hurling boisterous insults at each other. Now they rarely shared good times.

Cosell, the doting father and grandfather, could no longer abide Forte's unrestrained sexual appetite. Cosell had been the best man at Forte's wedding. Now he was unamused by Chet's flirting with the stunning young women who turned up on the *Monday Night* scene.

One Monday night, Forte was followed to Philadelphia by a statuesque blonde acquaintance. He set her up in the stadium for a honey shot. When he put the camera on her, she noticed it—having been through the routine before—and distinctly mouthed the words "Hi, Chet!" as the lens caught her in close-up. In the truck Forte almost leaped out of his skin: "Get her the fuck off the air!" he screamed. "My wife is watching!"

So was Cosell.

Cosell also took to grumbling in private about other colleagues who, he said, cheated on their wives.

Although he was fond of Simpson, he would sometimes, disapprovingly, label him a womanizer.

The case of Gifford was more complicated. Cosell often described Gifford's first wife, Maxine, as a lovely girl whom he and Emmy adored. He found it hard to accept Gifford's decision to leave her after she was stricken with multiple sclerosis. Emmy would tell him that Frank had agonized for years over Maxine's problems, and that those years had included some painful moments for Frank as well.

When Gifford subsequently married Astrid, Howard and Emmy established a warm relationship with her—so much so that she eventually sought Emmy's counsel when her marriage to Frank started to sour. Cosell found the whole business increasingly distasteful.

He had more reason than ever to quit. The "little monkey" debacle was fresh in his mind. So was the episode with Simpson in Buffalo. Emmy too was tired—tired of the tensions, the travel, and the tirades against her husband in the press.

Late in October, Cosell called Arledge. They went to lunch. The message was clear—Cosell wanted out.

For the first time, Arledge and the rest of the people at ABC Sports had begun to believe he meant it.

If Cosell had had enough of *Monday Night Football*, others had had more than enough of him.

Despite what Cosell thought, Gifford and Meredith were not out to get him. They were out to get away from him. They had no desire to play the heavies in the shows produced and directed by Cosell in hotel lobbies across America.

Al Michaels, Cosell's baseball partner, who once enjoyed a cordial relationship with him, now found it impossible to work with him. "It got to the point where he was sapping and sucking all the joy out of the job," Michaels said. "He was disgusted with everything. He didn't like working with the guys. He didn't like the whole sports syndrome. He just complained constantly. Everything was wrong. The weather stunk, everything stunk. He never wanted to be anywhere. He didn't want to go to the baseball game, the football game. He didn't want to be doing this next week. He didn't want to be in this hotel. He didn't want to be in this car."

Cosell, by this time, "had something terrible to say about everybody, every day," a senior ABC executive said. When he tried to figure out what was wrong, all he could come up with was "immaturity." Cosell turned sixty-five in 1983—by this point he was acknowledging his true age—but too many people at ABC had seen him act like a child on too many occasions.

Some of the amateur psychoanalysis went deeper than that. Gene Klein, an NFL owner who came to detest Cosell, said, "Howard is a hater. Certain people hate everything. Talk to any psychiatrist, and they tell you the person he really hates is himself."

For all the success, wealth, and acclaim he had attained, for all the bravado and bluster about his greatness, Cosell felt unfulfilled. He announced to the world that he had defeated all his enemies, conquered every obstacle, survived "on the precipice of professional peril every day of [his] life." But he was exhausted by the fight; his mood was perpetually gloomy, his soul apparently, inexplicably, tortured.

"There's no question that the magic was gone and Howard was a liability," said John Martin. "That was a view that was shared, mostly because Howard didn't want to do what he was best at, become that lightning rod. He became a very unhappy man."

Like many others who had been close to him, Martin hated to watch the decline of Cosell. "He had everything. Brilliance, articulation, happiest family man in the world, all the money. And still, there was some kind of insecurity, that paranoia that seemed to grip him. It was all beneath him and yet it wasn't; it engulfed him. There was a dichotomy going on that was really unbelievable. It was depressing to see it happen."

Howard Cosell had quit *Monday Night Football* more times than anyone at ABC could count. He'd quit after the first preseason; he'd quit after the first torrent of press criticism; he'd quit after the first season with Gifford; he'd quit in the early seventies over Gifford and Meredith ganging up on him; he'd quit in the late seventies over Gifford and Meredith ganging up on him; he was going to quit when Dennis Lewin was on the scene; he was going to quit when Terry O'Neil was on the scene; he had walked out of booths all over the National Football League during games; he'd quit to Forte, Ohlmeyer, Martin, Pierce, and Goldenson. Mostly, of course, he'd quit to Arledge.

Arledge had taken the spin around the floor with Cosell so many times that when they went to lunch after the World Series, he knew all the steps by heart. "Roone," Cosell said, "I'm not gonna take another day of this. I'll never walk into that booth again."

Arledge responded by quietly telling Cosell that he just needed to relax, maybe take some time off. It worked, if only temporarily. After a three-week hiatus, Cosell returned to the booth.

But Arledge left that lunch more convinced than ever that Cosell intended to walk away.

This time, Arledge was inclined to let him go.

For starters, Arledge thought Cosell's flailing against the sports establishment was more neurotic than noble. "Howard had become crazed about the NFL and Rozelle and Al Davis and the rest of it," Arledge said.

Arledge was also having a harder time than ever putting up with Cosell's downside—the gratuitous insults about Gifford, the drinking on the air that would never be tolerated in a lesser performer, and, perhaps most disturbing, Cosell's tendency to complain to Arledge's superiors. Cosell, Arledge thought, was circumventing his authority.

Arledge would cringe whenever he heard that Cosell had been running around the company talking to Fred Pierce or Leonard Goldenson. He felt he had stood behind Cosell, at his most principled and his most petty. He had turned away countless calls for Cosell's scalp, including some from within ABC management.

Whenever Cosell professed his undying loyalty to Goldenson, who, he said in public, was like a father to him, Arledge gritted his teeth. He remembered the calls years before from Goldenson, suggesting that maybe Arledge had made a mistake in putting Cosell on *Monday Night Football.* If credit for Cosell's survival was being handed out, Arledge sure as hell did not believe that Leonard Goldenson should be standing at the front of the line.

Arledge felt Cosell would never understand how often and how passionately he had backed him. Nor was he disposed by then to try to explain it to Cosell. The gulf between the two men had become so deep that explanations were impossible.

Yet Cosell never stopped pleading for Arledge's attention and approval. When Arledge responded, Cosell felt gratified— and yet he wondered whether he was just being manipulated as part of an elaborate scheme. Like some others who worked for the dynamic yet enigmatic Arledge, Cosell had come to think of him as Machiavellian.

Cosell appreciated what Arledge had done for him in Sports, but he felt cheated of the opportunity to share in the legitimacy that Arledge had earned in News. He still wanted to be an anchorman for ABC News.

Several months earlier, Cosell had sent Arledge a message, via an article by Tom Shales in *The Washington Post*—"If Roone wants to make 'World News Tonight' work, let him call me up and I'll anchor it."

Arledge didn't make that call. He didn't make any calls to Cosell as 1983 wound down.

Monday Night Football staggered into December with the ratings down by almost 20 percent from the last full season.

On the last weekend of the season, Cosell worked a Friday night game in Miami. The Dolphins crushed the Jets, 34–14, and he got some last licks in on Joe Walton.

No one knew—not even Cosell—that it was the last football game he would ever work for ABC.

Going into 1984, ABC faced the most awesome mountain of television production any network had ever attempted to scale, and Arledge would be leading the ascent.

He was scheduled to supervise a 250-hour sports double feature, the Winter and Summer Olympics. That was only the start. Arledge also had to oversee ABC News's coverage of the two political conventions that summer and the presidential election in the fall. Finally, he would produce ABC's first Super Bowl in January 1985, and, the next day, run the network's coverage of the presidential inauguration.

Seven years after taking over ABC News, Arledge commanded a television empire of unprecedented sweep and influence. He no longer worried about being taken seriously—not after bringing respectability to ABC News and creating such breakthrough programs as *Nightline*. He socialized with the power elite, counting among his friends the likes of Ethel Kennedy, Felix Rohatyn, Helen Gurley Brown, George Shultz, Swifty Lazar, and Henry Kissinger. Wheeling through Manhattan in his chauffeured Jaguar, he was a figure of unquestioned stature.

Under ordinary circumstances, Arledge would have relished

the challenges that faced him in 1984. But he began the year miserable and debilitated. He was separated from his second wife, Ann, after trying desperately to reconcile their differences. The breakup left him uncharacteristically depressed—and lonely. He was still in love with her.

Arledge was also ill with a thyroid condition. He looked terrible. He lost weight—more than he ever wanted to—and his usual healthy, ruddy glow disappeared for a time.

The first big event on Arledge's calendar, the Winter Olympics in Sarajevo, Yugoslavia, was a near disaster. Bad weather and poor early performances by American athletes sent the ratings into a tailspin. They recovered, but back in New York, one man seemed to be thoroughly enjoying Arledge's predicament—Howard Cosell. Word got back to Arledge that Cosell was delighted every time ABC stumbled.

Through the early months of 1984, Cosell went on with *SportsBeat* and planned his work in the Summer Games, where he was to cover boxing single-handedly. He was willing to cover amateur boxing, though in 1982 he had publicly and dramatically sworn off working any more professional fights.

In Los Angeles, Arledge choreographed his most spectacular sports extravaganza, providing his hands-on touch from his seat of authority in the ABC control center. The L.A. Games were another artistic and financial triumph for ABC.

Throughout the seventeen-day Olympiad, Arledge avoided direct contact with Cosell, dealing with him through the producer at the venue. After the Games, Arledge went straight on to Dallas for the Republican convention.

Cosell took a week off, then went to a meeting with Goldenson, where he told the chairman that he was going through with his plans to quit *Monday Night Football*. This time Goldenson did not try to dissuade him. They agreed that Cosell would continue to work other events at ABC, such as the World Series and the Kentucky Derby.

By this point, rumors of Cosell's retreat from the *Monday Night Football* wars were widespread. The situation seemed to be in limbo, with everyone waiting to see if Cosell would really go through with it this time and if Arledge would allow him to go.

The press then had a part to play, as it so often did with Cosell. When Larry Stewart, a reporter for the *Los Angeles Times*, called him about the rumors, Cosell, thinking ABC had made the news official, confirmed the story. The report the next day forced everyone's hand.

Arledge was furious. He felt Cosell had foreclosed his options; he felt his authority had again been circumvented.

Cosell thought that was ridiculous; he had made his intentions known ten times over, but Arledge had refused to act.

Their relationship, once so close, had become so twisted around their Olympian egos that they could no longer communicate at all.

To the very last moment, Cosell had been waiting for a call delivering a last-minute reprieve.

Arledge could not bring himself to pick up the phone. So he did nothing. He simply let the most wrenching termination of his career take its natural course.

As ABC Sports had geared up for the Summer Olympics, Ned Simon desperately needed a decision from his bosses—if only he could find a boss willing to make a decision.

Simon had been assigned to produce water polo, but he knew next to nothing about the sport. He wanted to go to Budapest for the world championships, where Olympic teams would be competing. He tried to get approval for the trip by going through what he thought were the right channels, but at ABC Sports in the early 1980s, there were no channels, right or otherwise. Simon was bumped from one executive to another, without getting an answer. He went so far as to track down Chuck Howard at the U.S. Open golf tournament at Winged Foot, but Howard said he was too busy to deal with the request.

Simon went to Hungary anyway. He paid for his plane fare out of his own pocket and shared a room with Tim Brandt, the water-polo announcer, who had permission to go. Simon was not trying to be a martyr; he just didn't want to get to Los Angeles and make a fool of himself.

Robbie Cowen, one of his friends in production, could not believe that ABC Sports was so unmanaged that Simon had had to pay his own way to Hungary. So, after Simon got back, Cowen circulated an unsigned memo about the incident through the department, all the way up to Arledge. Simon got reimbursed.

Simon's experience was one small sign of the rudderless state of ABC Sports, even as its executives made plans for the most colossal production in television history.

Arledge's absentee leadership had paralyzed and divided the Sports division. Decisions were put off and sometimes passed over. And the infighting among Arledge's deputies took on the flavor of Shakespearean drama, with every duke, count, and lord scheming to capture the throne, all to the detriment of the best interests of the kingdom.

Arledge himself deserved much of the blame. Though he was consumed by News, he could not cut the cord to Sports. It was a failing recognized even by his staunchest supporters at ABC. "He had diffused the responsibilities," Fred Pierce said. "There was a lack of clear-cut responsibilities."

Jim Spence, the senior vice-president and principal spokesman for the division, thought he was the heir apparent. But inside ABC, Spence could not exercise leadership; he was widely regarded as a visionless functionary, installed by Arledge to do the scut work.

Spence did his job and, for the most part, he did it well. He knew the talent contracts and rights deals inside and out. He was the detail man that Arledge could never be. Arledge respected his abilities and appreciated his loyalty—but limited his authority to administration and kept him away from production.

So Spence stayed in the hierarchy, though no one—other than Spence himself—ever believed Arledge could countenance him as a successor.

Instead, Arledge favored John Martin, a younger executive who had come up through the production ranks to become an Arledge protégé. He was below Spence in the organization chart and kept a low profile outside the company. But insiders knew that Martin, who was suave and smooth, unlike the blunt, often abrasive Spence, was the one who had Arledge's ear.

Martin himself knew it: "I really was on a dotted line to Roone on most of the production and programming aspects. I went directly to Roone on everything and caused all sorts of havoc by doing it."

Late in 1983, Arledge decided to act. He offered Martin the presidency of ABC Sports. But there was a catch: Arledge intended to retain ultimate say over Sports with a "group president" title. Still he pleaded with Martin to take the job. But his timing failed him. While Arledge had procrastinated, a protégé from the past, Don Ohlmeyer, had built his own television empire.

In 1982, Ohlmeyer merged his fledgling company, Ohlmeyer Communications, with Nabisco, creating a multimedia conglomerate that produced sports events, made television movies, bought commercial time, and did whatever else caught Ohlmeyer's fancy. He wanted to base himself in Los Angeles, but he needed a top executive to run the operation from New York; he also needed a solid number-two man for the company.

Ohlmeyer went after John Martin. Martin was going to be the second guy in either company, but Ohlmeyer had a piece of his to offer. Martin, citing "an offer [he] couldn't refuse," turned down a chance to be president of ABC Sports in favor of a chance to be president of Ohlmeyer Communications.

Arledge's next candidate came from outside ABC. It didn't matter that he'd never worked in television, that he had run nothing more sizable or influential than his own travel company for most of his professional life. From what Arledge saw of his organizational abilities as chairman of the Los Angeles Olympic Organizing Committee, he became convinced that Peter Ueberroth could run ABC Sports.

Arledge approached Ueberroth before the games in L.A. and asked straight out if he would be interested in being president of ABC Sports. Ueberroth seemed interested, so Arledge set up a meeting to offer him the job.

But again the timing was bad. Ueberroth was talking to Major League Baseball about becoming the commissioner. Arledge advised him to make a long list of demands that Arledge was sure the baseball owners would never agree to.

To Arledge's astonishment, they did agree to them. ABC Sports lost another presidential candidate.

Arledge looked around for someone else he felt he could trust. He decided to offer the job to his closest assistant—and friend—at ABC News, the division vice-president, David Burke. Burke also had no experience in sports television. He had worked in politics for the Kennedy family and former New York governor Hugh Carey. Then he worked on Wall Street. His strongest connection to sports was as a fervent, long-suffering fan of the Boston Red Sox.

But Arledge had a high regard for Burke's judgment and his leadership abilities, so he offered him the job as president of Sports. Burke was flattered and tempted. But he realized that he would be walking away from the number-two job in News under Arledge to take the number-two job in Sports under Arledge, and News appealed to him far more than Sports did. With some reluctance because of their close relationship, Burke said no to Arledge.

Arledge had run out of options. He had just one protégé left at ABC Sports, Jeff Ruhe. Ruhe, his former administrative assistant, had spent the year in Sarajevo and Los Angeles as coordinating producer of the Olympics.

Ruhe, a tall, handsome, classically mannered graduate of Stanford, fit right into Arledge's crowd. He married Courtney Kennedy, daughter of Robert and Ethel Kennedy. He was the second Arledge associate to be linked by marriage to Ethel Kennedy. Gifford's daughter, Vicki, had married Ethel's son Michael.

After the L.A. Games, Arledge wanted to move Ruhe back to New York, so that he would have a confidant at Sports when he wanted to avoid Spence. But Ruhe needed more seasoning before he could be considered for the president's job.

ABC Sports was still careening along with no driver behind the wheel.

11.

THROWN
FOR A LOSS

"It was no longer the Monday night show coming to town. It became a booth full of guys doing their job."—O. J. SIMPSON

In December 1984, Howard and Emmy Cosell sat down to dinner with Leonard Goldenson at a party at the elegant Four Seasons restaurant in Manhattan. As soon as they were served their soup, the ABC chairman confronted Cosell with a startling proposition.

"Howard," Goldenson said, "would you consider doing the Super Bowl for us?"

The suggestion could not help but swell Cosell's ego with delicious satisfaction. The 1984 *Monday Night* season had been a flop. The show lacked excitement. The ratings sagged. And even the critics had to admit that they missed Cosell.

Now the head of ABC, faced with the most important football telecast in the network's history, was acknowledging just how desperately Cosell was needed.

Goldenson elaborated. "I just don't want Simpson on the air any longer."

There it was—the admission that the man who had taken Cosell's place on *Monday Night Football* had proven to be an utter disappointment. It was impossible to replace Howard Cosell.

The chairman's offer stirred Cosell. He felt he owed a great debt to Goldenson, and he liked him enormously. To go back to the booth as a personal favor to Goldenson could be justified as a noble gesture. The lure of the biggest attraction in all of television was also undeniably powerful.

But Emmy was on the scene. The decision could not be made without her approval.

The Super Bowl held no attraction for Emmy Cosell. She knew the depth of Howard's animosity toward the pro-football establishment. She had to listen to him every day. Emmy told Goldenson they were through with the NFL.

"Emmy's right, Leonard," Cosell said, jumping in, the decision made for him. "I can't go back."

Then Cosell thought of something else. Besides, he added quickly, he could not be part of a move that would oust and embarrass Simpson, whom he still considered a friend, despite their emotional confrontation the previous year.

"I think you're being unfair," Cosell said gently. "You can't take the man off the air now, having gone all this time."

His mild endorsement of Simpson aside, Cosell felt compelled to unload on *Monday Night Football*. He ripped Arledge for having so much faith in his jocks, and for his wrongheaded confidence that the program could thrive without its one true star.

Goldenson, a small, fastidious man who had to look up to the looming Cosell, tried to defend Arledge. Arledge, he said, had always worried about how *Monday Night Football* would fare without Cosell. He couldn't convince Cosell.

All Cosell knew was that Arledge had never made the call to ask him to come back to *Monday Night Football*. To him, that amounted to rejection.

Cosell ate his meal with unbridled pleasure. He was in a buoyant mood all night. He left the restaurant with Emmy on his arm, feeling warm inside.

The Super Bowl was coming up and ABC knew that its coverage, no matter how elaborate and expensive, would be missing something terribly important.

Six months earlier, Roone Arledge had hoped that *Monday Night Football* would enjoy a whole new life without Howard Cosell. Frank Gifford and Don Meredith, who were still good friends, might flourish without the irritant of Cosell. O. J. Simpson was still new, but he was a star; he had great potential. There was, Arledge thought, no reason to panic. About the only problem demanding immediate attention was halftime. With Cosell gone, Arledge needed to find someone to do the highlights.

Gifford was not the answer. As oblivious as Arledge was to his friend's limitations as an announcer, and as distant as he had become from the day-to-day business of Sports, he knew it would be foolish to try to replace Cosell with Gifford. Gifford had plenty to do on the telecasts already; the last thing he needed was an additional burden that would subject him to unflattering comparisons with Cosell. This was not the time to risk damage to Gifford's tenuous self-confidence.

Of course, bringing in an outsider could also be viewed as a slap at Gifford.

Arledge did nothing for a while. He had been through his exhausting and stressful summer, with the Olympics, the political conventions, an operation to treat his thyroid condition, and a divorce. He had hoped to take a few days off in August. Instead he was required to attend what for him turned out to be a long, meaningless meeting of ABC executives on Amelia Island, off the coast of Florida, where it was hot, humid, and bug-infested. *Monday Night Football* was the least of his problems.

On August 29—five days before the first post-Cosell *Monday Night* telecast—producer Bob Goodrich, on behalf of Arledge, finally called Jim Lampley, a rising star at ABC Sports, to see if he might be interested in narrating the halftime highlights.

Lampley, then thirty-five, had enjoyed a charmed career at ABC. He was hired in 1974 after a national search for a college-age reporter to provide color from the sidelines of NCAA football telecasts. Boyishly handsome, clean-cut, and just off the campus of the University of North Carolina, Lampley was also bright, articulate, and ambitious. Eventually, he took on play-by-play assignments and anchored ABC's college-football scoreboard show. Arledge thought Lampley's work on the college-football show had been superb.

A *Monday Night* assignment could also be the plum that would help keep Lampley at ABC. His contract had two days to run when he heard from Goodrich. Terry O'Neil, still raiding his old shop, had offered him a job at CBS and wanted an answer soon.

Lampley was flattered, but less than enthusiastic about joining *Monday Night Football*. For one thing, he was surprised that the people in charge still wanted to do halftime highlights, which he felt had become passé. Most of Sunday's big plays had already been seen during CBS's and NBC's football coverage and on local news and sports shows on Sunday and Monday nights. Cosell made the highlights special because he was Cosell. Lampley wondered what he could do to make them work, though he didn't say anything at the time. With his contract in the balance, it seemed like the wrong time to express doubt.

What surprised Lampley even more was that the call from Goodrich had come so late. Everyone at ABC had known for weeks that Cosell was leaving. Now, just days before the first game, Arledge was finally getting around to deciding how to fill what amounted to nearly fifteen minutes of prime time on the most-watched series in sports television. ABC might consider halftime a plum, but Lampley thought it had become a step-child.

"It was astonishing to me," Lampley said, "that such a piece of time and such a valuable property would be treated so cavalierly. But it was a reflection of the fact that ABC Sports was, to some degree, an unmanaged entity in those days. Everything required Roone's attention, and Roone had no attention span."

Lampley decided to do the highlights. His agent thought the *Monday Night* assignment would enhance his value. It did. Lampley signed a new contract with ABC a few weeks later that paid him $700,000 a year.

If Lampley thought the highlights had become a stepchild, O. J. Simpson came to believe the whole show was being left unattended. For all the problems that he caused, Cosell had insisted—demanded—that his superiors pay attention to *Monday Night Football*. If they ignored Cosell, they did so at their peril. Now they could safely ignore the show.

"*Monday Night* was a neglected child," Simpson said. "It was left to fend for itself. No one was there to nurture it."

The season had begun with almost everyone in good spirits.

Gifford and Meredith were happy to be rid of Cosell, to be able to go about their work without having to listen to his droning litany of complaints. Most of the people on the telecast felt that, by the end, Cosell had become an intolerable burden. Lampley, the new arrival, said, "Everyone sort of relaxed and took a breath and said, 'Wow, it's over. Our long national nightmare is over.'"

Simpson was not so sure; he still considered Cosell a friend and mentor. As for Forte, he put the best face on things in public, telling one reporter that *Monday Night Football* "has a chance to last forever." In truth, he was apprehensive. Forte had always believed that Cosell made *Monday Night Football*. He was also unhappily aware of the shortcomings of the men remaining in the booth. Forte eventually concluded, "When Howard left, it really was the end, in a way, of *Monday Night Football*."

Cosell's absence was felt from the moment the show went on the air; his brilliant, high-intensity openings had set the stage for everything to follow. "He could make two eighty-five-year-old men playing marbles sound like the most exciting thing in the history of sports," Forte said. Now Gifford took over as the so-called host of the show, but even when the introduction was done on tape, he often had his usual trouble getting the words to come out right. Worse than that, he was unable to use his voice the way Cosell had to create excitement. The energy level of every show dropped even before kickoff.

Up in the booth, no one took command of the telecast. Gifford did his best, of course, but he was busy calling the game, getting in and out of commercials and promos, and keeping track of his names and numbers. He seemed looser at first, perhaps because he no longer had to worry about Cosell pouncing on his every mistake. But he was not able to lead Meredith and Simpson.

With Cosell gone, Meredith was expected by some outsiders to blossom into the show's most colorful personality. Instead, he floundered. He could no longer sit back and react to Cosell, so he just sat back. He was as lazy as ever, and he made almost no attempt to mask his indifference, showing up at production meetings wearing silly hats or crazy outfits. At Meredith's worst, one staffer said, "you could see how hungover he was. He didn't give a shit at all."

Once, Meredith brought in a blackboard with elaborate

fanfare. The crew expected some unprecedented X-and-O work out of Don. Instead, he spent the meeting chalking a lovely drawing of a rose.

Simpson missed Cosell more than anyone else did. Cosell had the ability to draw people out; Arledge said he could "make them better than they were." Before their falling-out in Buffalo and occasionally afterward, Cosell was unusually generous with The Juice, serving him up one softball question after another in an effort to let him shine. Afterward, they would have a couple of drinks and talk about the telecast. Now Simpson partied after the games with Lampley. They had a lot more fun, but Simpson's performance suffered.

Simpson also wanted everyone's role in the booth to be better defined, but he did not know where to turn for guidance. Forte was the strongest force on the show, he thought, but "Chet was not a fix-it person." Eventually, the announcers tried to work out some loose guidelines themselves; Meredith would comment on passing plays, O.J. on running plays. "But that was late in the year when we realized we weren't going anywhere," Simpson said.

Halftime also remained a problem. Lampley narrated the highlights from a studio in New York for five weeks until he was sent to the game sites by Arledge, who thought the telecast lost energy when it moved back to New York. When Goodrich suggested that he introduce the highlights from a camera position on the sidelines, Lampley rebelled. He wasn't thinking about the show, but about himself. "I've struggled for years to get away from the image of a young guy standing on the sidelines playing a subsidiary role," he told Goodrich. Goodrich agreed to let Lampley introduce the highlights from the booth.

Lampley was now openly opposed to building halftime around the highlights, suggesting instead a mix of sports news, features, and interviews. But Goodrich and Arledge both liked highlights, arguing that they had the distinct look of NFL Films and, in theory, a distinct narration on ABC. Lampley finally gave up, reasoning that his primary responsibility was to the college show. "It wasn't as if I had a ton of energy and time left over to fight this battle," he said.

No one seemed to have much energy or time for *Monday Night Football*. As long as the games were exciting, the telecast would be fine, but dull games inevitably produced dull television. For the first time ever, the appeal of _Monday Night Football_—ABC's most expensive and longest-running prime-time show—depended principally on the performance of the twenty-two men on the field wearing helmets and pads.

Forte's mantra—"I must've said it nine million times: We're in prime time, guys"—had been forgotten. As often as Forte would remind everyone that _Monday Night Football_ could not be just another telecast, that the games needed to be entertaining, that they needed, above all, to be different, even with all the cameras and technical wizardry and high-priced names in the booth, the telecasts were starting to look a lot like football on CBS and NBC. At the other networks, people thought ABC was looking worse.

Television critics and sportswriters agreed that the telecasts lacked spark. WITHOUT COSELL, IT'S NO SHOW, said a headline in _The New York Times_ after the season opener. Skip Bayless, a Dallas columnist, wrote, "It isn't the same without him. Now it's just another football game on Monday night."

In _Sports Illustrated_'s review, critic Taaffe called _Monday Night Football_ "just another NFL game in search of an identity." He described Gifford as "mistake-prone," Meredith as "not-so-funny-anymore," and Simpson as "unclear." With Cosell no longer available, Taaffe recommended that ABC go after John Madden.

The ratings also continued the slide that had begun in 1982. Cosell's absence was not the sole factor, but without him there was less reason to watch a lackluster game. A Sunday night game in mid-September between the Browns and the Broncos drew a shocking 9.5 rating—the smallest audience in the history of the series. The Dolphins-Bills matchup attracted a disappointing 14.9 the next night, and a week later a thrilling, high-scoring game between Oakland and San Diego did only slightly better, reaching 15.5. Now Madison Avenue, as well as ABC, was nervous.

Gifford, Meredith, and Simpson began to feel the pressure. "Those three guys were a little shell-shocked by the constant criticism and scrutiny," said a crew member. Goodrich kept thinking that the telecasts were improving, but he began to question his own judgment. "I thought the mix had potential for a long time," he said. "Toward the end of the season, I was wondering whether it was just me wanting it to work."

Even Gifford got testy. At a game in New Orleans in November, Lampley had arranged for ex-Raider quarterback Ken Stabler, who lived in the area, to come to the Superdome for a halftime interview. Gifford grabbed the interview for himself, telling Goodrich that he had covered Stabler for many years.

Later that season in Detroit, Simpson learned from what he called a "totally solid source" that the Lions were talking to Seattle's Chuck Knox about their head coaching job. Simpson broke the story on the air, but instead of giving him time to run with it, Gifford dismissed it as mere speculation. "Gifford almost reprimanded me on the air," Simpson said. "It was on and off the air, I'll bet you, in ten seconds." Gifford's intentions were good; he was worried that ABC could be embarrassed if O.J. was wrong. But the incident showed that communication in the booth had broken down, badly.

If there was one moment that encapsulated the entire season, it came in San Diego near the end of a dismal game in which the Seahawks were blowing away the Chargers, 24–0. Naturally, the hometown crowd was quiet. A decade earlier in Houston, a similar game had been the setting for Meredith's famous "Number 1" line, triggered by a fan's obscene gesture to the camera.

This time, during a commercial, Meredith and Simpson leaned their heads on each other and pretended to be falling asleep. Forte saw them and, laughing, said, "Hey, man, do that when we come back, do that when we come back."

When they came out of the commercial, there were the two announcers, apparently lost in a deep sleep.

About thirty seconds later, the phone rang in the truck. On the other end of the line was Arledge. He had been watching in New York, and he was extremely agitated.

"You don't make fun of the product," he snapped at Goodrich, "especially when the product is *Monday Night Football*. I don't care how bad the game is."

Coming from Arledge, that was practically an explosion. Arledge later delivered the same message directly to Simpson and Meredith.

Goodrich felt terrible. It was the only time in his years

as a producer that he had ever been the target of Arledge's anger.

Simpson said it was the first time, in all his dealings with Arledge, "that Roone had ever said a harsh word to me. So I was blown away. I was hurt."

Meredith didn't let it bother him.

Monday Night Football hit bottom on the night of October 8, 1984.

That evening at nine, NBC telecast a heavily promoted movie called *The Burning Bed,* starring Farrah Fawcett as a battered wife. The movie was an enormous success—attracting a 36.2 rating, making it the top-rated show in that week's Nielsens and the top-rated movie of the television season. No other program—not *The Godfather,* not *Gone With the Wind,* not Rhoda's nuptials, not *All in the Family* at its peak—had ever done so much damage to a *Monday Night* game.

That same night, CBS introduced a new situation comedy at nine called *Kate & Allie;* it soon developed into a hit show. Women now deserted the ABC games for *Kate & Allie* and CBS's *Cagney & Lacey,* shows with a feminist flavor that were perfect weapons to counter *Monday Night Football.*

On ABC, the Super Bowl–bound 49ers ran over the New York Giants, 37–10. ABC was run over too, as the game managed only a 14.6 rating, the lowest ever for a Monday night game.

The timing could not have been worse. The ratings for ABC's entire prime-time schedule came crashing down during the fall of 1984. After five consecutive years as a strong number two in the prime-time Nielsens to CBS, ABC plummeted to third. NBC, meanwhile, was on a roll.

Bill Cosby, who had been an early victim of *Monday Night Football* when his comedy-variety show on CBS was buried in 1972, was back on television with a spectacularly successful sitcom. Now Cosby, along with the rest of NBC's Thursday lineup, crushed ABC's occasional Thursday football games.

NBC's success spread to Mondays. The network scheduled female-oriented movies in the same vein as *The Burning Bed,* all created especially to run against football. Valerie Bertinelli was a nun who left the convent in *Shattered Vows,* Sophia Loren was the mother of a sick boy in *Aurora*, actress Theresa Saldana reenacted her experience as a crime victim in *Victims for Victims*—all dented ABC's Monday night ratings.

ABC's only solace was that the problems with sports ratings were not limited to Monday nights. For the second year in a row, fewer people were tuning in to Sunday NFL games on CBS and NBC. Ratings for college games were down too, as were ratings for most sports. Some people blamed it on the Olympics. After watching up to 180 hours of round-the-clock action from Los Angeles in the summer, viewers wanted a break from sports in the fall. But the true causes went deeper, deeper than the increased competition from independent stations, cable services, and videocassette recorders.

Ultimately, the people running the television sports industry—the networks, the leagues, the stations, the syndicators, and the cable services—had only themselves to blame for the problems that were about to engulf their businesses.

The sports boom was going bust because the networks, faced with spiraling rights fees, had responded by putting more sports on the air than viewers could possibly absorb. Led by ABC, the growth of sports programming had continued unabated since the early 1970s to the point where, in 1983, the networks ran 1,441 hours of sports—nearly 28 hours a week. More than 500 of those hours were devoted to football.

Sports viewing, as a whole, continued to grow, but the audience was spread over many more events. The sports glut reached its peak in 1984, thanks to the Olympics and the U.S. Supreme Court, which ended the NCAA's control over television rights to college football in June. Now fans could feast on a crowded menu of college games on Saturdays before the pros took over on Sundays. By Mondays, many had had their fill.

Only the last Monday night game of 1984—a thriller between two playoff teams, the Dolphins and the Cowboys—saved the season from becoming a total ratings disaster. Even so, *Monday Night Football* had its worst ratings ever in 1984. The series finished with a 16.9 average, down 21 percent from the record year of 1981.

The proof was in the numbers—the *Monday Night* phenomenon was finished.

*   *   *

If the flood of sports programming saturated the viewers, it positively swamped the advertisers. Suddenly, there were too many spots to sell and too few buyers.

John Lazarus, ABC's high-flying supersalesman, had seen the collapse coming. Six months earlier, at the L.A. Olympics, he had staged a lavish fling, the likes of which no one at the network ever expected to see again. "It was like Rome," said an ABC Sales executive.

The party lasted for more than two weeks. Each evening, ABC entertained more than twelve hundred people. It was a garish, indulgent, $2.1-million revel, the ultimate show-off celebration, hosted by a Sports sales division that had made the slick entertaining of clients a trademark. It was carpe diem fun on a Roman scale—but Rome was burning.

Even as ABC celebrated its financial triumph at the Olympics, desperation started to creep into the conversations between the sales staff and their clients. Massive holes needed to be filled in the commercial inventory of *Monday Night Football* for 1984.

Some felt Lazarus had oversold the Olympics to the detriment of *Monday Night Football*. Others believed the competing networks were dragging the football prices down. Whatever the reason, the partygoers were not buying.

The people at Miller beer, citing their commitment to the Olympics, told Lazarus they had to cut their spending on Monday nights and dropped their buy from twelve units a week to ten; Anheuser-Busch dropped down right along with them. For the first time in years, Busch also bought time on nonsports programs such as *Hill Street Blues*. Detroit's automakers also shifted dollars into other prime-time attractions to reach women car buyers as well as men.

Wherever they went all summer, Lazarus and his sales force heard the same thing: Prices were too high. The sales people began offering discounts, but, to their dismay, many buyers kept their hands in their pockets.

ABC began the season with more than 20 percent of the ads unsold in *Monday Night Football*. The sales people were having a brutal time selling the September games, which attracted smaller audiences. The Thursday games were being destroyed by Cosby and NBC. Prices fell lower.

"It was like a crash, like the stock market," said Steve Leff of Backer & Spielvogel, one of the networks' biggest clients. "They all of a sudden couldn't sell their product at the price they wanted. So they did the next best thing. They sold it for anything they could—which burst the balloon that had been built up over twenty years."

Panic set in. The networks turned to scavengers, buyers who would wait until the last minute to grab time at bargain rates. NBC and CBS offered 25 percent discounts on the NFL. Spots in college games that had sold for $60,000 the previous year were dumped at half-price.

ABC peddled spots on *Monday Night Football*, which had been priced as high as $185,000, for as little as $100,000. Network salesmen made a habit of staying at their desks until late on Friday nights, desperately searching for buyers. "You would call every client you thought could have a dollar to spend," said Michael Rubin, an ABC salesman in Chicago. "It was frightening." Even so, inventory remained unsold.

By now Lazarus had other worries. He was dragged into a scandal involving the man he had signed up to cater those classic Olympic parties, a friend named Robert Landau who also catered parties for *Monday Night Football*. Lazarus pledged ABC's money to a creditor of Landau's without the network's permission. Those Olympic parties turned out to be his own farewell blast. In late September, Lazarus's contract expired and he left ABC.

Sports sales was turned over to veteran J. Larre Barrett, then forty-six, who had worked for ABC since 1965. He had never seen a market in such disarray. However, he arrived too late to do anything but preside over the Friday night fire sales and tally up the numbers at the end of the year.

The numbers were disappointing, if not disastrous. *Monday Night Football* brought in about $145 million for ABC in 1984, down 15 percent from the previous year. It was barely enough to cover the NFL rights fee and production costs. The network got no return on its investment.

Barrett set to work on a plan for the 1985 season, but he suspected there was no way to squeeze more money out of the advertisers. No improvement was expected in the sports marketplace, and *Monday Night Football* prices would be depressed by the dismal ratings of the season just ended. About the most Barrett could hope for was to avoid another decline in revenues.

ABC was trapped on the NFL rights escalator—with the sponsors unwilling to pay for the ride up.

Roone Arledge was not about to hit the streets to sell ads for *Monday Night Football*, but he did have an idea for reviving the show.

In mid-September of 1984, Arledge invited Brent Musburger, the undisputed star of CBS Sports, to a discreet meeting at the St. Regis Hotel in New York. He had been in secret negotiations with ABC since February.

Musburger, then forty-four, was smart, well educated, and facile on the air, a journalist who could cover the big issues in sports. He had been a Chicago sportswriter before joining CBS, where he now hosted the network's NFL coverage and appeared on most of CBS's big events.

Arledge offered him a better package of assignments. Musburger could work ABC's major events, which included baseball's All-Star Game and World Series as well as the Super Bowl, and he would play a major role at the 1988 Winter Olympics, an assignment he had always coveted. Musburger would also be part of the announcing team on *Monday Night Football*.

Arledge had grown dissatisfied with Meredith and Simpson. He had made up his mind to get rid of one of them. Gifford would remain on play-by-play, as he envisioned it, while Musburger would be the host, take over halftime, and add journalistic punch, filling some of the void left by Cosell's departure.

The decision to woo Musburger had significance beyond *Monday Night Football*—it was evidence of the decline of ABC Sports. For the first time, Arledge felt he had to raid another network to revive his sagging prime-time showcase. He had pulled Gifford from CBS fourteen years earlier, of course, but that was less a talent raid than an invitation to a friend to join an already-jumping party. This time, the network that boasted that it was "recognized around the world as the leader in sports television" had to look down the street to improve its recognition factor.

The ABC offer flattered Musburger. "Everyone was aware of

the impact of *Monday Night Football*," he said. He also liked the idea of working for Arledge, who remained the dominant figure in sports television. He wondered, however, how Arledge managed to run both News and Sports. "I had doubts that he would be able to devote his attention to both," Musburger said.

They decided to meet again, but first Arledge set up a lunch for Musburger and Gifford. Gifford was gracious, and they got along fine. Musburger and his brother, Todd, who acted as his agent, then met Arledge and his top aides for another lunch at ABC's well-appointed suite at the Plaza Hotel. Things had reached the point where Musburger wanted to meet the people he would be working with at ABC.

The next day, Todd told ABC that Brent was "locked in neutral." CBS and ABC both had offers on the table worth more than one million dollars a year. Feeling the threat from ABC, CBS had stuffed its offer with goodies, including play-by-play on the NCAA basketball finals and college football. Todd and other family members recommended that he stay with CBS, but Brent liked the opportunities being dangled by Arledge. "I was inclined to go with ABC," he said.

By early December, Musburger was ready to make his choice. All he wanted was one last talk with Arledge, who had given him a phone number where he could be reached over the weekend. When Musburger called on Saturday, he learned that Arledge had left for a meeting in Hawaii with ABC executives. Musburger left a number, but he didn't hear from Arledge.

Arledge's inaccessibility was, by then, the stuff of legend in the television industry, but this missed connection had immediate ramifications. It reminded Musburger that he would never have an easy time tracking down the man in charge of ABC Sports.

"I have no doubt," Musburger said later, "that if Arledge had been totally focused on Sports, I would have left CBS." As it turned out, he decided to stay.

Leonard Goldenson had been unable to lure Howard Cosell back to football, but ABC's chairman remained determined to see to it that O. J. Simpson would not be in the booth during his network's first Super Bowl.

Goldenson was not a football fan, but he read the papers and occasionally watched on Monday nights. He knew he was not the only viewer who felt frustrated while trying to understand Simpson. "He spoke too fast," Goldenson said. "He wasn't getting through to the audience." Goldenson told Arledge to dump Simpson from the Super Bowl coverage.

Arledge felt that some of Simpson's critics outside ABC were racially motivated, but he was in no position to argue such a point with Goldenson. He had, after all, been thinking himself about taking Simpson off the package the next season.

For once, Arledge decided to deliver the bad news in person. With producer Bob Goodrich at his side, Arledge explained to Simpson that ABC had a tradition of inviting active players into the booth for big events such as the baseball playoffs and the World Series. Arledge assured Simpson that he would play an important role, appearing on the pregame, halftime, and post-game shows.

Simpson took it well, but his feelings were hurt. "O.J. was crushed," Goodrich said. "It was a big blow." In public, Simpson was statesmanlike, even though the game was being played in the San Francisco Bay area, where he had grown up, and involved his old team, the 49ers. "These were my guys," Simpson said. "I knew the players. I knew their tendencies. I knew more guys on that team than I knew on Buffalo." Simpson was admired within ABC for the way he handled the demotion.

The Super Bowl, a Rozelle creation, had long since become a television extravaganza, the most-anticipated, most-watched, most-analyzed program of the year. Over the years, CBS and NBC had engaged in a game of Super one-upmanship, competing in alternate years to see who could use the most cameras, spend the most money, sell the most advertising, and attract the biggest audience. Now ABC was joining the race and Arledge, naturally, felt he had to outdo his rivals.

The entire network had a stake in the game. After such a difficult fall season, ABC's accountants were looking for a Super profit. The slumping entertainment division was counting on a Super sendoff for its mid-season of prime-time programs, notably a husband-and-wife cop show called _MacGruder & Loud_ that premiered that night and was plugged, by unofficial count, fifteen times during the game. Peter Jennings, the anchorman of

ABC's *World News Tonight,* appeared briefly before the Super audience to promote the network's inauguration coverage—set for the following day—and chat a little about football before the kickoff. (That Jennings could say anything at all about football was counted as a minor miracle by those who knew that two months earlier, with a third of a season left, when Arledge first suggested that he appear at the Super Bowl, Jennings had replied: "Great! Who's playing?")

Forte carried the torch for ABC Sports. He took command of the technical preparations and, with the arrogance that had come to epitomize ABC Sports, scoffed at the notion that his *Monday Night* crew would be awed by the Super Bowl. "How can you be awed when you're doing *Monday Night Football* every week and forty, fifty, sixty million people are watching you?" Forte said. "The Super Bowl was really just another game for us."

Actually, ABC's Super Bowl production dwarfed anything seen on Mondays. Super Bowl statistics were tossed around so often that they numbed the mind, but the numbers issued by ABC to describe its hardware were unquestionably impressive. The army of ABC people who brought the six-hour spectacle to the public had at their disposal 19 stationary cameras, including 2 "super slow-mos," 5 hand-held minicams, 5 unmanned cameras, 17 videotape machines, 50 microphones, 1 helicopter, and 11 more cameras from remote locations, including one with American soldiers in South Korea and another in London, England, where the game could be seen on television beginning at one A.M. With ABC on the scene, it became the "Wide World of Super Bowls."

While there was no economic justification for ABC to pour millions of production dollars into a game that was guaranteed to draw a huge audience, that didn't matter. It would have been unthinkable for Arledge and ABC not to do the biggest and most extravagant of all Super Bowls.

Besides, ABC was already counting its profits. The first million-dollar minute in the history of television arrived on January 20, 1985, despite the ills of the sports advertising market. First Lazarus, then Barrett, had done a masterful job of selling; commercials in the game were priced at $500,000 or $525,000 per thirty-second spot, and they were all sold. Including the pregame and the postgame shows, the take came to $33 million, $7 million better than CBS or NBC had ever done.

San Francisco's 36–16 romp over Miami was an anticlimax for everyone except O. J. Simpson, who emerged as the unexpected star of the telecast. Simpson's pregame analysis was uncannily accurate, as he predicted that the 49er running backs would be a major factor in the game and that Roger Craig could be the team's "unsung hero." Craig went on to score three touchdowns, and ABC was so proud of O.J. that it offered a replay—though not in reverse angle—of his remarks. It was a sweet moment for The Juice.

The rest of the ABC coverage ran true to form. Gifford referred to Miami's wide receivers, Mark Duper and Mark Clayton, as "the two Dupers." Meredith's commentary was mostly of the "golly gee, gosh dang, I like it" variety. And Joe Theismann, Arledge's guest announcer for the game, tried to explain Dan Marino's passing problems by saying that "in this game, the working mechanism of the delivery doesn't exactly come the way you want it to"—meaning, evidently, that the young quarterback was tight. None of the trio offered much insight. In the press box, Simpson had all kinds of ideas, but he couldn't get them to the men in the booth. Afterward, he described the telecast as "smooth but not enlightening."

ABC was hoping for a record audience, given the appeal of the teams and their quarterbacks, Dan Marino and Joe Montana, as well as the cold weather in most of the country. Instead, the numbers were merely Super—a 46.4 rating and 63 share, ranking the telecast fifth among all Super Bowls.

Fifth place was not where Roone Arledge liked to be.

The party was over for Don Meredith.

After the Super Bowl, Arledge was sure he had seen enough of Meredith. "It became obvious after the season that Don really was not with it anymore and didn't care that much," Arledge said.

As for Meredith, he was ready to retreat to his beautiful new home in Santa Fe, New Mexico. He had probably hung around a little too long anyway, he thought. "We were on the road for fifteen years," he said. "That wears and tears on you."

Dealing with Meredith had never been simple, and his departure was no exception. Meredith's contract, which expired after the 1984 season, had a provision that required ABC to notify him well in advance of the 1985 season if he was going to be released. If the network did not give him adequate notice, ABC would be required to pay severance of more than $200,000 to Meredith.

Of course, ABC missed the cutoff date. Arledge and his men figured Don would understand. Of course, Meredith insisted on being paid.

"Legally, he was correct," said Irwin Weiner, Arledge's financial officer. "But, after all that we'd been through with Meredith—his leaving, his coming back, all the bullshit you go through with Meredith—I thought he was being an asshole."

Roone Arledge was puzzled. How could a company that small buy a company this big?

It was March 17, 1985. Arledge was in South Africa with *Nightline*, supervising a series of reports that would win acclaim and awards for the late-night news show. Fred Pierce had just called with some unsettling news: ABC was going to merge with Capital Cities Communications, a communications company that owned television stations, newspapers, and magazines.

Pierce tried to be reassuring. He had been led to believe that after the merger he would continue to run the ABC television network, the company's television stations, and its cable holdings. He described the deal as a merger of equals.

It was not. ABC was four times as big as Capital Cities, but not nearly as efficient. It had been beset by suitors for decades. Cap Cities, in contrast, was highly profitable and cash rich. It had agreed to pay $3.5 billion for ABC. The deal was a friendly takeover, but a takeover just the same.

Cap Cities was a famously lean company, the best-run media company in the nation in the estimation of Wall Street. Cap Cities' reputation for cost-cutting immediately provoked fears at ABC that spending would be slashed—and heads would roll.

Arledge hurriedly left South Africa to return to New York. From his point of view, the most encouraging news was that Pierce, who was probably his strongest supporter in top management, was going to remain in charge. The conquerors were going to begin their occupation early in 1986, so he had nine months to await the new regime.

*   *   *

In the spring of 1985, for the first time, Roone Arledge worried about the survival of *Monday Night Football*. "I felt that the future of the package was really in doubt," he said. Barring a dramatic increase in the ratings, he knew *Monday Night Football* was bound to lose money in the two seasons that were left on the rights deal negotiated with the NFL in 1982.

With so much football on the air, Arledge badly wanted to restore some luster to Monday nights. "We needed something," he said. "Howard was gone. Don was gone. And O.J. was questionable. Frank was having more and more to carry the whole show."

Arledge's options were limited. Gifford was entrenched in play-by-play. Simpson's Super Bowl performance had earned him another shot at Monday nights, but Arledge knew that O.J. was not going to bring more viewers to the set. And the man he really wanted to add to the booth, John Madden, was under contract to CBS. Madden might become available by the end of the year, but Arledge could not wait that long.

The ABC brain trust pored over lists of names, much as they had after Meredith first left in 1974. The glitter from one star name caught their eyes, just as it had back then—Joe Namath. Namath had long since retired from football. His last NFL pass— an interception—was thrown as a Los Angeles Ram during a Monday night game in 1977.

Namath, then forty-one, was thought to have bona fide charisma; he was perhaps football's most recognized face of the 1960s and 1970s. A brilliant quarterback, Namath was the first to throw for more than four thousand yards in one season. He led the Jets to an upset victory in Super Bowl III, a victory he had "guaranteed" in the press and a game that brought credibility to the AFL. But what made Namath a national celebrity were his extracurricular exploits. He signed a then-record $427,000 contract with the Jets in 1965; he fought with Rozelle over his interest in Bachelors III, a nightclub allegedly frequented by gamblers; he starred in notorious commercials for panty hose; and he fashioned a reputation as a playboy and bon vivant. Off the field, Namath was most often pictured emerging from a New York nightclub with a model or starlet on his arm.

While Namath's image as flashy, glamorous "Broadway Joe" did not endear him to all of Middle America, Arledge saw it as a plus. In the best of all scenarios, Namath would supply a combination of Gifford's sex appeal with Cosell's ability to command the spotlight. Namath also had extensive experience as a performer; since quitting the NFL, he had pursued an acting career, mostly starring in musical comedies on the straw-hat circuit from Long Island to Florida. He had also flopped once in prime time, playing a basketball coach in a short-lived NBC series called *The Waverly Wonders*. "Namath was our best shot at recapturing some of the magic," Arledge said.

There was, however, the matter of dealing with his lawyer, the pesky Jimmy Walsh, who insisted on negotiating a deal for Namath before allowing him to talk to Arledge. ABC could then interview Namath, put him through an audition, and turn him down if they liked, but the terms of the contract had to be set in advance. Arledge thought it was "the stupidest, ass-backwards way of doing a negotiation ever dreamed of," but he went along anyway. Walsh also insisted on a salary that exceeded $800,000 and on a two-year deal. "If Namath didn't work out, it didn't work out," Arledge said, "but it was worth the gamble." If Namath could do anything to help ABC protect its $290-million investment in the next two seasons of *Monday Night Football*, he would earn back his salary many times over.

But the man hired by ABC was not the glitzy Broadway Joe of the 1960s and 1970s. By 1985, Namath had mellowed, abandoning bachelorhood in New York for married life in Fort Lauderdale, Florida. When he wasn't touring with a show, he would while away his time fishing in the mornings, playing golf in the afternoons, and spending evenings at home with his new bride, Deborah Mays, a twenty-two-year-old ex-model and horsewoman. Mays was partly responsible for his new career; while watching a game together, she had been impressed by his remarks and suggested he try football commentary on television.

After meeting Namath, everyone on *Monday Night Football* looked forward to working with him. Those who expected him to behave like a big shot were pleasantly surprised: He was polite, modest, a true gentleman. Arledge, who had known him for years, had to keep telling Namath to stop calling him "Mr. Arledge." And crew members were delighted when, during a visit to a training camp to tape a feature, Namath stopped to sign autographs, toss around a football, and chat with kids in the crowd. "Namath was fantastic," said one staffer. "It took all of about five minutes to realize that this was a genuinely nice person."

Namath's hiring also grabbed media attention. "It attracted glamour right away," Arledge said. "At the press conference we had when you go from city to city, people would be lined up." The mood on the production team was upbeat. "I thought Joe was going to be terrific," Forte said.

If marquee value, good looks, and a pleasant personality were enough to succeed on *Monday Night Football*, Namath would have been a hit. Unfortunately, he lacked one necessary talent: He was not very good at talking about football.

Everyone knew Namath would need coaching. Goodrich brought him to New York for a couple of practice games with Gifford and Simpson; the results were mixed. Namath knew football, but he had trouble articulating his insights. Forte and Goodrich worked with him, stopping the tape, making suggestions, pointing out errors, and urging him to add some energy to his delivery.

He first appeared on the air at the Hall of Fame Game in Canton, a special occasion for the ABC team because Namath and Simpson were both being inducted into the Hall that day. Namath sounded nervous on the air, which was understandable on such a big day for him. But the next two exhibitions were only slightly better.

By the eve of the season opener, Goodrich knew he had a problem. Namath had hardly improved at all. "People had such high expectations," Goodrich said. "He wasn't the savior of *Monday Night Football*." Trying to buy time for his new star, Goodrich asked some critics not to review Namath until later in the season.

Most ignored the request. "Broadway shows are reviewed on opening night," one critic wrote. As Goodrich expected, the reviews were overwhelmingly negative. "For the most part," said *The New York Times*, "Namath's remarks were inane." The *New York Post* called him "disappointing" and "bland." Several critics ridiculed Namath's fondness for the adjective *heckuva,* as in "heckuva run," "heckuva pass," "heckuva game." Passes and runs that weren't "heckuva" were often "lousy."

Goodrich and Forte thought Namath's flaws could be mended with time. Like many newcomers to the booth, Namath had a tendency to state the obvious. One night, with the Bears holding a 30–17 lead over the Vikings, Namath said, "It looks like the Vikings will need two scores to pull this game out." When a team drove toward the goal line, he would tell the viewers that "they really want to score here." Forte and Goodrich thought they could work with him to eliminate the clichés. And they wrote off his "heckuva" hang-up to nerves.

What troubled them as the season unfolded was that Namath did not work harder. Goodrich urged him to arrive early for games to meet with the players, but Namath's wife was expecting their first child and he wanted to spend time with her. At a Monday production meeting, Forte was shocked when Namath admitted that he did not know who had won an important game the day before. "Maybe it was just once," Forte said, "but once was enough for me. I don't care if you don't watch the games, but know who won and lost."

The bigger worry—and the biggest surprise—was that Namath was nowhere near as colorful as his image. *Monday Night Football* desperately needed someone to stir the pot, get a little argument going, or offer a fresh point of view. Instead, Namath was unfailingly pleasant and mainstream, no different from Gifford and Simpson. Arledge wanted a live wire, but Namath was a dud. Arledge thought he came across as "bland and noncritical and nonfunny."

The booth was no longer an arena for conflicts, even friendly ones, among the announcers. Gifford, Simpson, and Namath got along well, which was fine, but they also agreed all the time, which was not. Watching from home, Don Ohlmeyer liked each of the men in the booth but thought the mix was dreadful: "All three of those guys love football, they like the players, and they're all their friends. It didn't work."

Sports Illustrated waited six weeks into the season to render its devastating verdict. William Taaffe wrote that "the show used to entertain us, inform us, make us laugh. Now it's more tiring than all the blather on Sunday afternoons."

THROWN FOR A LOSS ||| 317

The reviews became self-fulfilling. Wounded by the attacks, Namath and Simpson pressed harder. Gifford was also stung by the critics, and his errors drew more attention. One night at halftime, he introduced a feature about St. Louis Cardinals quarterback Neil Lomax by saying, "A lot of people don't know Steve Lomax . . ."

Forte seemed to give up. When Namath uttered a cliché or Simpson slurred his words, the director would just moan and bury his head in his hands.

Forte and the production side were slipping too. In a memorable game between Chicago and Green Bay, everyone on *Monday Night Football* was taken by surprise when Bears coach Mike Ditka inserted William "Refrigerator" Perry, the mammoth defensive tackle, into the backfield of his goal-line offense. When Perry was handed the ball and plunged in for a touchdown, there was no isolated camera on him—proof that the production team had been unprepared for the unorthodox play. No one had bothered to seek out Ditka over the weekend to hear his plans, even though he had a reputation as one of the more accessible and open coaches in the NFL. Staffers at the other networks who were watching the telecast were astonished.

Forte was also unhappy when one of his prize hand-held cameras on the sideline was eliminated as part of a cost-cutting campaign.

In a Dallas–New York game, for the first time in the history of *Monday Night Football*, ABC missed a touchdown. The coverage lingered too long on the quarterback who had thrown the ball.

Forte screamed louder than ever, but it was too late.

Frank Gifford was "a male mannequin, his voice still too weak and undramatic to have any impact. . . . He's not a natural performer, never was, never will be."

Don Meredith "rarely prepared for a telecast. . . . He'd try to compensate for his lack of knowledge by singing a song."

O. J. Simpson was not up to the job, proving again that "it was a mistake to take a jock and put him on the air."

And Roone Arledge was "obsessed with power."

The assessments of Howard Cosell could not have surprised

anyone who had spent much time with him in his later years on *Monday Night Football*. The only surprise was that Cosell chose to publish them at a time when he was still working for ABC Sports.

The first excerpts from Cosell's new book, *I Never Played the Game*, appeared in *TV Guide* in late September 1985. In the eyes of many executives at ABC Sports, he savaged his ex-colleagues on *Monday Night Football*.

The rest of the 380-page book was similar in tone. Cosell attacked Pete Rozelle and the NFL, the major-league baseball establishment, greedy franchise owners in all sports, the boxing business, corruption in college athletics, sportswriters, television critics, and anyone else who had ever committed the unforgivable sin of failing to pay proper homage to Howard Cosell. The book was vintage Cosell: brilliant in spots, entertaining, hard-hitting, self-serving, and, most of all, thoroughly self-absorbed. Every page was a variation on a theme: I was right and everybody else was wrong. The book could have been called *I Never Played the Game—But I Always Won Anyway.*

Almost all the attention given to the book went to his attacks on *Monday Night Football* and his fellow workers at ABC. The reaction was swift.

Days after the excerpts appeared, Jim Spence called Cosell to tell him that he had been removed from the announcers' booth at the upcoming World Series and reassigned to the pregame show. He did not tell Cosell that he was calling under orders from Arledge.

Cosell lashed back. He spoke in slow, measured tones, building to a crescendo. "Spence," he said, "forget me. You know better than that. I don't need you. I don't like you. I don't respect you. I have the ultimate contempt for you. I want you to know it. And I don't want to do the World Series."

Not long afterward, the network canceled *SportsBeat*, the low-rated sports-issues show hosted by Cosell.

The next time anyone in the ABC hierarchy heard from Cosell, he was speaking through his lawyer, Bob Schulman. "Howard wants out," Schulman told Irwin Weiner. ABC agreed to release him from his contractual obligations. Cosell walked away from more than two million dollars a year. He wanted nothing to do with television sports.

Cosell's *Monday Night Football* colleagues were stung by the book. Gifford was so deeply wounded that he never again spoke to Cosell, although publicly he kept his feelings in check. "The sad part is that he's so bitter, lashing out. I feel pity and sadness for him," Gifford said.

Forte, too, was hurt. Cosell had given him no credit for his contributions to *Monday Night Football*. They had been the best of friends, but Forte now called the book "an unadulterated piece of garbage."

Simpson was also upset, particularly with a section that had him crying during his phone call to Cosell after the Buffalo blowup in 1983. Simpson said he never came close to crying.

Cosell and his book were a plague on *Monday Night Football* for the entire 1985 season.

Gifford told a reporter, "He's haunting the people around the show."

Not all the news was bad for *Monday Night Football* in 1985. The ratings rebounded from the record lows of the previous season, for several reasons unconnected to the quality of the telecast.

This football season did not follow ABC's 180 hours of Olympics, as it had in 1984. Teams from major television markets—the Giants, Jets, Raiders, Rams, and Bears—were strong. And, to combat complaints about commercial interruptions, the networks and the NFL decided to squeeze their twenty- four minutes of advertisements into sixteen breaks rather than twenty-two.

The most anticipated game of the regular season, a December showdown between Dan Marino and the high-flying Miami Dolphins and Jim McMahon and the fearsome Chicago Bears, fell on a Monday night. The Bears, trying to become the first team to go unbeaten since Miami had done it thirteen years earlier, were upset by the Dolphins, 38–24, in a wild and exciting offensive battle that produced the highest *Monday Night Football* ratings of all time—a 29.6 rating and 46 share.

The ratings recovery came too late for J. Larre Barrett and his people in sales. Barrett had labored all spring and summer to sell *Monday Night Football*, with grim results. He had found a number of new buyers, including Ford, which returned to the package after a seven-year absence. But ABC, for the first time, had been forced to drop the price it was charging to franchise buyers. The brewers and carmakers paid $175,000 per spot in 1985, compared to $185,000 the year before. Slumps in the computer industry and on Wall Street only made matters worse.

As the season began, chunks of time remained unsold. The Friday night fire sales resumed, and *Monday Night* ad prices plunged to less than $100,000. Twenty-one games later, ABC sales had generated about $144 million in revenues.

It was not enough. The network had paid the NFL $140 million in rights fees. Even after cost-cutting, ABC spent nearly $30 million more to put the games on the air.

For the season, *Monday Night Football* had lost $25 million.

Near the end of 1985, Roone Arledge tried yet again to add some personality to *Monday Night Football*. He made a run at John Madden of CBS.

As in the case of Musburger a year earlier, Arledge was forced to admit that another network had fashioned a talent superior to anyone at ABC. Madden was universally recognized as the best NFL color man on television.

The former head coach of the Oakland Raiders, Madden managed to come across on the air as both a lovable, hilarious oaf and a knowledgeable expert on football. Unlike many analysts who were content during a replay merely to rehash the play, Madden, armed with O'Neil's Telestrator, took fans inside the action and explained why things happened, actually helping them to see the game better.

With Cosell gone, Madden was the only football announcer on television with the power to bring viewers to the set.

Arledge's efforts didn't get far. Although ABC was willing to pay Madden more than $1 million a year, it wasn't enough to persuade him to defect. He wanted $1.5 million to do *Monday Night Football* and ten to twelve other events. With the new bosses from Cap Cities about to arrive, no one wanted to make an expensive deal that could be subjected to second guesses.

The Cap Cities situation was occupying Arledge's mind. Pierce had been told by the new owners that they no longer wanted him to run the broadcasting operations, that he would be given only the network. "They wanted to change the ground rules," Pierce said. "It wasn't acceptable to me." He went on a skiing vacation, considered his options, and then quit when he returned in January.

Arledge was left unprotected. And he was disturbed that media accounts of the ABC takeover had singled him out as the personification of the network's free-spending ways. He had been responsible for much of the network's success, and much of its profits, for two decades. Now he was being typecast as the executive who commanded fleets of helicopters and limousines.

The week before Christmas, Arledge abruptly called Cosell one morning to invite him to lunch. They had not spoken since the publication of Cosell's book.

In the book Cosell had revealed, consciously and subconsciously, the depth of his twisted, twenty-year love/hate relationship with Arledge. He had somehow managed to dedicate the book to his boss and mentor, acknowledge his genius, and express a measure of gratitude for the support Arledge had given his career, while simultaneously charging Arledge with being power-hungry, manipulative, infatuated with jocks, and jealous of the celebrity that he, Cosell, had attained.

Of all the people Cosell had written critically about in _I Never Played the Game_, Arledge had displayed the least reaction—in fact, he had displayed no reaction at all. Whatever his true feelings about the book, he kept them to himself. His only response was precisely the one most likely to exasperate Cosell: He said publicly that he had not read it.

When Cosell took the call that morning from Arledge, he was instantly suspicious. "What do you want to do this for?" he asked nervously. Cosell was sure there had to be an ulterior motive behind the call, some reason why Arledge wanted to see him after so much time had passed. He agreed to meet Arledge that afternoon at the "21" Club, and he had no idea what to expect when he got there.

From the moment they sat down together, the encounter was strained. Cosell was terribly ill at ease. He did not let much time go by before he challenged Arledge's assertion that he had not read the book. "You'd be too curious," Cosell said. "You'd want to know what I said."

"Howard," replied Arledge, "I have a pretty good idea what you'd say."

One reason he had such a good idea was that he had read the excerpts from the book that were published in *TV Guide*. Those excerpts contained most of the harshest comments Cosell had made about his broadcast-booth partners, though not his nastiest words about Arledge himself.

So he could, in fact, discuss some of his objections to what Cosell had written.

"It's unfortunate and unseemly that you attacked all the people you worked with and I think it was a mistake," Arledge told him. "But the real tragedy of it is that what you had to say of a serious nature in the book nobody ever focused on."

"Well, that's your opinion," Cosell replied.

They stayed on late into the afternoon, talking on other subjects. But it was not a lunch suffused with the warmth of the season. Arledge sensed Cosell's discomfort. He seemed to be waiting for another shoe to drop. Arledge believed Cosell was expecting him to reach into his pocket and pull out some devastating statement on the end of Howard Cosell's association with ABC.

Arledge could not assuage that discomfort by assuring Cosell continually that the sole purpose of the lunch was the urge to break bread at Christmastide—and that he had nothing special in his pockets.

The encounter ended awkwardly on the sidewalk outside "21." Cosell tried one last time to get Arledge to admit that this talk of ignoring the book was all a sham.

"I still don't believe you didn't read it," Cosell said.

Arledge could only shake his head and laugh.

12.

SACKS AND
TURNOVERS

*BE REASONABLE: DO IT MY WAY.—sign on the desk of Dennis Swanson,
new president of ABC Sports*

In the first week of February 1986, Dennis Swanson, the
newly appointed president of ABC Sports, stood before a
meeting of the entire staff of the department—producers,
directors, announcers, p.a.'s, accountants, secretaries—about
eighty people in all. He had a message to deliver.

The marine had landed.

Standing with arms folded across his barrel chest, swaying
from side to side, the narrow slits of his eyes looking past
everyone in the room to points left, right, and above their heads,
Swanson laid it all out for them, straight—with just a hint of
relish:

This was his department now. ABC Sports was a financial
disaster and the new Capital Cities management had installed
him as the fixer. The fix would be immediate and it would be
total. Change was coming, and it would affect all their lives.
They would all work differently, and they would all live differently. The ABC Sports Country Club was closed, boarded up,
and slated for demolition.

"I didn't go to an Ivy League school," Swanson said, making
it sound like a boast. "I went to a land-grant college in Illinois

323

because my family didn't have the money to send me to an Ivy League school. I had to get into the marines to go through graduate school. I worked my way up."

He was setting himself apart from those in the department—Arledge, Spence, Howard, Forte, Ruhe, and others—who had gone to Ivy-type schools, implying that they were privileged brats who did not know the value of a dollar.

A new order was in charge, drawn not from the arrogant and profligate ranks of the network but from the lunchpail-carrying ranks of local stations, where people know what television is really all about—turning a profit.

"I've worked in Stations," Swanson went on. "A lot of you don't know much about Stations because you think you're so hot from having worked for the big sports network. But we do a little thing in Stations that maybe you're not familiar with either—we make money."

It sounded like reverse chic to some of those being taunted by Swanson. The Ivy Leaguers had screwed up, he was saying, and now the Station guy was going to teach them about humility.

"There's a fine line between professional pride and arrogance," Swanson pronounced. "We're not going to be arrogant anymore."

ABC Sports, as he saw it, had nothing to be arrogant about. The division had lost millions in 1985 and it was going to lose millions more in 1986. The quality of production, he thought, was nothing to brag about, probably no better than the other networks. And, he had heard, the work habits were atrocious.

"I'm old-fashioned in a lot of things," he said. "I think people should come to work on time. I think they should work hard while they are there. I think they should answer the phone before it rings three times."

Swanson said the department had been spendthrift, shelling out too much money in rights fees and in salaries, especially for production people.

"I'm only the president of this organization," Swanson said. "I'm not paid what Chet Forte's paid."

The comment stunned Forte. He could not believe that the first thing Swanson had said about him was that he made too much money, and, even worse, that his new boss had announced it in public.

Swanson was not through with Forte. He also ridiculed him for being captured in a *USA TODAY* photo wearing a gold medallion on his chest where a tie should have been.

Swanson's fusillade of sarcasm soon found other targets.

"We've got so many damn vice-presidents around here that you don't know when you're going to bump into somebody in the hall who's a vice-president of something," he said in mock amazement. "We've got a vice-president of production; we've got a vice-president of production *affairs*. We've got a vice-president for administration. Jesus, even Jeff Ruhe's a vice-president."

If anyone in the room had still missed the point, the mention of Ruhe, the Sports executive closest to Arledge, slammed it home. Swanson was openly going after the Arledge crowd. Finally, he got around to Arledge, the main target, the legend.

The Cap Cities people had removed Arledge from Sports and retitled him the "group president" of News and Sports, but the title was meaningless. Inside the company, most people knew on January 27, when the announcement was made, that Arledge had no authority over ABC Sports anymore. Many thought that his hold over News was tenuous, at best.

Swanson was not about to pay homage to the legend of Roone Arledge. Not once during the meeting did he acknowledge that Arledge had built ABC Sports into an American institution. Not once did he mention the vision, the innovations, the hands-on production of nine Olympics, winter and summer, the decades of profits. Instead, he made it seem as if the only thing legendary about Arledge had been his penchant for high living and fiscal excess.

"If Roone were Jimmy Carter's adviser," Swanson said, in a line that did not sound spontaneous to anyone in the room, "the U.S. would surely have gotten all its hostages out of Iran, because Roone always travels with two or three too many helicopters."

Swanson had come to bury the sports Caesar, not to praise him.

Before arriving at ABC Sports, Dennis Swanson had one claim to television fame: He had discovered Oprah Winfrey.

Swanson had been the general manager of WLS-TV, the

ABC-owned station in Chicago, when he spotted Winfrey on a tape that her producer had sent along with a job application. Swanson hired the producer and, more important, hired Winfrey to host WLS's moribund morning talk show. Once Winfrey got to Chicago, she became a media whirlwind. She went on to movies and magazine covers, and her talk show became one of the most successful properties in all of television syndication. Swanson did not have much to do with her stardom, but he had made it all possible. It was the sort of credit a television executive can ride a long way.

Swanson rode it to the job running ABC's stations division, which he assumed on March 12, 1985. Three days later, he turned forty-seven. Three days after that, his boss called to say that ABC was being taken over by Capital Cities, a company with the most profitable group of television stations in America. They did not need Swanson to tell them how to run Stations. He knew then that his life was going to change.

It changed for the better. Cap Cities surveyed the ranks of management at ABC and came away mostly disappointed. But they liked what they saw in Dennis Swanson.

What they saw was a no-nonsense guy with a reputation for taking on crises and resolving them. He was hard-headed and uncompromising. Cap Cities liked his style and they liked his background in Stations; he understood their business. They had a crisis in Sports and they needed a crisis manager. Mostly, they needed a guy whose sport was hardball.

The marines do not recruit softball players. Swanson's marine background—he left with a rank of captain—clearly made a mark on his personality. *Tough* became an adjective all but attached permanently to his name.

Born in a small California town called Wilmar, Swanson went to the University of Illinois on an engineering scholarship but switched to journalism after working at the student-run radio and television stations. After his three-year marine stint, Swanson picked up a graduate degree in communications from Illinois and set off for Cedar Rapids, Iowa, to work as a reporter and photographer on local news shows.

Swanson's climb through the business was steady, if not meteoric. He worked a couple of years at WGN, an independent station in Chicago, then moved over to WMAQ, the Chicago station owned by NBC, where he was a reporter, assignment editor, field producer, and sportscaster. After that he became an executive with a television-news production company in Chicago and New York.

When that company folded, Swanson, then thirty-eight, had to make a crucial decision. He had one offer to become a news executive at an ABC-owned station in Los Angeles, and another to go back on the air doing sports in Chicago. There had even been rumors that Swanson would be paired with baseball announcer Harry Caray to call the White Sox on radio. He took the L.A. offer and became news director, then station manager. His success there vaulted him to the general-manager job at WLS, which thrived during his two-year reign.

But, if Swanson had the brains, the drive, and the toughness to thrive in the trenches of television, no one knew whether he had the finesse to make it as a network executive. Nothing about him was smooth.

"Dennis the Menace," some called him. Swanson's deceptively boyish face was mounted on a big, round-shouldered frame. With his jowly, slightly mashed features and shambling gait, he looked like a gangly kid gone slightly doughy in middle age.

He didn't talk like a kid. Although he sounded like he had a perpetual cold, with the words coming out through his nose, Swanson always spoke with self-assured authority. He did not project warmth, he had a flashpoint temper, and he was blunt and decisive. An ABC underling who questioned one of his decisions got a swift reaction from Swanson: "You may be right, but I'd rather make a wrong decision than no decision at all."

Fred Pierce, who picked Swanson to run the ABC-owned stations, was impressed by Swanson's leadership abilities. "But Dennis is a little heavy-handed," Pierce said. "It's obvious he's an ex-marine."

Pierce also blamed Swanson for taking early steps at Sports that crushed toes unnecessarily. "He was myopic. He could only see his own problems. Dennis doesn't deal well with people."

Swanson did not believe he was hired to be nice to people. He believed he was hired to patch up a network division that had been hemorrhaging money.

"I don't give [people] a lot of sugarcoating," he said. "When you make the kinds of changes we had to make, there's no easy way to make them."

Nor did he care about winning friends at ABC Sports. As he told his staff, "Everyone does not have a vote here. This place is going to be run like a dictatorship. And I am the dictator."

Roone Arledge had been given the word on a Friday, the day that corporate executives usually pick to deliver bad news. The two top executives of Cap Cities, Thomas Murphy and Daniel Burke, told him that he had to give up control of Sports. They were giving the job of Sports president to Dennis Swanson, they said, and they were announcing it on Monday.

The Cap Cities executives tried to couch their decision in a positive light. ABC News, they said, was so important that it needed Arledge's full-time attention. Cap Cities was going to expect more from News—tighter management, stricter controls over spending, and, most important, more productivity, including pilots for new prime-time series.

Arledge had seen it coming, but the loss of Sports was still a blow. He had run ABC Sports for twenty-five years. It was his creation. It had been, for all those years, a central part of his life. Now he was being forced to let go of it, although there was one final production assignment that the company wanted him to take on. Cap Cities faced financial disaster at the 1988 Winter Olympics in Calgary, which the old management—including Arledge, of course—had overspent to acquire. They needed Arledge to make the best of the Calgary production. They also needed his name to help sell the Games to skeptical advertisers. Arledge agreed to remain as executive producer of the Calgary Games.

He would not, though, remain executive producer of anything else at ABC Sports, a move that erased the stamp he put on every sports program—as well as the checks he put in the bank every time the title was announced on the air.

Arledge had little to say in public about his new status, except to note that he had wanted to give up Sports for years. Of course, he had also wanted to anoint his own successor and to retain ultimate power over the division. This was not the way he had planned to step down from the throne.

*   *   *

From the moment Chuck Howard set eyes on Dennis Swanson, he knew that ABC Sports, the place where he had worked all his adult life, was about to be turned inside out and upside down.

"If you had walked out on the street and tried for six months to find a guy more different from Arledge," Howard said, "you would have been hard pressed to come up with somebody any more different than Swanson."

Swanson didn't flinch from the comparison. From the moment he took over, his every word and deed seemed designed to transmit the message that the Arledge years were over.

After searching the division for the proper number-two man to head up the production side, Swanson settled on the executive who had long been scorned by the Arledge crowd—Dennis Lewin. The choice of Lewin, the former *Monday Night* producer who had been intimidated by Cosell and Forte, shocked veterans at ABC.

But the appointment made sense for Swanson. Lewin was neither an Arledge intimate nor an Arledge favorite. He was a detail man, exceptional at organization, if not a dynamic leader. Swanson himself was going to provide all the dynamism needed by ABC Sports.

Lewin was not an Ivy Leaguer either. He was a Big Ten guy, from Michigan State. Dennis Swanson, of the Fighting Illini, liked Big Ten guys.

Forte, predictably appalled by the appointment, believed Lewin fit another of Swanson's needs—he was the executive most willing to accommodate Swanson. Or, as the always-blunt Forte put it, "If Swanson backs up, Lewin breaks his nose."

While Lewin was rising, Jeff Ruhe, Arledge's closest ally left in the department, was in trouble. Ruhe, a former special assistant to Arledge, had been named a vice-president of ABC Sports. He was being groomed by Arledge to take over.

In the months before the Cap Cities takeover, Ruhe worked under the illusion that he was heading for even bigger things under the new regime. He had been approached by Daniel Burke, the president of Cap Cities, who suggested that he take a special graduate-level management course at Harvard in the winter of 1986. Burke told Ruhe that ABC needed skilled managers and he was among the most promising they had.

Arledge opposed the idea. He wanted Ruhe to stay at ABC Sports to help him fight for the division. But Ruhe knew from talking to Burke that the revolution was coming, and that Arledge would be losing his influence over Sports.

Ruhe accepted Burke's offer, and the $22,000 Cap Cities check for the tuition. But Swanson was appointed just as he was about to leave for Harvard. That left Ruhe uncertain about his future, until Swanson came to him personally, assuring him that he could go to Harvard without worrying about what was going to happen that winter at ABC Sports. No major decisions would be made for some time, Swanson told him, and even if something was about to be decided, Boston was less than an hour away on the shuttle. He promised to keep Ruhe informed and involved.

A week later, Swanson was cracking jokes at a staff meeting about Ruhe being a vice-president. Shortly afterward, he named Lewin to the top production position—without a phone call, let alone a shuttle visit, to Ruhe.

When Ruhe heard the news, he was doubly stunned. He could not believe that Lewin, whom he considered a drudge, would now be his boss. He also could not believe that Swanson had broken faith with him.

When Lewin offered him a role in the 1988 Winter Olympics in Calgary, basically the same job that he had had in L.A. in 1984, Ruhe knew where he stood. He contacted Irwin Weiner, the top financial executive, and got out of his contract with ABC.

One more Arledge disciple was encouraged to make a mid-career change.

But ABC Sports was not filled with Arledge disciples. The division had deep reserves of disgruntled, frustrated staffers who had suffered for years under Arledge's absentee-landlord management. Once Arledge made it clear that his first love was News, many in Sports felt like members of a lower caste. They found Swanson gruff, overly cost-conscious, and occasionally petty, but they welcomed him anyway. He was accessible; he had clear authority; he was decisive; and all his energies were committed to Sports. ABC Sports was finally going to have an on-site leader.

"We now have a clear definition of who's doing what," one

executive said soon after Swanson's arrival. "That wasn't the case before."

Some insiders even believed that ABC Sports had needed a marine invasion, after all the irresponsible spending that had marked the early 1980s. Events had been acquired, they thought, that had no chance of making money. The division's losses in 1985, the down year after the Olympics, had been about $22 million.

Things looked worse for 1986. When Swanson was given the Sports job, he was also given a set of ABC projections that pointed to a $55-million loss. Cap Cities' accountants reworked those numbers in mid-February, and predicted that the Sports division would lose $82 million.

Worst of all, Swanson could do little in the short run to turn things around. He was saddled with money-losing rights deals for baseball, college football, and *Monday Night Football,* all of them negotiated by Arledge and Spence. He could not squeeze more money out of the advertisers. He could only save a nickel here, a dime there. "You add up enough dimes, you get a dollar," he would say.

One morning at about nine, a couple of ABC Sports veterans arrived at the office and heard a typewriter clacking in the president's office down the hall. They were surprised to find even a secretary at work so early, so they peeked down the hall to see what was going on. There was Dennis Swanson, typing a letter.

Frank Gifford did not know what to expect when Swanson summoned him to his office in late March. Outwardly, Gifford was cool, but inside he was apprehensive. For the first time in sixteen years, he was facing a boss he did not play golf with on the weekends.

Swanson and Lewin laid out their plans to him. They were dropping Joe Namath from *Monday Night Football.* They were dropping O. J. Simpson from *Monday Night Football.*

Lewin saw the flash of concern on Gifford's face, as though he expected the next name crossed off the show to be his. Lewin jumped in to reassure him.

We want to get down to a two-man booth, Lewin explained,

and we want to use people from in-house. We want you to move over to color, and we want to bring in Al Michaels to do the play-by-play.

Gifford was shocked. "I've been doing this for fifteen years," he said, immediately resisting the idea.

Lewin tried to be diplomatic. Swanson came on tough. They reminded Gifford that the package was losing money. It didn't make sense, they said, to pay Namath and Simpson all that money to do *Monday Night Football*—particularly since they didn't do it very well. Better, they concluded, to take the best guys they already had on the payroll and put them on ABC's most important event.

Gifford said he respected Michaels as a solid professional, but he made it clear—and he made it clear with some intensity—that he didn't like the idea of being forced to change roles after fifteen years of solid professional work of his own. At best, he said, he would have to think about it.

Gifford was hurt. Swanson, he thought, had been insensitive. He was the veteran on the package, the team player, and now he was being treated like a hired hand. No one had asked for his opinion. He didn't have a vote. The dictator had spoken.

"I thought it was precipitous, to say the least; not handled well at all," Gifford said.

The shake-up came at a trying time for Gifford. His mother was gravely ill in California, and he was spending much of his time at her side. He couldn't even think about football. He left the confrontation with Swanson and flew back to L.A. to be with her.

Lewin was headed the same way. He flew to Los Angeles the next morning. He had two meetings on his schedule, the first with O.J. Simpson, and the second with Al Michaels.

Lewin had known Simpson for fifteen years. He was not going to enjoy removing him from *Monday Night Football*. But he did have a consolation prize to offer: Simpson could become the analyst on ABC's college-football package. Swanson's broom was also sweeping out Frank Broyles, who had been the college color man for nine years. Of course, the college job was going to carry only about one third of the $600,000 salary that went with O.J.'s prime-time exposure on Monday nights.

Simpson took the news gracefully. He accepted Lewin's

explanation that ABC wanted to try a new approach. With Namath out too, Simpson felt he could not take it personally. But he never saw himself as an all-purpose football color commentator, so the college job had little appeal. He told Lewin he would consider it anyway.

Then Michaels met Lewin for dinner. Swanson's decision-making process had been so swift that Michaels had only the slightest hint that something was up with *Monday Night Football* that might involve him. Still, he was surprised when he realized that he was going to get the *Monday Night* job.

It wasn't that Michaels did not think he deserved the promotion—far from it. He had been convinced for years that he was the most talented broadcaster in all of sports. But Michaels had never considered the *Monday Night* play-by-play job attainable, not under the old regime, not with Gifford holding such a privileged position.

Lewin laid out the scenario, then had some more good news for Michaels. Ken Wolfe was going to be named the new producer of the show. Wolfe was Michaels's closest friend at ABC Sports.

Naturally, the offer delighted Michaels. He was ready to accept, but Lewin explained that Gifford was balking at the change. No announcement could be made until the situation with Frank was resolved.

Michaels, a man of limited patience, would have preferred not to wait.

In the 1980 Winter Olympics, as the clock ran down on the biggest upset in American sports history—the victory of a bunch of college kids from the United States over the greatest hockey team in the world, the Soviet Olympic team—Al Michaels shouted out a phrase destined to be remembered by every one of the 51 million viewers who shared the moment on television:

"Do you believe in miracles? YES!"

Michaels himself did not believe in miracles. He had a different sort of faith. He believed in the greatness of Al Michaels.

By 1986, Michaels, then forty-one, had made believers out of millions of sports fans. More important, he had won over the hierarchy of ABC Sports. He was blessed with enormous on-air talent; he cared passionately about sports and broadcasting; and he worked with near-obsessive dedication. Al Michaels had become the best play-by-play announcer in sports television.

That had been the single driving goal of Michaels's life— virtually from the cradle. When Al was five, living in the Flatbush section of Brooklyn not far from Ebbets Field, his father, Jay—a theatrical agent in New York and later in Hollywood—took him to his first ball game. Most of the five-year-olds in the park spent such days staring into center field and dreaming of becoming Duke Snider. Al Michaels spent his day staring into the radio booth dreaming of becoming Red Barber.

"I wanted to be an announcer from day one," Michaels said. "I never wanted to do anything else. It never wavered."

After high school in Los Angeles, Michaels chose to attend Arizona State, not for the education or the weather but because the campus radio station covered ASU's big-time football, basketball, and baseball programs. He refined his skills for four years as the main voice of Arizona State sports. He married his high school sweetheart after graduation, had a short and unhappy experience as a color commentator with the Los Angeles Lakers, and eventually landed blissfully in Hawaii, where he found a job broadcasting minor-league baseball.

Bliss gave way to ambition. In 1970, Michaels made the jump to Cincinnati, where he became a rookie announcer for the Big Red Machine. After one year, Michaels was doing a few innings on NBC's national telecasts of the World Series.

Three years later he moved on to San Francisco and the Giants, and two years after that, ABC Sports hired him as a part-time backup baseball announcer. In January 1977 he went to work full-time for the network.

By Michaels's standards, his early career at ABC amounted to a monumental struggle to achieve his rightful place of honor.

"My first full year in '77 I didn't do the Series," he said, "which should have been a warning to me that I was going to have to fight for things"—things he believed should have been his by sheer force of his talent.

Keith Jackson got the Series assignment; Michaels got "pretty angry, pretty upset." By the time the 1979 Series came around, with his contract almost up, his anger had become a threat: "I let it be known in no uncertain terms that were I not to be part of the World Series now and forever more, I was out of there."

ABC took the awkward step of dividing the assignment, giving Michaels the games played in Pittsburgh and Jackson the games in Baltimore.

Still, Michaels's fight for recognition went on. Even after his triumph at Lake Placid in 1980, ABC refused to satisfy Michaels's longing to be knighted with a premier role in a major sport.

Some of the assignments he was getting—high diving, amateur wrestling, the B-games on college football—were starting to get him "a little crazy," Michaels said. "I mean, I'm still not remotely there. I'm still getting whacked around politically."

In 1982, Michaels saw Jim McKay with *Wide World,* Gifford with NFL football, and Jackson with college football, and wondered why he had nothing of his own. So he confronted Jim Spence.

"You have to explain this to me," Michaels said heatedly to Spence. "What the hell's the problem? What the fuck is going on with you?"

This time he got a commitment that baseball was all his. A year later, when Arledge was in the middle of his dance with Brent Musburger, Michaels sent out another unhappy message and was given a new five-year contract that took his salary into the one-million-dollar range.

Along the way, Michaels was becoming the prototype of the contemporary play-by-play man. He was smooth, articulate, and unselfish on the air, taking pains to draw out his color commentators, especially Jim Palmer and Tim McCarver on baseball. He was also superbly prepared, especially after he had a satellite dish installed in the yard of his home so that he could watch numerous sports events and keep up on players from all over the country.

But even as he established an unassailable professional reputation, his personal reputation was undergoing reevaluation within ABC. Everyone had liked Michaels at first. He was friendly, easygoing, fun to be around. Even Cosell enjoyed his company.

That did not last. Cosell and Michaels soon became bitter personal enemies. Others declared a plague on both their houses. Caught up in his success, Michaels began to act like a star and demand that he be treated as one, getting more hung up on hotel suites and limos than anyone else at ABC Sports.

"He started becoming a prick and a prima donna," said one co-worker. "He got more and more that way. If people give him what he wants, he's a good guy. If they slip up a little bit, then he's bad-mouthing them, ripping them."

Michaels's work earned him stacks of exceptional notices in the press. But the occasional, mostly mild knocks he took often outraged him out of all proportion. He would complain angrily not only to the writers, but often to their editors too.

To many of his colleagues, this reaction made no sense. Michaels was at the top; he had nothing to fear from a few negative comments. He was beginning to display a hypersensitivity to the press reminiscent of Cosell, the man he disparaged so vehemently. And, unlike Cosell, Michaels had many more fans than foes in the press.

What Michaels did not have was recognition beyond the fairly narrow world of sports. Unlike Cosell and McKay at ABC, Madden and Musburger at CBS, and Bryant Gumbel and Bob Costas at NBC, he had not become a personality outside the broadcast booth.

Cosell ridiculed Michaels's inability to emerge as anything but a sports figure, saying he had broadcast the single greatest event of all time—the American hockey victory—and walked away from it obscure instead of celebrated.

Michaels loved being inside the booth too much to volunteer for studio work, which would have enlarged his public profile. But when Dennis Lewin turned up on his doorstep with the invitation to speak to 30 or 40 million people every Monday night, Michaels found himself especially excited by the prospect of all that week-to-week exposure. "My work was now going to be more visible to a larger audience than it had ever been before," he later said.

The *Monday Night Football* lineup was far from settled. Joe Namath had to be released. Nobody thought he had worked out on the air, and he had no long-term ties to ABC. It was a cut-and-dried business decision—for the moment.

Swanson had one of his aides call Namath's lawyer, Jimmy Walsh to tell him that Joe would not be back. Namath had signed a two-year contract, so ABC still owed him $850,000 for 1986.

The two Dennises running ABC Sports turned next to the production side, which Swanson felt had deteriorated badly.

Forte was kept on as the director. His reputation still carried him. Besides, ABC was not well stocked with ace football directors. Most people in the department believed the list began and ended with Forte.

But Bob Goodrich had produced the show for six turbulent years, longer than anyone else in *Monday Night* history. Everybody, including Goodrich, believed the show needed a new man in charge in the truck.

Ken Wolfe had all the right qualities. He was young—thirty-three—smart, good with people, and experienced, after years of producing the B-games on college football. And his friendship with Al Michaels didn't hurt.

Wolfe also had something in common with Chet Forte—he too had been an All–Ivy League guard in basketball. Wolfe, a six-foot-two-inch native of Brooklyn, had graduated from Harvard in 1974 with no delusions of NBA grandeur. He headed off to play in Europe, but returned after one season to join ABC as a production assistant.

Working his way up to associate director and associate producer, Wolfe handled many major assignments—the Olympics, baseball, boxing, college football—but never *Monday Night Football*. He was the first producer the show would have since Year One who had no previous experience on the telecast.

Wolfe learned immediately that "the nature of the business had changed," as he put it. He was going to have to produce a new, slimmed-down version of the show. *Monday Night Football* was no longer the spoiled child of ABC Sports. Swanson had cut off its allowance.

There would, he decreed, be no more limos, no more posh hotel suites, no more staff hand-holders in the booth and the truck, no more cushy extras of any sort. None of that affected the product that went out over the air, but other economies did. The number of cameras, which had peaked in 1984 with twelve, was down to eight for some games in 1986.

Wolfe dutifully doled out the operative explanation to the press: "We're getting back to basic football."

That, of course, was "back" to a place where *Monday Night Football* had never been before.

Swanson's no-frills plan still lacked a crucial component. Frank Gifford, upset and insulted, was on the West Coast saying nothing about whether he intended to accept Dennis Swanson's decision to alter his *Monday Night* duties.

But another voice of protest was heard. In his only public comment on any of the convulsions at ABC Sports, the department he had built into an industry landmark, Roone Arledge denounced the treatment being given to his friend Frank Gifford.

"If it's perceived as a demotion," Arledge told the New York *Daily News*, "and I don't quarrel with the perception, Frank has been ill-served. He is one of the people who stood very tall in some difficult times, particularly last year. After 15 years he deserves a lot better and it's worth reconsidering the move."

Arledge conceded that he had not been consulted on the decision, confirming that his "group president" title was meaningless. He had completely lost authority over the Sports division.

But Arledge still considered Gifford his closest friend. "I have a strange criteria for judging people," Arledge would say. "If I were arrested by the Turkish authorities on a trumped-up drug charge and I could make one phone call for help, Frank Gifford would be on a very short list. He wouldn't sleep until I was out."

Now, for the sake of his friend, Arledge was willing to speak out—even though the gesture exposed his own demotion.

"Frank held everything together last year," Arledge said. "It's a shame if there's any implication that he was less than totally professional."

The comments brought no reaction from Cap Cities. Dennis Swanson had nothing to say, but his silence made it clear that his decision was not going to be reconsidered. Later, Dennis Lewin said of Arledge's protests, "He's entitled to his opinion."

Gifford, meanwhile, sorted through his options. The changes at ABC Sports came as one of his friends, Susan Winston, was installed as a special consultant to CBS News for that network's beleaguered morning show. Gifford had worked with Winston when he had filled in as host of *Good Morning America*, a show she produced. Winston was interested in bringing Gifford to CBS.

He waited almost two months before making his decision, months plagued by concern about his mother and a final unpleasant phase of his marriage to Astrid. The breakup landed his name in scandal-sheet headlines. He had begun a serious new relationship with a New York talk-show host named Kathie Lee Johnson—and Astrid went public with her scorn for the openness of that relationship.

At the same time, Gifford was discreetly negotiating with Swanson, whose approach had softened considerably.

The key to his return, the thing Gifford wanted, was the assignment as official host of *Monday Night Football.* Wolfe said, "Frank's feeling was, 'I've been here sixteen years. All these people have come in and out. I'm still the voice of *Monday Night Football.'* It was something of an instinctual reaction. 'Hey, I'm moving here, moving there, moving to analysis. But I should still be the host.' "

Swanson came to agree. He said, "I can't imagine *Monday Night Football* without Frank Gifford. Frank is still the soothing voice, the face people tune in to see."

He eventually signed Gifford to a new five-year contract at about $1.1 million a year. The contract specified that Gifford would host the show—open every game and halftime show— in addition to doing the color commentary.

Gifford discounted the money as an inducement. "I've done very well and do very well outside this. But this is what I focus on. This has been part of my life. And quite frankly I'm very proud of it."

He could back up the pride. Gifford had done more *Monday Night Football* games than anyone else. Through all sorts of personal tragedies, including deaths in his family, he had never missed a Monday night game. The show had become a part of him he could not easily shed.

In May, ABC announced that Frank Gifford would be the sole analyst on *Monday Night Football.* A few weeks later, Swanson met a group of television critics in Los Angeles, where he was asked to explain all the changes in the booth. He praised Gifford and Michaels, saying that the two of them should produce "a higher quality on-air presentation than we've had, and it's just that simple." Then, almost as an afterthought, he said: "It just seemed to me the least amount of risk involved in that decision, so that's why we did it."

It was a revealing comment. Unlike Arledge and so many of the people who built ABC by taking chances on unorthodox ideas or unusual personalities, Swanson tried to minimize risk.

He was not a gambler who made gut decisions; he was a businessman who made calculated ones.

The code word for Frank Gifford's performance in 1986 was *adjustment*. As in, "Frank was making the toughest adjustment of all." That was the official reaction of Ken Wolfe. Privately, Wolfe admitted he was "playing the game a little."

Everybody played the game a little during the 1986 season. The name of the game was: "Pretend This Is Working."

They had to pretend that *Monday Night Football* was working despite an analyst who did not analyze, a director who was tired of directing, a budget that was stretched to the breaking point, and a schedule that turned into a disaster.

The production staff split into factions, with Michaels, Wolfe, and the other newcomers setting themselves apart from Gifford, Forte, and the rest of what was left of the old *Monday Night* crowd. Neither faction trusted the other. And neither was happy with the quality of the telecasts.

Gifford's shift to color commentary was the most glaring problem. Almost nobody believed it was working well. One of the major powers of the old ABC Sports called it "the worst move in the history of sports television."

Gifford's weaknesses were exposed as never before. For the first time, he was not sharing the booth with someone despised by a sizable portion of the public—Cosell—or someone less able to talk articulately about football—Simpson or Namath. And he was being asked, for the first time at ABC, to analyze and comment on the game. His tendency to apologize for the players and the league, only a minor drawback when he was doing play-by-play, became a flaw that could not be ignored.

Gifford had finally lost his renowned ability to escape unscathed as the invective from the public and press came flying at the show. *Monday Night*'s Teflon man had become the Velcro man: Every insult stuck.

The press commenced firing at will in the Hall of Fame Game in August and never let up. Gifford took a terrible beating.

In a *New York Times* review of the opening game, Michael Goodwin said, "He used the word 'great' eight times. 'Spectacular' and 'tremendous' each were called upon twice, while 'superb' and 'extraordinary' were also used. 'Good' was about as close as he came to criticism."

In the Atlanta *Journal*, Hubert Mizell wrote, "The Al Michaels–Frank Gifford tandem has been as inadequate as a Band-Aid on a decapitation. . . . Gifford obviously knelt at some jock altar and dedicated his life to protecting players, protecting coaches and protecting the NFL."

In the *San Francisco Chronicle*, Herb Caen said in his column that "Gifford is about as colorful as cream cheese on white bread and now that English is our official language, could be in big trouble."

And in *The Washington Post*, Norman Chad, in what was mostly a *favorable* review of *Monday Night Football*, said that Gifford had started the season "by shifting his collection of clichés from one end of the broadcasting booth to the other. Gifford might be the only person capable of both surviving a nuclear attack and having something nice to say about the weather the day after. . . . He is to NFL telecasts what Ricardo Montalban is to *Fantasy Island*—a congenial guide to good times, taking us on a carefree trip in which we encounter only great athletes, nice guys and wonderful rivalries."

Ironically, Arledge's old charge to take football out of the cathedral and expose it to irreverent commentary had come back to haunt his fondest friend. Gifford was still doing analysis the softball way he had two decades—and a lifetime of television—earlier at CBS. Now the critics would not stand for it.

Gifford stood up stoically under the barrage, saying he was not reading the reviews. When asked about the criticism, his main defense contained both a kernel of truth and an effective plea for patience and sympathy. "Going to color man was something I was asked to do," Gifford told Rudy Martzke in *USA TODAY*. "It's totally different."

Inside, Gifford was in pain. "It was tough," he said. "It was a struggle all year."

He did not get much help—or much sympathy—from Al Michaels or Ken Wolfe.

On the air, the chemistry between the announcers was bad from the beginning. "Al just didn't bring Frank in," one *Monday Night* veteran said. "They would never develop any controversy."

Off the air, Michaels and Wolfe displayed scorn for Gifford—as long as Frank was not around.

Michaels was careful to play the role of team player in public. He spoke warmly of Gifford in the press, blaming any problems on that arduous "adjustment" Frank was being asked to make. In Gifford's presence, Michaels was solicitous of his feelings, even to the point of occasionally asking for Frank's assessment of how well he was doing on play-by-play or wondering if Roone had told Frank what he thought of the show.

But Michaels and Wolfe had little respect for Gifford. Michaels seemed to resent that Gifford had the assignment of opening the show; he wanted to do it himself.

"Al thought Frank was a bumbling idiot," a longtime crew member said. "For Frank to be opening the show, Al thought was ridiculous."

Once, soon after Norman Chad's stinging slam on Gifford appeared in *The Washington Post*, Michaels walked up to a crew member in the hotel, pulled a clipping of the review from his pocket, and asked, "Want to slip this under Frank's door?"

Another staffer reported a similar experience, saying Michaels pulled out some of Gifford's bad notices and joked about them.

Michaels charged later that any and all people relating such incidents were "trying to stir things up between [him] and Frank." He called the stories about the clippings "a complete, bullshit fabrication."

But Chet Forte disputed Michaels's denial. "Al backstabbed Frank all season," Forte said. "If he says he didn't, he's a liar."

Wolfe was neither as forceful nor as open about his disdain, but he too was frustrated with Gifford. He would bad-mouth him in the control room, shrugging his shoulders and making it clear that while he was stuck with Gifford, he wasn't happy with him.

Forte found himself in the strange position of defending Gifford as the season began. They were the Old Guard, after all, and Forte stood up for Gifford when Wolfe or Michaels complained about Frank's mistakes.

But Forte and Gifford had never been close; they were an odd couple at best. By mid-season, Forte had abandoned his defense work on Frank's behalf. Gifford slid into isolation from the rest of the crew, and so did Forte.

Forte and Wolfe were having their own problems. Forte, as usual, wanted to run the show. Wolfe was the slightly nervous newcomer, and he usually deferred to Forte. But Forte was worn out by all the hassles, especially the aggravation of working with Gifford.

"Sometimes I just had to leave the truck and get out," Forte said. "Howard was unbelievable and there is no comparison. But Frank, whether he was too intense, whether it was his personal problems, with his mother's illness, a lot of personal things, it certainly affected Frank. Because Frank was atrocious. Atrocious. Not even passable. . . . Thirty, forty takes on the opening. I mean, that's unbelievable."

Forte, in his seventeenth year of directing football on Monday nights, was running on empty. "Chet careened from caring to not giving a shit," said a crew member. "You just knew he didn't give a damn anymore."

He started displaying his boredom and disgust in public, complaining to the press that Cap Cities' austerity program had taken the fun out of working at ABC Sports. "I don't think you'll see any limousines tonight," he told a reporter.

Nobody was seeing limousines in 1986. It was the year of the Toyota, as Michaels put it. The p.a.'s were told to book cheap hotels, which the stars and production staff despised.

Michaels took it worst. "Here's a guy who, when he was young, working his way up, saw all these limos and Grade A treatment, and when he finally got there it was all taken away from him," a staff member said. "He found himself riding around in rental cars."

Forte flew into L.A. one time to be greeted by a young gofer driving her own car—a 1976 faded-blue VW bug. They had a fifty-five minute ride to Anaheim, so the woman tried to break the ice with a joke, saying, "Not a limo, huh? Would've brought the Rolls but it had a flat." Forte was not amused.

The games themselves did nothing to improve anyone's mood. Few were exciting, many were one-sided, and several were routs. The best game on the schedule, a mid-season showdown between the powers of the NFC East, the Giants and the Redskins, turned into a ratings fiasco, due to circumstances beyond ABC's control. The seventh game of a cliffhanger World Series between the Mets and the Red Sox was wiped out by rain on Sunday night and had to be rescheduled to Monday. "Basic football" on ABC was annihilated by exciting baseball on NBC. The game drew a pitiful 8.8 rating, effectively ensuring that the season-long rating would fall again.

Later in the season, a *Monday Night* telecast in Washington set a new record for longevity, concluding at 12:57 A.M. in the East. The game was equally numbing, a clunky 14–6 win by the Redskins over the 49ers. Though few stayed up to watch, Michaels and Gifford had one of their best nights together, getting off several funny lines inspired by the slow-motion play.

Midway through the third quarter, Forte flashed a graphic: "It's Tuesday." At 12:30 Michaels welcomed the audience tuning in after Johnny Carson. Gifford suggested that they order in brunch. At one point Michaels said the two teams had been penalized more than Ivan Boesky.

Dennis Swanson thought most of the humor was great, but he disliked Forte's graphic. He dressed down the director about it.

One viewer who expressed outright boredom with the *Monday Night* package in 1986 was the recently departed Joe Namath. He told a reporter from *Newsday* that the games were dull, that the announcers were missing too many things, and that he wished he were there to help out.

Swanson, who saw the comments, dashed off a pungent note to Namath informing him that ABC, which had been paying his salary, was terminating his contract for "unprofessional conduct." Namath sued soon after, and the case dragged on for more than a year.

As the season lumbered to a conclusion, the mood on the telecast grew dark. Swanson was talking publicly about all the money the package was losing. ABC, he said, would abandon the most famous franchise in sports television unless the network could get a better rights deal with the NFL. "We can't be in the business of subsidizing pro football," he said.

The uncertainty about the future of *Monday Night Football* made it more and more difficult to get up for the games.

Before a game in Cleveland, the crew found a new diversion. With the pricey hotels downtown now out of range of the new budget, the caravan moved out to a hotel near the airport with one notable attraction—a nine-hole miniature-golf course in the courtyard.

On Sunday morning, Forte and Wolfe, along with two p.a.'s and Billy Edwards, the longtime sideline assistant who signaled the television timeouts, began a putting tournament. With Forte involved, money was soon riding on the outcome. Gifford joined in briefly, but not successfully. A cold November breeze blew on the players, but they pressed on. They played for about two hours, and agreed to work in another hour the next morning before the eleven o'clock production meeting.

The stakes escalated in the morning. Bets of $100 and $150 were riding on individual putts. Forte was in his element, dashing around the little green-felt fairways, scraping his opponent's crotches with his putter at opportune times. The scheduled hour for the production meeting came—and went. The producer and director were still playing miniature golf.

The announcers wandered by. Michaels was invited to play but declined. Crew members watched and waited for the meeting. The golf game went on.

It didn't end until well after three P.M. By then, the production meeting was long forgotten.

Dennis Swanson had demanded an end to the screaming in the production trucks. He said it was unprofessional. But everyone knew that the champion screamers of ABC Sports, Chet Forte and Chuck Howard, also happened to be the production people with the deepest loyalties to Roone Arledge. With Jeff Ruhe and Jim Spence gone—Spence had cleaned out his desk the moment he heard he had been passed over and Swanson had been named president of Sports—some people suspected Swanson had targeted Forte and Howard.

Howard had reason to be suspicious. He had lost his job as head of production to Lewin. And Swanson had once cornered him and asked him how often he talked to Arledge. "It's none of your fucking business," Howard told his boss.

Resentful as he was, Howard decided to be straight with Swanson. He went on to tell him that he was not a close friend of Arledge.

"You don't know me," Howard said. "What you're concerned

about—and I know what you're concerned about—is that you think I'm gonna call Roone and bitch to him about something that's going on or undermine you. Hey, I don't operate that way. If I've got a bitch with you, you're gonna hear about it right up front. I'm not gonna be calling fucking Arledge behind your back."

Whether or not Swanson believed him, Howard's days at ABC Sports were coming to an end. In November, Swanson and Lewin heard about a screaming confrontation between Howard and an associate director. Lewin made inquiries, then approached Howard. Howard became the next ABC veteran to go to Irwin Weiner about a severance arrangement.

Somehow Forte hung on. Swanson had taken him aside once to tell him he was a great director, which softened the impact of his first insulting remarks about Forte's salary. But Forte was thinking of quitting. He wanted to go into business on his own and write a book about his career.

Forte went public with some complaints. Near the end of the *Monday Night* season, he crossed a line—he compared Swanson's rule unfavorably to Arledge's.

"In our heyday, it was, 'Do what you want. Get all the cameras you can,'" Forte told Joe Lapointe of *The Detroit Free Press*. "We stayed in the best places. We traveled first-class. It was a lot more fun. It was the good times. You didn't care how much money you spent, because you were making money.

"Roone is gone," Forte went on. "Jim Spence is gone. Chuck Howard is gone. Who's next? My contract is up in 1988, before the Olympics. I don't know where I'm going to be in 1988 when it comes to television." He liked Swanson, he said, but he also called him a "tough son of a bitch."

Forte also complained about the spending cutbacks that left him with fewer cameras and about the lousy games. "It's been a very frustrating year, overall," he said. "It just has not been a fun year. It's bad enough trying to keep my crew up when it's 21–0 at halftime. You're giving them pep talks. 'It's still prime time, guys. It's still on the air!' It's been low on the fun scale. It's been the worst. I cannot remember a series of games as bad as this year."

When Swanson saw the story, he erupted. He didn't call Forte. Instead, he called Ron Konecky, Forte's lawyer and agent, to complain. Lewin told Forte that Swanson was "very upset."

"Dennis," Forte replied, "I'm sorry but that's what I believe. That's what I believe this business is coming to."

Forte thought ABC Sports had never been in worse shape. He had been frustrated with Arledge, he had been through monumental battles with Chuck Howard and Jim Spence, but he respected them all. They stood for something, he would say. He especially missed Arledge. Forte, for all his braggadocio, felt secure when he knew Arledge was watching. "I don't want to sit there like God," he said. "I want somebody to critique me. And the critique guy in my area was Arledge. I had the best."

Now, he thought, nobody cared about production, nobody even knew production. "They don't have anybody with guts anymore," Forte would say. "Plus they don't have talent. That's the key thing. You don't get piss in this business without any talent."

The final blowup came after the last *Monday Night* game of the year in Miami. Swanson told Wolfe and Forte to stop over in Memphis on their way back to New York to survey the site of the opening game of ABC's new college-basketball package—a detour that Forte thought was a waste of time. Basketball coverage, he thought, was routine; you put a camera at each end of the court, and two others on the sides. He called Lewin and said, "This is crazy! How many people do you need on a survey?" Then he flew back to New York.

Swanson had seen enough. He demanded an explanation. Forte was tired of explaining himself. "At the end, I really wanted to get out," he said. He resigned from ABC in January.

Two months later, Forte suffered a massive heart attack. He needed extensive bypass surgery to save his life.

13.

ALL IN THE
GAME

*"If we have a good football game, we get good ratings. If we have
a great football game, we get great ratings. And, if we have a bad
football game, we get lousy ratings."*—FRANK GIFFORD

At the party inside the Shedd Aquarium, across the street
from Soldier Field in Chicago, the fish looked more excited than
the guests.

The guests were the ones with tickets in their pockets. They
were on their way to the most talked-about event of the summer
of 1987 in the Windy City and one of the most eagerly anticipated
games in NFL history, a showdown between the Chicago Bears
and the New York Giants, the Super Bowl champions of 1986
versus the Super Bowl champions of 1987.

None of the electricity generated by the game was evident
around the hors d'oeuvres, where men dressed in business suits
engaged in muted conversation. Others stared at the sea life
floating by the glass panels of an enormous fish tank in the
center of the room. In deference to some of the deeper-water
fish, the lighting was dim. There was no music. It wasn't that
kind of party.

This was the new brand of *Monday Night Football* party, a
match for the new brand of *Monday Night Football*—less osten-

tatious, less raucous, and less extravagant. It reflected the new management style at ABC Sports. Dennis Swanson had set out to project a back-to-basics image. "We can't go into a negotiation with people, and ask them for rights-fee relief, and then travel around in limousines and throw big parties," he would say.

The guests were mainly advertising clients, many of whom had paid a premium to buy into what ABC had expected to be its biggest *Monday Night* opener ever. They sat around at small tables covered with white tablecloths, talking among themselves. Several wondered if Oprah Winfrey would show up.

She didn't.

Neither did any of the stars of *Monday Night Football*. Swanson appeared briefly and shook a few hands—the only visible evidence that the function had any connection to the show or to ABC Sports.

The star of the evening was a medium-sized hammerhead shark.

As the guests drifted over to the stadium long before kickoff, they did not seem disappointed. The party was far from memorable, but the big game was still coming up. That was what really counted.

As the final days of the NFL's $2.1-billion five-year television-rights agreement arrived during the winter of 1986–87, the top network executives on Broadcast Row were in a rebellious mood. After years of playing the supplicants to the NFL, this time, this winter, they were finally going to stand up to Pete Rozelle.

They had no choice. The networks were going to lose more than $70 million on football in 1986. ABC alone had lost $25 million, about the same as 1985, despite all of Swanson's efforts. Every time a game went on the air, the network went another $1 million or so into the red. No other program in the history of network television had lost so much money.

Swanson was determined to bring that to an end. "We are going to be asking for relief," he said. "There's no question about that." The other networks issued similar declarations. Forget any increases, they warned Rozelle.

Rozelle, for his part, had to contend with his owners. Each

team was getting about $17 million in television money in 1986, an average of 60 percent of its revenues. Art Modell of the Browns spoke for his fellow owners when he told reporters, "I cannot go backwards. I must go forwards."

Rozelle and Modell knew that the only solution was to turn to cable television—the competitive force that had done so much damage to the networks in the first place. "We knew we had to take less money from the networks," Modell said, "but you can only do that by adding a new source of revenue." The NFL was ready to adapt to the changing landscape of television.

Throughout the fall, Rozelle, Modell, and Val Pinchbeck, the NFL's veteran television executive, met with executives of the leading cable interests—ESPN, Home Box Office, Showtime, USA Cable, Ted Turner's Superstation WTBS, and a consortium of cable-system operators who had joined together specifically to pursue pro football.

None of that pleased the networks. For pro football to succeed on cable, they knew the cable services would need a strong schedule of games. None of them was going to pay for Green Bay against Tampa Bay. What's more, NFL games on cable were sure to become an appealing alternative to entertainment shows on the networks. "If cable does damage to our audience," said Gene Jankowski, the president of the CBS Broadcast Group, "we're only going to pay less the next time around."

Cap Cities/ABC had the least to lose from a cable deal, provided that the winner was ESPN, the all-sports cable network. Cap Cities/ABC owned 80 percent of ESPN; the parent company's interests were watched over by Herb Granath, the onetime *Monday Night* ad salesman who was in charge of all of ABC's cable investments. The other 20 percent of ESPN was owned by RJR/Nabisco, which was represented by Don Ohlmeyer, another *Monday Night* alumnus. Ohlmeyer had become a key consultant to ESPN.

Launched in 1979, ESPN had been ridiculed for years as a minor-league player in sports television, especially when it filled time with broadcasts of rodeo, softball, and full-contact karate. But the company, after posting $100 million in losses through its first six years of operation, climbed into the black in 1985. And ESPN quickly broke to the head of the pack among the cable operators seeking to deal with the NFL.

By the first of the year, the new rights deal had begun to take shape. The NFL would sell the NFC games to CBS, the AFC games to NBC, the *Monday Night* games to ABC, and a Sunday night package to cable. Swanson was determined to get rid of Thursday night football; Rozelle agreed that the so-called specials had been a flop.

Then, to the delight of the NFL, a new player entered the game—the fledgling Fox Broadcasting Co., which was beginning its drive to become the fourth television network.

Fox, bankrolled by media baron Rupert Murdoch, made a serious run at *Monday Night Football*. At the time, the new network had little to offer its stations beyond the late-night rantings of talk-show host Joan Rivers. The NFL in prime time would give Fox instant credibility as well as a solid beachhead on Mondays from which to expand.

Murdoch and Barry Diller, Fox's hard-nosed chairman, went to see Rozelle. They also made their position public. "We'll take ABC's contract and sign it now," Diller said. In 1986, ABC had paid $150 million for twenty-one games, or $7.1 million a game. Near the end of the negotiations, Diller offered close to $9 million a game, but Rozelle did not want to take the risk of working with a new entity with a weak station lineup.

Naturally, he did not tell that to Swanson.

ABC was up against the wall—just as it had been in 1970, when Rozelle had used the threat of Howard Hughes's syndicated sports network as a sledgehammer.

So much was at stake. As the third-place network, ABC would be devastated by the loss of *Monday Night Football*, one of its few remaining prime-time ratings successes. Fox would probably make inroads into ABC's affiliate lineup on Mondays.

There was a lot at stake for Swanson too. "Do you want to be known as the president of ABC Sports and the man who lost *Monday Night Football*?" he said later. "You want that written on your tombstone? Not me."

ABC finally made the deal, agreeing to pay $360 million over three years. The price tag came to $7.5 million a game—more than the network had paid in 1986, despite all of Swanson's bluster.

Swanson was uncomfortable with the numbers. "I felt they

had squeezed more dollars out of us than we wanted to pay," he said. "We were at risk." His only consolation was that this package did not include the unattractive Thursday games.

ESPN, meanwhile, won the cable package with a bid of $153 million for the three years. They would get eight Sunday night games in November and December, ending ABC's monopoly on prime-time NFL action.

Only CBS and NBC negotiated price reductions—CBS to $450 million, NBC to $360 million, both down about 7 percent from 1986. They were also getting less for their money. With so many of the best matchups set aside for prime time, the Sunday afternoon schedules were starting to look like leftovers.

Fox came away empty-handed. The Fox people hoped for relief from an investigation by the Federal Trade Commission, which spent months trying to decide whether the NFL was obligated to sell its games to the highest bidder. Fox officials suspected that the three major networks had pressured the league to keep football out of the hands of their newest competitor.

Rozelle had not exactly been humiliated. In fact, as he flew to Hawaii for the annual NFL owners meeting, he felt that this negotiation had been his toughest and most satisfying. The NFL would take in nearly as much money from television in 1987 as it had in 1986. No one—except Rozelle himself—had expected that.

In the spring of 1987, ABC Sports had an opening for a football commentator.

The opening was not on *Monday Night Football*. Unlike most of the critics, Swanson was satisfied with Gifford and Michaels. He said repeatedly that they would return as the *Monday Night* team if ABC negotiated a new rights deal with the NFL.

But college football had lost its analyst, Tim Brandt, who jumped to CBS when Swanson passed on an option to renew his contract at a substantial increase in pay.

The two ABC Dennises swiftly concluded that the best candidates were working for the other networks. Lewin's first choice was Dan Dierdorf, who had been considered for some college work on ABC a couple of years earlier.

In two years at CBS, Dierdorf, a former St. Louis Cardinals

lineman, had made a precipitous climb, becoming a network play-by-play man as a novice, then in his second season ascending to the job of analyst on CBS's number-two team—putting him just behind John Madden in the ranks of color commentators at CBS.

Lewin phoned Dierdorf's agent, Art Kaminsky, just to find out if Dierdorf was even free to talk to another network. He was surprised to learn that Dierdorf was immediately available.

Dierdorf had negotiated a long-term contract with CBS in 1985, but he had never signed it. He was upset with some of the terms, including an option that provided only a $250-a-game raise in 1987.

Lewin could scarcely believe his luck. He brought Dierdorf and Kaminsky to a meeting in New York and offered Dan the job as lead analyst on ABC's college-football package.

Dierdorf, already a savvy media veteran, respectfully declined. He did not figure that a number-one college-football job at ABC represented a step up from a number-two NFL job at CBS.

A couple of weeks later, Lewin called again: Would Dierdorf be interested in the college job, plus a role hosting the halftime of *Monday Night Football*?

Now the offer was starting to sound interesting to Dierdorf. Not interesting enough to accept, but interesting enough to consider.

While waiting to hear back, Lewin and Swanson talked the situation over. They liked Dan Dierdorf; the more they talked, the more they wanted Dan Dierdorf. *Monday Night Football* had worked with three in the booth before, hadn't it?

In April, Kaminsky called Dierdorf with good news. ABC had offered him that third chair—vacant for one year—in the booth on Monday nights.

After a few formalities with CBS, where the news that the Dierdorf contract did not have a Dierdorf signature on it enraged CBS executives, a place was reserved in the *Monday Night* booth for Dan Dierdorf.

At 290 pounds, Dierdorf was an extra-large presence before he even went on the air.

Dan Dierdorf, who had been a not-too-serious history major at the University of Michigan, knew his football history inside and out. He also knew quite a bit about *Monday Night Football*'s history and he was flattered by the ABC offer.

"I was the first ex-jock to be in the booth because I was a broadcaster, not because I was a marquee ball player," he said.

He was hardly a scrub ball player, of course. Dierdorf had made All-Pro five times, and he was considered the best interior offensive lineman of his day.

But Dierdorf became an announcing star on television the old-fashioned way—he earned it.

He had always found it absurd that football players did so little with their lives in the off-season. He considered football a part-time job and decided early in his professional career to learn broadcasting from the bottom up.

Born in 1949, Dierdorf grew up in Canton, Ohio, home of the Pro Football Hall of Fame, with a love of the game and a sense that he could go as far as dedication and hard work could take him.

He starred at the University of Michigan and, in 1971, was drafted in the second round by the Cardinals. The team eventually grew into a playoff contender but never erased the franchise's enduring mark in the annals of sports history: The Cardinals were the only long-established team in a major American sport that had never won a postseason game of any kind.

Dierdorf shrugged off the disappointments and took advantage of his celebrity status in St. Louis. He began doing a talk show on radio in 1975. He was bright, with an easygoing on-air style and a natural sense of humor. The show grew into a local institution, so Dierdorf had his second career in place long before his football days ended.

When Dierdorf retired after the 1983 season, he did not try to jump into television commentary. He recognized that "most ex-jocks, when they went with a network, got offered a three- or four-game package. Some became stars, but more often they got chewed up and spit out."

Dierdorf decided it would be wiser to develop some expertise as a color commentator before taking on the networks, so he started with radio football. He did forty college and pro games in 1984, a schedule that had him flying all over the country on football weekends. He once called three games in thirty-six hours.

By the next fall, he was ready for the networks. A tape of his work had found its way into the right hands. They belonged to Terry O'Neil, who was still running the football coverage at CBS.

O'Neil had an unexpected problem. One of his top play-by-play men, Frank Gleiber, had died of a heart attack. O'Neil called Dierdorf, telling him he was thinking of "investing the time and money in a guy with no bad habits to teach him play-by-play."

Dierdorf liked the challenge. O'Neil, who still had no compunction about spending his network's money, set up Dierdorf with complete crews, including a color partner, stat-man, and spotter, for three preseason games that were pure practice sessions. Even Arledge at his height had never sprung for more than one dry-run game.

Satisfied, O'Neil sent Dierdorf out as a play-by-play man. Dierdorf did well, well enough to be in O'Neil's plans for the following season. But O'Neil stopped making football plans for CBS in 1985. He lost a power struggle within CBS Sports and left the network.

The new boss, Ted Shaker, liked Dierdorf, but believed he had more potential as a color commentator. He boosted him to the second team behind Madden. "It was the best thing that could have happened to me," Dierdorf said.

As everything fell into place in Dierdorf's professional life, his personal life was marred by tragedy. In January 1985, the second child of his second marriage, a two-month-old daughter named Kelly, died in her crib from sudden infant death syndrome.

Dierdorf responded to the crushing grief by working even harder. He kept his radio show, continued all his football announcing jobs, then began anchoring sports reports for a St. Louis television station. His wife, Debbie, finally made him cut back out of fear that he would have a heart attack.

When Dierdorf arrived on *Monday Night Football*, he was experienced as a broadcaster and totally confident that he could handle the job. He was prepared to deliver everything that ABC wanted—personality and humor, as well as insight, and a deft hand with the Telestrator, O'Neil's favorite toy from CBS that Swanson wanted to import to *Monday Night Football*.

Dierdorf was unsure about just one thing: He wondered how Frank Gifford would take the news that he was now going to have even less to say on *Monday Night Football*.

*   *   *

ABC had every reason to believe that 1987 would be the comeback season for *Monday Night Football*. The network was pleased with the announcing team. It had shed the Thursday/Sunday package. And the schedule delivered by the NFL was, in the words of Ken Wolfe, "ridiculously good . . . almost a can't-miss proposition."

Pete Rozelle had gone out of his way to revalidate the NFL's most important television franchise. Beginning with the Giants-Bears showdown, the schedule was stocked with playoff teams.

The personable Dierdorf eased comfortably into the mix. He got along so well with Michaels off-camera that no one had any doubts the chemistry would carry over onto the air. "I'm in tune with Al," Dierdorf said, "because Al and I are semicrazy."

Gifford was not playing the same tune, but he was still on the team. He was getting used to making adjustments—the *Monday Night* cast had changed every year since 1982—and he would give his best effort. He had nothing but wonderful things to say about Dan Dierdorf.

While Dierdorf attracted all the attention, a new player was brought into the truck as well. Veteran Larry Kamm became the first director to take over the chair occupied by Chet Forte since 1970.

Kamm was a journeyman director who had worked every one of ABC's nine Olympics since 1964 and had toiled for many years on *Wide World*. Even Forte predicted that he would get by on Monday nights, because he had Chet's hand-picked camera crew behind him. Forte was also convinced that Kamm lacked talent; he felt he would need all the help he could get.

That sounded like sour grapes, but by the end of the preseason, most of the crew members were ready to agree with Forte. Kamm was regarded as a hack director, oddly obsessed with low-angle shots and sluggish when trying to capture fast-developing plays.

Kamm did not aid his cause by being, in the words of one staffer, "so stuck up nobody can stand him. . . . He thinks he's the greatest. Everyone else thinks he's terrible."

Michaels put so much into his work and cared so deeply about the quality of the telecasts that he would occasionally take subtle shots on the air at Kamm if the director put up a bad shot or made a bizarre cut. Wolfe's relationship with Kamm began badly, and stayed that way all season long.

If Kamm was one weak link on the production team, Gifford remained the other—though he was growing more comfortable as an analyst and winning respect for his dedication, if nothing else, from Michaels and Wolfe. They still made fun of Gifford behind his back, but it no longer seemed malicious. "Some of the things could be pretty derogatory, but they were mostly laughing it off," said a crew member. "It wasn't nasty."

After watching a videotape of the highlights of the Giants 1986 season that had been voiced over by Gifford, Wolfe joked, "Gifford's the only guy who can make a championship year sound boring."

The Giants-Bears opener paid off on the field; it had big names, big plays, and big hits. The game also delivered a big audience, but ABC was disappointed. The network had hoped for record ratings, but the 23.7 rating fell short even of the previous record for an opening game. ABC salespeople began to wonder if the new television ratings system, the Nielsen "people meters," which required more active participation by viewers, contained some antisports bias.

But the sales department had much more to worry about than the new push-button ratings system. Looming over the season was the threat of another players' strike, something no one believed could possibly happen when the season started.

It happened at midnight on September 21, before the second game of the comeback year of *Monday Night Football* had ended.

During halftime of the game between the Patriots and the Jets, the intransigent representatives of the owners and the players came on the air, laid out their cases, and indicated there was no longer any hope of avoiding a strike. Dierdorf blasted everyone involved, saying neither side seemed sorry about the strike.

Monday Night Football returned two weeks later—not with the NFL, but with "replacement players." The NFL owners, trying to break the players' union, resumed the season after missing a week, using players picked up from minor leagues, waiver lists, bars, and construction jobs.

That night, a promising matchup between the Giants and the 49ers became a bogus game between reject players. The "scab" players, as the regulars called them, put on the worst show in *Monday Night* history, a contest that turned out to be a gross mismatch. The 49ers had taken the strike seriously and lined up a representative team, while the defending Super Bowl champions were a pathetic joke.

ABC concentrated on covering the strike. It was a wise move, although Michaels and Gifford found it strange to be interviewing team owners and striking players while the game was going on. One interview went on even as a touchdown was scored.

The first strike game was memorable for a shot of a Giants replacement player sound asleep in mid-game on the sideline. "That about sums this one up," Michaels said. Gifford tried to explain how the guy weighed three hundred pounds and was just worn out.

Everyone on the crew was distressed by what the strike was doing to their season. Wolfe said, "We could have broken records. . . . It hurt us quite a lot." Dierdorf called the strike "destructive to everyone involved. . . . It was very disappointing to have it happen, and in our Super Bowl year."

Michaels took it hardest. He also took it personally. He felt the league was foisting a fraud on the public; it offended his sense of professionalism. "I had a personal problem dealing with that," he said. "The thing that really disturbed me was the league was able to get away with it."

The next two weeks brought more strike games, which ABC tried to take seriously. But everyone at the network, from the executives to the production staff to the salesmen, believed that the powerful momentum built into the schedule had been immobilized by the strike.

Once the strike ended, ABC's ratings began to rebound. But viewers came and went, depending on who was playing and how the games unfolded. When teams like the Giants, the Cowboys, and the Raiders fell out of the playoff chase, the ratings for their games slid. The season finale, New England against Miami, became a dud when Indianapolis clinched the division title in the AFC East on the previous day. Even as the quality of the production improved—and it did improve, as the season progressed—there was no evidence that viewers were tuning in to watch Michaels, Dierdorf, and Gifford. Now, the game was the thing.

That was fine with the sports television critics. They also embraced Dierdorf as a fresh, appealing new voice. Rudy Martzke of *USA TODAY* called ABC's hiring of Dierdorf "the announcing coup of the season." In *The New York Times*, Michael Goodwin said that Dierdorf "brought a much-needed dimension to the show," and that he and Michaels "seemed to have some personal chemistry." Gifford suffered by comparison. Goodwin called him the "odd man out . . . who is being kept on beyond his time. On the railroads superfluous staffing is called featherbedding."

Still, no matter what the critics or his critical colleagues thought, *Monday Night Football* needed Frank Gifford. He was the last link to the glory years, the glamour years. That became apparent to the production assistants when they checked into hotels. As the p.a. would order newspapers for the staff, the hotel clerk would usually have no reaction to the names of Kenny Wolfe, Larry Kamm, and Al Michaels. The name Dan Dierdorf would often attract a puzzled look, and a request for the spelling. The mention of Frank Gifford, however, would invariably elicit instant recognition and genuine excitement. Gifford remained the only *Monday Night* star with a profile that reached beyond the sports fans.

Ratings at season's end were solid, though they failed to meet expectations. ABC had first projected an average 18 rating for the season, but after getting the schedule, they revised that up to 19.9. *Monday Night Football* finished with a 17.8. The season average was driven down by the strike, but, even so, ABC's sales people were disappointed in the numbers.

Still, the sports advertising marketplace was on the mend. Jim Wasilko, a Swanson ally who was installed as the head of Sports sales early in 1987, had gently pushed ad prices up to $200,000 per spot, higher than ever before, and most of the games were sold out.

Monday Night Football was making money again, though not very much. ABC generated a little more than $9 million in sales per game, but once agency commissions, production, and talent costs were subtracted, there was barely enough left to cover the rights fee. Swanson said the show made a "modest" profit. Other sources said the network made $5 to $7 million.

All year long Wasilko felt that the sports marketplace remained fragile. Looking ahead to 1988, he saw the Winter and Summer Olympics, which would absorb hundreds of millions of advertising dollars. As for *Monday Night Football* in 1988, he said, "I can't tell you we're going to make money."

As Dennis Swanson considered the state of ABC Sports midway through 1987, he felt he had turned things around. "This job has actually gotten to be a little bit more fun lately," he said. "The future of our business is very good." ABC Sports was going to make money for the first time since the glorious Olympic year of 1984. Swanson's problems, though, were far from over.

In September, he took a sudden, unplanned sabbatical. His departure followed what many sources reported was a blowup at a Cap Cities budget meeting, when Swanson lost his temper and screamed obscenities at a financial officer for nit-picking his department budget. Swanson never commented on his leave of absence.

The outburst shocked some people, but it pleased many in the Sports division. They interpreted it as the boss standing up for them. With ABC Sports no longer losing money, they thought, Swanson was resisting demands for further austerity.

He also was under enormous personal strain. His college-age son had been struck and almost killed by a car; it was feared for a time that he might never walk again. One of his sports colleagues said the incident had pushed Swanson near the edge and precipitated the explosion in the Cap Cities meeting. Swanson spent the next few weeks at home.

Michaels, meanwhile, had an explosion of his own. It came during the World Series, which had been a success by any measure—the ratings, the reviews, and the quality of the telecasts. Michaels's play-by-play work was superb.

But a Minneapolis *Star-Tribune* feature writer named Bob Lundegaard rattled Michaels by tuning in to the games on a satellite dish and listening to his between-innings comments to dish viewers. When Michaels read in the next day's paper that he was bad-mouthing his Minnesota hotel and denigrating the series, he called the paper in a rage. He insisted—to no avail—he had been joking. That night on the between-innings satellite feed, Michaels delivered a vicious, prolonged diatribe against Lundegaard. He called the reporter a "scumbag" and implied that he was on drugs. ABC cut off the sound.

No one, though, suffered a more public embarrassment during the fall than director Larry Kamm. He was assigned to direct the New York City marathon, which had become a favorite television event for serious runners. Somehow, ABC missed the shot of the winning runner crossing the finish line—a blunder so incredible that it produced screaming headlines in the city's tabloids the next day. Kamm was mortified.

Swanson had turned around the business of ABC Sports, but at what cost? As he focused on the balance sheet, most ABC productions had become indistinguishable from those of the other networks. Some were clearly worse; the golf coverage had become an industry-wide joke, as ABC missed key shots and misidentified players during major tournaments. *Wide World* was living on its reputation; the ratings fell and, in mid-season, ABC announced there would be an overhaul in 1988.

There was no escaping it anymore. ABC Sports' famous boast that it was "recognized around the world as the leader in sports television" had become just that—a boast.

Al Michaels fired his agent, Barry Frank, late in 1986. He was not getting enough exposure, he thought, and he knew Frank had helped another client, CBS's John Madden, to become a media celebrity with lucrative endorsement deals and best-selling books. Michaels, still a relative unknown outside of sports, felt he deserved as much.

His new agent was Art Kaminsky, who'd made such a good deal for Michaels's new partner, Dan Dierdorf. Kaminsky went to work and negotiated a long-term contract for Michaels that was worth $1.5 million a year. Michaels now earned a higher salary than anyone in sports television except CBS's Musburger.

Dennis Swanson announced the deal a few days before ABC's telecast of the Super Bowl in San Diego. He also announced that Dierdorf's contract—he was making $900,000 a year—had been extended. Both men were tied to ABC through the early 1990s.

Swanson did not want anyone to miss the implication of the double signing. He reminded reporters that Gifford had signed a long-term deal (he was making $1.1 million) that would keep the *Monday Night Football* cast intact for the next few years.

It would be the first time the series had achieved any measure of stability since Howard Cosell walked away from the booth.

Super Bowl XXII, like the four that preceded it, was a Super Rout.

The Washington Redskins, led by quarterback Doug Williams, cannonaded the Denver Broncos with five touchdowns in the second quarter. The final score was 42–10.

Frank Gifford, summing up ABC's disappointment in the second half as the game degenerated into a one-note bore, said, "If it was a fight, the ref would stop it."

ABC's *Monday Night* crew lavished all its technical and verbal skills on the game and was pleased with the results. The game looked clean; no important moments were missed. Despite the lack of suspense, the announcers believed they had called their best game of the season.

Swanson agreed. After the game, he praised his team. In the cool San Diego evening, he walked out of Jack Murphy Stadium with Michaels, his arm draped paternally around the shoulders of his highest-priced talent.

Most reviewers applauded the production. ABC got high marks for its replays and commentary, and Dierdorf drew raves; he was singled out as the star of the telecast for his quick eye, which spotted a Redskin fumble that wasn't called, and for his quick wit, which enlivened the tedious second half.

Some reviews described Dierdorf as the best thing to happen to *Monday Night Football* in years. That was as much good news as the show had generated since the record rating season of 1981. ABC was in the mood for a giddy celebration.

But, by the morning after, Super Bowl XXII had left both ABC Sports and the NFL with a punishing hangover. The rating for the game had plunged to a 41.9, the lowest of any Super Bowl since 1974 and well below the number promised to advertisers. Even worse, Nielsen reported that the game had recorded a 62 share—the worst in the twenty-two-year history of the Super Bowl.

Most previous Super Bowls had achieved shares between 70 and 80, meaning that between 70 and 80 percent of the people watching television at the time had been tuned to the game. Even taking into the account the changed television environment, the many new outlets of video competition, the all-new ratings system, and the competitive weakness of ABC, one conclusion was inescapable—more people than ever before were watching something other than the Super Bowl on that special Sunday in January.

Whatever the merits of the coverage—and ABC's basic football approach had pleased committed sports fans and sports television critics—ABC had failed to attract uncommitted viewers. Many of the viewers who had once flocked to *Monday Night Football* for entertainment, controversy, unpredictability, craziness, and just plain fun were no longer attracted to ABC's solid, but unspectacular, brand of gridiron action.

The limits of the back-to-basics style were most glaring during ABC's pregame show, which was a critical embarrassment and a ratings fiasco. The show was unimaginative, plodding, sloppily produced, and utterly lacking in entertainment value. Keith Jackson, the play-by-play war-horse, was miscast as the host; he had no ties to professional football, no talent as an interviewer, no hope of injecting any fun into the proceedings. The pregame show's 14.3 rating was the worst, by far, in Super Sunday history.

The game telecast was smoother and more professional, of course, but no more compelling than the pregame show. Michaels's enthusiasm, Dierdorf's humor, and Gifford's good-guy appeal went only so far with viewers. The announcers failed, for example, to explain in any real detail why the game had turned around so dramatically in the second quarter and how the Redskins were able to maintain their dominance. They also missed the opportunity to exploit to the fullest a couple of natural story lines—the frustration of Denver's John Elway, a bona fide superstar who was being denied a Super Bowl victory for the second year in a row, and, more important, the record-setting performance of Doug Williams, who was making social history as the Super Bowl's first black quarterback. Surely Cosell would have made more out of Williams's roots at all-black Grambling College, his suffering in Tampa Bay, his departure for the USFL, and his struggle, even during the season just past, to win the Redskins' starting job.

The halftime and postgame shows were also filled with missed opportunities, notably at the end of the telecast when ABC declined to air an arty, highly produced closing. Arledge had made the classy closing flourish an ABC trademark since the 1976 Winter Olympics from Innsbruck, which ended with a glorious music-video montage of the Games' highlights set to the soaring chorus of Beethoven's "Ode to Joy." NBC and CBS immediately began putting their own finishing touches on major events.

ABC had prepared a closing feature for Super Sunday about Doug Williams and Redskins coach Joe Gibbs, but ended the coverage without using it. Instead, ABC Sports signed off with a fuzzy shot of a crowd of Redskins fans celebrating in Washington. Not a single face could be discerned in the mob.

The final image was the furthest thing from up close and personal; it was remote and impersonal. Nor was it original. It was the same chaotic crowd scene displayed after every major sports win, every season, every year. This was the routine of celebration; the drill of victory.

Roone Arledge watched the show in his Manhattan apartment. He had ideas, as always, about the telecast, and, since old habits die hard, he could not help analyzing the coverage. He might have been tempted to pick up the phone to call the booth with a suggestion for the producer or for his friend Frank. He didn't. The Roone phone had been disconnected. Instead, the group president of ABC News and Sports sat back and did his best to enjoy the game—as a spectator.

14.

WHATEVER HAPPENED TO *MONDAY NIGHT FOOTBALL?*

"Turn out the lights. The party's over."—DON MEREDITH

When *Monday Night Football* premiered on ABC, American soldiers were still dying by the thousands in Vietnam, the Beatles had an album on the charts, Hondas were still just motorcycles, and R. J. Reynolds was still telling television viewers that Winston tastes good like a cigarette should.

Eighteen years later, the series was still thriving—in a medium in which programs that last three or four seasons are considered long-term successes. By 1988, *Monday Night Football* had been on the air longer than any other show in prime time except *60 Minutes*.

The *Monday Night* story, in a sense, is the familiar story of show-business success in America. *Monday Night Football* rocketed into prime time, growing so hot so fast that it was bound to cool down, fueling so many big egos and such high expectations that it courted self-destruction.

In the beginning, there was only magic. There was Arledge, with the vision to transform a football game into a potent stew of drama, comedy, and soap opera; and Cosell, with the personality and talent to bring new viewers to the set. There was Gifford, with his jock expertise and sex appeal; and Meredith, with his country wit. There was Forte, with his technical brilliance; and Ohlmeyer, with his ability to lead. There was also a company, ABC, that was willing to gamble, and an industry, sports television, ready to be awakened.

In its glory days, the show made television come alive. *Monday Night Football* delivered a weekly burst of spontaneous, unpredictable entertainment that stood out amid the droning blandness of prime time.

What followed was the phenomenon: fame and acclaim and riches. Sports television exploded into a billion-dollar-a-year industry, powered by the genius of Arledge. "The bottom line on Roone is he made the sports television business what it is today," said Barry Frank, who worked for Arledge at ABC and went on to make his own fortune as a sports agent and entrepreneur. "Without him, we'd all be making fifty thousand dollars a year selling suits at Barney's."

But the fame and acclaim and riches did not satisfy Arledge. Nor did they calm the restlessness that had perpetually plagued Cosell and Meredith. They all wanted something more, something that mattered in a way that covering football games on television never could.

And so they looked elsewhere, to news or the variety stage or Hollywood. Swelled wallets led to swelled heads, and a sense of shared purpose was destroyed by pockets of petty selfishness. Everyone spent less time and energy on *Monday Night Football*. They saved their best creative impulses for newer, more exciting ventures.

Monday nights, inevitably, lost their magic; magic is always a fleeting effect. ABC's technical wizardry was quickly copied, and the charisma among the personalities wore off. Still, even after the banter turned bitter, Cosell, Meredith, and Gifford held the stage for a remarkably long time, first on the strength of their individual talents, finally on nothing but their lingering reputations. Arledge, the one man who might have been able to conjure up some new tricks, was busy performing on another stage.

But this show-business story does not have the familiar ending. Unlike other entertainment phenomena of the 1970s—disco dancing, Burt Reynolds, *Charlie's Angels—Monday Night Football* did not fade away. It had grown from a television show into an institution, too valuable to ABC and the NFL to kill off.

The show had to go on, to survive not by evolving into a higher form of television but by reverting to a lower one.

By the early 1980s, *Monday Night Football* had slid into reverse.

The business of sports television suffered along with it. So did the Big Three networks that had long dominated the American television industry. When ABC was taken over by Capital Cities, the company built by visionaries fell into the hands of sober men with eyes focused squarely on the bottom line.

Monday Night Football needed a new infusion of creativity; it got Dennis Swanson. Swanson knew how to make money, but he did not know how to make television. He did the best he could, but his options were few.

Even if he had wanted to, Swanson was not going to find another Cosell to inject new life into the show. No one would ever be Howard Cosell again—not even Howard Cosell. All that Swanson could do was try to stabilize the show's vital signs.

He prescribed a weekly dose of "basic football"—solid, respectful coverage. It was the kind of coverage provided by the other networks on Sunday afternoons, the kind of undistinguished coverage that had been scorned by the creators of *Monday Night Football*, who had insisted that they were going to be different.

The wheel had turned completely. Back in 1970, *Monday Night Football* had shown contempt for the sports establishment by declaring that the show, not the game, was the thing. ABC's provocative, irreverent style irritated some hard-core fans and many of the sportswriters who served them. But casual fans and young viewers flocked to the show.

Now the new men of *Monday Night Football* were announcing that the game reigned supreme. That pronouncement warmed the hearts of the traditionalists, while leaving the casual fans utterly cold.

ABC's coverage and commentary were thoroughly professional and occasionally entertaining, especially after the arrival of Dierdorf. But the show was free from even a hint of controversy, and not a soul talked about *Monday Night Football* past Tuesday.

That was not likely to change unless ABC could somehow

find another Arledge, another young gambler with ambitions and energy and ideas and the will to make things happen. Or, at the least, it would not change until the company created an environment in which ideas could be nurtured and risks taken—if a big, well-established company like Cap Cities could ever create such an environment.

It was a question that intrigued Arledge himself. "This industry is at a crossroads," he said. "Networks did not get to be networks just by being good bottom-line investments. They didn't get to be the institutions they are in this country just by cost-cutting.

"It's a little bit like the person who was hit by a truck, and you're lying bleeding in the streets, which, in a sense, all three network television companies were. You need people to come in and save your life. You need a paramedic to come in and revive you. But once you're revived, you need somebody with dreams and you need vision and you need leadership."

Dreams and vision and leadership were exactly what *Monday Night Football* needed, but at ABC Sports they were in dwindling supply.

Monday Night Football was still there every week in the fall, surviving and sometimes thriving—when the Bears were on the schedule or a playoff spot was on the line. The fans came out; the lights went on; three men talked; the action unfolded; the money rolled in.

Same night, same network, same name. But it was not *Monday Night Football* anymore. It was football on Monday nights.

Epilogue

Pete Rozelle, though occasionally rumored to be in ill health, continued to preside over the National Football League. The television contract he negotiated in 1987 would serve its purpose: to keep the league on sound financial footing for another three years. His only worry—and it was a minor one—was a lingering Federal Trade Commission investigation into the process of awarding the television rights.

Herb Granath, the salesman who so creatively packaged *Monday Night Football*, was promoted to president of ABC Video Enterprises in 1982. One of his chief duties was supervision of ESPN, the all-sports channel that is 80 percent owned by ABC. It became the NFL's outlet for Sunday night football on cable TV.

John Lazarus, the gregarious sales executive who followed Granath, emerged from the cloud that hung over him after his departure from ABC into another prominent position: head of sales for the fledgling Fox network. He left that job shortly after Fox failed to land the *Monday Night* package to join a sports marketing and production company.

Dennis Swanson entered his third year as president of ABC Sports promising new prosperity for the division. He signed all his top talent—Michaels, Gifford, and Dierdorf on football; Tim McCarver and Jim Palmer on baseball; Jim McKay on horse racing and golf—to extended-length and lucrative contracts and planned to focus his attention on improving the production side. Swanson did not play a major part in the key ABC Sports production of 1988, the Calgary Winter Olympics.

Dennis Lewin, former producer of *Monday Night Football*, continued to serve as the executive in charge of production at ABC Sports and played an important production role in Calgary.

But to many inside the division he remained the reliable executive who had trouble escaping his image as an uninspiring leader.

Don Ohlmeyer, the most dynamic producer *Monday Night Football* ever had, achieved more individual success than any other graduate of the program. His company, Ohlmeyer Communications, continued to make movies for television and packaged sports programs. But Ohlmeyer lost a major part of his empire in 1988 when he split with Ross Johnson and RJR/Nabisco. Ohlmeyer Communications ventured into television syndication in early 1988 with a new late-night talk show. Ohlmeyer made the deal himself to secure the host, who had been reluctant to return to television. The show was called *Howard Cosell: Speaking of Everything.*

Terry O'Neil, the intense young man whose days producing *Monday Night Football* were cut so abruptly short, formed his own production company after he lost the power struggle at CBS Sports. But O'Neil Productions faltered in early 1988. O'Neil closed his New York office and set to work on his next project: a book about his experiences in sports television.

Bob Goodrich, the *Monday Night* producer with the longest tenure, took over as producer of ABC's main game of college football in 1986. He experienced a series of professional highs and lows in 1987–88, taking much of the blame for ABC's problem-plagued golf coverage, then winning praise for his work producing the Alpine ski coverage in Calgary.

Chet Forte, the master sports director whose energy provided so much of the visual excitement of *Monday Night Football,* recovered from his heart attack in early 1987 and went to work at his own sports production company, LaRose-Forte Productions. He professed happiness at independent work, but he missed the action of the truck. Before the 1987 season he asked Michael Weisman, the executive producer of NBC Sports, to think of him whenever he had a shortage of directors. Weisman put him on three late-season games. Weisman was happy to have Forte—"He even brought his own limo," Weisman said.

In the summer Forte began directing a new prime-time football show: arena football on ESPN.

Fred Williamson never regained the cinematic fame that had

preceded his brief employment on *Monday Night Football,* but he continued to star in, produce, and direct low-budget but profitable action movies, many filmed in Italy, where he lived. His more recent titles include *The Messenger* and *The Big Treasure.*

Alex Karras enjoyed steady show-business success in Hollywood after his tenure on *Monday Night Football.* He appeared in several theatrical films, most notably *Victor/Victoria,* and starred for four seasons in his own situation-comedy series on ABC, *Webster.*

O. J. Simpson remained a familiar face on television thanks to his commercials for Hertz. He was also a regular on an HBO comedy series called *First and Ten.* Simpson was no longer associated with football on television, but he had invested wisely and was financially secure. He was also keeping a close eye on his eldest son, a big, fast running back approaching college age.

Joe Namath was still involved, deep into 1988, in a lawsuit seeking his second year's salary from ABC. But Namath re-emerged on television calling games for NBC in the 1987 season. The network paired him with one of its top play-by-play announcers, Marv Albert. After a somewhat rocky start, Namath improved enough to be selected to work a playoff game for the network.

Al Michaels completed a run of high-profile sports assignments by calling the ice-hockey competition in Calgary. He received his usual store of compliments from the critics for his solid work.

Don Meredith lived a life of uncomplicated pleasure in Santa Fe with his wife Susan, who handled the few professional interests he maintained. Meredith did no sports work and little acting. He did take to the stage for a special benefit performance of *The Odd Couple* in Santa Fe in 1986. His co-star: Frank Gifford. (Frank played Felix, Don played Oscar.) Meredith came back for a *Police Story* special on NBC in 1987, and he still did a few commercials. Susan Meredith reported that some friends were pressing Don to consider a run for governor of New Mexico.

Frank Gifford, the *Monday Night* survivor, endured more hostile reaction from the press over his performance as co-host—with his third wife Kathie Lee—of ABC's late-night reports from Calgary. Gifford remained secure at ABC, having patched up all his problems with Dennis Swanson, who now spoke of Frank in glowing terms as the soul of the *Monday Night* broadcasts. But with the emergence of Dan Dierdorf into stardom, even Gifford's defenders began to wonder what useful role he could serve in a three-man broadcast team. ABC had other assignments for him, including the main-host role on a revamped *Wide World of Sports*. As he approached his sixties, Gifford remained a fixture at ABC Sports.

Howard Cosell returned to television in January 1988, not in prime time, not live, and not speaking of sports. His *Speaking of Everything* syndicated program ran in many places in the dim hours past midnight. But Cosell was back in front of the cameras, conversing with and confronting guests, most of whom seemed to be his close friends. One of the first to appear on the show was a friend of long standing whom Cosell seemed delighted to have brought back into his life: Roone Arledge. Cosell, in a typical gesture, wiped away all the differences that had separated them. He praised Arledge lavishly in public statements and began his show with Arledge by calling him a giant in the television industry. Arledge and Cosell toasted each other with champagne after the taping. Three months later, the show was canceled, a victim of low ratings and a lack of advertiser support.

At about the same time, his nationally syndicated sports column was dropped by its home newspaper, the New York *Daily News*. Cosell, who turned 70 in March 1988, was left with only one professional outlet, his daily network radio commentary. He spent his working days still taking dozens of calls in his small office in the Burlington Building in Manhattan. Cosell continued to call it "the nerve center of sports in America."

Personally, he faced his most severe crisis when his beloved wife, Emmy, became seriously ill.

Roone Arledge began perhaps the last of his Olympian years with another marathon stint behind the controls of ABC's ninety-four hours of coverage from Calgary. It was a brief sports interruption in a career now devoted entirely to ABC News. In 1988, that meant presiding over another presidential primary season, two political conventions, and the presidential election in November. Calgary was a mixed experience for Arledge. The ratings success more than validated his faith in the Olympics as an event of unprecedented appeal for television and confirmed again the level of impact he has had on the tastes of the American public. Some of the telecasts earned high praise, but the games as a whole were not judged to be an artistic success. They simply went on too long and contained too many commercials and too little drama to stand up to the elevated standards Arledge and ABC had set for themselves during previous Olympiads.

Having created and established popular and critical successes such as *Nightline, 20/20,* and *This Week with David Brinkley,* Arledge had also attained a level of considerable influence in television news. How much longer he would remain in position to wield that influence for the benefit of ABC was a question he was not discussing in public as he planned the extensive news coverage of 1988. Some of his closest associates speculated that Arledge would soon abandon the world of network TV for some new, more stimulating challenge—if he could ever find one that promised the kind of action and impact that made Roone Arledge's pulse race faster.

A Note on Sources

Most of this book is based on the firsthand reporting of the authors. We used books and magazine and newspaper articles as a starting point for our research and, in a few instances, as sources of quotations or eyewitness accounts of past events.

Books that provided background include *Supertube: The Rise of Television Sports* by Ron Powers, *The Thrill of Victory: The Inside Story of ABC Sports* by Bert Randolph Sugar, *The League: The Rise and Decline of the NFL* by David Harris, and *Super Spectator and the Electric Lilliputians* by William O. Johnson, Jr. Howard Cosell's three books—*Cosell*, *Like It Is*, and *I Never Played the Game*—were also valuable.

Other sources that were helpful include *Playboy* interviews of Roone Arledge, Howard Cosell, and Don Meredith; an Arledge interview by Nancy Collins in *New York* magazine; an account of the meeting between Cosell and Spiro Agnew in the *National Observer;* and several articles by William Taaffe in *Sports Illustrated.* Several sports television critics have covered *Monday Night Football* over the years; their stories and reviews were also helpful, and we have tried to credit them in the book.

The quote from Howard Cosell that precedes Chapter Three comes from an article by Jim Barniak in the Philadelphia *Evening Bulletin.* The quote from Don Meredith that precedes Chapter Seven comes from an article by Edwin Shrake in *Sports Illustrated.* The quote from Howard Cosell that precedes Chapter Ten comes from an article by Lesley Visser in *The Boston Globe.*

Acknowledgments

We would like to thank Jim Landis and Jane Meara, our editors at William Morrow & Co., for their support, assistance, and enthusiasm. We would like to thank our agent, Richard Pine, for his encouragement and fast work in getting this book off the ground.

Most of the material on which this book is based comes from interviews. We talked with nearly 150 people in the television industry. Many were interviewed more than once.

We wish to give special thanks to Roone Arledge, whose cooperation was essential, and Howard Cosell, who was generous with his time and, of course, his opinions.

Other sources who were especially helpful include Steve Bozeka, Dick Buffinton, Robbie Cowen, Dan Dierdorf, Dick Ebersol, Chet Forte, Frank Gifford, Leonard Goldenson, Bob Goodrich, Jack Graham, Herb Granath, Steve Hirdt, Chuck Howard, Keith Jackson, Alex Karras, Jim Lampley, John Lazarus, Steve Leff, Dennis Lewin, John Martin, Jim McKay, Al Michaels, Don Mischer, Art Modell, Don Ohlmeyer, Terry O'Neil, Fred Pierce, Val Pinchbeck, Pete Rozelle, Jeff Ruhe, Ned Simon, O. J. Simpson, Dorrance Smith, Dennis Swanson, Jim Wasilko, Irwin Weiner, and Ken Wolfe. Several others who prefer not to be named also have our thanks.

Many people at ABC helped open doors for us. We're grateful to Elise Adde, Irv Brodsky, Dick Connelly, Nancy Dobi, Kim Edmonds, Larry Eldridge, Rick Giacalone, Tom Goodman, Julie Hoover, Tom Mackin, Patricia Matson, Jeff Tolvin, and Bob Wheeler. Jim Heffernan gave us access to the extensive library of the National Football League.

Throughout the project, friends, relatives, and others were

375

helpful in a variety of ways. Thanks to Richard J. Carter, Jr., Ruth Pollack Coughlin, Beaufort Cranford, David Harp, James Houston, Doug Kelly, Jeanne McAllister, Pat McGuire, Frank Murphy, Catherine Carter O'Neill, Alex Thomas, Gerard Uehlinger, and Irene Weinstock.

Finally, and most important, we want to thank our wives, Beth Keating Carter and Karen Schneider, and our children, Caela and Daniel Carter and Sarah and Rebecca Schneider Gunther. Besides providing invaluable help, they were remarkably patient and loving, and always there when we needed them.

Index